Chipmunk
xx

INSTITUTIONS, RELATIONS AND OUTCOMES

INSTITUTIONS, RELATIONS AND OUTCOMES

A Framework and Case Studies for Gender-aware Planning

Edited by

NAILA KABEER
RAMYA SUBRAHMANIAN

kali for women

1999

Institutions, Relations and Outcomes
A Framework and Case Studies for Gender-aware Planning
Published by
Kali for Women
B 1/8 Hauz Khas
New Delhi 110 016
Tel/Fax: 91-11-686-4497
Email: kaliw@del2.vsnl.net.in

ISBN 81 85107 98 X

Typeset by SJI Services, B 17 Lajpat Nagar II,
New Delhi 110 024
Printed at Raj Press, R 3 Inderpuri, New Delhi 110 012

Contents

Introduction vii
NAILA KABEER AND RAMYA SUBRAHMANIAN

Section 1. FromFeminist Insights to an Analytical Framework

1. From Feminist Insights to an Analytical Framework
An Institutional Perspective on Gender Inequality 3
NAILA KABEER

2. Beyond Myths
The Social and Political Dynamics of Gender 49
RAJNI PALRIWALA

3. Every Blade of Green
Landless Women Labourers, Production and Reproduction in South India 80
KARIN KAPADIA

4. "More Equal than Others?"
Gender Bias in the Constitution of Bureaucratic Merit in the Indian Administrative Service 102
SAROJINI GANJU THAKUR

5. "Brother, There are Only Two Jatis—Men and Women"
Section 125 Criminal Procedure Code and the Trial of Wifehood 147
MAITRAYEE MUKHOPADHYAY

6. Gender, Poverty and Institutional Exclusion
Insights From Integrated Rural Development Programme (IRDP) and Development of Women and Children in Rural Areas (DWCRA) 166
NAILA KABEER AND RANJANI K. MURTHY

Section 2. From Concepts to Practice

7. From Concepts to Practice
Gender-aware Planning through the Institutional Framework 197
NAILA KABEER AND RAMYA SUBRAHMANIAN

8. "Should I Use My Hands as Fuel?"
Gender Conflicts in Joint Forest Management 231
MADHU SARIN

9. Closing the Gender Gap in Education
The Shikshakarmi Programme 266
SHOBHITA RAJAGOPAL

10. From Private to Public
The Emergence of Violence Against Women as An Issue in the Women's Development Programme, Rajasthan 288
KANCHAN MATHUR

11. Too Big For Their Boots?
Women and the Policing of Violence Against Women 312
POORNIMA CHIKARMANE

Section 3. Following Through the Process

12. Following Through the Process
Implementation, Monitoring and Evaluation 339
NAILA KABEER AND RAMYA SUBRAHMANIAN

13. Gender Training Experiences with Indian NGOs 361
RANJANI K. MURTHY

14. Lessons Learned
Gender Training Experiences with the Indian Government 392
RAMYA SUBRAHMANIAN WITH NAILA KABEER, KANCHAN MATHUR, SHOBITA RAJAGOPAL AND SAROJINI GANJU THAKUR

Notes on Contributors 408

Introduction

NAILA KABEER AND RAMYA SUBRAHMANIAN

The idea for this book came out of a major training initiative organised jointly by the Government of India and the Department for Overseas Development (DFID, then the British Overseas Development Administration) and managed by the British Council. The objective of the Gender Planning Training Project (GPTP) was to familiarise a mixed constituency of development researchers, trainers and practitioners with a methodology for integrating a gender perspective into the policy and planning process. The project was intended to work at a number of different levels. At one level, it was intended as a straightforward training of trainers in a gender analytical framework. At another level it was intended to feed into gender training and advocacy around gender issues among people who were directly and indirectly active in the formulation and implementation of policy. At yet another level, it was intended as a contribution to the ongoing debates in India and the rest of the world about what we mean by gender equity and how we achieve it in development practice. Consequently, the participants in the project were drawn from multiple constituencies within the Indian context - researchers, trainers, NGO practitioners and government officials drawn from different levels of the bureaucracy. In addition, we also drew in as resource persons a range of different actors with valuable insights into these questions.

The Institute of Development Studies (IDS), Sussex, was approached as the academic partner in this project on the basis of its pioneering role in the field of gender training. One of the first international courses offering training in gender analysis for development policy to development researchers and practitioners was held at the IDS over a decade ago. The methodology that has evolved as a result of this long experience of working with participants from all over the world seeks to avoid sweeping generalisations on the basis of particular cultural values and beliefs. At the same time, it focuses on some of the commonalities which cut across cultural diversity. Consequently, it draws attention to those features of social relationships in different parts of the world which appear to be particularly implicated in the constitution and reconstitution of gender inequality: to the role of ideology, often sanctified in the name of culture and tradition, in legitimising, and thereby concealing, the injustices embodied in gender relationships, and to the importance of the material underpinnings of women's dependence. The methodology also moves the analysis of gender beyond the boundaries of the household. Although family and kinship relations play a central role in the creation of gender inequality, they are part of a larger institutional quartet which also includes the state, the market and the community. In particular, the framework highlights, in a way that many gender training frameworks in use in the international agencies do not, that the state and development agencies are not neutral players in the processes of exclusion and inclusion but rather an active force for better or worse, depending on the interests that they represent. By encompassing these different institutions, the training process was also able to touch on different aspects of participants' lives, both professional and personal.

The first section of the book lays out the basic elements of the institutional framework. Kabeer's piece provides an introduction to the key concepts which make up the framework, drawing attention to the interlocking relationships between the rules, resources, practices and power through which social inequalities of gender, caste and class are played out in different institutions in the Indian context. The chapter by Palriwala focuses on the household and kinship relations as a central arena in this process and the way in which these vary by class, caste and region. Kapadia draws on her field work in rural Tamil Nadu to demonstrate how gender inequalities are built into the apparently neutral forces of demand and supply in the labour market. Mukhopadhyay's contribution focuses on another purportedly neutral areana: the state in its judiciary capacity. Her analysis shows how rules apparently intended to protect women's interests do so only partially because they define women as dependents rather than full citizens. The problems caused by this equivocal view of women's status in the eyes of the law are further compounded by the interpretation of legal 'rules' by powerful individuals. Thakur's chapter also looks at the state but this time at the rules and norms through which the Indian Administrative Service is constituted. The IAS is an organisation which sees itself as based on merit and is supposed to be gender neutral in its recruitment and promotion procedures and terms and conditions of work. Its rules and norms are intended to reflect this. Thakur's analysis makes the point that in a world where women and men are socially constructed as different and unequal actors, apparent gender neutrality in rules will often result in gender-biased outcomes. The final chapter in this introductory section by Kabeer and Murthy provides an institutional analysis of two major credit interventions by the government. It points to different categories of gender disadvantage which explain the very partial success of these programmes in achieving their stated goals and demonstrates why targeting women does not by itself constitute a gender-aware intervention.

The next section opens with a chapter by Kabeer and Subrahmanian which applies the institutional framework to the analysis of a variety of development interventions. It is organised loosely around the logic embedded in the goal-oriented approaches to planning but eschews the rigidity often associated with such approaches. The other chapters in this section are case studies illustrating how an institutional analysis might help illuminate different aspects of gender inequality in policies and programmes. Clearly, the sectors and issues dealt with in these chapters do not by any means exhaust the developmental relevance of a gender analysis nor do they necessarily deal with the most critical questions. They were selected on the basis of the areas of expertise of some of the participants and resource persons who worked on the GPTP but they help to provide examples of how rules, resources, practices and power interact in the construction of social inequalities in different arenas of development.

Sarin looks at class, caste and gender interests embodied in the government's approach to joint forestry management: she identifies who gained and who was excluded from the benefits of the programme and why. Mathur and Chikaramane offer different perspectives on an issue which is increasingly being given recognition as a critical factor in the reproduction of gender inequality in low, middle as well as high income countries: domestic violence. Mathur provides an analysis of grassroots mobilisation around the issue while Chikaramane deals with attempts by the state to improve its record on policing domestic violence against women. Rajagopal's. chapter highlights the elements that need to be taken into account if the provision of educational services is to be gender-sensitive, drawing on the experiences of an innovative programme in Rajasthan.

Clearly, the gender-awareness in policy design is a necessary but not a sufficient condition for ensuring gender equity in the policy process. As the institutional framework makes clear, the agencies which are entrusted with implementing redistributive policy goals are often a part of the problem rather than of the solution. The opening chapter in this section points to the danger of conscious as well as unconscious forms of resistance within the implementation process that hamper the translation of gender equity goals into the intended outcomes. It suggests a number of tools to alert agencies to the likelihood of such resistance, including ongoing monitoring to ensure it is not allowed to sabotage their interventions. The next two chapters bring us back to the specific interests of the GPTP. They deal with experiences of gender training as a particular form of development practice intended to create a constituency for gender equity among development practitioners and to minimise resistance. Subrahmanian synthesises the experiences of a number of the people involved in the GPTP in using the framework in the context of training government officials, while Murthy summarises her experiences in the NGO sector.

This book is not intended as a training manual, or as an academic project. Rather, it seeks to persuade a wide and mixed audience with an introduction to a particular methodology for looking at gender inequalities in everyday life and within the policy process and with a number of case studies which provide different entry points into the use of this method. It is also intended as a tribute to all those who contributed in their own special and individual ways to a very unique project. We remember all the members of the GPTP "family" with a great deal of affection and this book is dedicated to them.

We would also like to give special acknowledgment to some of the people involved in the design, management and delivery of the project. First of all, our thanks to our collaborators in the Indian government, Mr Ramani, Mrs Kiran Agarwal, Dr N.C. Saxena, Mr A.K. Arora, Kalpana Amar, Mr Mandoliya and Mrs Margaret Alva. Mrs Sarojini Thakur played a leading role in the transfer of our training activities from IDS to the Lal Bahadur Shastri National Academy of Administration (LBSNAA). We thank Ms Judy Walker from DFID for her very active support for the project. From the British Council we would like to thank Cathy Stephens, Sue Beaumont, Ann Bailes and, of course, Cedric Langham. We are grateful also to Maitrayee Mukhopadhyay and Kiran Bhatia who worked on the IDS team and to Urvashi Butalia, our editor at Kali for Women. Finally, our very special thanks to the person who nurtured this project beyond the call of duty in her capacity as manager of the project on behalf of the British Council, Ms Kamal Singh.

Section 1

From Feminist Insights to an Analytical Framework

1

From Feminist Insights to an Analytical Framework

An Institutional Perspective on Gender Inequality

NAILA KABEER

Introduction

In recent years, there has been a proliferation of analytical frameworks intended to facilitate the integration of a gender perspective into the policy process in response to two sets of concerns. On the part of gender advocates, it has represented a recognition that, unless the insights from feminist scholarship and activism are synthesised and systematised, so that their relevance for policy and planning is easily apparent to those who are practically engaged with these activities, such insights will play a minimal role in informing policy design and influencing its outcomes. On the part of policymakers, on the other hand, it comes from the recognition that the 'gender-blindness' of past policy efforts has entailed avoidable developmental costs and an interest in analytical tools to ensure that the same mistakes are not repeated in the future.

In this chapter I will be laying out one attempt at systematising some of the insights from feminist scholarship from this body of work which tries to retain the complexity and politics of this scholarship, but in a framework that will allow those not familiar with this scholarship to conduct their own analysis in the context of institutions and cultures which they know best. The chapter draws on earlier versions of the framework contained in Kabeer (1994a) and Kabeer and Subrahmanian (1996) but here attempts to adapt it more explicitly to the Indian context. Its aim is to promote an understanding of the deeply-entrenched institutionalised nature of gender inequalities, the power relations which they express, their relevance to the policy domain and the different forms of gender advocacy which have emerged to address these inequalities. At the same time, it makes clear that there is no single correct way of 'doing gender' in the policy domain: all that a framework can do is provide policy makers with a different 'window on reality' from their accustomed one and hope that it will make a difference in the way that they design and execute policy in the future. Feminists, as Sandra Bartky points out, do not ask different questions from everyone else; they ask the same questions differently.

Nature, Culture and Society: Different Views on Gender

One of the major reasons for the 'gender-blindness' of past policy relates to assumptions and ways of thinking which have allowed the relationships between women and men to be invested with the appearance of an eternal, unchanging and unchangeable aspect of the human condition. One such assumption relates to a widespread tendency to conflate sex and gender. Yet there is an important distinction between the two, one that is fundamental to the way in which a great deal of feminist thought has evolved and gender advocacy for social change has been formulated. It also lies at the heart of the framework we will be developing in this chapter and I will offer a very simple account here of the difference between the two which informs both the framework and the analysis in this book. *Sex* is taken to refer to those basic biological attributes which differentiate the male and the female of the human species, attributes which largely relate to their reproductive organs. The male and female of the human species are very similar to each other in other aspects of their biology: they both need food, water, sleep, clothing and shelter for basic survival; they are both helpless when they are very young and grow gradually more helpless as they get older. They are both capable of making sense of their world and of acting purposively on their conditions to change them. *Gender* is taken to refer to the full ensemble of norms, values, customs and practices by which the biological difference between the male and female of the human species is transformed and exaggerated into a very much wider social difference. The tendency to conflate *sexual difference,* which is biological, with *gender difference,* which is social, gives rise to a view that all observed differences in the roles, capacities and aptitudes attributed to men and women within a given context are rooted in their biology and hence cannot be changed.

Different societies differ, of course, in the specific social interpretation that they give to biological difference. Some societies allow large areas of overlap in the lives of men and women while others are organised in ways which maintain a very rigid segregation between the world of men and the world of women, what men do and what women do. What they tend to share is the idea that their way of organising roles and relations between women and men is the 'natural', and hence the only, way of doing it. In many South-east Asian societies, it is believed that women are naturally more commercial and concerned with money and they play a prominent role in trade and commerce. In much of South Asia, of course, women are considered to be hopeless with money, and financial matters are entrusted to men. In many parts of sub-Saharan Africa, cultivation is hoe-based and it is largely women who use the hoe. So deep is the view that hoeing is women's work that an official from Ghana once told me during a training course of a local saying to the effect that if a man touched the hoe, he would become emasculated. In South Asia, on the other hand, cultivation is largely plough-based and ploughing is seen as men's work. Indeed, women are forbidden to touch the plough because their bodies are considered to be polluting. (The implications of this taboo are clearly spelt out by Jayoti Gupta who points out how recent land reforms in West Bengal under a socialist government were premised on the socialist ideal of 'returning land to the tiller', an ideal whose male bias became manifest in the automatic exclusion of women from rights to land although, Gupta's analysis makes clear, many women would have been prepared to till their own land in the face of social disapproval (Gupta, 1997)).

The biologistic views about differences between women and men are significant in the development context because they sanction views about the appropriate distribution of resources and responsibilities which are often difficult to budge. Thus men and women are prevented from doing certain things or receiving certain benefits, not on grounds of proven ability or inability, but *because* they are men or women. This differentiation on the grounds of biology is inequitable as well as unnecessary when it leads to gender inequalities in well-being and opportunities, as well as to gender differences. Examples of this abound in development literature.

Yates (1994), for instance, notes a Ghanaian national education policy document that resorts to biological determinism in order to justify the delivery of gender segregated vocational education:

> By their very make up biologically, nature has made women comparatively more delicate than men physically. There are therefore some trades which do not suit women. If our women by their vocational skills will develop muscles and look masculine, sooner or later they will look physically like their husbands .... Skills which require physical strength do not often suit women. Vocational skills which require deft hands, aesthetics and accuracy of taste by tongue and many such are those which suit women. Examples are hairdressing, dressing, cookery, ordinary or advanced processing of various commodities .... (cited in Yates, 1994 p.104).

This statement provides a useful illustration of the instability of the distinction between sex as a biological attribute and gender as a social difference since it starts out by asserting a biological argument—nature has made women more delicate—but goes on to use this purported biological difference to argue against forms of activity which would apparently negate biology so that women will develop muscles and start to look like their husbands! Ghana, it should also be noted, is a country where women are known to work extremely long hours in the field, engage in their own independent enterprises and generally exercise considerable economic autonomy.

If declarations of biological difference are used on some occasions to exclude women from project benefits, they can also be used on other occasions to bring them into a project on exploitative terms. A documentary film of an irrigated rice project in the Gambia records how project rules redistributed land from women to men for rice cultivation with the expectation that women would work as unpaid family labour on their husband's rice lands whereas previously they had cultivated rice on their own independent holdings. Stressing the need for female labour to the rice irrigation project, the project manager explained, 'Women are better than men as far as transplanting is concerned and they are also better than men as far as working in the water ... so quite frankly we expect a lot of labour from women' (cited in Carney, 1988, p. 63).

However, the accelerating dissemination of knowledge about different societies of the world as a result of the revolution in global transport and communications, has made it increasingly difficult to sustain the idea that there is something 'natural' about the organisation of the gender division of roles and responsibilities in any particular community as we get to know how different it is in the next community. Resistance to any form of change in gender relations has increasingly taken on the rationale of the 'sanctity of culture'. The discourse of 'culture' is the obvious next line of defence when arguments based on the discourse of 'biological difference' start to look shaky since it accommodates the defence of the very same gender division of roles, responsibilities and privileges that the earlier arguments on the grounds of biological difference were used to defend. However, defence of the status quo on the grounds of the sanctity of culture is of a very different order to defence on the grounds of biological differences. Beliefs about biological difference are beliefs about *facts*, based on what we know, or think we know, about the objective state of the world. Beliefs about the social implications of biological difference can be countered by sound evidence to the contrary. For instance, it was not that long ago that it was believed in the UK that not only were girls not as brainy as boys, but that they were not even brainy enough to deserve education. Today, as girls outperform boys in UK schools, we now *know* this is not the case.

A defence based on the sanctity of culture, on the other hand, moves us away from disputes over *facts* to disputes over *values*. Culture represents a particular way of organising social life and the values that go with it. It consequently represents the privileging of one set of values over others. We are no longer arguing about how we think the world *is* but also how we think it *should* be. Culture, in other words, does not have an independent existence, like biological difference, 'out there' somewhere, regardless of how we view it. Culture exists precisely in how we *view, evaluate and attempt to organise* the world around us, including, of course, how we view, evaluate and organise biological difference. Cultural values exist in the hearts, minds and belief-systems of the men and women who subscribe to them, give them meaning and reproduce them through their practices over time. As such, they are an important source of people's identity and sense of 'community'. And as these meanings and practices change, culture also changes.

Those who defend gender inequality on the grounds of culture often fail to perceive just how much culture has been changing. We have only to look at the way things were done in the subcontinent in our grandmothers' time, in our mothers' time and in our own time to realise how much culture has changed for many of us. Some of it has been unintended change, occurring in response to changing material circumstances. A number of authors (including Palriwala, this book; Kapadia, 1995) have pointed to the 'sanskritisation' of culture in the southern states of India through the spread of marriage-related practices associated with the upper Brahmana castes in the north. Such practices, the seclusion of women after marriage, marrying outside the kin group, payment of dowry, the fall in the status of kin related through the mother and the rise in the status of kin related through the husband, has led to the same patterns of discrimination against girl children in the southern states that used to be confined to the north. No individual or set of individuals set about to make these changes happen, but they did happen and they represent a profoundly different way of doing things in the south.

Other forms of changes in culture are purposive, the result of deliberate interventions attempting to bring them about. The clauses in the Indian Constitution which guarantee equality to all citizens, the adoption of various measures to bring about such equality, can be seen as an example of such purposive interventions in a culture in which caste and gender inequality occupy a central place. It is precisely because culture is a set of *values* that the Constitution can contest those aspects of culture which are no longer considered acceptable in the present context and seek to replace them with the values of democracy, equality and citizenship. However, cultural contestation will only occur when dissent is possible. As long as the upper castes in India monopolised the power to define the culture of their community, we were given a view of the caste system as based on natural justice that went largely unopposed. But once dissenting views began to be heard, once a sufficiently organised dalit movement began to challenge the premises of the caste system, it was revealed for what it was: an arbitrary and unjust way of organising social life. As long as men are given sole authority to define culture within their communities, we are given a particular view of what culture means. Here, too, as dissenting voices begin to gather strength, culture becomes revealed as one among many ways of organising relationships between women and men within the family and in the wider community, and a particularly unjust one.

The various social movements in India, including the women's movement and the dalit movement, can be seen as the organised voices of dissent, the public contestation of dominant cultural meanings and values and hence the embodiment of an alternative set of cultural meanings and values. But dissent also occurs on a more everyday basis outside the realm of organised politics. Kapadia (1995) came across it in her conversations with rural women (in Tamil Nadu) whose perceptions of the kinship and family relations as being inimical to women's interests were expressed in a local saying which only women voiced: *Sondam sudum* (kinship burns!). I came across it too in my interviews with women factory workers in Bangladesh who rejected the view that they were breaking purdah by going out of the home to work and offered their own alternative definition: 'The best purdah is the *burkah* within oneself, the *burkah* of the mind. People only say that working violates purdah in order to keep women down' (cited in Kabeer, forthcoming).

Mathur's contribution to this book presents a more elaborated account of contested views of culture in her description of the aftermath to the sati (immolation) of Roop Kanwar, the 18-year old Rajput girl from the village of Deorala in Rajasthan. Many in Rajasthan and across the country, including those described as the middle-class intelligentsia, condoned the death on the grounds that it had been a 'voluntary act' on her part. Others defended it more vehemently and aggressively and Mathur notes how Rajput youths marched through the streets of Jaipur with swords in their hands, ostensibly as an assertion of their cultural identity, but also as a show of strength to those with dissenting views.

Yet there were many in India and specifically in Rajasthan who asked what definition of culture justified the death by burning of a woman, however 'voluntary' the act was seen to be. Mathur cites the responses of the sathins, or women workers, of the Women's Development Programme (WDP) in Rajasthan who, through their experience in the field, had begun to question the 'sanctity of culture' on issues where it so clearly violated women's rights. It could, of course, be said that these women had been indoctrinated as a result of their contact with 'middle class feminists' who worked in the WDP but why should they be regarded as any more 'indoctrinated' in their views than the Rajput youths who marched to defend a definition of culture which put the interests of men first and subsumed a woman's identity so totally in that of her husband that her life was considered valueless when he died? The Rajput youths marched with swords to defend *their* cultural identity; the WDP sathins campaigned with the women's movement to defend what they believed to be important to *their* rights and dignity as women. The Rajput youths claimed to speak on behalf of 'the community' but they were also defending male privilege. The women claimed to speak on behalf of women and they were defending women's rights. Who was right? Who decides?

A view of ethics, of what is right and wrong, what is just and unjust, what is acceptable and unacceptable, is therefore at the heart of gender analysis, however neutrally it may be presented. Culture, as a set of values, plays an important role in creating a shared set of answers to some of these ethical questions and therefore constitutes an important source of people's sense of belonging, of identity and of community. Many aspects of culture are worth defending not only on the grounds of identity, but also because of the ethical values they embody. But culture is not indivisible, monolithic, immutable. Aspects of it are in the process of change all the time. Gender inequity embodies cultural values, and indeed is a cultural value, which women in particular have now begun to challenge. Clearly, in cultures where the essence of gender inequality is the silence or 'mutedness' of women, the idea that they should begin to speak for themselves is a radical break with the past and as such, constitutes a major threat to those whose sense of themselves, and of their place in the world, is constructed around a social order in which women are silent and men speak on their behalf. These are people who are unlikely to be swayed by these new voices, however persuasive, and often take refuge in the defence of the sanctity of culture. Indeed, the sanctity of culture is often defended by defining the very *idea* of dissent, and its claim to a hearing on grounds of human rights, equality and justice, as alien to the culture and hence a threat to its sanctity.

However, there are many others who have begun to question the justice of determining the life chances of individuals purely on the basis of their gender, particularly when it entails such glaring asymmetries at the level of basic survival and well-being, and it is for them that this book is intended. The framework in this chapter and the analysis in the rest of this book draws on the insights and experiences of a range of people active in challenging these injustices in order to provide a way of thinking about gender issues for those who are still relatively new to this arena. The main objective of the framework is to draw attention to the processes by which biological difference of sex is translated into social inequalities of gender in different societies. These processes begin for every individual from the day they are born, since whether they are born into a culture of son preference or where daughters and sons are equally valued, will shape a great deal of their experience of life from that day onwards, although it will not fully determine it. For the purposes of this book, I will be concentrating largely on examples from the Indian context, drawing primarily from some of the contributions in the book.

The Institutional Construction of Gender Inequality

As I have noted earlier, the concept of *gender* emerged as a way of distinguishing between biological difference and socially constructed inequality while the concept of *gender relations* sought to shift attention away from looking at women and men as isolated categories to looking at the social relationships through which they were mutually constituted as unequal social categories (Whitehead, 1979; Elson, 1991). Gender relations are an aspect of broader social relations and, like all social relations, are constituted through the rules, norms and practices by which resources are allocated, tasks and responsibilities are assigned, value is given and power is mobilised. In other words, gender relations do not operate in a social vacuum but *are products of the ways in which institutions are organised and reconstituted over time*.

The organisation of family and kinship in households and extended family networks are the primary sites of gender relations but the processes by which gender inequalities are socially constituted are not confined purely to household and family relationships. They are reproduced across a range of institutions, including many of the policy-making agencies whose avowed objectives are to address the different forms of exclusion and inequality within their societies. For this reason, the framework that we have developed for the analysis of gender inequality is one which focuses on the *institutional construction of gender relations* and hence the institutional construction of gender inequality. Frameworks are useful tools in the face of complex and dynamic societal realities if they can help draw attention to the key issues which must be explored in order to achieve certain analytical objectives. In relation to the objectives of this book, our framework is intended to direct attention to the existence of gender inequalities in the prevailing distribution of resources, responsibilities and power and to analyse how they are thrown up by the operations of the institutions which govern social life.

What are these institutions and how do they construct gender relations as a relation of difference and inequality? A simple definition of institutions could see them as a framework of rules for achieving certain social or economic goals; organisations refer to the specific structural forms that institutions take (North, 1990). For analytical purposes, it is useful to think of four key institutional sites—the state, the market, the community/civil society and the domain of family/kinship. Thus the state is the larger institutional framework for a range of legal, military and administrative organisations; the market is the framework for organisations like firms, financial corporations, farming enterprises and multinationals; the community is made up of various supra-family groupings, including village tribunals, political factions, neighbourhood networks and non-governmental organisations, which exert considerable influence over its members in particular domains of life; while households, extended families and lineage groupings are some of the ways in which kinship relations are organised.

Few institutions profess explicitly to ideologies of inequality; where inequalities are observed, they tend to be explained in terms which legitimate and justify them. Thus, inequalities within family and community tend to be attributed to natural difference, divine will, culture and tradition while inequalities within firms, bureacracies and other public bodies are rationalised as the operation of neutral market forces or merit-based rules of recruitment and promotion. Many of the official ideologies through which institutions describe themselves tend to get uncritically reproduced in social science text books, in public policy and in popular discourse, while the compartmentalised nature of the social sciences has led to the treatment of the key institutions as somehow separate and distinct from each other, the subject matter of different disciplines. Some familiar examples of how institutions are characterised in the social sciences, and often in popular consciousness, are given below but it is the role of analysis to move beyond the 'official' ideologies professed by, or attributed to, different institututional arenas to a critical empirical scrutiny of the actual rules and practices through which their different organisational forms are constituted.

Official Constructions of Institutional Ideologies

Institutional site	Official ideologies
State	Securing the national interest/ Equality of all citizens
Markets	Profit maximisation/ Securing commercial interests
Community	The moral economy/social networking
Kinship/family	Altruism, sharing and caring

Such an analysis would make clear that, although different organisations may operate with their own distinct 'ways of doing things', there are certain common norms, beliefs and values which cut across the different institutional sites, leading to the systemic and widespread construction and reinforcement of certain social inequalities. While literature on institutions and their organisational forms suggests that they vary considerably from each other and across cultures, it also suggests that they can be usefully analysed in terms of a number of generic constitutive components: *rules, activities, resources, people* and *power*. These are elaborated below.

'Deconstructing' Organisations

Rules (or how things get done): What is distinctive about institutional behaviour is that it is rule-governed rather than idiosyncratic and random. Distinct institutional patterns of behaviour inhere in the official and unofficial, the explicit and implicit, in norms, values, traditions, laws and customs which constrain or enable what is done, how it is done, by whom and who will benefit. The institutionalisation of rules has the advantage that it allows recurring decisions in the pursuit of institutional goals to be made with an economy of effort; their disadvantage is that they entrench the way things get done to the extent of giving them the appearance of being natural or immutable.

Activities (what is done): The other side of the coin to institutional rules is the generation of distinct patterns of activities. Indeed institutions can be defined as 'rule-governed' sets of activities organised around the meeting of specific needs or the pursuit of specific goals. These activities can be productive, distributive or regulative but their rule-governed nature means that institutions generate routinised practices and are reconstituted through such practices. Institutional practice is therefore a key factor in the reconstitution over time of social inequality and, in the final analysis, it is institutional practice which will have to be changed if unequal relations are to be transformed.

Resources (what is used, what is produced): All institutions have the capacity to mobilise resources and institutional rules govern the patterns of mobilisation and allocation. Such resources may be human (labour, education and skills) material (food, assets, land, money) or intangible (information, political clout, goodwill, contacts) and they may be used as 'inputs' in institutional activity or represent institutional 'outputs'.

People (who is excluded and included in institutional activities): Institutions are constituted by specific categories of people. Few are fully inclusive, despite their professed ideologies. Rather, institutional rules and practices determine which categories of people are included (and which excluded) and how they are assigned different tasks, activities and responsibilities within the production process and different resources in the allocative processes of the institution. Institutional patterns of inclusion, exclusion, positioning and progress express class, gender and other social inequalities.

Power (who determines priorities and makes the rules): Power is rarely diffused equally throughout an organisation, however egalitarian its formal ideology. The unequal distribution of resources and responsibilities within an organisation, together with the official and unofficial rules which legitimise this distribution tend to ensure that some institutional actors have the authority to interpret institutional goals and needs, as well as the ability to mobilise the loyalty, labour or compliance of others. Thus power is constituted as an integral feature of institutional life through its norms, rules and conventions, its allocation of resources and responsibilities and its customs and practice. The outcomes of institutional practice, including its reconstitution over time, will reflect the interests of those with the power to make the rules as well as to change them.

Applying the Framework to the Analysis of Institutions: Some Examples

The narrow application of these concepts to the analysis of an organisation will help to highlight the way in which these inter-related elements operate to produce unequal gendered outcomes; a broader focus will illuminate how gender and other social inequalities are mutually constituted within and across institutional sites. The family, as a specific form of kinship-based organisation, is a primary institutional site for the construction of gender relations because it is where the process begins by which biological difference is reconstituted as gender inequality. In much of the Indian subcontinent, particularly its northern plains, and including Bangladesh and Pakistan, son preference is a long established cultural value so that from the moment of birth itself, a girl is treated not just differently from a boy, but less favourably. The degree of discrimination may vary from family to family but it is widespread enough to show up in the statistics as marked gender differentials in nutrition, food allocation, health status and health expenditure, education, mortality rates and life expectancy. The same cultural values and practices also exclude women from the public domain, constraining their ability to make a contribution to the family economy and hence defining them as economic liabilities, thereby justifying the unequal treatment meted out to them within the family.

Kinship norms and rules play an important role in structuring marriage practices: in the Indian context, they intersect with the norms of caste and class to determine who will marry whom, at what age, which direction resources will flow at marriage and whether the newly-married couple will live with the husband's family, the bride's family or set up their own separate household. We call these rules and norms *institutional* because they are not determined or chosen by any individual; they exist at the level of the larger collectivity of community or society. Individuals who infringe them are seen as 'deviant' in some way and can incur a penalty. However, these rules and practices vary even within the Indian context, as the contribution by Palriwala points out.

Thus in south India cross-cousin marriage is more frequent and couples are as likely to reside with the bride's family as with the groom's while in northern kinship patterns, kin and village exogamy tend to be practised so that women marry outside their kin and village and take up residence with the groom's family as stranger-brides. These differing practices are believed to have considerable influence in shaping or patterning the forms of power and inequality experienced; for instance, the greater gender egalitarianism observed in south Indian kinship systems in which women are not separated from the support of their natal kin, as compared with the greater gender subordination of women in the north Indian system where women are ideologically and physically separated from their natal kin. Furthermore, the intertwining practices of female seclusion, strict controls over women's mobility and dowry which constrain the economic contributions of women in northern kinship systems further tend to undermine their personal autonomy vis-a-vis men within the family and community.

Where men are culturally defined as the main or sole breadwinners (as in northern India) they are also likely to be favoured in the intra-household distribution of resources (property and inheritance) and claims on the household product (consumption and investment). Through an analysis of food distribution practices in Rajasthani households, Palriwala throws light on one mechanism by which cultural norms translate into a hierarchy of claims to produce the kinds of discriminatory outcomes typically found in the state: adult males have first priority, with the male head of house as 'first among equals'. The old and the young, particularly young sons, are next in priority, with the young sons often given priority over the elderly. Since it is women who are responsible for cooking and serving food, any shortages or feelings of discrimination are blamed on them, even though the order of distribution is culturally sanctioned and beyond the choice of the individual woman. The higher levels of female mortality compared to male in almost every age group, which translates into overall gender inequalities in life expectancy, reflect this broader structural devaluation of women. Palriwala traces, in the Rajasthan context, how male property rights and the ability to contribute economically, juxtaposed against women's propertylessness and seclusion from the market, produce a view of women as economic dependents and hence residual claimants on household resources. Women are penalised as economic liabilities by a culture that has defined them as economic liabilities.

Kinship and family relationships are 'gender-ascriptive' (Whitehead, 1981) in the sense that all relationships between members are defined in inherently gender terms and spell out the claims and obligations entailed in that relationship. Taking the simplest example, while the parent-child relationship is gender-neutral as a concept, in reality, it refers to highly gendered relationships between mothers, fathers, daughters and sons, which are enacted by individual women, men, girls and boys at the individual level but which are also governed by cultural norms and values which spell out how they treat each other and what they can expect of each other. However, as I noted earlier, the norms and values which help define and structure relationships and behaviour within the domain of family and kinship are not the products of individual families and kinship groups but of the larger social collectivity. Consequently, they are carried over into other institutional domains, many of which purport to be, and are represented as, gender-neutral. An example of the way in which the schooling system, which certainly does not set out to reinforce gender inequality yet does so, was given to us by Gayathri Devi from the Education Department in Karnataka, who participated in the Gender Planning Training Project and provided us with a content analysis of primary school textbooks (from Std. I to Std. V) in her state. It revealed that activities/occupations described in relation to boys/men and girls/women were highly skewed, with around 40 different occupations and activities attributed to boys/men compared to around 11 attributed to girls/women. The list is reproduced on the facing page.

The analysis also found an extremely skewed gender distribution of adjectives used in textbooks from Class I to V, with around 17 different adjectives used in relation to boys/men (good, active, brave, patriotic, orphaned, clever, gallant, courageous, peace-messenger, adventurous, heroic, poetic, omnipotent, intelligent, talented, extraordinary, bold) compared to three or four for girls/women (kind, great mother, devoted mother). Do these adjectives reflect the reality of lives of boys and girls, men and women, in India, or even in Karnataka alone, or are they, like the the Ghanaian national education policy document cited earlier, merely a

	Male	Female
Std. I (activities)	Brushing, swinging, bathing, writing, planting, wood-cutting, bursting crackers, buying flowers, pushing rocks, playing, flying, sleeping	Eating, cutting, buying flowers, going to school, feeding the goat, sending children to school
Std. II (occupations)	Farmer, mechanic, fishing, driver, potter, physical instructor, carpenter, grocer, mason, weaver, king, bomber, postman, policeman, headmaster, soldier, teacher, tailor	Shopper (buying fruit etc), waitress (serving food etc)
Std. III	Shopkeeper, postman, watchman, teacher, farmer	Flower seller, teacher
Std. IV	Leaders, social reformers, snake charmer, watchman, minister	Singer
Std. V	Engineer, artist, freedom fighter	

projection of the class and gender biases of those who wrote the textbooks? And if education is an important route by which children learn about themselves, their place in society and what life might hold for them, what messages are these textbooks giving girls and boys about their future?

Various other examples of the way in which gender norms are reconstituted in institutional domains which are believed to be gender-neutral are provided in the contributions in the book. Kapadia's chapter describes this in relation to agricultural labour markets in Tamil Nadu. While women's involvement in agricultural labour markets is very much higher in the southern states than in the north, there is still a gender segregation of tasks in the agricultural production process which spills over in the labour market. Sowing and ploughing are defined as 'male' activities while carrying and weeding are seen as 'female'. While the cultural meanings invested in this particular division of labour give it the appearance of being 'natural', dictated by biological difference, Kapadia notes how arbitrary some of these classifications can be. 'Breaking the soil' with the plough or a large hoe were seen as 'male' but digging up the soil during weeding was defined as 'female' because it involved the small hoe.

Kapadia also notes that men were paid double the female wage for the same period of field labour, a differential that both women and men agreed was justified because men did the more demanding work. However, given that men were ploughing the earth sporadically and women were carrying soil ceaselessly, she suggests that this owed more to ideological perceptions than to objective reality[1]. An additional consideration behind the unequal wages was that it would have been considered deeply humiliating for a man to be paid the same as a woman, even for the same work. A differential had to be observed to signal the superior status of men. There was thus a 'gender premium' to wages. The mechanisation of ploughing had eroded a key source of male waged labour but the power of these cultural definitions placed a strong brake on the extent to which men were prepared to cross over the gender divide and take up 'female' tasks. On the rare occasions where some women had taken up a vacant 'male' job out of need, they were still paid the 'female' wage.

The chapters by Thakur, Chikarmane and Sarin all testify to some of the ways in which government institutions reproduce gender inequalities in their membership (the 'people' element in the framework) through rules and regulations which are implicitly or explicitly gender-biased. Thakur notes how norms from the domestic domain intruded into the bureacratic domain so that, until 1972, the IAS's recruitment rules discriminated very explicitly against married women because the responsibilities of wife and officer were seen as incompatible. Still prevalent are more implicit forms of discrimination by which field posts are typically given to male officers and desk jobs to female officers in certain states. There is nothing in the rule book that requires this; it reflects rather the way in which rules are interpreted. Women were only permitted to join the Forest Service in the late seventies and are still not permitted to become forest guards. Indeed, Sarin points out, that despite the shift to 'joint forest management' and the language of 'people's participation', forest departments retain the 'parmilitary organisational structure' they inherited from a period when their role was to guard the forests from the people.

Chikarmane notes the rules, norms and procedures by which the police force in the country remains almost totally male. Women were first inducted into the police force to deal with women and this segregated mentality remains embedded within its rules. Recruitment is not open to women in most states but limited to the number of posts available for women police: recruitment rules thus serve as the first point of segregation and women make up less than two per cent of the police force in most states. While in principle, promotional avenues were the same for women and for men, the restricted posts for women meant that possibilities for promotion were far more limited than for men. The result is a highly masculine police force and police stations which inhibit half of the country's population from seeking protection or redress. The gender-biased effects of this on police attitudes and practices are noted by both Chikarmane and Mukhopadhyay and Chikarmane also documents how it affects women's attitudes and practices in relation to the police. Rajgopal's chapter offers some insights into how the rules, norms and practices embedded in the government's delivery of primary education intersect with the rules, norms and practices of the wider community in Rajasthan to ensure that only particular groups of officially eligible school-age children viz. boys, especially those from upper caste households, benefit from the availability of this resource.

An analysis of the intersecting ways in which different institutions draw on and reproduce, norms and beliefs about gender, class and caste thus also helps to explain how resources get distributed, who gains and who is excluded. Kabeer and Murthy identify three forms of gender disadvantage which are likely to be relevant in a variety of different contexts but which are explored here in relation to access and benefits from government credit programmes for the poor. The first relates to what we call *gender-intensified disadvantage* and refers to the fact that for any given category of disadvantaged groups in society, women, by and large, suffer from all the disadvantages of men of their class but in an intensified form as a result of direct gender discrimination in the allocation of resources and responsibilities. Thus, for any given class, women are more likely to be assetless, illiterate and socially isolated than men, because of the way in which norms and practices define their access to these resources. The second relates to *gender-specific forms of disadvantage* and reflects the specific ways in which gender defines women as a subordinate category within a given cultural context. It refers to the operation of cultural norms and practices which are subscribed to all those who share a given culture but which may be operationalised differently across class and caste. Thus, in the Indian context, gender-specific forms of disadvantage relate to women's primary responsibility for housework, regardless of what other forms of work they undertake, the greater constraints put on their public mobility and the 'polluting characteristics' attributed to their bodies. But these forms of disadvantage may play out differently for different castes and classes.

The third category relates to *imposed gender disadvantage* and refers to the fact that while gender inequality may be constructed through different norms and varying realities for different social groups in society, some groups have more power than others to assume that their own norms and their own realities are universal and to impose them in the way in which goods and services are distributed within society. The chapters in this book provide various examples of imposed gender disadvantage in the evidence of middle-class, male, urban biases which characterise the design and delivery of education (Rajgopalan), credit (Kabeer and Murthy), forest produce (Sarin), legal justice (Mukhopadhyay) and government employment (Thakur).

Any organisation can be scrutinised both through the framework outlined above and an analysis of its official rules and unofficial norms. Together with the allocation of resources and responsibilities which these generate between different categories of people, the framework can help to understand the pattern of hierarchies embodied by the organisation, where power lies within it and who exercises it. Thus the gendered 'outcomes' of organisational practice—*who gets what, who does what, who decides, who gains and who loses (which men and which women)*—can be understood through a 'snapshot' analysis of its rules, resources and practices (See Figure 1). As the contributions in this book make clear, an analysis of 'rules', in particular the official ones, gives us only part of the picture as far as understanding inequitable outcomes. Equally, if not more, important is the analysis of the process by which written rules and unwritten norms and beliefs come into play in the everyday interactions by which organisational goals are translated into practice.

Figure 1: Gender relations (as outcome)

RULES NORMS, CUSTOMS, RIGHTS, RESPONSIBILITIES CLAIMS OBLIGATIONS	RESOURCES AS INPUTS, RESOURCES AS OUTPUTS	ACTIVITIES ROLES, TASKS LABOUR	COMMAND & CONTROL (HIERARCHIES OF POWER AND DECISION-MAKING)

Clearly, in this context, the question of power and authority is critical to understanding whose meanings and whose interpretations will prevail in the final outcomes. In the narrow organisational sense, power will be concentrated more densely in those members of an organisation who are favoured by the rules as far as resources and authority (i.e. recognised power to make decisions) are concerned. In the broader social sense, however, power is not formally rule-defined, but is most likely to be exercised by those who are able to mobilise these resources over a range of organisational domains. We see an example of this in operation in Mukhopadhyay's contribution where she traces the way in which wives' ability to get the maintenance payments due to them under the law were frequently thwarted because husbands were able to mobilise a shared understanding of women's fitness/unfitness as wives to win the support of the police, the lawyers and the judge to ensure a verdict in their own favour. Here it is not just the individual resources of the husband which determine his ability to secure a favourable outcome but his ability to mobilise ideological support from relevant male strangers with influence in the 'official' domain.

It is *precisely* because men from any given social class are more able in general than women from the same social class to mobilise resources from a broader range of organisational domains—the intimate and personalised organisations of family and kinship to the increasing more distant and apparently impersonal organisations of community, market and state—that gender relations are constituted as relations of power.

Understanding gender inequality through such an institutional perspective helps emphasise the complex ways in which organisational rules, cultural norms and routinised practices from different institutional sites intersect to produce and sustain such inequality across society. It also helps make a number of other points which need to be borne in mind when attempting to address such inequality through policy interventions:

- On the one hand, it reminds us that gender inequalities are deeply institutionalised in largely unquestioned aspects of organisational practice. Gender relations often appear immutable and given because gender inequalities cut across institutional sites; because of the taken-for-granted nature of the practices through which gender inequalities are institutionalised; and because of the powerful and 'eternalising' ideologies which justify these inequalities and keep them in place.
- On the other hand, if organisations are constituted and reconstituted over time through the routinisation of specific rules, norms and practices, then they can be transformed by challenging and renegotiating organisational rules and practice.

Needs, Interests and Institutional Change

Strategies which will help to challenge the institutionalised basis of gender inequality have to be premised on understanding of how organisations in different social domains get reconstituted as relationships of inequality over time and, hence, where an impetus for change is likely to emerge. Institutions, the rules they embody, the memberships they create, the resources they distribute and the practices they generate survive over time because they serve the interests of a sufficient number, or a sufficiently powerful number, of their membership. The rules, norms and practices of an organisation require its members to perform certain obligations in return for certain claims. Defined by the rules and norms of the organisation, these claims and obligations set up certain *needs* for different members, if they are to fulfil what is required of them, and thus contribute to how that organisation is reproduced over time. Where institutional relationships are constituted in gender-ascriptive terms, such as those associated with family and kinship, these claims and obligations will also be defined in gender terms and will generate gender-specific needs, including the *practical gender needs* of everyday life.

However, while other organisations are not inherently gender-ascriptive, we noted examples of how they tend to reproduce gender norms, practices and inequalities through their organisations. This often takes the form of acknowledging the relevance of certain gender attributes and needs, but not others. Thus, employers may justify paying higher wages to male workers because they are socially defined as the primary family breadwinner while they may refuse to provide child care facilities at the work place for women workers on the grounds that it is their private domestic responsibility. In other words, needs are not neutrally interpreted: some needs are given social recognition by an organisation. Men's role as breadwinners is translated not simply into the 'need' for a job but also the need to pay them more than women, regardless of productivity and regardless of whether the woman might in fact be the sole or primary breadwinner of her family. Women's role as carers does not, however, easily translate into a recognised need for child care facilities in the work place. It is thus through the 'politics of needs interpretion' that biases of states, markets and non-governmental organisations reproduce the inequalities of the inherently gendered institutions of family and kinship.

Rajgopal's chapter analyses how the official primary school delivery system in Rajasthan was designed in such a way as to ignore not only the class and caste disadvantage which differentiated the population of school-going girls and boys, but also ignored the gender-specific needs and constraints which affected the ability of girls to attend school. The gender composition of teachers, the timing and location of classes, the content of the educational curriculum and indeed, every aspect of the educational system made no allowances for the social constraints, domestic workloads and livelihood roles which particularly prevented girls from poorer households from participating in the schooling system. The result was that Rajasthan is one of the poorest perfomers in the country as far as basic literacy is concerned and the poorest performer as far as female literacy is concerned. However, drawing on the experience of an innovative educational programme which explicitly addressed the biases in the rules and practice within the official educational system, Rajgopal offers evidence that a more imaginative design of public policy can help reverse long-standing forms of discrimination.

Sarin's contribution to the book provides an analysis of how class and gender inequalities come together in shaping the definition of 'needs' in the context of social forestry. Although the Indian government has adopted the idea of joint forest management with the community, it tends to operate with a very undifferentiated notion of community, ignoring the existence of differing, and conflicting, needs and interests within the community with regard to forest produce. Women from poorer families rely on collecting forest produce for cooking fuel, so that while it is the collective needs of the family for cooked food which underpins the need for firewood, it is constructed as women's practical gender need since they are responsible for finding this firewood. However, forestry policy has prioritised the *community's* need for timber over the needs of poorer families for cooking fuel. The result has been to transform poorer women into 'forest offenders' as they attempt to bypass these rules, something that brings them into direct conflict with men and women from wealthier households who are now 'forest police' since they have alternative sources of fuel and stand to benefit from the sale of timber.

As long as existing organisational arrangements meet the needs of a sufficient proportion, or a sufficiently powerful proportion, of its membership—*and no better arrangement appears feasible*—there will be little incentive to seek to renegotiate the rules and the organisation in question is likely to be reproduced over time in a relatively unchanged form. However, in as much as existing practice embodies gender inequalities in the distribution of allocative and authoritative resources, women and men benefit unequally and are likely to have very different and often conflicting *strategic gender interests* in defending, resisting or transforming these rules. Thus, if Figure 1 is taken to provide a 'snapshot' of gender relations within specific organisations and helps to explain the gendered *outcomes* of organisational practice at a particular point in time, Figure 2 draws attention to *process* over time: the reconstitution of gender inequalities in an unchanged form because of the combined presence of powerful interests in promoting unchanged practices and the absence of any countervailing interest groups strong enough to challenge them.

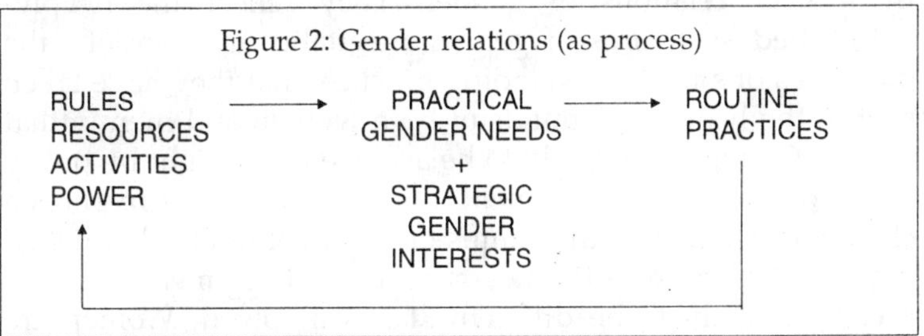

We use the terms 'practical needs' and 'strategic interests' to make a distinction between the manifest and underlying aspects of gender inequality in our analysis of gender-aware policy interventions, a distinction which crops up in a number of forms in this chapter and in the rest of the book:

> *practical gender needs* refer to those which are manifest in everyday life as a result of the asymmetrical gender division of resources and responsibilities.
>
> *strategic gender interests* are a product of the underlying structural inequalities which give rise to these needs.

Needs tend to be associated with dependency status in policy discourse; interests, on the other hand, entail a recognition of the rights of the individuals and hence their ability to define their own goals and priorities. While needs and interests refer to different dimensions of desired outcomes, they are clearly inter-related in practice, since the capacity to make choices rests on certain prior needs being met and the way in which prior needs are met will shape the extent to which people are able to make choices for themselves.

Molyneux (1985), who coined the distinction between practical and strategic, gives examples of the kinds of changes which might serve women's strategic gender interests: the abolition of a coercive gender division of labour, of unequal control over resources, measures against male violence, respect for reproductive rights, the establishment of political equality; and ending the sexual exploitation of women. Each of these changes addresses the ways in which women are constrained, by the fact of being women, from making choices. However, each of these changes also goes to the very heart of the power relations of gender. They reflect the deeply-entrenched structures of gender inequality in a society, the outcomes of such long-standing practice, that they have taken root in the hearts and minds of both women and men in that society. Change is unlikely to be achieved overnight by policy diktat or declarations of intent, not only because it requires a change in the hearts and minds of women but also because it requires a change in the hearts and minds of men. But here there are likely to be different stakes involved. Women are demonstrably more open to the idea of change in this field because they have much to gain from a more egalitarian organisation of gender relations. Men, on the other hand, have a collective interest *as men* in organisations of social life which give them a privileged status: they do not only have a strategic gender interest in resisting attempts at transformation, but also have the greatest *capacity* to resist such transformation.

The idea that men and women might have conflicting gender interests is one that makes many people deeply uncomfortable because gender relations are so closely associated with the intimate relations of the family and have been so widely constructed as natural, harmonious and unproblematic. Yet we constantly come across evidence that such conflict does exist. It is this sense of antagonistic gender interests that is expressed in the statement by Farzana, the Muslim woman seeking to get maintanance from her husband whose story is told in Mukhopadhyay's chapter. Her lawyer tells her that she would have been better off married to a Hindu since she could not have been divorced so easily. Farzana points out that she would been ostracised by her community if she married outside it to which the lawyer responded that all *jatis* were the same, they were all Indians. Farzana's response is unequivocal: 'Brother,' she says 'there are only two jatis: men and women'.

Antagonistic gender interests are also in evidence in Bina Agarwal's report of the reaction of the Minister of Agriculture to her seminar on gender and land rights at the Indian Planning Commission in 1989: 'Are you suggesting that women should be given rights in land. What do women want? To break up the family?' (cited on p. 281 in Agarwal, 1994). And while the women's movement in India has identified dowry both as an expression of women's devalued status within the family, and as a cause of violence against them, often resulting in death, they are unlikely to receive a great deal of support from the Indian bureacracy in this since men within the bureacracy can count on receiving extremely generous dowries, *precisely* because they are in the bureaucracy.

We see various aspects of male gender interests played out in the contributions by Mathur and Mukhopadhyay, both in the exercise of male power in its ugliest and most violent form, but also male power as the routine mobilisation of the biases implicit within institutional rules and practice (Lukes, 1974). Mukhopadhyay provides accounts of how the rules of the law are interpreted in practice for women, focusing on the law which guarantees 'dependent' members of the family (aged parents, wives and children) the legally enforceable right to maintenance if it can be proved that the household head is not living up to his obligations. The law itself is, of course, a recognition of an existing social reality: that certain family members are rendered dependent on others by the operation of social rules and the way that the law is intepreted will determine the extent to which the effects of this dependent status are mitigated or reinforced. Mukhopadyay traces the way in which shared views about women's rightful place influenced how both the police and the courts treated disputes between husbands and wives, and defined the officially recognised as well as unofficial grounds on which wives gained, or were denied, the right to maintenance. Women lose the right to maintenance if they marry or take up a job since they are now defined as someone else's dependent or they are defined as independent. However, they could also lose the right to maintenance if it can be shown that they were not beaten or tortured in any way by their husbands, apparently the only grounds which the court recognised as justification for a wife to leave her husband. And the only evidence that such abuse had occurred was testimony by the police.

Mathur's contribution tells us the story of Bhanwari, a WDP worker, who was gang-raped by a group of upper caste men from her village for her temerity in seeking to implement the government's ban on child marriages and how the crime was treated by the police, the local courts and then the Supreme Court. She traces the kinds of class, caste and gender biases that came into play in the exercise of power and allowed a small number of men to rely on other men (particularly with shared caste interests) to uphold their shared gender interests when these came into conflict with those of a woman (who also happened to be from a lower caste to themselves). Indeed, one of the arguments used by the defence to suggest that the rape could not have taken place invoked explicitly caste interests: it suggested that since the offenders were upper caste men and included a Brahmin, and Bhanwari was from a lower caste, the rape could not have taken place.

However, entrenched male privilege within an institution does not imply that change is impossible. Institutions have to be constantly reconstituted through the practices of different actors, all of whom bring a range of identities and interests to bear upon their practice. It is precisely the potential for conflict and contradiction arising out of diverging interests within an organisation which may give those with a stake in transformation the impetus and strength to challenge the 'rules of the game'. Here it is important not to fall into a feminist version of 'women-as-homogenous-category' which assumes all women perceive an identity of interests and will act as advocates for the same forms of change. Women carry identities other than those of gender and some women may benefit sufficiently from the workings of an organisation to find change threatening. Or their stake in defending a system of rules and practices may change over time as they move from positions of relative powerlessness to positions of relative power.[2] Equally fallacious is the other side of the coin to the delusion of universal sisterhood—that of universal brotherhood. Even if men as a collectivity may benefit from a specific configuration of rules, norms and practices within an organisation, individual men may not. Like women, men also carry identities other than their gender and even their gender identities may have contradictory implications. As direct beneficiaries of unjust rules and practices, they may support them but as fathers, husbands or brothers to those who suffer the effects of such injustice, they may not. Moreover, many men are capable of rejecting injustice, regardless of who benefits or loses from it, *because it is injustice.*

Bhanwari's husband appears to be an example of such a man. As Mathur points out, in a society where husbands tend to reject 'violated' wives because they have been dishonoured, the fact that Bhanwari's husband stood by her after having been made to witness her gang-rape was unusual enough in itself to be used in court to cast doubt on his evidence: the argument of the defence was 'In our society how can an Indian husband whose role is to protect his wife stand by and watch his wife being raped?' Mathur also points out that while it was a male judge who acquitted the accused and hence dismissed Bhanwari's charge of rape, it was another male judge who spoke against the court's decision at a demonstration organised by women's groups.

In other words, while institutions and structures may embody male bias, and promote male power, at the individual level, men are no more homogenous than women, and many will prove valuable allies in the struggle for change. While some may contribute to it on grounds of a perceived injustice or on grounds of compassion, others may do so because they may recognise that there are long-run, and frequently hidden, material as well as emotional 'costs' to being a man, of a different kind to those of being a woman. In the context of my training experiences, individual men have often spoken of the pressures they always face to 'get to the top' of the pecking order; the pressure to perform sexually; and their fear of failure as a breadwinner in the event of lack of promotion or redundancy. In her analysis of the gendered constitution of the Indian Administrative Service, Thakur notes the long hours of work men are often required to put in to prove their commitment to their jobs at considerable cost to their personal lives and to the lives of their wives and children, in contrast to the very different expectations—and concomitantly different constraints—which are placed on women officers who are seen as having prior obligations to their families.

All of this is to caution against the portrayal of gender interests in essentialised terms, but it is not to deny that women are likely to have a much greater stake in social transformation in the direction of greater gender inequality. The deep entrenchment of male privilege within specific organisations and within society at large suggests that women are likely to be in the forefront of any fundamental challenge to the system and its most effective advocates, so that transformatory strategies will generally entail creating the conditions where the potential for such challenge can be articulated, mobilised and acted upon. Hence the point we made earlier: the struggle to achieve gender equity in development policy is in the ultimate analysis a *political project* and it is essential to think tactically as well as strategically about how it is to be achieved.

This means the need to recognise that most women need resources to cope with the constraints of the present situation before they can take on the task of transforming that situation. Hence, rather than posing a dichotomy between the everyday practical needs generated by the prevailing gender division of resources and responsibilities and longer-term strategic gender interests, both can usefully be seen as different aspects of the same question: *what* the priorities for gender-aware policy should be and *how* they should be operationalised. Women's practical gender needs and the ways in which they are met then become inter-related dimensions of strategic interests—needs point in the direction of satisfying choices, while interests refer to expanding control over the conditions of choice (see Jonasdottir, 1988, for an excellent discussion of interest theory). The capacity of those who have a stake in challenging the status quo to deal with this resistance cannot be taken for granted; it has to be built up through processes of empowerment. The idea of strategic gender interests can therefore be given a processual definition: meeting daily practical needs in ways that transform the conditions in which women make choices is a crucial element of the process by which women are empowered to take on the more deeply entrenched aspects of their subordination. This relates once again to the point we made earlier: that the transformatory potential of an intervention lies as much in the *means* through which needs are satisfied and opportunities created as it does in the precise *ends* which inform a policy intervention.

Engendering the Mainstream Policy Agenda

The importance of political considerations in attempting to bring about gender-aware development is well illustrated by looking at some of the ways in which feminist advocates have sought to influence the policy process, from both within mainstream international agencies as well from outside. As we shall see, these efforts can be distinguished not only in terms of their overall goals but also in terms of the basis on which they seek to make their claims. In particular, efforts to make development policy more gender-aware have been fuelled by two different, although not necessarily incompatible, types of considerations (Elson, 1992; Jahan, 1995).

Integrationist tactics: Integrationist advocacy has sought to emphasise how a concern with the advancement of women can contribute to the achievement of agendas set by those who may have no particular concern with women's needs and interests. To use Jaquette's terms, integrationist advocacy can be seen as an attempt to shift the basis of claims on behalf of women from the earlier emphasis on *need*, always a more discretionary form of claim and one most easily ignored in situations of competing claims, to an emphasis on *merit*, which attempts to redefine the basis of women's claims in terms of which are compatible with institutional priorities (Jaquette, 1990). Its advantage is the short-term payoff, but its achievements are likely to be circumscribed within predetermined parameters set by institutional rules.

Transformative or agenda-setting strategies: Transformative advocacy is based on the recognition by some gender advocates that in male-dominated organisations, the 'rules of the game' are likely to throw up notions of merit which are loaded against women (a point made in some detail in Thakur's chapter). Transformative strategies are more politically ambitious because they are about changing the rules, rather than playing by them. In development terms, they go beyond seeking to integrate gender issues into the development agenda and seek to transform the agenda and broaden its goals to enable it to address issues of social justice. More crucially, they seek to give women a much greater role in setting the agenda in the first place. Because of the more radical goals, transformative strategies require a more nuanced and complex set of tactics: theoretical arguments which challenge established ways of thinking; creative proposals for alternative ways of doing; and political mobilisation to ensure more participatory and responsive decision-making structures (Elson, 1992).

Forms of Gender Advocacy in Development Policy

Overall goal	Policy intervention		
	Gender-neutral	Gender-specific	Gender-transformative
Integrationist	✓	✓	****
Transformative	****	✓	✓

Integrationist Advocacy: From Needs to Merit

Integrationist tactics by gender advocates began as a response to the segregated and marginalised status assigned to women's concerns in mainstream policy agendas prior to the emergence of Women in Development (WID) advocacy. At that time, development efforts were dominated by the drive for economic growth, generally backed by state intervention. Within this agenda, men were identified as the key economic agents, and hence the focus of mainstream development policies, while women were brought in primarily under the state and private welfare efforts in their familial roles as mothers, wives and dependants or else as 'deviants' from familial roles: destitute and abandoned women and prostitutes. This gender segregation within the policy domain was the main target of the early WID critique and explained their emphasis on *integration*. What women were to be integrated into varied according to what the mainstream agenda was. As the stress on economic growth of the early decades of development gave way in the seventies to a concern with poverty and basic needs, integrationist efforts sought to demonstrate that women were predominantly represented in the ranks of the 'poorest of the poor' and were largely responsible for meeting the family's basic needs. By the eighties, the ascendance of neo-liberal ideologies in the international arena led to a renewed emphasis on economic growth, this time with the stress on market forces, and integrationist gender advocacy accordingly shifted to 'efficiency'-based arguments, stressing the critical significance of women's economic contribution in any effort to maximise returns to economic growth. This has been associated with the emphasis on women's role in market-led recovery as food producers; as microentrepreneurs; and as the key earners of foreign exchange in an era of trade liberalisation and export-orientation.

More recently, as the limits to the market as prime allocator of resources have become more evident, there has been a growing emphasis on the human factor in development. For the World Bank, this has taken the form of a re-focus on poverty and the promotion of labour-intensive strategies backed by public investment in human resources as the key to poverty-alleviating growth. The UN agencies have sought to promote a human-centred development but with less of an emphasis on the market as the key institutional mechanism for ensuring growth and more space for public action. Although 'women' as a category is now more routinely included within such discussions, it is often on a token basis; gender advocates within these agencies, therefore, have to continue to explicitly draw out the gender implications of these broader policies. Consequently, a narrower version of *mainstreaming* is concerned with highlighting the gender dimensions within the current policy preoccupations of official development agencies.

Advocacy for Transformation: From Merit to Justice

Alongside these integrationist efforts, there have been parallel efforts by gender advocates, scholars and activitists, often outside the official agencies, to move beyond the task of integrating gender issues into mainstream development to the more challenging task of transforming the meaning of development from a gender perspective. As Elson (1991) points out, one reason why male bias continues to persist in development thought and planning is because a gender approach has frequently been reduced to 'adding women on' without seeking to question mainstream ways of thinking and operating. As long as these ways of thinking and doing remain intact, the potential for a more gender-aware development remains severely curtailed.

Early attempts at a transformative approach took the form of the demand for equality. The 'welfare' approach had been heavily criticised by early WID advocates because it equated women primarily with reproduction and ignored their critical role in production. Pointing to the adverse effects of development for women, early advocates argued for *equality of opportunity* for women within the development process. However, the redistributive connotations of the demand for equality—and in particular its pertinence to the institutional practices which led to the reproduction of male dominance within most development agencies—meant it never went beyond the level of rhetoric in most of these agencies (Buvinic, 1983). In any case, it was also increasingly realised that formal equality of opportunity within institutions which had evolved around the assumption of the male institutional actor would always work against women: as the case of Pauline Neville-Jones, a high-ranking woman who recently resigned from the British Foreign Office after being passed over for promotion, appeared to demonstrate, there is no need for active discrimination against women when the culture of an organisation can be relied on to reproduce the gender status quo (*The Observer*, 11 Feb. 1996).

More recent advocacy to transform development practice has therefore focused on the nature of institutional rules and practices and the way in which they embody male agency, needs and interests. Some feminists have stressed the significance of women's labour and responsibilities in the production of human resources and the extent to which existing policies and institutions have taken them for granted. Others have pointed to the gender-blindness of laws which have been constructed on the basis of formal equality, or equality premised on the notion of the 'sameness' of women and men, where the male actor is held to be the norm. Kapur and Cossman (1993) suggest that a *substantive*, as opposed to a *formal*, concern with equality in law, would require taking legislative account of the ways in which women are different from men, both in terms of biological capacities, as well as the socially constructed disadvantages women face relative to men. Similarly, in the context of development, I have noted the implications of the social construction of biological differences, and the associated division of resources and responsibilities, for the needs, interests and constraints experienced by women and men (see Kabeer, 1994). I have suggested that gender *equity* has to be premised on the notion of social justice rather than on a search for *formal equality of opportunity*; gender equity requires recognition of the unequal constraints and opportunities which underpin gender differences in the ability of women and men to define their own goals and exercise agency in pursuit of these goals. Within a framework of substantive equality and gender equity, welfare investments to assist women in the reproduction and care of human resources and efficiency investments to ensure the optimal use of their productive potential have to be seen as complementary, rather than competing approaches, to a human-centred development.

We can also identify the first signs of a transformative version of the *mainstreaming* approach in the efforts of a number of development agencies to address their own procedures of recruitment and promotion. Such moves may not have gone far enough—the comment of one gender advocate on the basis of her experience within the UN system would probably apply across the board to most development agencies: "We'll know we have equality when a mediocre woman has as much chance of success within the system as a mediocre man." But these moves represent an important change from the early days of advocacy when there was considerable resistance by male-dominated agencies to the equality agenda because of its redistributive connotations for agency practice. It is significant that many of the same international agencies which were so resistant to the demands for equality in the seventies are now taking steps to achieve a greater gender balance in their recruitment and promotion practices. Ultimately, however, mainstreaming is more than a question of numbers of women in an organisation and in high places, although that clearly helps. It is only when the attempts to shift gender perspectives and women's concerns from their marginal location, in both institutional and ideological terms, to the centre of the development agenda, leads to a process of rethinking of institutional rules, priorities and goals and substantial redistribution of resources that mainstreaming strategies can be considered to have had a transformative impact on development practice. The ultimate test of 'mainstreaming' is when the mainstream agenda itself has accommodated a world where women's needs, interests and abilities *also* matter (see Jahan, 1995, for further discussion on mainstreaming).

Following on from, and subsuming, the demands of equality, equity and justice are strategies which stress the *empowerment* of women. Empowerment is about questioning the notion of selfhood that women and men bring with them to their everyday development activities and the extent to which it is premised on a sense of self-worth and dignity. Empowerment processes seek to bring about changes in the distribution of material and symbolic resources and opportunities between women and men within the development process but also—and crucially—to bring about changes in the beliefs and values which they have assimilated in the process of acquiring a gendered sense of selfhood where these consitute a constraint on their capacity for exercising agency in their own lives (Batliwala, 1994 and Kabeer, 1994, for more detailed discussion on strategies for empowerment).

Moving from Gender-blind to Gender-aware: Policy from a Different Perspective

The aim of the framework and analysis in this chapter and in the rest of this book is ultimately a practical one. We hope that by providing a systematic way of analysing gender inequality and showing the welfare, efficiency and equity costs that it entails, those who are influential in making and implementing policies in government and non-governmental organisations with a mandate to address these various goals will be enabled to analyse for themselves the relevance of gender in their work. In this final section of the chapter, I want to use the preceding discussion to make the point that there are a number of different ways in which a gender-aware perspective can be translated into policy, depending on the forms of advocacy which are most likely to be effective or the goals of policy which are most likely to be realisable. I started this chapter by pointing out how a great deal of *gender-blindness* of past policy reflected particular assumptions about biological difference and cultural determinism which allowed policymakers to perceive men as the key development actors and to privilege their needs, interests and priorities in the way that they designed policy. *Gender-aware* policies, by extension, are those which are based on the recognition that development actors are women as well as men, that men and women are constrained in different, and often unequal ways, as potential participants and as beneficiaries in the development process and that they may consequently have differing, and sometimes conflicting needs, interests and priorities.

We have discussed how gender-blindness is often rooted in the taken-for-granted norms, biases and prejudices so that there is a persistent need for 'reality checks' by policymakers, practitioners and analysts between their assumptions and practices and the reality on the ground. However, rethinking assumptions and practices from a gender perspective does not necessarily lead to the adoption of policies which go straight to the heart of the unequal relationships between women and men. The extent to which interventions which result from gender-sensitive analysis will also have transformative outcomes will reflect the combined effects of the predisposition of individual planners, practioners and the institutional constraints within which they must function, the socioeconomic contexts in which they seek to intervene and the possibilities which it offers. Consequently, under the broad rubric of gender-aware policies, we can distinguish different kinds of interventions, differentiated by whether they are seeking to achieve 'integration' or 'transformation'. One corollary of this distinction is that debates about the generic virtues of 'integrated' versus 'women-specific' programmes miss the point. Instead, an intervention has to be designed on the basis of the needs or opportunities which have themselves been prioritised on the basis of gender-aware analysis and the political feasibility of particular forms of change so that as the following schema shows, *formally* gender-specific interventions can be *substantively* distinguished by the integrationist or transformative intent of their goals.

Linking Goals and Interventions

Overall goal	Policy intervention		
Integrationist	Gender neutral	Gender-specific	***
Transformative	***	Gender-specific	Gender-transformative

The main thrust of 'integrationist' advocacy is to point out that men and women have different roles and make different kinds of contributions and that these have to be built into policy design to ensure the most effective use of development resources (see Overholt et al., 1985, for a framework for gender analysis which embodies an integrationist perspective). Such advocacy tends to promote *gender neutral* policies based on the idea that an accurate assessment of the existing gender division of resources and responsibilities will ensure that policy objectives are met as effectively as possible within a given context. In countries where there is a significant tradition of independent female farming, a gender neutral agricultural policy aimed at improving agricultural productivity would design its extension services to reach both sets of farmers. In other contexts, where female seclusion is more widely practised and men dominate field-based agricultural work while women are engaged in homestead farming, a gender-neutral agricultural extension service which aimed at improving agricultural productivity would entail services which encompass information and inputs pertaining to both cereal crops grown in the field as well as horticultural crops grown on homestead farms. Gender neutral policies have often been advocated from within integrationist frameworks and hence reflect the strengths and limitations of such advocacy. They reflect an improved informational basis but not a greater political awareness. They are premised on the recognition of the different roles, resources and responsibilities of men and women and hence target the appropriate actors in the development effort, but they leave the existing divisions of roles, resources and responsibilities intact. They prioritise the practical over the strategic.

Integrationist advocacy can also lead to *gender-specific* policies which are intended to target and benefit a specific gender in order to achieve certain policy goals or to meet certain gender-specific needs more effectively. This category of policies differs radically from the older gender-stereotyping, which targeted men for production-related interventions and women for welfare-related interventions, if it is based on an accurate analysis of the prevailing division of labour, responsibilities and needs rather than on planners' biases and preconceptions. The gender division of labour in most societies entails the assignment of differing tasks and responsibilities to women and men in the pursuit of household survival and security and consequently generates gender-specific practical needs and constraints. Gender-specific policies may result from a recognition of these differing needs and constraints. Boserup's advocacy that greater attention be paid to education for women as a way of closing the growing productivity gap between men and women and the resulting gap in their ability to benefit from development, is an example of advocacy which might lead to a gender-specific response. Similarly, recognition that women may be held back from participation in mainstream development by lack of control over their fertility may lead to the rise of family planning efforts targeted at women. Home-based income-generating projects for women in societies where strict norms of female seclusion are observed, with related restrictions on women's mobility, may be the appropriate and gender-specific responses to objective constraints. Thus, the difference between a women-specific intervention being regarded as gender-aware rather than gender-blind rests on the difference between one which is based on prior assumptions about 'proper' roles for women and one which is based on the analysis of gender-specific needs and constraints.

However, gender-specific interventions need not be limited to integrationist goals. They can also be thrown up by transformative advocacy which seeks to address not the manifestations of gender inequality but also their underlying causes. Some examples of *gender-transformative* interventions which take a gender-specific form may help to make the distinction between 'integrationist' and 'transformative' clearer. If we take the case of female circumcision, an intervention which address it purely in terms of its implications for women's health is an example of a highly needed, gender-specific intervention but one that is likely to leave the practice itself intact. However, it takes on greater transformatory potential if the health intervention is also accompanied by an attempt to raise the issue of women's rights over their own bodies: circumcision is, after all, generally done *to* one person on the authority of another and usually without the consent of the former. If mothers are seen as the front-line agents in arranging for the circumcision of daughters, then mothers may have to be the obvious front-line in the campaign to stop female circumcision. However, longer transformation will clearly require men to become advocates for such change as well.

While feminist activists were among the first to promote women's groups as a means of bringing women together in the struggle for social change, the formation of women into groups has been taken up in a wide variety of development interventions for the more effective integration of women. Indeed, in Bangladesh, where the now widespread practice of group-based lending to women was pioneered, there is a striking contrast between the insistence on group formation in the context of credit delivery whose goal is the creation of women entrepreneurs who must presumably compete with each other to be successful, and the denial, with government backing, of the right to organise to women working in the garment factories who presumably have a collective interest in organisation. It is clear that the formation of women's groups in the context of development efforts is a gender-specific strategy which can have more limited integrationist or more open-ended transformatory ends in mind.

However, transformative strategies do not necessarily entail women-specific interventions. Returning to the earlier example of school textbooks, we noted that they offered a very biased, and very unreal, model of gender for boys and girls. A gender-aware revision of the textbooks would clearly have important implications for the messages about gender role models for boys as well as girls. A gender-neutral revision of a textbook would entail a fairer representation of girls and boys in the illustrations and text, engaged in the kinds of activities that they typically engage with in the given context. A gender transformative revision, on the other hand, might seek to show boys more often taking part in domestic activities and girls aspiring to non-traditional roles in order to seek to question, rather than merely reproduce, the gender division of roles and responsibilities.

The transformatory potential of symbolic representations should not be underestimated. An anti-liquor agitation mobilised by rural women in Andhra Pradesh was sparked off by the reading materials distributed in a literacy campaign which showed the plight of a poor village woman whose husband drank away his wages at the local liquor shop. As Batliwala, (1994) points out, the example encouraged women to raise questions in the literacy classes about their own status and their potential to act. Equally, however, the practical and political difficulties of realising the transformatory potential of an intervention should not be underestimated. The field of development is littered with the remnants of policies which started out with good intentions and then foundered because of the failure to follow them through. The analysis of the programme entitled DWCRA (Development of Women and Children in Rural Areas) by Kabeer and Murthy in this volume provides some examples of how this might happen as they trace the different moments at which an intervention is conceptualised, formulated, communicated and then implemented.

This attempt to categorise different policy interventions according to their underlying objectives is thus intended as an analytical, rather than a prescriptive, tool. *Gender-transformative policies* are likely to be politically challenging because they inevitably require men to give up certain privileges or take on certain responsibilities in order to achieve greater equity in the development process. They may offer a 'win-win' outcome in the longer run, but in the shorter run, they are often perceived in 'zero-sum' terms. And since most women would prefer not to live in antagonistic relationships with men, most are unlikely to welcome forms of intervention which sharpen these antagonisms unnecessarily or in ways which increase their insecurities. The different approaches therefore should not be seen as mutually exclusive; one may be used as the only viable possibility or as a precursor to another. In situations where extreme gender bias in planning has been the norm, merely shifting to a more neutral approach may constitute a major step forward. In other situations, transformative strategies can take a gender-specific form, sometimes focusing on women, as we have seen, and sometimes on men e.g. interventions which seek to strengthen male responsibility in family planning, given the predominant (and indeed sole) focus on women in most family planning programmes, or attempts to conscientise men in gender issues such as wife-beating and dowry. In yet other situations, redistributive policies may end up being counter-productive if male resistance is not accurately anticipated and there is a backlash against women who should have benefited. In such contexts, welfare or poverty approaches, stressing needs rather than interests, may often prove to be the politically most feasible *entry point* for raising gender awareness within the policy arena because of their apparently non-threatening concerns; however the *means* used to implement the approach will determine whether it remains a purely welfarist measure, leaving intact the underlying causes of gender inequality, or whether it contributes to longer-term strategic change. Planning for transformation entails strategic thinking and a grounded sense of what is possible.

This means therefore that we need to move away from the dichotimised and prescriptive thinking implicit in the way that concepts such as access/control and practical/strategic have often been put forward in gender analysis (Overholt et al.; Moser, 1989) to more processual ways of asking about the relationship between an intervention and its likely impact. The key question about 'access' to resources is not 'control', but about *the difference it makes* to shifting gender inequalities. To focus purely on control ignores the multiple ways in which gender inequalities are manifested in everyday life and narrows the question of 'impact' down to a single dimension (see Kabeer, 1998, for further discussions of this point). Similarly, we need to ask how practical daily needs can be met in a way which can start to shift structural inequalities rather than setting up a 'hierarchy of needs' in which the grand 'strategic' takes political precedence over the mundane 'practical'. Because empowerment has many different dimensions, it cannot be captured through unidimensional or hierarchical measures: the focus of policy design where women's empowerment is a consideration has to be on its likely *transformatory potential*, on the difference it can make to the lives of men and women and on the significance of this difference in terms of the structural inequalities of power.

Conclusion: Let a Thousand Flowers Bloom!

These arguments and rationales for the promotion of gender issues in the policy arena clearly offer different bases for claiming resources with differing degrees of transformatory potential. However, it is also important not to reify the various categories. Gender relations are far too differentiated across cultures, and far too fluid within the different cultures, to permit for easy or universal policy prescriptions. The primary contribution that scholarship, advocacy and activism in this field can make is to analyse the main barriers to gender equity and social justice in different contexts and to develop appropriate strategies for dealing with them. If planning for transformation requires strategic analysis and a grounded sense of what is possible, as we suggested earlier, then the *how to* of policy is as important as the *what*.

There is no clear, unilinear path to social transformation and many of the contributions in this book tell us this. They point to attempts by the state, by NGOs and by activists to transform the conditions of women's lives but they also point out how often such attempts remain half-hearted and piecemeal or else founder in the face of age-old inequalities. However it is also clear that no single intervention can be expected to shift these ancient forms of discrimination, however promising its performance. What holds out more promise for the process of transformation than any single intervention is the variety of such interventions which are being carried out in India, and in many other parts of the world today, and the difficulties of containing within manageable boundaries the myriad changes which they unleash. The rape which Bhanwari suffered as a result of her challenge to the discriminatory practices of the upper castes in her community is an age-old response by men to challenges to their patriarchal power. But her response in taking the perpetrators through the legal system of India to the highest court in the land suggests that such privilege is in its turn now being challenged. The courts of the land will either have to transform their rules and practices so that they become more neutral in adjudicating between conflicts of caste, class and gender or they face becoming discredited in the eyes of the people they are intended to serve. Bhanwari may have not received the justice she hoped for, but she blazed the path for other women behind her in their search for social justice.

Notes

[1]The point that gender differentials in agricultural wages reflect ideological valuations rather than economic ones was made to me by a female agricultural labourer in Bangladesh (see Kabeer, 1994, p. 152).

[2]The classic example in the South Asian context is that of a woman moving from the position of being a new daughter-in-law among her husband's family to becoming a mother-in-law to a son's wife.

References

Agarwal, Bina, 1994. *A Field of One's Own: Gender and Land Rights in South Asia* Cambridge and Delhi: Cambridge University Press.

Batliwala, S., 1994. "The Meaning of Women's Empowerment: New Concepts from Action" in G. Sen, A. Germain and L.C. Chen (eds.) *Population Policies Reconsidered. Health, Empowerment and Rights* Harvard, Mass: Harvard University Press.

Buvinic, M., 1983. "Women's Issues in Third World Poverty: A Policy Analysis" in M. Buvinic, M. Lycette and W.P. McGreevey (eds.) *Women and Poverty in the Third World* Baltimore: John Hopkins University Press.

Carney, J., 1988. "Struggle over Land and Crops in an Irrigated Rice Scheme in the Gambia" in J. Davidson (ed.) *Agriculture, Women and Land. The African Experience* Boulder, Colorado: Westview Press.

Elson, D., 1991. "Male Bias in Macro-economics: The Case of Structural Adjustment" in D. Elson (ed.) *Male Bias in the Development Process* Manchester: Manchester University Press.

———, 1992. "Gender Issues in Development Strategies" in *Women 2000,* No. 1, New York: UN Division for Advancement of Women.

Gupta, J., 1997. "Voices Break the Silence: Women Define Their Rights and Demands with the Changing Land Relations in West Bengal" in *Journal of Women's Studies,* Vol. II, No. 2, Calcutta: Women's Studies Research Centre.

Harrison, E., 1995. "Fish and Feminists" *IDS Bulletin* Vol. 26(3).

Jahan, R., 1995. *The Elusive Agenda: Mainstreaming Women in Development* London: Zed Books.

Jaquette, J.S., 1990. "Gender and Justice in Economic Development" in I. Tinker (ed.) *Persistent Inequalities* Oxford: Oxford University Press.

Jonasdottir, A.G., 1988. "On the Concept of Interests, Women's Interests and the Limitations of Interest Theory" in K. B. Jones and A.G.Jonasdottir (eds.) *The Political Interests of Gender* London: Sage Publications.

Kabeer, N., 1994. "Training as Activism: Reflections on the Gender Planning Training Programme in India" paper presented at the pre-Beijing Conference at the University of East Anglia.

———, 1994a. "Gender Aware Policy and Planning: A Social Relations Perspective" in M. Macdonald (ed.) *Gender Planning in Development Agencies: Meeting the Challenges,* Oxfam U.K.

———, 1994b. *Reversed Realities: Gender Hierarchies in Development Thought,* London and New York: Verso Press, Delhi: Kali for Women.

———, 1998. "Can Buy Me Love? Re-evaluating the Empowerment Impact of Lending to Women in Rural Bangladesh" IDS Discussion Paper, Institute of Development Studies, Sussex.

———, and R. Subrahmanian, 1996. "Institutions, Relations and Outcomes: Framework and Tools for Gender-aware Planning" IDS Discussion Paper No. 357, IDS, Sussex.

Kapadia, K., 1995. *Siva and her Sisters. Gender, Caste and Class in Rural South India* Delhi: Oxford University Press.

Kapur, R. and B. Cossman, 1993. "On Women, Equality and the Constitution: Through the Looking Glass of Feminism" *National Law School Journal (Special Issue on Feminism and Law)* National Law School of India University, Bangalore.

Lukes, S., 1974. *Power: A Radical View* London: Macmillan Press.

Molyneux, M., 1985. "Mobilisation Without Emancipation: Women's Interests, State and Revolution" *Feminist Studies* Vol. 11 (2): pp. 227–54.

Moser, C.O.N., 1989. "Gender Planning in the Third World: Meeting Practical and Strategic Gender Needs" *World Development* Vol. 17(11): 1799–825.

North, D., 1990. *Institutions, Institutional Change and Economic Performance* Cambridge: Cambridge University Press.

Overholt, C., M.B. Anderson, K. Cloud and J.E. Austin (eds.), 1985. *Gender Roles in Development Projects* West Hartford: Kumarian Press.

Whitehead, A., 1979. "Some Preliminary Notes on the Subordination of Women" *IDS Bulletin Vol. 10 (3):* pp. 10–13.

Yates, R., 1994. "Women and Literacy: Contested Agendas in the Functional Literacy Programme, Ghana" Ph.D. dissertation, University of Sussex.

2

Beyond Myths

The Social and Political Dynamics of Gender

RAJNI PALRIWALA

Introduction

The idiom of kinship is all-pervasive in South Asia. Family and community are metaphors for the most sacred and most natural of relationships—between children and parents, wife and husband, sister and brother, devotee and god. These are the relationships which provide emotional security, material support, care, a sense of belonging, status, legitimacy and social identity. Simultaneously, the concrete experiences of women, young and old, reveal that the family-household and community have been, and are, spheres of inequity, constraint, oppression, even violence, embodying interests and power relations differentiated by gender and age. It is this duality and contradictoriness of the most intimate and most social of relations which lies at the heart of any attempt to understand and transform gender relations in South Asia.

The complexity is intensified by the diversity in kinship patterns and domestic arrangements among regions, between religious and 'ethnic' communities, castes, and classes, as well as between rural and urban spheres. These diversities overlap and cross-cut. Further, the apparently unchanging foundations of everyday life—kinship, marriage, family—have been changing over time, usually very subtly. The growing possibility and necessity of dealing with people without consideration of their kinship links is worth noting in this regard. Yet assertions of 'eternities' and uniformities in values and practices are central to the force and meaning of domestic arrangements and community. These are rooted in the 'common sense' of culture as given and gender relations as biologically based. It is only in going beyond these myths that the social and political dynamics of gender may be understood.

The discussion on the diversity and mapping of cultural regions in South Asia suggests a critical dividing line between the Sanskritic north and the Dravidian south (Karve 1968; Dumont 1957; Crane 1967; Kolenda 1967; Mandelbaum 1970; Libbee 1980; Sopher 1980; Dyson and Moore 1983; Palriwala 1994; Agarwal 1994). In this, the north-east is left out, which unfortunately, for want of space, will be true for this essay also. In terms of indicators of women's well-being, such as sex ratio, literacy, and kinship patterns, as discussed below, the south appears more favourable to women.

Juvenile sex ratios indicate that the preference for sons and patriliny is even stronger in the north than in the south. Two broad but related explanations can be given for this—cultural and economic. The first focuses on Brahmanical values favouring sons and men. Disaggregating the data, we see that in Tamil Nadu the sex ratio for the non-Sanskritic scheduled caste groups is higher than for others. However, in Rajasthan the ratios are more adverse for the scheduled castes than for others, with a much greater fall in the figures for the 5–9 age group as compared to the 0–4 age group, clearly indicating discrimination against girls amongst them (Agnihotri 1996). Either Brahmanical values have engulfed these castes or a second explanation has to be looked for, one which relates to the economic value of sons and men.

Work participation rates indicate that the availability and accessibility to individual paid employment and wage labour is even lower for Rajasthani women than it is for Tamil women, diminishing their economic value for their families. Furthermore, as discussed later, even as overall unemployment has been increasing, the differences between male and female employment have widened considerably. Scheduled castes—more than any other group—are poorer, have few family resources, and are dependent on wages. Thus it would appear that not just caste and status values, but also material pressures and the perceived economic worth of women orient the family and kinship system.

The pattern of widowhood also reflects the north-south divide (Drèze 1990), within the relative deprivation and inauspiciousness which largely marks widowhood in India. The proportion of widows in the rural female population and the ratio of widows to widowers in the north, especially the northwest, tended to be much lower than in the southern states in 1981.[1] This appears paradoxical, conveying the message—"More widows in the south? That's bad"! However, Drèze links the regional variation to (1) the stronger survival advantages of adult women in the south vis-a-vis adult men in the south (especially Kerala) and women in the north. This is reflected in the higher life expectancy of southern women and better female-male ratios; (2) the slightly larger age gaps in mean age at marriage between wives and husbands in the south; (3) lower widow remarriage rates in the south than in the north (see below); and crucially (4) the better survival chances of *widows* per se in the south than in the north and northwest. The first and the last in particular are compatible with a less women-hostile south.

As against the above, how are we to understand the reports of female infanticide among castes in Tamil Nadu which did not practise it earlier and the decline in juvenile sex ratio in some districts of that state (Chunkath and Athreya 1997)? Further, the women's movement, the Committee on the Status of Women in India, and other studies have highlighted the spread and inflation of dowry and the occurrence of dowry deaths in almost all groups in India. In other words, the contrast between the anti-women northern family and the women-benevolent southern family may hold only as a first approximation. We are directed to the possibility of an emerging or deeper unity underlying important differences in gender relations in the two regions.

What, in kinship relations and domestic arrangements, can explain the above? Firstly, our comparisons cannot be based on single features, which may contradict each other as high sex ratio and low widow remarriage do in parts of the south. Rather we must probe the interrelations between practices and groups, such as marriage patterns, domestic arrangements, employment opportunities and caste. Crucially, these features must be placed in their wider social and historical context if their meaning is to be understood.

In order to do so, this essay starts by examining household patterns in Rajasthan and Tamil Nadu at the macro-level. It then elaborates a case study of kinship networks and intra-household dynamics in Rajasthan, focusing on authority relations in the spheres of consumption and family finances. This leads to a discussion of family ideology, specifically the notion of 'family good'. Comparisons with Tamil Nadu again emerge, focusing in particular on shifts and the factors behind them. In conclusion, I explore the dynamic link between the sex ratio and the situation of widows.

Household Arrangements and Gender Relations

Domestic arrangements are central to the organisation of gender relations. Popular sayings, tales, drama and literature as well as sociological writings tend to reflect the view that women experience the complex/extended/joint household as more oppressive than the simple/elementary/nuclear one.[2] The implicit and at times explicit suggestions are that joint living is concomitant with stronger family sanctions, patriliny and patriarchy. In this section various kinship and economic features associated with contrasting household patterns will be elaborated. This essay supports the view that family sanctions are stronger in regions of joint household living, but not that patriliny is weaker in elementary living arrangements. At the outset we may note the relatively high incidence of joint household living in various districts of Rajasthan, including Sikar, as compared to the low incidence in most districts of Tamil Nadu in 1961 (Kolenda 1967; 1987; 1989).[3] The residential unity of patrikin and their wives (Shah 1973) is highly valued in the north.

Marriage practices and domestic organisation

In this sub-section regional differences in norms and practices of marriage and divorce are related to variations in the incidence of joint living. It is crucial to note the importance of marriage in peoples' life trajectories and in gender relations in India. Marriage is near universal, but more so for women than for men, and more so in districts where joint family living is more common (Kolenda 1987). Marriage continues to have material, social, and symbolic meanings and consequences which are asymmetrical in terms of their implications for females and males in at least three significant ways.

First, selfhood, respectability and status are tied to wifehood and motherhood in more exacting ways than they are to being a husband and/or father. A single man or a man without children is seen as unfortunate, but a woman in a similar situation is inauspicious, possibly dangerous. Second, marriage remains embedded in community, caste and religious codes. Thus inter-community marriages may be growing, but intra-caste, arranged marriages continue to be the norm. Wedding rituals and prestations, such as dowry, in becoming more elaborate and expensive, simultaneously act as markers of community and make daughters a burden. Third, and linked to this, is the significance of ideologies regarding female sexuality in ordering practices of kinship, family and marriage. Women are reified as the guardians and conduits of family and community honour, purity, and status in all South Asian religions. The control of marriage, particularly of girls, is central in bounding and resuscitating the community.

A corollary of the above is that marital ties are embedded within the wider kinship network, particularly those which flow out of marriage-affinal ties. At the same time, the characteristics of spouses, such as relative age, educational and income level, seniority in household, shape intra-household relations and are relevant to women's bargaining powers within their marital homes. Thus, in the (northern) high joint-living districts, where the age at marriage of girls, but also of boys, is low compared to that in the (southern) low joint-living districts (Kolenda 1987), young married couples are likely to live with the senior generation. Adolescent marriage, joint family living, the control of daughters-in-law, and family sanctions seem to go hand-in-hand.

Another important feature of the north-south divide was that among most southern castes the preferred spouse was an actual or classificatory relation, though in practice often this was not possible. The emphasis was on the reinforcement of existing kinship ties, rather than an extension of the community of cooperation. Women tended to be married into families they were related to or knew members of, into families considered of equivalent status. In contrast, among Hindus in the north there has been a 'traditional' prohibition on marriage between kin. The emphasis is on the spread of affinal ties within the caste, and among high status groups on the ideology of hypergamy—marrying daughters into a superior group/family. The last stresses a hierarchy between wife-takers and wife-givers, accentuating the hierarchy between husband and wife. However, this ranking was not entirely absent in the south, especially among Brahmans. Kapadia (1995) suggests that marriage could create a hierarchy even between close cross-kin who had been social equals. The greater age gap between older husbands and younger wives (where age means seniority and authority) in the south is also pertinent here.

Concomitant with the above is the practice of intra-district and intra-village marriage in the south as against the rule of marriage into another village in the north (Libbee 1980). Kolenda (1968; 1987) has suggested that these aspects mediate a woman's bargaining power within the household and her ability to move out of the oppressive joint household, thence affecting the incidence of joint living. In the northern districts where joint households are more common, non-kin marriage (among Hindus) and patrilocal residence are more prevalent. This ensures a geographical separation between a woman and her natal kin and her greater incorporation into her marital household, which increases with class and caste status, and joint family living. She starts life after marriage among strangers, with few, if any, kin nearby who she and her husband can easily call on for support, material or moral. It is the man's patrilineal kin who constitute the couple's everyday world, who intervene in household disputes, and who provide both the community of cooperation and the community of sanction, whereas in non-Brahman Tamil Nadu the wife's kin is likely to fill this space. Though even in Tamil Nadu "when there are marital problems, it is usually the interests of the male that prevail" (Kapadia 1995:14), marriage between kin and within the village softens the patriarchal implications of patriliny as found in the north.

In a context where most females recorded as household heads were not currently married, their percentage was slightly higher in the southern low joint family districts (Kolenda 1987). Widow remarriage, particularly to a younger brother or kinsman of the late husband, seems to have been more common in the north than in the south, indicating the greater control of the widow by her in-laws.[4] In south India non-Brahman widows are more likely to return to their natal homes, but north Indian Hindu women cannot easily do so. Furthermore, while divorce rates are low in India, the percentages of divorced females were greater in districts with low incidence of joint living. Kolenda (1987) suggests that in the latter women were allowed divorce, and could even initiate it, which is not the case in districts with high incidence of joint living.

This parallels oft-made correlations between upper castes, Brahmanical values, joint living and hierarchical intra-familial relationships on the one hand, and lower castes, elementary households, easier divorce, and a relative freedom and independence for women on the other. However, we must note that this 'freedom' was not even based on an independence of mere subsistence. Furthermore, it could be double-edged, for men could also divorce or desert with more impunity, and with a greater possibility of remarriage. In both Rajasthan and Tamil Nadu the increase in associated expenses is making divorce and remarriage more difficult for lower caste men and women (Palriwala 1990; Kapadia 1995). However, this does not mean a strengthening of marriage bonds, family or community sanctions, or of joint living. Women's organisations have been indicating that the desertion of wives and children has increased phenomenally across the subcontinent.

Economic trends and shifts in marriage and household patterns

The last trend points to the interrelations between economic processes and kinship and gender relations. Kolenda (1987; 1989) found that households dependent only on agriculture or household industry appeared to be more characteristic of the high joint-living Rajasthan districts than the southern districts. The former districts also have a higher than average farm size and more large holdings, while the latter have a much higher percentage of landless. This appears to indicate that joint household living is more likely where households are also production units and the supply of non-family labour low, increasing the pressures to optimise family resources and labour, male and female; that 'family feeling' is swayed by material considerations. Where individuation of resources and work has gone further, norms of joint household living and thence family support and sanctions have weakened (cf. Sharma 1989).

The household pattern, the nature of intra-familial relations, and women's ability to live independently of marriage—whether as divorcee or widow—are closely linked not only to kinship rules and moral codes, and to women's relative influence within the kinship network and community, but also to their access to information and material resources—economic independence—and their value as workers. Literacy levels for women remain low—strikingly so in Rajasthan. In both regions, patrilineal inheritance has been the norm, but in the south women have had slightly better access to land[5]—as daughters without brothers or as widows, facilitating households independent of their in-laws. However, across the country, land reform did not give women land, even as it deepened processes converting family property into objects and resources owned by individual men. While a factor contributing to joint living has weakened, women's rights to and access to property are now more closely tied to individual men, increasing their dependent status and decreasing their bargaining power.

Female labour force participation is much lower in the high joint-living districts of Rajasthan than in the southern districts, where veiling norms are not prevalent, suggesting that the recognition of women as workers is more likely in the latter. However, labour force statistics do not capture the intensity and extent of female family labour. In some regions, the last has increased with agricultural developments and male emigration. While many more women are wage earners in Tamil Nadu, two contradictory trends are discernible in both regions. On the one hand, women's earnings/work is crucial for the survival of poor households and, on the other hand, more and more households are dependent on individual male earners. Men, upper castes, and upper classes are better placed to obtain the more secure, remunerative, and prestigious non-agricultural jobs. The latter require education, contacts, money and social skills in which women, the lower castes and the poor are at a disadvantage.

Various studies indicate a shift away from kin marriage in the south. Economic and social differentiation within and between kinship networks, following education and the switch from household enterprise to individual jobs, and the spread of dowry, are among the factors. Kapadia argues that the decline in kin marriage and 'more dowry marriage with "strangers", is undermining women's traditional status' (1995:14–15) in non-Brahman groups, increasing the hierarchy between wife and husband, women and men. The emerging employment structure not only further devalues women as workers, it alters the relations between family members, reinforcing perceptions of property as male right, of female dependence and the preference for sons, even as it may discourage joint living.

In the next section, I elaborate on these processes and practices primarily through material on cultivating households of rural Sikar, Rajasthan (Shekhawatis), drawing occasional comparisons with Tamil Nadu. Through the discussion I address two frequently raised and critical issues. The first is that if the family is an arena of oppression for women, why do they seem particularly concerned to maintain and foster kinship ties and values? Why do they invest so much of themselves in family relations? The second is the apparent transparency of women as the primary oppressors of other women within the family in India.

The Dynamics of Kinship and Gender Relations in Rajasthan

The focus now shifts from household composition to kinship networks and intra-household relations. In dealing with the changing conditions of land, labour, commercialisation, and male migration, Shekhawati men and women act to maintain and enhance social networks, both reinforcing and manipulating patrilineal principles and gender relations. These structure, and are in turn shaped by, intra-household negotiation over consumption and food distribution and the control of finances.

Social networks and patriliny

Community ties and social networks are central to the economic and social strategies of Shekhawatis. The overlapping and mutually supporting networks of kinship, caste and clientage, albeit with altered contours and new members, have been given a fresh life by economic trends. As the absolute necessity for employment-related emigration and non-agricultural incomes have spread in Sikar, traditional forms of security have been reinforced even as new avenues are sought. Villagers foster ritual kin relationships and patron-client ties with a view towards future loan, leasing and/or labour/employment needs.[6] Avenues and symbols of upward mobility and high status are expressed through an extended social network. This entails acquisition of a surplus to enable expanded gift exchange, conspicuous consumption, and hospitality. New income sources both depend on and make possible the maintenance of community ties. As discussed in the last section, men, upper castes and the richer classes have better access to the new income and employment opportunities.

The most important segment of the Shekhawati villagers' social world remains their links through blood or marriage, neighbours, patrons and clients. Maintenance or enhancement of status and the support of this community entail either the power to set new norms or conformity to its social forms and values, cast as tradition and the ways of the elders. These include the normative division of gender roles, and a morality pinned on women's behaviour and modesty, despite shifts in veiling and seclusion practices (See Palriwala 1990).

Central to this social ethos are notions and conventions of patriliny and patri-virilocal residence. Patriliny defines group membership, identity and inheritance of property. Rights and interests in the family are contingent on membership, dictating the separation of women from the family property (Palriwala 1990). The family is a patrilineal descent group with a core of patrilineally related men—agnates—women being necessary, but transient and peripheral. Daughters move to their marital families, and daughters-in-law are of another line.

Group membership and relationships are validated and marked, in conjunction with status, through the gatherings at rituals, (especially weddings) and gifts, particularly among kin and affines who form the core of one's social group and identity (cf. Gough 1956; Dumont 1957). Women are the conduits for gift exchange between patrilineal groups, and this very quality undermines their integration into any one patrilineal group. With ambiguous kin group membership and dual loyalties to both their natal and their marital groups, Shekhawati women can receive only maintenance and 'gifts', and not a property share. This ambiguity is manipulated to dilute women's rights, except where their reversionary rights are used to prevail over claims made by "avaricious" kinsmen. Among Muslims, daughters' Shariat right to a half share is voiced as a residual right or a gift from a generous brother to a destitute sister. This has intensified with the post-Independence legislation giving limited rights in their fathers' property to daughters, the increasing pressure on and demand for land, and the individuation of property.

Patri-virilocal residence, and women's residential practice in particular, continuously reiterates transience, ambiguous membership and contingent rights (Palriwala 1990; 1991). For a fair length of time new brides and young married women move to and fro between their natal and conjugal homes. It is perhaps the most difficult period of their life, when as young girls they make their home among strangers (cf. Karve 1958). While it is difficult to assess changes in this, it would appear that back and forth visits have become more frequent. This may be related to the continuing low age at marriage, the reduced distance between affinal villages, improved transport in terms of roads and bus services, the absences of migrant husbands, but particularly the increasing demand for unpaid family workers in agriculture. Different segments of their kin assert their rights over young women, who move between villages, working where and when required, their contribution to any one 'family' thus depreciated. Women themselves wish to maintain their natal ties.

Gough (1956) suggested a contrast between the more complete incorporation of Tamil Brahman women into their marital homes/lineages, through assimilation to their husbands, and the lesser incorporation of non-Brahman women. Incorporation strengthened rights in the marital home, but weakened access to the safety-net of the natal home. However, ambiguity in group membership of Shekhawati Muslim and non-Brahman Tamil women seemed not to carry as strong negative implications as it did for Hindu women in Rajasthan, perhaps because of the cross-cutting of blood and marriage ties. In the social world of non-Brahmans in Tamil Nadu the matrilateral kin to an extent outweighed the patrilineal kin, stengthening women's value and bargaining power in the kinship circle (Kapadia 1995).[7] The shift away from kin marriage, mentioned earlier, is undermining this, indicating changing notions of community, as well as the strategic expansion or shrinkage and use of community and kin.

Economic exigencies and new social pressures are being met with shifts and manipulations, unmasking tensions which are often an exacerbation of earlier stresses on women. The apparently fixed rules of patriliny allow for manipulation, particularly between various lateral and lineal ties, between generations, and between affines. This can enable the exclusion of the extended kin group and women from property. The lack of economic and social alternatives for women means their persisting dependence on family ties. They recognise that relationships are their only resource and security, even as their kin attempt to restrict the scope of their responsibilities towards them.

Intra-household authority

Women's options and strategies in such a context are explicated through an examination of intra-household relations, in the following pages. Assuming a joint household, normatively, the head is always the senior-most male adult. All members are expected to submit to the head's authority in labour allocation, distribution of consumption, income pooling, cash expenditures, and actions seen as affecting the social relations of the household. The head is to consult other household members, particularly men and senior women. Ideally, nobody questions the head once he takes a decision. The presumption is that he has the most complete knowledge regarding household matters and his decisions are motivated by family interests.

The women of the household are under the triple authority of the senior woman—the wife or the mother of the male head of the household—their husbands, and the head. Rules of avoidance and segregation between the sexes lead to the appearance of separate but interlocking lines of authority. In practice, the authority of the male head depends on his age and the kinship composition of the household. Youth and very old age, widow(-er)hood, or absence due to migration generally reduce the control of both the male head and the female manager. In the absence of adult household men, a woman manager is expected to be guided by male kin, her dead husband's and her own.

The management of various spheres of activities rests primarily on that household member who has the knowledge and the responsibility of ensuring the work is done. In many household operations no real decision is taken or if so, not by an individual household. The senior woman, as long as she is capable, is in charge of housework, day-to-day consumption and livestock production. Differences over agricultural work could be between men, between women and/or between men and women. Friction over work is usually expressed in terms of a perceived discrepancy between work performed and access to consumption. Conflict over "work in the house" appears to be between women, even where dissension among male agnates underlies it.

Control over consumption

This and the next sub-section examine the dynamics of food consumption and control, which we will see are both indicative and a metaphor for intra-household power, distribution and relationships. Our focus is on the nature of women's agency in this sphere.

Generally, it was held that (senior) women manage the household grain stocks. Control was limited for both women and men by the fact that at least 55 per cent of households did not grow enough grain, let alone all food items, for their annual requirements (Palriwala 1990). Women managed only that grain which was brought to the house, and could not deny men access. Substantially, they were dependent on men buying and stocking grain for household use from 'their' earnings. Through barter, women could secretly acquire items of small value denied to them.

Commercialisation was diversifying men's options, but whittling away women's control. Surplus households, and others also, sold their produce in the wholesale market in the town, but proscriptions on their mobility hindered women in this. Men conducted and controlled the sale of agricultural products and could veto women's assessments. Thus, even in the village context, women were hampered in undertaking transactions. Despite the ideal of prior consultation, there were incidents where women remonstrated with a son or husband selling grain for alcohol, and were ignored or even beaten. As a last resort, women could call on their natal kin to intervene, not necessarily with success.

A common saying was that a household was made or broken by the skill and thrift of its womenfolk in managing household stocks. A range of women argued, "There are few women who do not wish their marital households to prosper. Ultimately we do not gain by frittering away household goods on ourselves or on those who are not members of our households." They continued to be dependent on their families for subsistence. Their personal status was linked to their reputation as skilled housewives. In accepting the idea of family needs, they pointed to differences in perceptions of these needs. They insisted that many so-called frivolities were often essential in ritual gift exchange, necessary for both their daughters' well-being and maintenance of the household's status. Men would blame women if the household 'lost face' because these gifts were not given. At the same time men wasted money on many useless personal expenses.

Serving food, especially non-cereal items, was a right women jealously guarded, backed by pollution norms. However, it also became a responsibility, such that the onus of providing the means of consumption often fell on women, further constraining their control. The extremely limited availability of waged employment for Shekhawati women, in contrast to that in Tamil Nadu, did not help. Saradamoni and Mencher (1982) and Kapadia (1995) also point to the dependence for consumption in labouring Tamil households on women's wages, even if the menfolk were earning, with women feeling more keenly the responsibility for feeding children.

The social and economic context defined women as ultimately dependent on their personal influence over household men. This was magnified with the growing significance of individual male incomes in the household economy. Day-to-day consumption was one of the few areas in which women exercised some authority. They used it to instil in young children a recognition of their mothers' power (cf. Minturn and Hitchcock 1963). They used it to try and ensure that sons and nephews were favourably disposed towards them. Influential women had been successful in the above. Contradictions in norms and women's direct responsibility meant that strains over consumption were likely to get expressed in anger with or conflict between women. Suspicions were strongest where the woman manager was variously linked to the men of the household, especially as sister, daughter, wife, sister-in-law were increasingly cast as individual obligations.

The possibilities of discrimination were largely limited to special foods and/or through a reduction of the woman's own consumption. Avenues of manipulation were used to obtain items of daily consumption for household members, particularly children. Etiquette dictated that a person accept what was served, and the server take into account the former's status. The earner and the household head, however, could demand and direct. Children protested perceived favouritism or demanded hidden extras. A woman could face the "reprehensible" situation, of a young son physically forcing her to give him some delicacy. In situations of deficit, tensions over suspected discrimination and intra-household conflicts tended to increase. This, rather than women's power, was a factor in the larger percentage of elementary households among poor peasants and labourers (of which lower castes were a significant proportion) than among middle and rich peasants.

How are these manoeuvres, these negotiations to be understood? In Kolenda's framework (1967), the high incidence of the joint family indicates that Shekhawati women had little bargaining power and hence were unable to bring about household partition. Within that, intra-household day-to-day consumption was one area women hoped to control in the course of their life cycle and could manipulate to a limited extent.[8] They exercised a circumscribed power, primarily over the work and consumption of daughters and daughters-in-law. The knowledge and hope of future authority, the apparent exercise of autonomy, gave women an interest in the system, adding to its strength. However, the agenda and the options within which women exercised authority were not set by them (cf. Lukes 1974). The constraints of the macro structures and cultural codes were concretised through women's life-time dependence on husbands and sons, as well as the normative rights of men, the owners, to all household products. The possibility of physical force being used against them further limited women's ability or desire to control, transgress, or change.

The discourse and practice of food distribution

Caste and religious codes, land ownership and class, occupation and migration characteristics of households affect their composition and division, the division of labour, intra-household food distributon, the attainment of seniority and headship by women and men, and modify patterns of control and absolute levels of consumption. Variations in practice reflect the flexibility of 'uniform' norms and emerge through people's relationships and dealings with the concrete conditions of life. In looking at this, the parameters affecting women's consumption levels in particular are elaborated.

The distribution of food was governed by rules and values, witnessed and practised from infancy onwards.[9] Kinship status—in terms of patrilineality, generation, age seniority and sex—contribution to household income and work, and the particular context of social relationships, delineated intra-household access to consumption. These dimensions could either reinforce or contradict each other in practice. Adult male agnates had first priority, but the male head of household and the person who "earned" were first among equals, particularly in the case of delicacies and "nutritive" items. Conflict in priority could emerge if the head and the main "earner" were not the same.

The old and children had a right to food as agnates and/or because of past or future labour. Kinship and family solidarity dictated support to agnates, the old, the sick and the young. The old had reared, supported and established the present generation, passing on the basis of livelihood, property and a way of life (cf. Parry 1979). However, the young, specifically sons, were the future support, the heirs, and represented familial continuity and success. The young were likely to be given priority over the aged.

Hence, with the old and the sick, there was often bitterness and suspicion, especially where family assets and possible inheritance were minimal. Where the senior generation was represented by an old widow, this tension was perceived as an extension of the mother-in-law/daughter-in-law relationship. The daughter-in-law had probably suffered discrimination and harrassment at her mother-in-law's hands. Also, mothers-in-law socialised new brides into their roles as household managers and food distributors. An oft-repeated saying was that an old woman, by the example of her behaviour with her mother-in-law, had taught her daughter-in-law to mistreat her. Even if poverty led to insufficient food for all, or the male head or "earner" decided that the old be given only the basics, it was the woman responsible for cooking and serving who was blamed.

Most people denied discriminating against girls. "Children are children, whether male or female." "As children daughters are a greater help than sons so why should they be discriminated against?" Many said that daughters cared more for their parents than sons did. Yet sons were the embodiment of the family's future, and could be favoured with the justification that they must quickly grow and work for the whole family. The mother-son bond, viewed as especially tender (cf. Gore 1962; Madan 1965; Pocock 1972; Das 1976), was favoured by women as their one emotional support and material security. A woman's hope of achieving status in her marital home was through her sons (cf. Hershman 1981). Furthermore, since a large percentage of households were complex, the girl's mother was often not the person serving food. Other household women seemed to give in to demands of nephews or grandsons more easily than those of nieces and granddaughters.

Evidence contrary to the statements regarding lack of discrimination is overwhelming. Sikar is among the districts in the country with the lowest ratio of young girls (under-tens) to young boys (Miller 1989), even though the overall sex ratio is above the all-India average. The higher overall sex ratio may be related to male emigration and the lower sex ratio in the under-ten age group to discrimination between baby girls and boys in food and medical care, as well as differences in nutrition of mothers, of sons and of daughters. Alternatively, these contrary sex ratios represent a new trend of devaluation of, and bias against, female children, perhaps being replicated now in Salem, Tamil Nadu (Chunkath and Athreya 1997). Hypothetically, selective discrimination against later-born girls rather than all female children would appear to hold.[10] What stands out starkly is that in explicating family and gender relations, love and calculations of material interest cannot be taken as mutually exclusive (Goody 1984).

New mothers, especially of sons, pregnant women, and all other men and women were said to follow in priority in that order. "If the mother of sons did not eat well, who would?" it was exclaimed. Part of the new mother's nutrition depended on food gifts from her natal home. The person who cooked and the youngest daughter-in-law, often one and the same, ate last and this itself acted against her even if there was no conscious discrimination.

The rights of women in different castes and classes to consumption were discussed in terms of their work contribution. Women, who were in seclusion and hence did not labour in the fields, would say that women of the cultivating and labouring castes had a right to eat because they worked, whereas if nobody gave them (i.e. the ones in seclusion) food they could not protest as they did not work or earn. Female work and hence requirements were valued lower than male work and the requirements of women were presumed to be less than those of men. Women questioned the relative valuation of some but not most tasks. Thus while they would argue that the female chore of weeding was underestimated relative to what young household men did, the strictly male work of ploughing was accepted as the most taxing. Kapadia (1995) similarly found that labouring women in Tamil Nadu endorsed the view that male work was harder, but resented their exploitation through work contracts by their menfolk. Dual residence also acted to minimise daughters-in-law's rights of consumption, through obscuring and denying their labour contribution in each place of residence (Palriwala 1991).

Male migration and control of household finances

We can now examine directions of change in familial relations through the dynamics of intra-household financial management in the context of male migration and the growing dependence on male earnings. The latter not only affect household composition and intra-household relations, but usher in a further decline in women's well-being and value.

Ideally and in practice, cash earnings are part of the household pool, under the control of the male head. In households which barely met their subsistence requirements or earned little cash income, this control had little meaning, but conflict could be intense. Three categories of women's earnings were not part of the household pool: income from the sale of clarified butter, from female crafts and the earnings of daughters. These were classed as women's personal income, to be spent as they desired.

However, women tended to spend their earnings on "household" requirements relating to their work responsibilities, such as food and gifts to married daughters. Declining economic resources and the absence of migrant husbands at times of crisis strengthened this tendency. Further, proceeds from sales undertaken by men entered the household pool. Yet, even a household at a bare survival level could not claim a daughter's earnings, despite rights to her labour. Her earnings could be saved towards her trousseau or prestations she must take to her marital home.

As mentioned earlier, consultations preceded expenditure decisions, especially on the taking of loans, selling or pawning household assets (particularly jewellery), and/or using women's income. With constraints on female mobility and the widely held belief that village women knew little beyond their kitchen and their animals, it was said that men "knew best". Women were expected to remind men of social obligations, including gifts at life cycle ceremonies and to visiting affines. Blame for default was placed as much if not more on women than on men, but the final decision lay with senior men and the household head.

Employment-related male emigration in Sikar had increased phenomenally. Only migrants absent for long stretches, a year or more, remitted large portions of their earnings. Individual male earners, particularly if their earnings were regular, substantial and entailed emigration, kept a portion for 'personal' expenses. Where the household head was a migrant, day-to-day management was no longer in his control. However, the dependence on his individual earnings had tilted the balance of power further in his favour. His presence was all-pervasive even in his absence and, if in addition he was able to return frequently, he kept firm control over the purse strings.

Among the labourer castes and Muslims, households tended not to be joint. The woman managed the land and related tasks, organised credit and consumption, and fulfilled the household's social obligations. Transactions were usually along established ties. Written communications had a new importance, forcing a greater dependence of illiterate women on the male kin of their husbands. However, women were making decisions and at times in opposition to their husbands. They argued that their absent men could not know nor be explained the complexities of a situation. Some argued that they were better planners and more sensible than their husbands, who also silently recognised this. "In their next letter, our husbands express their anger at being crossed, but it fades by the time they return."

Despite the variation in women's financial authority among the Muslims, the difference between them on the one hand and the cultivating and ex-landlord castes on the other was striking. Not only was the factor of long-term and distant (to the Gulf) male migration important, among Muslims the conjugal tie tended to receive more emphasis than among the middle and upper Hindu castes. Though the hierarchy between husband and wife was clearly articulated, many a Muslim woman was confident that she had only to persuade her husband and not contend with his entire family. This could be related to weaker family sanctions with elementary household living, lesser household resources, and the absence of household enterprises (including agriculture); to women's independent craft income; to patterns of cross-cousin and parallel cousin marriage which affected the nature of relationships; and to their rights, however minimal, in their father's property as discussed earlier.

Many of the male earners were junior emigrants. Complex household living continued to be admired and practised widely in Shekhawati, along with the maintenance of extended ties. Joint householding could work to the econmic and social advantage of both the temporary migrant and his village-based father/brothers. The migrant's wife remained under the authority/protection of his parents and/or brothers. However, an increasing tension between an individual's control of his earnings and the control of household resources and income by the household head was manifest. The migrant developed new tastes and priorities. Fathers complained that they had given life to and invested in their sons, but now the latter were making no contribution to the household. Both migrants and their village-based kin felt they were subsidising each other.[11]

There was a greater tendency for sons to form independent households in the lifetime of both parents rather than wait till their death. There was a decline in the mother's ability to keep her sons together once their father was dead (Palriwala 1990). Crucially, if households were dividing sooner, junior men and women were gaining control of their respective spheres earlier.

The dependence on individual wages had also complicated the relationship between junior women and other household members and between husband and wife. On the one hand, migrants' wives often had more petty cash than women from households where the income source was a household enterprise or traditional service, even if in a similar or higher income bracket. This could also be true in comparison to middle and poor peasant men. To avoid tensions, gifts from migrant husbands had to be kept a secret from other household members (cf. Parry 1979). On the other hand, a woman had had some independent knowledge of village-based household income and how it was spent. Kin sanctions had operated more directly and easily to ensure that a man did not neglect his household or his wife and children.

Furthermore, the treatment within the household of a junior emigrant's wife depended on him fulfilling his familial obligations. It was more difficult for her to follow or influence household decisions in his absence. Mobility constraints and norms of modesty increased her social dependence on his immediate network. In some cases, other household members felt that the emigrant's wife had become 'uppity'. Even as aspirations of status grew, the threat of the woman being seen as unchaste and losing status loomed larger.

Overall, the influence/control over household consumption and expenditure of an emigrant's wife depended on the pattern of migration and remittances, level and sources of income, household composition, and presence of close kin of the husband. She was more dependent on the individual man, her husband and his kin, on what he told her regarding his income and on what he sent or bought her, on his being pleased and approving of her behaviour. There was a growing gap between her contribution and that of her husband to the household budget and resources. This in itself reduced possibilities of autonomy and reinforced the link between her consumption levels and fulfilment of ascribed roles (cf. Maher 1981). Kapadia (1995) has suggested that in Tamil Nadu these shifts have led to the spread of upper caste values of the submissive, self-sacrificing woman and a more conservative gender discourse.

Working for the "Family Good"

Gender, age and kinship hierarchies were the parameters within which intra-household work contribution, consumption requirements and authority were worked out, moderated by caste and class. Labour contribution was articulated as a determinant of rights to the products of labour and consumption. However, not only were interpersonal relations and preferences a factor in actual intra-household distribution, the significance of labour was transcended by income contribution and, crucially, the parameters of patrilineal male kinship and ownership of property. Ultimately, the "good of the family" was seen to entail the well-being and upward mobility of the property-holding male agnatic core (coparceners). They had first rights to consumption and defined household needs and expenses, while women had no legitimate needs outside common household needs.

In the family ideology, men and women, young and old were essential and had to give and receive their due, which was however inherently differential. Whether daughters or daughters-in-law, they had secondary rights, in congruence with their peripheral status in the family/coparcenary and residual rights in land, and linked to their "contribution" to the "family". The owner had first rights to the harvest from his land—part of his identity—as against the worker. Similarly, the lineally ascendant male agnate had prior claims to a child, though there was recognition of the "labour" the mother contributed in bearing and rearing the child. The male child and the father were expressions of each other, not to be lightly separated. This differed among non-Brahmin Tamils, where the marriage claims of matrilateral kin on their daughter's/sister's children had diluted patrilineal ties and weakened the patrilineal coparcenary. Though the last was rarely a householding unit, values of extended kinship held.

Economic inequalities had increased and the right to pursue "traditional" forms of status, such as dowry marriage, were "democratised" in both Shekhawati and Tamil Nadu. However, unlike in the south, neither political developments nor shifts in land ownership and new economic opportunities had seriously affected caste hierarchies in Shekhawati. Developmental processes and the paucity of employment were, on the one hand, resuscitating social networks, collective household strategies, and occupational multiplicity. On the other hand, they were individuating and objectifying patrilineal property, creating the basis for individual rights, and demarcating and valorising individual earners, almost entirely men.

In Tamil Nadu also, male non-agricultural employment has gained in importance. Disagreements over valuation of labour, income contribution, consumption and "sharing" are sharpening. Even as differences over family strategies and the needs of various household members are magnifying, the above trends are acting to devalue women and strengthen men's value and consumption rights as against theirs. Rather than being questioned, behavioural constraints on women have been reinforced or expanded. Contradictory practices tended to be resolved by the upwardly mobile groups in favour of practices supportive of patriarchal forms (cf. Chowdhry, 1994, on widow remarriage).

There has been a shift in emphasis from a patrilineal "family" in which women were necessary dependents to individual male control of property. A woman's rights in her "family" were even earlier linked to the rights of her father/brother and/or husband and her interpersonal relations. Her rights have been narrowed and fixed more firmly on these individuals and her work contribution. The daughter and sister are increasingly cast as individual liabilities rather than a strategic resource, even in castes in which their labour was recognised.

This is clearly linked to the diffusion of dowry and inflation in marriage and other ritual gifts among most castes, which are continually calling on women's rights in their natal home (CSWI 1975; Srinivas 1987; Palriwala 1984). Dowry and gifts to a daughter lessen the immediate economic viability and wealth of her natal household. This is ever more a contradiction between gifts to, and desires for, an individual's, a daughter's, "happiness" and the long-run economic advancement of the giver and/or his household. Conflicting pulls over social gain through investment in one's social network and fulfilment of obligations to kin versus the economic rationality of restricting the latter to immediate household members, or even oneself, have sharpened.

Women's labour is seen to defray the expenses incurred in providing them with marital gifts rather than contributing to household subsistence, continuity and mobility. Daughters-in-law are valued for the goods they bring in. Thus, a vicious cycle has been established: the devaluation of women's labour for the 'family' and thence her rights to consumption, the justification of dowry in terms of a woman being an economic burden, and demands for prestations feed into each other.

Conclusion

Against this background I return to initial issues I raised regarding widows and sex ratios. State and popular perception in India assume "family support" for the aged and the widowed. It has been argued that the great majority of the old continue to live with and are taken care of by a son, even in the rural south where the incidence of extended families is relatively low (Caldwell et al., 1988: 193). However, studies also show the importance of economic resources in terms of land, business, or wages in ensuring the well-being of the old and the widowed. Further, the possibility of "reproductive failure", of no surviving son when the parents are old, is greatest where the need is most—among the poor and landless (Cain 1986).

Single person households consist preponderantly of widows (Palriwala 1994). Studies also indicate the intra-household neglect of widows. Their lower nutritional and health status and life expectancy were largely a result of the loss of property, the experience of economic decline, and the loss of family support, which characterised women rather than men on widowhood or marital breakdown (Drèze 1990). New economic and demographic pressures, including declining family resources, inflation, low wages and high unemployment, add to this. Widows with sons, widows who were household heads, widows in such households with property and widows who could work and earn, experienced the least vulnerability.

The intra-household treatment of widows is influenced by various factors including notions of the widow's ritual and social inauspiciousness, interpersonal relations and their history, her age, her ability to contribute to the household, class and caste/religion and her ability to assert her rights vis-a-vis her dead husband's kin. Hindu widows in the north relative to Muslim and southern widows, experience a more drastic post-marriage separation from the natal home, making support from the latter more tenuous, diminishing also their ability to influence the kinship network on the whole. Muslim and southern women have a slightly better access to paternal property, of which however there may be little. The positive aspects for Muslim widows are offset by the greater restrictions on their labour and employment, in common with north Indian Hindu women.

For women, the dread of widowhood deeply influences their perspective on life. A lack of resources, employment, any state support system and the absence of an individual identity, define their options. The cultural and economic logic to women's desire for sons, their investment in the emotional bond with them and their rivalry with their daughters-in-law, thus becomes clear. In a patrilineal, patrilocal society, sons are their security, if despite being good and chaste wives (following *patidharma* among Hindus), they are widowed. Producing sons is part of their *patidharma,* for who will take care of their husbands if they should predecease them? It is their investment for their daughters' futures, for who will take care of them if they are widowed? Sons are desired not only for spiritual reasons, but because of the mundane experiences of women and their loved ones in this world.

Most crucially, the growing importance of male wages/salaries, and men's greater access to paid employment has meant a greater valuation of men and of sons. Daughters have to be married into other families, that too in a context of declining kin and uxorilocal marriage, and spiralling expenses on dowry and rituals associated with daughters. These are undoubtedly factors in the female foeticide and infanticide reported in the last decade among non-Brahmin castes in Tamil Nadu. The previous male bias in the social structure has been strengthened and spread.

Women's economic dependence on husband, son and kin has intensified. This has crucial implications for their manoeuvrability and valuation and hence for their consumption rights, as well as for the form in which obligations to them were to be fulfilled and the readiness to do so. Tensions between women—between mother-in-law and daughter-in-law or between sisters-in-law—and the control they exercised on each other have increased. Critically, the vulnerability of some categories—the landless, widows, divorced and abandoned wives—has intensified. Their networks of support are individualised and weakened, with little attentuation in the systems of sanction controlling them.

Notes

[1]Kolenda, 1987, seems to indicate a somewhat different situation emerging from the 1961 census.

[2]Most uses of 'family' in everyday language and in the social sciences assume a group of persons related to each other through 'blood' or marriage. It is important to distinguish household from family. The operational social science definition of a household includes those sharing a common hearth and a common roof. However, economic criteria may rest on common budgeting, through joint resources and/or pooling of income. Thus two or more brothers, with their wives and children, who live in one house, but have separate hearths and do not pool their income could see themselves as separate households, though one family. Any detailed examination of changing family-household structures will have to consider three related dimensions: (1) Family ideology, including notions of kinship and cultures of post-marriage residence; (2) varied economic and cultural regimes and economies of scale, as well as class, caste, urban-rural and regional variations in composition; (3) the developmental cycle/process, which emerges through the interplay of familial and status ideology, demography, economics, and debates, the elementary/simple family-household is taken to include households of a single person, unmarried siblings, a parent or couple with/without children; an extended/complex/joint household contains at least two or more married couples or persons and may in addition contain unmarried or widowed kin.

[3] The 1961 Census tabulated the composition of a 20 per cent sample of households (hearth groups) on the basis of which Kolenda (1987) constructed three indices of joint household living.

[4] It may be noted that widow remarriage has been associated both with regions harsher to women and those which are less so (cf. Chowdhry 1994).

[5] See Agarwal (1994) for an overview of regional patterns in women's land rights in South Asia.

[6] This is also the case, with somewhat different contours and intensities, in Tamil Nadu. See Gough; Good 1991.

[7] Matrilateral kin/affines may not have the same significance in Rajasthan as, Kapadia argues, for Tamil non-Brahmans. However, their ritual, symbolic, and social importance in the lives of outmarried women, their husbands and his kin, across a range of castes, must not be underestimated. Affinal relations were viewed as above the economic competition and petty jealousies of agnatic and day-to-day ties. Hence

they were just arbiters and a source of assistance, both material and moral. As in Tamil Nadu, affines were gifts-givers par excellence. Contemporary trends in dowry and the inflation in affinal prestations have distorted this.

[8] Leach (1962) argues that in any kinship system, if it is to be viable, there must be areas open to individuals to manipulate to their own benefit.

[9] Women (and men) are socialised into society and culture. They operate from within a habitus, from within "a community of dispositions... schemes of perception, appreciation and action, which are acquired through practice" (Bourdieu 1977: 97), making for a male-biased conformity even while apparently allowing choice.

[10] Dasgupta (1987) argues that discrimination of female children is related to family-building strategies of parents. She found that rather than a uniform discrimination against girls in the Punjab, discrimination was determined in particular by serial order. Most mothers wanted at least one daughter to help them in the house. She relates the discrimination to the differential economic and social value of sons and daughters.

[11] Shifts in household composition reflect changes in intra-household relations. Studies on the impact of an increasing dependence on individual, non-agricultural, non-village occupations and income have put forward contradictory conclusions. For discussions of the problem-ridden debate on the decline or otherwise of the Indian joint family, see Shah 1973; Kessinger 1974; Madan 1976; Parry 1979.

References

Agarwal, B., 1994. *A Field of One's Own: Gender and Land Rights in South Asia* Cambridge: Cambridge University Press.

Agnihotri, I. and R. Palriwala, 1996. "Tradition, Family, and the State: The Politics of the Contemporary Women's Movement", in T.V. Sathyamurthy (ed.), *Social Change and Political Discourse in India: Structures of Power, Movements of Resistance: Vol. 3: Region, Religion, Caste, Gender and Culture in Contemporary India* New Delhi: Oxford University Press.

Agnihotri, S., 1996. "Juvenile Sex Ratios in India", *Economic and Political Weekly* XXXI (52): 3369–82.

Bourdieu, P., 1977. *Outline of a Theory of Practice* Cambridge: Cambridge University Press.

Cain, M., 1986. "The Consequences of Reproductive Failure: Dependence, Mobility, and Mortality among the Elderly in Rural South Asia", *Populations Studies*, 40: 375–88.

Caldwell, J.C., P.H. Reddy and P. Caldwell, 1988. *The Causes of Demographic Change: Experimental Research in South India* Madison, Wisconsin: University of Wisconsin Press.

Chowdhry, P. 1994. *The Veiled Women: Shifting Gender Equations in Rural Haryana 1880–1990* New Delhi: Oxford University Press.

Chunkath, S. R. and V.B. Athreya, 1997. "Female Infanticide in Tamil Nadu: Some Evidence", *Economic and Political Weekly* XXXII (17): WS21–WS28.

Das, V., 1976. "Masks and Faces: An Essay on Punjabi Kinship", *Contributions to Indian Sociology* n.s. 10:1–30.

Dasgupta, M., 1987. "Selective Discrimination Against Female Children in Rural Punjab, India", *Population and Development Review* 13(1): 77–100.

Drèze, J., 1990. "Widows in Rural India", Development Economics Research Programme Discussion Paper Series, No. 26. London: Suntory-Toyota International Centre for Economics and Related Disciplines, London School of Economics. Mimeo.

Dumont, L., 1966. "Marriage in India. The Present state of the Question—III: North India in relation to South India", *Contributions to Indian Sociology* 9: 90–114.

———, 1957. *Hierarchy and Marriage Alliance in South Indian Kinship* Occasional papers of the Royal Anthropological Institute of Great Britain and Ireland, No. 12. London: RAI.

Dyson, T. and M. Moore, 1983. "On Kinship Structure, Female Autonomy and Demographic Behaviour in India", *Population and Development Review* 9(1): 35–60.

Good, A. 1991. *The Female Bridegroom: A Comparative Study of Life-Crisis Rituals in South India and Sri Lanka* Oxford: Oxford University Press.

Goody, E., 1984. "Parental strategies: calculation or sentiment? Fostering practices among West Africans", in H. Medick and D.W. Sabean (eds.), *Interest and Emotion: Essays on the Study of Family and Kinship* Cambridge: Cambridge University Press.

Gore, M.S., 1962. "The Husband-wife and Mother-son Relationship", *Sociological Bulletin* XI(1,2):91–102.

Gough, K., 1956. "Brahmin Kinship in a Tamil village", *American Anthropologist* 58(5): 826–53.

Hershman, P., 1981. *Punjabi Kinship and Marriage*. Ed. by H. Standing. Delhi: Hindustan Publishers.

Kapadia, K., 1995. *Siva and Her Sisters: Gender, Caste, and Class in Rural India*. Oxford: Westview Press.

Karve, I., 1958. *Kinship Organisation in India*. Bombay: Asia Publishing House.

Kessinger, T.G., 1974. *Vilayatpur, 1848–1968. Social and Economic Change in a North Indian Village* Berkeley: University of California.

Kolenda, P., 1967. "Regional Differences in Indian Family Structure", in R.I. Crane (ed.), *Regions and Regionalism in South Asian Studies: An*

Exploratory Study Duke University Monographs and Occasional Papers Series, No. Five.

———, 1987. *Regional Differences in Family Structure in India* Jaipur: Rawat Publications.

———, 1989. "The Joint Family Household in Rural Rajasthan: Ecological, Cultural and Demographic Conditions for its Occurrence", in J.N. Gray and D.J. Mearns (eds.), *Society From the Inside Out: Anthropological Perspectives on the South Asian Household* New Delhi: Sage.

Leach, E., 1962. "On Uncertain Unconsidered Aspects of Double Descent Systems", *Man* 62 (214): 130–34.

Lessinger, J. 1990. "Work and Modesty: The Dilemma of Women Market Traders in Madras", in L. Dube and R. Palriwala (eds.) *Structures and Strategies: Women, Work and Family* Delhi: Sage Publications.

Libbee, M.J. 1980. "Territorial endogamy and the Spatial Structure of Marriage in Rural India", in Sopher, D.E. (ed.), 1980.

Lukes, S., 1974, *Power: A Radical View* London: Macmillan.

Madan, T.N., 1965. *Family and Kinship: a Study of the Pandits of Rural Kashmir* Bombay: Asia Publishing House.

———, 1976. "The Hindu Family and Development", *Journal of Social and Economic Studies* 4 (2): 211–231.

Mandelbaum, D.G. 1970. *Society in India* Berkeley: University of California Press.

Maher, V., 1981. "Work, Consumption and Authority Within the Household", in K. Young, C. Wolkowitz and R. McCullagh (eds.), *Of Marriage and the Market* London: CSE Books.

Mencher, J. and K. Saradamoni, 1982. 'Muddy Feet, Dirty Hands: Rice Production and Female Agricultural Labour' in *Economic and Political Weekly*, XVII (52): A149–A167.

Miller, B.D., 1989. "Changing Patterns of Juvenile Sex Ratios in Rural India, 1961 to 1971". *Economic and Political Weekly* XXIV(22): 1229–36.

Minturn, L. and J.T. Hitchcock, 1963. "The Rajputs of Khalapur", in B.B. Whiting (ed.), *Six Cultures: Studies of Child Rearing* New York: John Wiley and Sons, Inc.

Palriwala, R., 1990. "Production, Reproduction and the Position of Women: A Case Study of a Rajasthan Village", Unpub. PhD. Diss, University of Delhi.

———, 1991. "Transitory Residence and Invisible Work: A Case Study of a Rajasthan Village", *Economic and Political Weekly* XXVI (48):2763–72.

———, 1994. *Changing Kinship, Family, and Gender Relations in South Asia: Processes, Trends, and Issues* Leiden: Women and Autonomy Centre, University of Leiden.

Parry, J.P., 1979. *Caste and Kinship in Kangra* Delhi: Vikas.

Pocock, D., 1972. *Kanbi and Patidar: A Study of the Patidar Community of Gujarat* Oxford: Clarendon Press.

Shah, A.M., 1973. *The Household Dimension of the Family in India* Delhi: Orient Longman.

———, 1988. "The Phase of Dispersal in the Indian Family Process", *Sociological Bulletin* 37(1&2): 33–47.

Sharma, U., 1989. "Studying the household: Individuation and Values", in J.N. Gray and D.J. Mearns (eds.), *Society from the Inside Out: Anthropological Perspectives on the South Asian Household* New Delhi: Sage.

Sopher, D.E. (ed.) 1980. *An Exploration of India: Geographical Perspectives on Society and Culture* Ithaca, New York: Cornell University Press.

Srinivas, M.N., 1976. *The Remembered Village* Delhi: Oxford University Press.

———, 1987. *The Dominant Caste and Other Essays* Delhi: Oxford University Press.

3

Every Blade of Green

*Landless Women Labourers, Production and Reproduction in South India**

KARIN KAPADIA

Introduction

Recent research regarding women's economic contribution and modes of conceptualising it, has found not only a strong tendency on the part of men to minimise their wives' contribution but also that women themselves are often socially conditioned to undervalue and underreport their own work (Bruce and Dwyer, 1988, p. 15). Even where women make a major economic contribution, this is often not socially recognised and, therefore, not enumerated in economic surveys. This may be why the major involvement of lower-caste landless labourer women in agricultural work in South India has largely gone unrecognised. This 'social blindness' has been shared by social scientists to a surprising degree, so that, for instance, even feminist researchers assume that it is primarily in Africa, rather than Asia, that one finds a high visibility of women in key economic activities' and a remarkable 'explicitness of differential male and female income streams within the household' (Bruce and Dwyer, 1988, p. 12). However, both these phenomena equally characterise landless women

*This essay originally appeared in the *Indian Journal of Labour Economics*, Vol. 35, No. 3, 1992. The publishers are grateful to the editors for permission to reproduce it here.

labourers in Tamil Nadu, so 'Asia' is not so distant from 'Africa' after all. We have yet to recognise the enormous diversity of socio-economic and cultural patterns within the area we call 'South Asia'.

Here I discuss key aspects of the economic contribution of 'untouchable' caste Pallar women in the village of Aruloor in Lalgudi Taluk, Tiruchirappalli (hereafter 'Tiruchi') District, Tamil Nadu. These 'untouchable' Pallar women live in two contiguous streets, Periyar Street and Kamaraj Colony, just west of the Three Streets area where the caste-Hindu Muthurajahs live. There were around 110 Pallar households in this Pallar area of south Aruloor in 1987–88. Most families were landless and many were very poor (Kapadia, 1990). Almost all were dependent on agricultural wage-labour for a living.[1]

Remarkably, it is Pallar women who today form the major part of the agricultural labour force in the area. Even more remarkable, they contribute a far larger share of their incomes to the household than their husbands do, and far more regularly. For this reason I argue that their labour and their earnings are crucial to the survival of their families. These women are major providers and breadwinners: this fact is implicitly recognised and positively valued in Pallar culture, but not in the discourses of the dominant culture, which denigrates manual labour and especially the participation of women in such labour. Nor has this work been recognised by policy makers and planners.

In the first part of this essay I describe the double burden of women. Thereafter, I draw on Joan Mencher's research and compare it with my own findings. I then go on to discussing changes in the work participation of women and men which have led to a 'feminisation of agricultural labour' in the area. Here I also briefly compare Gillian Hart's observations on Muda within the situation in Aruloor. This is followed by a description of the sexual division of labour; in a subsequent section I discuss gender-differential payments in agriculture and in the final section I return to the issue of differential contributions to the household, and its implications.

Recruitment to and Organisation of Domestic Labour

Double Burden of Pallar Women

The Pallar woman plays the role of breadwinner in addition to doing all the household work. Pallar men don't normally assist women in these tasks. Thus the normal timetable of a Pallar woman is to be up by 7 a.m. and off to the fields after breakfasting on cold rice porridge (*kunji*) by 7.30 a.m. It takes half an hour on average to get to the field site, maybe less. From 8 a.m. to 12 noon she and the other women in her 'coolie' group labour, for example, at weeding or transporting manure or soil. At noon they ought to break off, but because of the scarcity of work, it became common (from October 1987 onwards) for employers to demand that labourers work an extra hour until 1 p.m. for the same wages (Rs. 5).

When she returns home the Pallar woman washes dishes and eats some more cold *kunji*. Most Pallar families can afford only one main meal a day and this she cooks in the late afternoon or evening. She spends the afternoon doing other household tasks like washing clothes, cleaning the house and caring for young children. She has her bath in the river and she might rest if she has no other housework. In the evening the women of neighbouring houses sit together, on their front door steps or right in the middle of the street and chat. After the meal which is eaten quite late, at about 9 p.m., everyone goes to bed by about 10 p.m. During the continuing drought all bathing and washing of kitchen untensils, clothes and children became a very difficult task because there was no water in Aruloor's river or in the street pumps. The women had to trudge out to the fields to find a pumpset from which water was flowing. So the relatively leisurely afternoons I describe seldom occurred, nor did they exist during the busy months of full employment. When transplanting of the *samba* crop occurred (the months of October and November) and when the *samba* harvest took place (mid-January to mid-March) many women only entered their homes at night to eat and sleep, utterly exhausted from ten to twelve hours of intensive labour. This was when extra homestic help was most essential, primarily to provide childcare and, secondarily, to cook and do the housework. So virtually no female child attended school during these months because her labour was needed at home.

Differential Wage-Contributions to the Household

In October, 1987 my Pallar research-assistant and I initiated a daily census in which we asked every woman in the two Pallar streets (Periyar Street and Kamaraj Colony) what work (both domestic/subsistence and waged) she had done, how much she had earned and how much her husband had contributed from his wages. This daily census continued until the last week of May, 1988. It provided overwhelming evidence for the claim that Pallar women had been making all along, namely that their husbands gave them little of what they earned, usually less than half, while the women themselves normally gave their entire wages towards supporting their families.

Pallar men do contribute towards their households but on a fairly irregular basis. Their wives normally had no idea how much their husbands had earned that day because their husbands did not tell them—that is why our survey only listed husbands' contributions and could not detail husbands' earnings. Given that it is women who contribute virtually their entire earnings on a wholly regular basis, it is arguably they, and not their husbands, who are the family's main support. While Pallar men's contributions to domestic income were limited and irregular, they did not hesitate to demand that they be fed every day. This discrepancy between the contribution made by men to the domestic economy and their consumption of the domestic product was a central reason for quarrels between women and men. As a sign of their frustration or because of genuinely inadequate food provisions, women sometimes refused to cook or could not cook for their husbands. This situation was normally met with physical violence from the husband who was quite often drunk.

I provide two samples from the census of earnings and contributions in October, 1987 in order to illustrate the difference between lean and good times and between the contributions made by women and men. The first sample is of four days in early October just before water was released into Aruloor's Panguni river (a tributary of the Kaveri). No water meant no work, so during these days, as in the preceding weeks, very few women and men found jobs and earnings were low (see Table 1). As my assistant and I went on our census round, the women would bitterly say: 'You ask did we go for work today! Where is the work? There is no water, so no work. Don't trouble us now. Come back when the water comes. *Then* we'll tell you about work!'

The highest female earning in these lean days, between 2 October and 5 October, 1987 was Rs. 9, the daily wage of Rajambal (of Household No. 72), a skilled worker in her mid-50s. But she earned this not in Aruloor but by commuting daily by bus to paddy fields near Srirangam where she did eight hours transplanting work per day. The fields belonged to the relatives of a wealthy Muthurajah widow (of the Muthurajah Three Streets in Aruloor) for whom Rajambal's husband was irrigation supervisor.

The highest contributions from men (Rs. 50 on both 4 and 5 October) were exceptional: in both cases the money was given for the specific purpose of buying parboiled rice (*pulungal arisi*) from the Government ration-shop where it appeared on 4 October. On both days only a single contribution of Rs. 50 was made by one man towards rice-buying and the great majority of women had to buy the family's rice ration solely out of their own earnings. Lohambal, a widow, had to pawn her kitchen pots, including her large stainless steel *kodam* (water pot) to get Rs. 60 to buy rice. Ration-shop rice is of poor quality but the Pallars have to buy it because it is considerably cheaper than open-market rice. Thus the Pallars, whose labour actually produces the finest rice in Tamil Nadu, have to live on the worst rice the state produces—the irony is striking and not unnoticed by them.

There are normally two paddy crops a year, in this area of Lalgudi Taluk, which has traditionally been part of the 'rice-bowl' of South India, well-watered by the tributaries of the Kaveri River. The first crop, the *kar*, is grown between July and September, while the second crop, the *samba*, which is of better quality, takes longer to grow—it is normally grown between October and January/February. However, a long-running drought that was in its fourth year in 1987 had had dire consequences and for the fourth year running the *kar* crop failed, due to lack of water. So, as Table 1 indicates, in the first week of October, 1987 only a few labourers found work harvesting the *kar* crop as there was so little to harvest. Normally payment for agricultural work is in cash, only paddy harvest work is paid in paddy.

Paddy contributions from men (in both Table 1 and Table 2) are remarkably lower than those from women because many Pallar men sold their paddy for cash for drink. Women never did: this harvested paddy provided rice of quality far superior to the Government ration-shop rice, which is why Pallar women treasured the harvest paddy—as, indeed, everyone in Aruloor who had access to it did. I was constantly told that shop-bought rice was never as tasty as home-produced rice.

Table 2 indicates how dramatically earnings and numbers of women and men employed increased within four days of the first appearance of the prayed-for, longed-for water. The number of women in waged work more than doubled between 5 October and 12 October (rising from 37 to 83) and the number of men who contributed to the household doubled (rising from 14 to 28). But, as always, some men continued to give nothing at all in household contribution. Remarkably, while the amount of cash earned by women more than tripled (going up from Rs. 109 to Rs. 336) the amount contributed by men only doubled (from Rs. 132 to Rs. 288).

In our daily evening census we were often told that the husband had earned a wage that day but had contributed nothing. Thus when we asked a woman what her husband had contributed that day, we often elicited a reply like the following: 'He's given me nothing: he spends it all on drink! And he's drunk half the time. He only comes home to eat and sleep.' Many women were deeply frustrated by such behaviour.

The pattern of contributions to the domestic budget from women and men in Table 1 indicates that between the second and the fifth of October men's total contributions exceeded women's total earnings every day. This is because men's wages are much higher than women's. For this reason, even though only some men made contributions and almost none gave his entire earnings, women's wages were so low in comparison that they added up to less. Between the tenth and the

Table 1: Female Earnings & Male Contributions (Drought)

	Women's earnings					Men's contributions				
1987 Date	No. of Women	Cash high (Rs)	Cash low (Rs)	Cash tot. (Rs)	Paddy tot. (Mar)	No. of Men	Cash high (Rs)	Cash low (Rs)	Cash tot. (Rs)	Paddy tot. (Mar)
2 Oct	28	8	0.50	122	-	13	35	0.60	152	-
3 Oct	27	9	1.00	109	3	10	35	5.00	132	-
4 Oct	44	9	1.00	173	6	13	50	5.00	219	-
5 Oct	37	9	1.00	147	3	14	50	5.00	189	4

Table 2: Female Earnings & Male Contributions (Enough water)

	Women's earnings					Men's contributions				
1987 Date	No. of Women	Cash high (Rs)	Cash low (Rs)	Cash tot. (Rs)	Paddy tot. (Mar)	No. of Men	Cash high (Rs)	Cash low (Rs)	Cash tot. (Rs)	Paddy tot. (Mar)
10 Oct	68	9	1	281	4	25	35	5	221	2
11 Oct	80	5	1	303	7	25	10	5	211	2
12 Oct	83	8	1	323	8	28	35	5	274	*
13 Oct	76	8	2	336	10	27	35	5	288	*

Key: Mar : Marakkal
tot. : total
(a local measure)
(*Men tended to sell their paddy for cash for drink)

high : highest single wage/contribution
low : lowest single wate/contribution

thirteenth of October, however, this pattern changed (Table 2) because, with the coming of river-water, the transplantation of the *samba* paddy crop swung into action. Consequently, during these transplanting days women's earnings exceeded men's contributions every day. Both female earnings and male contributions increased in the following weeks when there was virtually full employment for both sexes. Full employment only exists during the months of transplanting and the months of harvest: this is when demand for labour is at its peak.

Significantly, while male contributions never included the wages of a male child because young boys did not participate in adult male waged labour, female earnings regularly included the wages of female children, who often participated in adult female waged labour and were paid the adult female wage.

Pallar women in Aruloor contributed virtually 100 per cent of their earnings to the household, in sharp contrast to Pallar men. They saw nothing extraordinary in this and it appears that Pallar women in the neighbouring villages of Nannikal and Pettupatti did likewise. Indeed, the extensive research of Joan Mencher (1985, 1988) on landless agricultural labourer households suggests that this differential pattern of high contributions from women earners and low contributions from men earners is typical and widespread, not only in Tamil Nadu, but also in the neighbouring southern state of Kerala and elsewhere.

She discusses her detailed surveys of rural landless labouring households in Tamil Nadu, Kerala, West Bengal and elsewhere in several articles (Mencher, 1979, 1980, 1982, 1985, 1988). Her data on landless households details the share of earned income contributed to the household by wives and husbands and very clearly shows that women contribute a much larger percentage of their incomes. Her findings for the Tamil Nadu districts that neighbour Tiruchi District show that:

(1) in Thanjavur, wives contributed 99 per cent, husbands 77 per cent
(2) in South Arcot (1), wives contributed 99 per cent, husbands 77 per cent

(3) in South Arcot (2), wives contributed 96 per cent, husbands 71 per cent

(Mencher, 85, pp. 362–3).

She comments: 'What is most significant in these figures is that in every case, the proportion of income contributed by wage-earning women to the household is far higher than that of their earning husbands' (Mencher, 1985, p. 365). She, therefore, concludes that policy planners and governments must 'pay more attention to female income. The contribution of our female informants is crucial for family survival, even in households where there are working males' (1985, p. 366). My data from Aruloor entirely support these conclusions.

Pallar Men and Technological Change

On the one hand it was true that Pallar women often spoke of the problems caused by excessive male drinking and that violence against women was a visible phenomenon in the Pallar street. On the other hand there were good reasons why Pallar men might feel frustrated and depressed and, therefore, have recourse to alcohol. Among contributory causes, the central one was probably the impact of technological change.

C.P. Chandrasekhar (forthcoming) has pointed out that researchers who study rural populations need to be clear about what phase of agricultural development they are in. He has noted that an area that has reached a peak of Green Revolution development makes intensive use of High Yielding Varieties (HYVs) of seeds, fertilisers and pesticides and invests in improved irrigation—during this phase there is an increased demand for labour due to intensive cropping. However, Chandrasekhar notes, this phase of the Green Revolution is generally followed by a quite separate phase of mechanisation, in which agricultural labour is displaced and labour demand falls. This appears to be the phase that agriculture in Aruloor is in at present. Within the short period of about fifteen years, ploughing in Aruloor has been almost entirely mechanised. Haruka Yanagisava has noted that there was no mechanisation of ploughing at all in Appadurai and Mela Valadi (villages fairly close to Aruloor) in 1979 when he carried out fieldwork there (Yanagisawa, 1984). Thus a dramatic change has occurred in male agricultural employment in the area within a very short space of time.

Ploughing was traditionally the male activity par excellence—and consequently Pallar men have, within the last decade, suddenly been stripped of their major agricultural task. Virtually no other task has been mechanised, however, in sharp contrast to the mechanisation that has revolutionised wheat farming in the Punjab. No female task has so far been touched by mechanisation, possibly because the very low wages that are paid to women labourers make the mechanisation of female tasks unnecessary and uneconomic—as yet. However, Mencher has noted, with some degree of alarm: 'At a conference on women and rice cultivation in 1982 at the International Rice Research Institute, descriptions were presented of ... labour-saving innovations, such as herbicides (to eliminate weeding), hand-operated transplanting equipment (which would reduce the number of women needed to transplant by a factor of six), and very simple harvesting equipment.... It is possible that these innovations will come soon to Tamil Nadu and Kerala. Such changes, blind to gender dynamics in income processes and to the class structure of the society, have the potential to do profound damage to large numbers of households' (1988, pp. 99–100). This prediction holds true for Pallar households in Aruloor: Mencher's alarm is well justified.

Traditionally ploughing was done by one man using a wooden plough and a team of buffaloes (or bullocks). Ploughing up paddy-fields prior to transplanting was a central occupation of Pallar males, who received comparatively high wages at Rs. 15 a 'furrow' (*yer*) for this specialised task. An acre of paddy-field required eight furrows to turn the soil, four lengthwise and four breadthwise. The job was usually done by four teams of oxen, thus four men were involved and each earned Rs. 30 for the job which needed three to four hours work. This meant that the landholder paid Rs. 120 to plough up a paddy-field in preparation for transplanting. When tractors were first introduced for ploughing in the Aruloor area, some fifteen years ago, they cost more than Rs. 120 to plough a field. Today, however, a small, mechanised power-driller called a 'hand-tractor' ('*kai*-tractor' in Tamil) can be used to plough a field at less cost (Rs. 90 to Rs. 100). directed by one man who walks behind, holding it. Small tractors have also come on the scene, undercutting the cost of traditional ploughing. Thus, in the space of fifteen years a great change has occurred, for about 90 per cent of ploughing in Aruloor is mechanised today, according to the estimates of Pallar informants. In this way Pallar men have lost their most profitable job.

Though Pallar men have faced steadily decreasing opportunities for work, unlike Pallar women, they do not readily cross the sexual division of labour in order to take up 'female' work, because they would lose status if they did. The fact that young Pallar boys are not drafted into adult male labour also suggests that there is far less demand for male agricultural labour today, in the area.

Transplanting, however, has not been mechanised, nor has weeding; consequently there is more 'female' work than 'male' work available today in paddy cultivation. Pallar women have more work available to them than men, not only in the cultivation of paddy but also with regard to sugarcane and banana. This 'feminisation of agricultural labour' is a striking feature of work in Aruloor today, but it is not a unique phenomenon for it has been well documented in other areas too. Thus in Vadamalaipuram in Ramanathapuram District, Venkatesh Athreya noted that while the average total of days of employment for men was 200 days, for women it was 215 days (1984, p. 96). He continued: 'The decline in average casual employment for male workers from eight months to 200 days appears to be related to the tractorisation of much of ploughing work. The significant increase in average duration of female casual employment between 1958 and 1983 appears to be the outcome of more intensive cropping and higher yields arising therefrom' (1984, p. 96). The Vadamalaipuram employment situation thus closely resembles that in Aruloor, and for the same reasons.

The fact that Pallar women are far more independent of their men than women of other castes, may be another reason for the apparent frustration and lack of morale of many Pallar men. Whether they want to or not, unlike men of higher castes, they are forced to occasionally depend on the wages of their wives, given that Pallar women are more steadily employed. This suggests that a deep contradiction exists between the ideal self-image of Pallar men and reality: they like to see themselves as authoritative and in control, but in fact have to regularly depend on their wives' income. This may contribute to their depression and frequent drunkenness.

It also exacerbates the tendencies induced by their socialisation as children. If such a rigid sexual division of labour did not exist between 'female' and 'male' tasks, boys could perhaps be socialised into light 'female' wage-work as easily as girls are. However, the sexual division of labour is unlikely to crumble easily, not only because of the strength of cultural tradition, but also because there is too little work available even for the women.

The Sexual Division of Labour

The sexual division of agricultural work in Aruloor is a cultural construction, but, like all successful cultural constructions, it has assumed the appearance of 'God-given' fact and is regarded as 'natural' and dictated by human biology.

The central sexual divide in agricultural labour was between activities like sowing and ploughing, which were defined as 'male' activities and activities like carrying and weeding, which were seen as 'female'. Tamil cultural rationale defined all digging with the large hoe (*mumbti* from *'mannu-vetti'*: 'breaking the soil') and ploughing, as 'male' labour. A fairly explicit symbolic parallel was set up between Tamil ideas of sexual intercourse and procreation of the one hand, and agricultural activities on the other. A typical image of sexual intercourse (particularly strong in upper caste discourse) was that of the male 'seed' that entered the female's 'field' to germinate and develop into a baby. Thus, the 'sowing of seed' both in sexual intercourse and in agriculture was seen as a quintessentially male activity. Digging or the 'breaking of earth' (*'mannu-vetti'*) was a similar activity, identified with the invasive male, while the female was identified with the dormant but nurturing earth. Though Pallar informants stated that digging was a 'male' activity, an exception was made for the 'digging of weeds' (*kallu-kothradhu*) of certain crops (especially banana and sugarcane); this was defined as a 'female' task. The rationale was that such weed-digging did not involve the use of the large hoe (*mumbti*) so it was not really 'breaking the earth', and was, therefore, not a 'male' activity.

With women's work a parallel between what is viewed as 'biologically female' and as appropriate agricultural work is quite explicit: pregnant women carry their babies for ten lunar months before delivery and after child-birth they carry and suckle their babies for many more months. Therefore, carrying is seen as a peculiarly female task. Further, to carry an object for someone expresses the inferiority of the bearer to the person whose burden she bears. Thus carrying a burden is typically the task of a social inferior. Here it is not sexual hierarchy but social hierarchy that is enacted. In Tamil society women are the inferiors and the 'servants' of men, hence, in agricultural activities in Aruloor, it was primarily women who bore burdens.

These ideas were reflected in daily life and on ceremonial occasions too—in ritual processions it was women who carried the burdens of ritual gifts (*seer*) on their heads while the men normally carried nothing at all. If a man—of any caste—had to carry something, he carried it in his hands, on his shoulder or on his back, never on his head. To do so was to carry something 'like a woman', that is 'like an inferior' and thus to provoke derision. There were a few exceptions to this general rule, however, given that it was felt that the easiest way to carry heavy loads was on the head. So at the paddy harvest both women and men carried their immensely heavy loads of paddy on their heads. At the banana harvest too, the *tar* (banana clusters), which were extremely heavy, were carried on the head by both sexes.

In these ways the agricultural labour, connected with Aruloor's three main crops of paddy, banana and sugar cane, was sexually divided so that all carrying, weeding and transplanting were 'female' jobs, while digging (with the large hoe) and ploughing were solely 'male'. Harvest work required both sexes, some tasks were performed jointly while others were segregated.

Very significantly, as a general rule, jobs that carry higher status are 'male' jobs. Thus paddy harvest work is sexually divided so that sieving and winnowing, which are very tedious jobs, are 'female', whereas the important but easy task of finally measuring the grain out is strictly 'male'. All male jobs are always paid considerably more than female jobs.

These are the general principles on which agricultural work is sexually divided. These gender boundaries are normally not transgressed: ploughing, especially, is entirely taboo to women. I learnt (after assiduous enquiry) of only one Pallar woman in a distant village (Pichandarkoil) who had been widowed and who had chosen to plough her own fields because her male kin demanded excessive payment to do so. She had been virtually ostracised by her community for appropriating this male prerogative. Pallar informants in Aruloor who heard of her were amazed at her daring.

With the sole exception of ploughing, however, women actually can and do perform 'male' jobs in the privacy of their family farms. Thus, *when no male wage is at stake,* Pallar men are perfectly happy to let women perform 'male' labour. Further, due to the continuing drought in Tamil Nadu and to the consequent shortage of agricultural work (which depends on water) Pallar women occasionally crossed the gender divide and performed 'male' jobs, if Pallar men did not take them up. My Pallar informants reported a team of Pallar women from another village doing heavy *mumbti* (digging) work—'male' work—in that village, while in Aruloor itself women occasionally did 'male' digging jobs if they became available. Remarkably, despite the dire straits their families were in, unemployed Pallar men never took up 'female' jobs: they preferred to depend on their wives' wages. Also, they would have lost face if they had performed 'female' tasks. So the crossing of boundaries in the sexual division of work was in one direction only, of women crossing to 'male' jobs whenever these became available.

The division of agricultural tasks by age did not formally exist in Aruloor because all jobs were defined as adult jobs and paid an adult wage. Those who were too young or too old for the rigours of fieldwork were automatically excluded from it. It was mainly in domestic labour that children (particularly female children) participated. But young girls aged about eleven and upwards were recruited into adult wage labour regularly by their female kin. In order to participate they had to be dressed up as 'adult women' in a *sari*, because customarily only post-pubertal (i.e. 'adult') women were allowed to do agricultural work. Those Pallar women who were too old for wage labour would cut grass for sale as fodder or they would graze goats. They never sat idly at home because they had to support themselves: among the impoverished Pallars there were no joint families, only nuclear households.

Payment for Agricultural Work

The most striking feature of agricultural wages—apart from their meagreness—is the huge degree of sexual differentiation involved. For daily work, which consisted of four hours of field labour from 8 a.m. to 12 noon, women were paid Rs. 4 before October 1987 and Rs. 5 thereafter (having successfully negotiated a higher wage)[2]. For a similar four hour 'daily work' period, men were paid Rs. 10. Thus men were not just paid more but more than double the female wages. However, my Pallar informants felt that there were various reasons for this: on the one hand both women and men agreed that men ought to be paid more 'because their work was harder' and, on the other hand, it was generally felt that it would be deeply humiliating for a man if he was paid the same as a woman *even* for the same work. Therefore, a differential had to be observed, simply in order to secure the superior status of the man. Indeed, we will see how (male) employers willingly gave a 'gift' or 'extra' payment to men, but never to women.

It is extremely interesting that most women—at least formally—endorsed the ideology that male work was paid more because it was 'harder'—particularly since this assumption was obviously often not true. Digging the earth ('male' work) might appear harder work than carrying soil ('female' work) but the two jobs are paced very differently and, therefore, digging is not necessarily more exhausting. For instance, when a field has to be levelled, two men might be hired to dig out the earth that is then carried (in baskets on the head) by a team of eight women to the site that has to be raised. The men dig a little and then rest, but the women have to carry their baskets to and fro almost unceasingly, often under a blazing sun. In these circumstances men's work does not appear harder, but the men get Rs. 10 each and the women only Rs. 5 each. Yet the women do not complain about this.

On the other hand, they did complain about and sharply resented the way in which Pallar men regularly exploited their wage labour. This happened in the context of contract (or piece-rate) work where Pallar men regularly recruited Pallar women who were often their own kinswomen and even their own wives. Where a mixed sex group was required for a contract job it was automatically the men who appropriated the position of authority, recruited the workers and negotiated the deal. Men 'took charge' because they normally did in any mixed sex social interaction. Contract work differs from fixed wage daily work in being much more highly paid. However, this higher pay never reached the women because men 'talked' the contract. That is, the men negotiated the higher wage per worker with the employer, but then they kept this wage secret from the women and paid them instead at the daily work time rate (Rs. 5) even though the women were working longer hours, and faster. Where much longer hours than the standard four hours of daily labour were required, the women workers were paid a little more, but still far less than what the men paid themselves. I was told that if the women were paid Rs. 8 each then you could be sure that the men were getting at least Rs. 20 each. Because women knew that they were being exploited in this way, there preferred to negotiate their contract work themselves in separate all-female work-groups: this was increasingly the case. Contract work used to be far rarer than daily work in Aruloor, and elsewhere in Tiruchi District, (Athreya, et al., 1990, pp. 139–46), but today it is increasingly common (Kapadia, forthcoming b). There has been a corresponding increase in the frequency with which women negotiate their own contract work, in order to cut out men and men's special 'cut' altogether.

So exploitation does not merely exist between high-caste employers and low-caste labourers, it also often exists between Pallar men acting as proxy employers and the Pallar women they recruit. It is intriguing that in these wage-labour contexts, the exploitation of Pallar women's labour by Pallar men, though it is a central fact of domestic life, is not accepted or tolerated by women in the sphere of work. This suggests that Pallar women feel that the values of the work place are different from those of the home. They are apparently willing to tolerate domestic exploitation of their labour because this is legitimised by a whole constellation of Pallar cultural imperatives that define their roles as women and mothers. But these cultural norms also emphasise their role as providers for their children: this sets up a sharp contradiction when the men they are required to respect as their husbands become their exploitative proxy employers. Outright conflict with husbands over wages is avoided by not entering into their employment: all-female contract work groups are the answer that women have found.

When the boundaries of the sexual division of labour are crossed, this is generally by women who take up vacant 'male' jobs. This appears to be because the responsibility of providing for their children is felt much more keenly by women than by men. However, on those rare occasions when a woman performs waged 'male' labour she is not paid a 'male' daily work wage (Rs. 10). Instead, though she had done a man's job, she gets a woman's daily work wage (Rs. 4). Thus, when Bathma, a strong, young woman of about 25, did a 'male' digging job with the large hoe one day, she was paid only Rs. 4 and not Rs. 10. She was not aggrieved: when my assistant and I asked her what she thought about it, she simply said that she had known from the first that she would not be paid a man's wage. Thus even for waged 'male' work a woman is paid less than a man and accepts this as normal.

The literature on Tamil paddy agriculture has claimed that there is one complex of tasks for which women and men are paid exactly the same for the same work, namely, for harvest work (Saradamoni, 1987; Mencher, 1982). This is not the case in Aruloor where I, too, was told that there was exactly equal pay for both sexes for harvest work, but found that this was, in fact, not quite true.

On two occasions during harvest work total pay for women and men differs. The first occurs when the paddy has been threshed (by both women and men), measured out and poured into sacks. On this occasion the women labourers leave for home to cook dinner, leaving their male harvest-partners (fathers, husbands, brothers or sons) to collect their share of the paddy 'wage'. The men then load the paddy sacks onto a cart or carry them into the owner's house (if the threshing has occurred on his doorstep). At this point they are always awarded an extra 'gift' of paddy 'for this job'; they sell this paddy immediately and spend the money on drink before going home. It is said that they are paid more than the women for the extra job of loading or carrying. This is arguably true, so in this case the extra pay may be justified.

However, the second event at which men are paid 'extra' (by their male employers), is particularly striking because they do no extra work at all. This happens the following day, when the final task of threshing the hay (to glean the remaining grain) is done. This consists of the trampling of the hay by cattle and thereafter the sieving and winnowing of the grain by women. On this occasion it is glaringly obvious that it is the women, not the men, who deserve the 'extra' pay, for it is the women who labour for hours while the men just sit around or sleep. On one occasion in the Pallar street, when the employer had given the men the expected 'gift' I heard one of the women say, ironically, to the man who was receiving it, '*We've* done all the work, but *you're* getting the extra pay! Won't you give us some of it?' The man receiving the extra paddy was not a whit embarrassed: he totally ignored her and, without pause, proceeded to sell the paddy on the spot for money for drink. Thus it seems that even when no differential wage is clearly justified, a differential wage is deliberately paid through a 'gift' to male labourers by their employers.

This extra pay might, on the one hand, be seen as ostensibly protecting the higher status of Pallar men: that is, it protects them from the indignity of equal pay with women. But, on the other hand, it subtly underlines the implicit co-option of Pallar men into the system of patronage dominated by upper caste male employers. Employers are virtually always men. This is inevitable in a patriarchal society where both authority and property are vested in men. The 'extra gift' that male employers give male workers also serves to emphasise the indebtedness of Pallar men to their masters. The bonds of patronage that exist between upper-caste employers and Pallar men are ancient. Today they are most clearly embodied in the fact that Pallar irrigation supervisors (*tannir pachararvar*) are virtually all men. This job, the only agricultural salaried job that is available, is virtually reserved for men. It is the modern incarnation of the ancient job of *pannaiyal*, the bonded farm servant, who was male. Thus women were traditionally excluded from being *pannaiyal* in their own right—they could only share in this work if married to the farm servant.

Today, however, the situation is more complex. Formally, the marginality of women workers appears to continue, for almost all irrigation supervisors are still men. But actually things are changing: most Pallar men used to be *pannaiyal* but in recent times only a few have retained jobs as irrigation overseers. Meanwhile the feminisation of labour has meant that employers actually depend more on women labourers than on men to get work done. Therefore, though Pallar women have been and continue to be excluded from the male system of work-patronage, they are simultaneously in a stronger bargaining position than Pallar men because it is their labour that is in greater demand. In such a context, women workers are likely to resist exploitation by employers more staunchly than men do, and this is indeed the case in Aruloor, as is attested by the fact that agricultural wages were pushed up through a strike initiated by the women's work groups (Kapadia, forthcoming a).

Gillian Hart made an important observation when she noted that in Muda in rural Malaysia the greater ability of women workers to organise collectively, as compared to that of men, was among other factors, related to their exclusion from a system of male patronage (1991, pp. 114–15). The Pallar women of Aruloor provide yet another example of the superior organising ability of women workers as against men workers in a Tamil context that has remarkable points of similarity with that described by Hart (1991).

The Profits of Production and the Ideologies of Reproduction

In conclusion I turn to the relationship between capitalist agricultural production and reproduction in the subsistence sphere. Though in 1987 and 1988 small-scale agricultural production in Tiruchi District was becoming increasingly unprofitable due to the continuing drought, large-scale farming remained profitable. For several decades large-scale agricultural production in the Tiruchi and Thanjavur area had been transforming itself into an agro-business where the agricultural producer was a capitalist entrepreneur who employed an increasingly proletarianised labour force.[3]

Remarkably, all transplanting work in the Aruloor area is done by Pallar women: every blade of green in the paddy field was planted by the hand of a Pallar woman. The relations of reproduction of the Pallar household depend on the recruitment of Pallar women to the fields and of Pallar women and female children to the household. Only the co-opting of female children as surrogate mothers allows women with young children to participate in full-time agricultural work. The work available to Pallar men has steadily fallen. Given that the wages of both women and men are very low and that men normally give only part of their earnings to the support of their households, this means that the earnings of Pallar women and the unwaged work of both women and female children are absolutely essential to Pallar subsistence. Ironically, they are equally essential to the capitalist agrarian economy.

The crucial point is that the profitability of agricultural production is based not only on the recruitment of Pallar men at very low wages, but even more on the recruitment of Pallar women at even lower wages and of female children at no wages at all. It is, on the one hand, the unwaged labour of women and young girls which maintains, and reproduces the Pallar household and, on the other hand, the meagre wages of Pallar women and men, that together maintain the profits made by the large landholders and agrarian entrepreneurs. In short, it is the unwaged subsistence labour of Pallar women and children that subsidises the profits of capitalist farming.

Supply exceeds demand in the rural agricultural labour market, consequently wages in Aruloor stay low (well below the minimum wages enshrined in government legislation) while profits stay comparatively high. The shift towards cash crops (especially banana—see Athreya, 1984, p. 70) has resulted in Pallar and other landless-labourer groups earning decreasing supplies of paddy. Mechanisation has decreased male work, but precisely because female labour is so cheap, there is, at present, not much incentive to mechanise further. Low wages and scarce work have trapped the Pallars in a cycle of deprivation in which children are recruited to household and wage work and, therefore, have virtually no chance to get an education. The Pallars have been steadily impoverished and almost pauperised over the last few decades and if better-paid jobs became available to them elsewhere they would probably migrate. However, with no such possibility in sight at present, they remain where they are and continue to subsidise the profits of capitalist agriculture.

The differential employment prospects and contribution to the household of Pallar women and men makes it clear, however, that the burden of family survival falls much more heavily on the shoulders of women. It is their unstinting contribution of their entire earned incomes to the family budget that keeps their families from destitution. As Joan Mencher has warned, if the enormous contribution of landless labourer women to family income is not recognised and if their agricultural work is taken away from them through state-subsidised innovation in technology, the result could be disastrous. Policy makers and planners must take due note—those hands that plant the green blades in South India's paddy fields are hands that, in the words of the Chinese proverb, 'hold up half the sky'.

Notes

[1]Fieldwork was carried out in Tiruchi District from January 1987 to May 1988 with further visits in December 1988, December 1990 and January 1991. Aruloor, Nannikal and Pettupatti are pseudonyms.

[2]See details in Kapadia (forthcoming a).

[3]See Gough (1991, 1989) for a detailed analysis; see Kapadia (forthcoming c) on the increasing landlessness of agricultural workers.

References

Athreya, V., 1984. *Vadamalaipuran: A Resurvey* Working Paper No. 50, Madras: Madras Institute of Development Studies.

———, G. Djurfeldt and S. Lindberg, 1990. *Barriers Broken: Production Relations and Agrarian Change in Tamil Nadu* New Delhi and London: Sage.

Bruce, J. and D. Dwyer, 1988. 'Introduction', in D. Dwyer and J. Bruce (eds), *A Home Divided: Women and Income in the Third World* Standford: Stanford University Press.

Chandrasekhar, C.P., forthcoming. *Agrarian Change and Occupational Diversification: Non-agriculutral Employment and Rural Development in West Bengal.*

Gough, K., 1981. *Rural Society in Southeast India* Cambridge: Cambridge University Press.

———, *Rural Change in Southeast India* Delhi: Oxford University Press.

Hart, G., 1991. 'Engendering Everyday Resistance: Gender, Patronage and Production Politics in Rural Malaysia', *Journal of Peasant Studies*, 19: 1, pp. 93–121.

Kapadia, K., 1990. *Gender, Caste and Class in Rural South India* Ph.D. Thesis, University of London.

———, forthcoming a. 'Mutuality and Competition: Female Landless Labour and Wage Rates in Tamil Nadu'.

———, forthcoming b. 'Discipline and Control: Labour Contracts and Rural Female Labour'.

———, forthcoming c. 'Pauperizing the Rural Poor: Landless Labour in Tamil Nadu', *Economic and Political Weekly.*

Mencher, J., 1980. 'The Lessons and Non-lessons of Kerala', *Economic and Political Weekly*, 41–43, pp. 1781–802.

———, 1985. 'Landless Women Agricultural Labourers in India', in IRRI, *Women in Rice Farming*, Gower: Aldershot.

———, 1988. 'Women's Work and Poverty: Women's Contribution to Household Maintenance in South India', in D. Dwyer and J. Bruce (eds), *A Home Divided: Women and Income in the Third World* Stanford: Standford University Press.

Mencher, J. and K. Saradamoni, 1982. 'Muddy Feet, Dirty Hands', *Economic and Political Weekly*, 17, pp. A149–A167.

Mencher, J., et al. 1979. 'Women in Rice-Cultivation', *Studies in Family Planning* 11, pp. 408–12.

Saradamoni, K. 1987. 'Labour, Land and Rice Production', *Economic and Political Weekly*, 22, pp. WS2–WS6.

Yanagisawa, H. 1984. *Socio-cultural Change in Villages in Tiruchirappali District, Tamil Nadu, India,* ILCAA, Tokyo University, Tokyo.

4

"More Equal than Others?"

Gender Bias in the Constitution of Bureaucratic Merit in the Indian Administrative Service

SAROJINI GANJU THAKUR

Hitherto, public administration studies have been dominated by the Weberian model of the rational, merit-based bureaucracy. The result was a subject that was technical, vocational and prescriptive: devoted to the refinement and transmission of generally agreed norms, rules and guidelines about how good administration should be undertaken. This model, likened to that of a machine, was "premised on the primacy of mechanisms associated with **'organisation'**: hierarchy, duty and authority" (Moore 1992) and therefore seen to function on the basis of impersonality and neutrality. Within this framework, differential outcomes for men and women within an organisation were attributed to the workings of an objective body of rules, norms and practices. There can be little doubt that organisational processes determine the manner in which the bureaucracy is constituted and perpetuated. This chapter focuses on analysing these processes to understand the nature of gender relations in the bureaucracy. It also examines the extent to which the bureaucracy reflects and reinforces the biases of larger society and is responsible for creating, maintaining and reproducing these.

In India, the bureaucracy represents one of the most potent and pervasive interfaces with the state. The specific focus of this study is the Indian Administrative Service (IAS), a bureaucracy which has often been labelled as the successor to the colonial Indian Civil Service (ICS). In numerical terms it represents a minuscule proportion of the bureaucracy in India[1]. It is significant because it controls decision-making positions at both levels of the government, the centre and the state. Selected through the process of competitive examination which is common for most higher levels of bureaucracy that function under the control of the central government, officers of the Indian Administrative Service are then allocated to state cadres for the duration of their career lives. At various intervals in their careers they can be on secondment to the central government for a fixed period of time after which they revert to the state cadres. The service is categorised as an all India service because of its federal character. Although, while serving in the state, the officers function under its control, the rules which govern their careers are applicable throughout the country. The pre-eminent position of this bureaucracy results in its being used as a model and standard for the bureaucracy at various levels in the rest of the country, and as a mirror of the underlying ethos that influences its structures, norms and values.

While the functioning of the IAS, in its initial phase, was to a large extent determined by the 'tradition' it inherited from the ICS, which consisted of powerful service class values, and "the essential attributes of that complex character—the English gentleman"[2] (Potter 1996), its composition differed significantly on two counts. Firstly, democratic provisions in the Constitution of India guaranteeing "equality before the law" and "equality of employment opportunity"[3] allowed entry to women into what had been a male bastion, and secondly, the provisions for positive discrimination in favour of the socially disadvantaged Scheduled Castes (SC) and Scheduled Tribes (ST)[4] led to the enactment of certain quotas for their entry into service. As a result, women competing in a common examination with men can qualify for entry on the basis of merit. Needless to say, however in view of reservations for the SC and ST categories the standards for entry are different both for men and women.

This study will focus upon the ways that men and women within the service perceive gender issues in their own lives and careers, as well as in the organisation of the IAS as a whole. While the consistently low rates of female recruitment are directly relevant to the overall numbers of women in the service, that issue emanates from a broader societal context and will require a separate study.[5] The purpose of this paper will be to explore the manner in which the rules and practices of the service (both formal and informal) impact on those men and women who are already within the service. It will examine the extent to which the bureaucratic structure is gender neutral, whether it provides equality of opportunity for both sexes or whether it is responsible for maintaining or creating and perpetuating inequalities between male and female officers which, in turn, contribute to gender-biased bureaucratic culture.

Gender, as the central concern of this paper, is only one element within a larger framework of civil service reforms. Recently a paper focusing on various aspects of IAS reform was written by the faculty of the LBS Academy and, in a sense, this study arises out of the analysis offered in that earlier paper (LBSNAA 1995, p. 1–24). The effort here simply represents a second level of analysis which centres on the manner in which the organisation of the IAS is itself a gendered entity, and on the various issues that affect men and women in their work as well as at home.

Study Methodology and Sample

It is also necessary to situate this study in relation to other studies that have examined issues of women in the IAS. The earliest of these is Nisha Sahai-Achuthan's "Women in the IAS (1948–74): A Study of Their Socio-Economic cum Academic Background, and Attitude to Marriage and Career." More recently, M.N. Prasad et. al. have published a paper entitled "Do Women in the IAS Face Discrimination", and the Department of Administrative Reforms and Public Grievances has undertaken a study of "Women in the Civil Services".

While the methodology used in all the studies is roughly similar (all, including this study, use a questionnaire as the means of gathering primary data) the present study differs in several significant ways. In the first place, this study draws upon a larger response base than any earlier ones. Additionally, it departs from earlier efforts in that responses from both men and women have been solicited—of the three other studies cited, only the Prasad et al. paper used male respondents as well as female.

Looking at these papers as consecutive steps in an ongoing effort, however, the most startling thing is not the differences between them, but the similarities. As the findings of these reports are roughly staggered over time, it is surprising how little the issues of concern have changed over the years. And in almost all cases the findings of this, the most recent study (covering up to the 1995 batch), confirm the earlier trends.

Here, I will first elaborate on the nature of the sample and draw a profile of the respondents. The main body of the analysis will then focus on the manner in which bias enters into the functioning and operation of the IAS.

The Sample

As the purpose of this study was to be suggestive, not definitive, we started out with a small but representative sample of IAS officers, sending questionnaires to approximately one sixth of the total number of IAS officers (800 out of 5,000). Although as the national training institute the LBSNAA runs frequent courses for IAS officers of various batches and cadres, we thought it best to solicit replies through the mail as we felt this questionnaire should be answered on a voluntary basis. The officers were addressed directly rather than through formal channels of control.

In the process of selection, one of our concerns was that the sample be representative of the distribution of officers over cadres and batches. To achieve this, for each cadre we calculated the cadre strength as a percentage of the overall service. We then computed that percentage out of 800, and sent it to that number of people in the cadre. In terms of batches, we were interested in receiving input from all levels of seniority, so within each cadre questionnaires were distributed equally among seniorities: i.e. a roughly equal number of questionnaires were sent to officers of each batch.

Where our sample does not represent the profile of the overall service is in regard to male/female representation. Because our questionnaire (Annexure-I) was primarily focussed on examining the gendered nature of the civil service and how experiences of male and female officers differ, it seemed necessary to seek responses from an equal number of men and women. The total number and distribution of women in the service was such, however, that in some cadres (as well as overall) the number of men who received questionnaires was greater than the number of women.

While we felt confident of the sample we had selected, as it was characteristic of the service, one problem that we encountered was with the mail. We chose the names for the sample from the civil list and used the addresses from the same. Unfortunately, due to the incomplete and sometimes out of date nature of these addresses, approximately 100 of the questionnaires that we mailed out were returned to us.

Luckily, however, we did end up with a sample that was quite representative. Out of the 124 respondents, 41 are women and 83 are men. We have respondents from every cadre (barring Kerala), and the overall cadre strength is also fairly representative. In addition, there was at least one respondent for every batch from 1961-1994. (see Annexure 2)

Explicit Bias in Bureaucratic Rules

Important insights into the gender ethos of the service can be gleaned from looking at the assumption about gender relations which underlie its rules, both at present and in the past. Two kinds of bias can be distinguished. Gender biased rules are those which explicitly introduce different conditions of service for women and men in ways which discriminate against one or other. The second form of bias emerges out of the way in which rules are interpreted so that apparently gender-neutral rules, interpreted in terms which either impose unwarranted gender differences or deny warranted ones, end up having gender-discriminatory outcomes. In this section, we deal with the former form of bias.

Although the formal ethos of the IAS is that of a merit-based organisation, in reality, its rules and norms suggest, often explicitly, that the ideal IAS officer is, or certainly was, male. The process underlying this resembles that described by Acker:

> The closest the disembodied worker doing the abstract job comes to a real worker is the male worker whose life centres on his full-time, life-long job, while his wife or another woman takes care of his personal needs and his children. The woman worker, assumed to have legitimate obligations other than those required by the job, did not fit with the abstract job.

Many of the more overtly gender biased rules have been abandoned or changed in the light of greater gender-awareness within the government as well as challenges by individual officers. But changing rules does not always change the underlying ethos which gave rise to them and it is worth noting what these rules have to say about prevailing perceptions of gender roles and responsibilities within an influential section of the Indian government. This point is illustrated by looking at the rules of marriage which characterised the IAS for many years after its inception, as well as by analysing some of the assumptions about the construct of the 'family' in those cases where both husband and wife were working as government servants.

While Article 16 of the Constitution opened the doors of civil service jobs to all women by ensuring "equality of opportunity for all citizens in matters relating to employment or appointment to any officer under the State," there was an underlying assumption that if a woman got married it would be difficult for her to cope with the dual roles of wife and officer. Consequently, the promise of Article 16 was betrayed by Rule 5(3) of the 1954 IAS Recruitment Rules which read:

> No married woman shall be entitled as of right to be appointed to the Service and where a woman appointed to the Service subsequently marries, the Central Government may, if the maintenance of the efficiency of the service so requires, call upon her to resign.

This rule was only deleted in 1972. Although information on the extent to which this rule was actualised is not available, what it did indicate was a governmental attitude which defined the roles of 'officer' and 'wife' as mutually incompatible.

The Indian Foreign Service (IFS), a sister service, was even more stringent in its rules. Rule 18 denied appointment to married women until 1973. Another provision stated that:

> a woman member of the service shall obtain the permission of the Government in writing before her marriage is solemnised. At any

time after the marriage, a woman member of the Service may be required to resign from service, if the Government is satisfied that her family and domestic commitments are likely to come in the way of the due and efficient discharge of her duties as a member of the service.[7]

Because of this rule women did resign from service or remain single, and it was only in 1979 that the rule was challenged in a case (AIR 1979 SC 1868) by Miss C.B. Muthumma. In his decision, the judges cited the "naked bias" of the rule and the "traumatic transparency" of such "discrimination against women".

The implicit assumption behind both the IAS and IFS rules was thus that "family and domestic commitments" were solely a women's responsibility. In both cases, it was assumed that a woman's place was in the home and that women had a prior commitment to a set of socially-ascribed domestic obligations rather than these being left to individual choice and negotiations with the family.

The rationale for rules governing the *privileges* for couples in government service also stem from a dominant view that the family be treated as a unit. While a couple working as government servants are treated at par in theory, and there is no *explicit* gender bias, implicitly the normative basis is of the family headed by the male officer and the women's earnings being viewed as supplementary. Simply by virtue of having a spouse in government, one of the officers is expected to abdicate his or her individual entitlement to certain privileges. These privileges include Leave Travel Concession (LTC), Home Travel Concession,* house loans from the government etc., and some allowances.

The IAS rules follow those of the Central government. In this context, the House Building Advances Central Civil Service (CCS) Rule No. 1 (reproduced below) appears to be conspicuously unfair:

---

*Leave Travel Concession is a privilege extended to civil servants to travel at government expense once in four years to any town in India with their family. Home Travel Concession is provided once in two years to visit one's home town.

> *When both the husband and wife are Central Government servants:* If both the husband and wife are Central Government servants and are eligible for grant of advance, the advance will be admissible to only one of them.

Similarly, when it comes to Leave Travel Concession (LTC), the government may have recognised that the husband and wife can have separate home towns, but if both husband and wife are Central Government servants:

> a) the children can claim the concession as members of the family of any one of the parents in a particular block;
>
> b) the husband or wife who avails LTC as a member of the family of the spouse cannot claim LTC independently for self.

The fact that it is usually the wife who waives her entitlement is clear when we see that women officers have repeatedly cited this disadvantage. At least five women officers married to other IAS officers referred to the limited benefits because of the rule that only one officer can claim benefits like Leave Travel Concession (LTC), Home Travel Concession (HTC), House Rent Allowance (HRA), House Building Advance (HBA). As one officer put it, it would seem that when two officers marry "the government extracts double the work but gives half the perks."[8] This can "encourage couples to live together or get technically divorced" in order to avail benefits like any other officer. If an officer performs all of the duties expected of an individual officer, then he or she should also be afforded all of the privileges granted to an individual officer. As one officer put it, "The rules weigh heavily against couples in government service and these benefits are not seen as a benefit at all."

While source constraints have often been cited as the logic for limiting benefits, it seems equally reasonable that if *two* members are contributing to the government system, they should be entitled to a better quality of life for themselves than in those cases where only one member of the family is working. One alternative is to rationalise allowances, rather than impose rules which benefit one officer and discriminate against the other. If husband and wife are both officers of the same seniority and they are individually entitled to a house of a certain category, they could be allowed a house that is one category higher. In practice there are states (Uttar Pradesh, Andhra Pradesh and Himachal Pradesh) which have allowed both husband and wife house building advances for either separate houses or the same house. Why should couples not be allowed two LTCs, Home Building Advances (HBAs) etc. if they can afford it? Why should the entity of one officer, usually the female one, have to be subsumed?

The rules also assume similarity in the situation of couples and individuals, and do not take sufficient account of the situation of single, divorced/widowed women or men. For instance, the issue has been raised that the provisions of the General Provident Fund (GPF) rules do not enable single women to withdraw funds easily, and that in many states there are no priorities for allotting accommodation for single women. In fact, in the Government of India there is a "Ladies Pool" in house allotment which allows women some priority. One suggestion would be to provide for similar rules in those states where they do not already exist to prioritise single women (for these purposes the definition of single women should include married women who are having to set up an establishment on their own).

Similarly, although in the Government of India there are clauses which permit officers to retain their accommodation (one below entitlement) during study leave, this is not true in all the states. This issue has been cited by a woman officer as an impediment to her having been able to take study leave—if the leave had been taken the officer would not have had a place to house her family!

Biased Interpretation /Outcomes of Bureaucratic Rules

In addition to explicit bias in bureaucratic rules, the second form involves the outcomes of rules which are supposedly "gender neutral". Who are the men and women who join the IAS? Are they from the same background? And are the implications for both the same? An understanding of this is critical because one of the ways that the bureaucracy perpetuates certain ideas and attitudes about gender is through the categories of men and women that it ultimately attracts and selects.

Family and Education

This section will establish the profile of the men and women in our survey both in terms of family and educational backgrounds. Table 1 focuses on the social distribution of respondents.

Table 1: Social Distribution of Respondents

Caste	*Male*	*Female*	*Total*
SC	10	2	13
ST	6	1	4
OBC[9]	4	2	9
General	63	36	98
Total	**83**	**41**	**124**

Based on the questionnaires of female respondents, it is clear that women IAS officers are on the whole from a fairly homogenous background. Women officers tend to come from an urban background where the parents—or at least the fathers—are primarily employed in government (usually at the higher levels), professional occupations or in the army. Whereas this finding is in accordance with the findings of earlier studies, what is surprising is the lack of change in the nature of the social background of women officers. In our sample there was not a single case of a woman from a purely agricultural background, and of the two female officers from the SC, in one case the father was in the IAS, and in the other both parents were in government service (teaching). Of the other categories, two OBC women officers got in before reservation (both from Tamil Nadu) and there was one ST woman officer whose father was educated to Class III.

In terms of educational background, all of the female respondents came from urban, English medium (for the most part convent) schools. Eleven (out of 41) female respondents had mothers who were professionals. So it is clear that, on the whole, only certain women have access to the kinds of social advantages (i.e., education, positive role models, etc.) which would enable them to sit for the civil service examination. It would also seem that reservations till 1995 have not actually made an impact in terms of attracting rural, and/or socially disadvantaged women. Despite the fact that the IAS may offer various reasons for attracting women—the respectability, the security of the work environment and the lack of alternate careers especially in the earlier years of the IAS—it has not succeeded in attracting women from various backgrounds.

In contrast, the backgrounds of the male respondents are more varied. From the total number of respondents (83), 22 came from agricultural backgrounds where the parents had low levels of literacy. Out of these, 13 came from SC/ST backgrounds and four from OBC. In the case of the three SC/ST with non agricultural backgrounds, the fathers were all in government service. There were four respondents from the OBC, but all of them entered service before reservations for OBC took place.

In order to see how (and if) the profile of male IAS officers from the non-reserved category changed over time, we sorted the questionnaires into pre- and post-1979 batches. In 1979, the nature of the IAS examination changed so 1980 has arbitrarily been chosen as a convenient dividing point. Of the pre-l979 batches, out of the 35 male respondents who did not come from an agricultural background only seven had fathers who worked outside of government (as politicians, lawyers etc.). In the post-l980 batches, out of the 23 respondents who were not from agricultural backgrounds, six were from non-government backgrounds. This would indicate that the children of government servants at some level aspire to be in government service themselves. There are very few entrants with backgrounds where the parents are professionals—i.e. in the private sector, business, or politics etc.

Taking the figures from male and female respondents together, it would seem that efforts to enable people from diverse educational backgrounds to enter the service (by changing the nature of the examination, etc.) has primarily benefited men. In view of the unequal access to education of men and women—particularly in rural areas—it will take time for quotas to reach women from backgrounds different to those of women presently joining the IAS. And even in the case of men, most are from backgrounds where parents were in government service at one level or another.

Regardless of the issue of whether IAS officers derive their power from their position, caste, class or gender (and undoubtedly it is a combination) the truth of the matter is that women have yet to reach a critical mass in the service. As Kantor suggests, when there is less than ten percent of a group (in this case women) in an institution, it is not representation but "tokenism". The fact that women have remained at only ten percent of the officers in the IAS since its inception means that they are in some ways still interlopers in what is, for all intents and purposes, a male service.

Marriage

The differences in backgrounds between male and female respondents may, in part, impact upon the kind of marriages that they are likely to have. If so, the issues discussed in the previous section may explain the following tables:

In our sample, nine out of 35 married women had arranged marriages (25 per cent). Of the 26 whose marriages were not arranged, 19 are married to other officers in government. For the most part, the spouses were officers also belonging to the

Table 2a: Numbers of Arranged/Non-arranged Marriages Among Female Respondents by Occupation of Husband

Occupation of Husband	*Arranged*	*Not Arranged*
Government	4	18
Private sector	3	5
In the home	0	0
Not given	2	3
Total	9	26

Table 2b: Numbers of Arranged/Non-arranged Marriage Among Male Respondents as Correlated to Occupation of Wife

Occupation of Wife	*Arranged*	*Not Arranged*
Government	14	9
Private sector	9	5
In the home	34	6
Total	57	20

AIS or Central Services. In contrast, of the 77 married men 57 had arranged marriages (74 per cent), with only 20 whose marriages were not arranged. It is also relevant to note that the overall number of single women in the sample was higher then that of single men (six women as compared to four men).

It must also be appreciated that marriage does not affect women and men in the IAS neutrally, particularly given the predominance of patrilocal marriage in the Indian context. Perhaps a beginning could be made by allowing women to change to the state/cadre where their spouse is working irrespective of whether he is with the government or not (provided this change is not to the home cadre).

The fact that women have fewer arranged marriages than men and are also more likely to marry another government officer has several implications. In the first place, for women there is an underlying pressure and preference for getting married within government, as otherwise it would be difficult for them to socially cope and manage their careers. In fact, the present rules so strongly favour and accommodate spouses who are both in government service (particularly in the matter of cadre changes) that this phenomenon has entered common parlance and is now known among the younger recruits as "CBM"—cadre based marriages.

For those with a spouse in the private sector, however, the possibility of a cadre change does not apply. In practice, then, this rule discriminates against those who get married outside government. The phenomenon of the husband resenting his wife's status and career is so common that M. K. Kaw, an IAS officer of the 1964 batch mentioned this in an essay entitled "Ladies, Gentlemen, Spinsters", commenting, "a major complication is marriage. Though we have pretensions of being modern, yet the *pratiloma* marriage where the wife is superior in status to the husband still carries an aura of transgression."[10] (Kaw 1993, p. 23) Though this essay is written in a humorous vein, it is a realistic summary of the many marriage-related difficulties that women within the service face. In some instances, and particularly before the mid-seventies, women quite often remained single or were forced to terminate their marriages. At least one officer wrote about this, saying: "I had to sacrifice my marriage as my husband could not take my success." It appears that male respondents are far more likely to conform to traditional practices in the matter of marriage than women.

Additionally, the allottment to certain cadres makes it difficult for women to even think about marriage at all (except to a fellow government servant). As one respondent notes, cadre allocation has not only led to her separation from her family but also has meant "difficulty in social integration, especially in venturing into marriage." In another case, a woman commented that: "I've made friends for a lifetime, but my family life (e.g. marriage) was out of the question. Especially when the Department of Personnel suggested marriage as the solution to the problem of getting a cadre change."

Biased Practices in Government

While gender biased outcomes and impacts of the selection process have been defined, the biases also affect the careers and the personal lives of men and women in the IAS. The findings as represented in the questionnaire responses can be divided into two broad categories—the nature of postings and the conditions of service (See Tables 3a and 3b).

While the issue of postings has been cited most often by both men and women, there are others too which indicate the gendered nature of certain practices.

Gender Stereotyping of Postings

As Table 3 indicates, the general perception among IAS officers is that there is gender stereotyping in the nature of posts held by men and women. What is more interesting, however, is that while 64 per cent of the respondents, the majority of both men and women, felt that gender stereotyping was a general phenomenon, the number of women who felt that they had been affected personally was significantly higher than the number of men.

In terms of people's perceptions regarding what posts are typically given to women and men, respondents felt that posts in the Women and Child Directorate and those related to Social Welfare were most often given to women. Social sector posts which have traditionally been labelled "soft" (especially Health, Rural Development and Education) were also listed as

Table 3a: Rules/Practices Cited by Male Respondents

Rule/Practice	*Number of times cited*
Postings/Transfers	15
Long Hours	12
Low Salary	9
Inefficiency in Govt. Functioning	3
Paternity Leave	2

Table 3b: Rules/Practices Cited by Female Respondents

Rule/Practice	*Number of times cited*
Postings	9
Leave	5
Cadre	5
Leave/Travel Concession	5
Facilities	2
Field Conditions	1

generally being given to women. To a lesser extent, these were followed by Secretariat postings such as Personnel. One senior officer observed that "even within social sectors, posts concerned with 'economic and financial' principles are viewed as male preserves, as if women cannot master such subjects unless they are financial advisers with accounts backgrounds. If at all women get an opportunity to work in male preserves they are given personnel, housekeeping and co-ordination jobs and invariably asked whether they have science and maths qualifications. This is a question rarely put to a male."

The nature of stereotyping in posts held by men covered three specific areas: field postings, regulatory administration, and "sensitive" postings which have public dealings. Many women felt that the more "challenging" jobs were given to men, as were posts involving "money deals". In a sense, however, the issue of "stereotyping" kinds of posts held by men is not entirely relevant: because men comprise the majority of the service, and almost all posts are held by a man at one point or another. As one female respondent stated "the job

Table 4: Is There Gender Stereotyping in the Nature of Posts?

	In General		*For you personally*	
	yes	no	yes	no
Men	41 (54%)	34 (46%)	1 (1.3%)	74 (98.7%)
Women	31 (84%)	6 (16%)	8 (21.6%)	29 (79.3%)
Total	72 (64%)	40 (36%)	9 (9%)	103 (91%)

[Total number of respondents answering this question = 112]

opportunities for men are immense. They can work both in economic and social sectors and can quickly claim 'expertise' in either sector. Men are 'large' enough in numbers to be sprinkled in all types of posts."

There was also recognition that field postings in areas with poor infrastructure and communication facilities, and which often involve physically arduous touring, were given to men. It was generally understood that women officers are usually posted in the field later than their batchmates, and that sometimes women themselves prefer not to take on certain posts. The routine nature of indoor and official work is often preferred in that it allows women to better manage the other aspects of their lives (like children, husbands, in-laws etc.).

Another interesting point that emerged out of the questionnaires was that the nature of gender stereotyping varied from state to state. Men from Jammu & Kashmir and officers of both sexes from Haryana, Punjab, and in some instances Uttar Pradesh, consistently stated that field posts were typically given to men, and "secretariat and non-risky jobs" of the "desk" type were given to women. From the AGMUT cadre (Arunachal Pradesh, Goa, Mizoram and Union Territories) respondents reported that men were given postings where greater physical effort was required in terms of arduous touring, and also that women are more likely to get posted in areas where basic comforts are assured. In some states—Himachal Pradesh, Gujarat, Maharashtra—it was noted that this kind of stereotyping did not take place. Of the women who replied that they did not feel there was gender stereotyping in the nature of posts held, several specifically stated that this view only applied to their state governments—Tamil Nadu, West Bengal, Andhra Pradesh—and that stereotyping seemed more likely in the case of the central government. On the other hand, women who have worked in Haryana and Punjab have, until recently, felt discriminated against as they were never given postings as District Magistrates. Others felt that there "may be some stereotyping as one moves up." From this data, one factor that emerged was that the nature of gender stereotyping of posts tended to correspond with the overall situation of gender disparities within the particular state. This correspondence underscores the fact that the IAS and the way it functions is part of a wider societal context, and thus cannot be looked at in isolation.[11]

Cadre allocation

Cadre allocations for men and women have generally followed 'neutral' principles and have depended on the numbers of vacancies for categories in the various states, the seniority of the officer in the merit list and a roster system which operates. This affects both men and women. When appearing for the examination, candidates have to indicate whether, if successful, they would like to be considered for allocation to their domiciliary (home) state. If they do, the actual allocation to one's home state is dependent on the availability of vacancies in the catogory one belongs to (general, SC, ST or OBC) and one's position in the merit list of the examination. The higher you are, the more chances there are of being allocated your home state. If there are no vacancies in your home state at present, a roster system operates which allocates candidates to various states depending on the number of vacancies available. This roster operates alphabetically and therefore, in no way takes into account the candidate's state of origin or choice. Normally, since cadres are allotted to officers, the only legitimate reason for a change can be through 'marriage' to another IAS officer when the couple can be adjusted into either of the cadres that they are in, or a third cadre of their choice if they are accepted. However, one cannot get a change to one's home state by marriage. Since cadres determine where one spends the majority of one's career, their allocation is fraught with long-term consequences. In fact many marriages between officers offer take this into consideration. Cadres are categorised as 'good' or 'bad' depending on the distance from one's place of origin etc. All other cases to change to one's home state are 'exceptions' on health grounds or other reasons, though normally such requests are not entertained. The Government of India vacillated about its policy of allotting provincial cadres to women. Its initial system of permitting zonal options was favourable to women. In this context, it is worth considering the manner in which the government's changing policy towards women in 'dangerous' cadres utilises stereotypical ideas of women. There has been much vacillation in the last few years about the policy of the government towards women posted in the disturbed areas of the North East and Jammu & Kashmir. For many years women were continuously posted in these places, but with the ambush of an female Indian Police Service officer (Ms. Vandana Malik), this policy was reversed. A government order, which is no longer applicable, entitled women who were outsiders to opt for an alternate cadre after initial allottment. As a result of this, many women who had served for years in the North East were able to opt for cadres of their choice.

Although this policy has now been reversed, it is worthwhile examing the two assumptions on which it was based: namely, that the risks likely to be faced by women and men are unequal, and that such risks could be faced by insider women but not by those who were outsiders. These assumptions, in fact, placed men in an unequal position and perhaps can be seen both as an instance of reverse discrimination, and as a bureaucratic manifestation of the same protective role that the north Indian father displays towards his daughter. Such thinking regarding women's safety in the North East vis-à-vis men's is probably arbitrary. However, the situation that presently exists is that outsider women who are now being posted to the North East feel that women in the batches immediately preceding them have been advantaged in some way.

A further implication of the earlier policy was that women in the North East cadres who belonged to the North East felt more isolated within their cadres and, as a result, also felt demoralised (personal communication with two insider women from the North East). Ironically, women who are insiders from these states and who may want to work there are often being assigned to outside cadres. For instance, there has recently been a woman officer from Nagaland allotted U.P. cadre, and another from J & K allotted Maharashtra cadre. As the above clearly illustrates, a consistent policy (which is sensitive to the needs of men as well as women) needs to be formulated and implemented at all levels.

Distribution and Level of Satisfaction of Men and Women in Different Posts

While the above section looked at perceptions of postings, this section will explore the nature of posts that are actually being held by women. An analysis of the nature and distribution of posts held by the officers in our sample is tabulated below. In Table 5, only posts held for periods longer than one year were analysed.

Table 5: Nature of Posts Held[12]

Type of Post	*Male*	*Female*
Social Sector	38 (6.57%)	54 (20.3%)
Regulatory	122 (21.1%)	53 (19.7%)
Finance and industry	62 (10.7%)	21 (7.92%)
International organisations	0 (0%)	2 (.75%)
Field	254 (43.9%)	85 (32%)
Public sector	40 (6.92%)	11 (4.15%)
Development	62 (10.7%)	39 (14.7%
Total	578	265

It is clear that the most significant difference in the nature of posts held by men and women who have responded was that while women predominate in social sector postings (20.3 per cent of all the postings held by women), men predominate in field postings (43.9 per cent of all postings held by men) which also confirms the perceived gender stereotypes. In development it would appear that women have a slight edge, whereas men seem to occupy a higher percentage of posts in the regulatory and public sectors. What is most interesting about these figures, however, is that while only 1.3 per cent of men felt that they had personally been affected by stereotyped postings (see Table 3), 21.6 per cent of women felt so. (In practice, therefore, the range of posts open to women appear to be narrower than those available to men.)

As far as the level of satisfaction men and women derive from their posts is concerned (see Tables 6a and 6b), it seems that in terms of overall careers men seem to derive greater levels of satisfaction from their postings as a whole: 44 per cent of men rated their postings as 4 or 5 (which indicates the greatest level of satisfaction), as compared to 31.3 per cent of women. On the other end of the scale, 40 per cent of women rated their postings in the lower 1–3 category, whereas only 25 per cent of men rated their level of satisfaction in the lower scale. A comparative view, however, reveals that in certain areas there are some significant differences between men and women's levels of satisfaction. Two such areas are regulatory administration and field posts where the levels of satisfaction derived by men are significantly higher than those derived by women. It is interesting to note that although fewer women had the opportunity to work in public sector administration and finance, given a chance these postings gave them as much satisfaction as postings in the social sector.

It would be a mistake, however, to accept this issue uncritically. The level of satisfaction is a complex of factors which includes many variables—the nature of the working environment, relationships with colleagues, etc.—and in this sense may not be an accurate reflection of the actual substance of a post. For instance, the fact that women received a lower level of satisfaction from field postings than men did not necessarily imply that women simply "don't like the job". As the

Table 6a: Level of Satisfaction with Postings: Male Officers

Type of Post	*Level of Satisfaction*					*Total*
	1	2	3	4	5	
Social sector	5 (13.15%)	2 (5.3%)	6 (15.7%)	14 (36.8%)	11 (28.9%)	38
Regulatory	13 (10.65%)	9 (7.4%)	21 (17.2%)	39 (31.96%)	40 (32.8%)	122
Finance and industry	4 (6.45%)	2 (3.22%)	16 (25.8%)	18 (29%)	22 (35.5%)	62
International organisations	0	0	0	0	0	0
Field	8 (3.14%)	10 (3.9%)	31 (12.2%)	77 (30.13%)	128 (50.4%)	254
Public sector	2 (5%)	0 (0%)	5 (10%)	12 (30%)	21 (52.5%)	40
Development	1 (1.61%)	1 (1.61%)	18 (29%)	10 (16.1%)	32 (51.6%)	62

[1 = lowest level of satisfaction, 5= highest]

Table 6b: Level of Satisfaction with Postings: Female Officers

Type of Post	*Level of Satisfaction*					*Total*
	1	2	3	4	5	
Social sector	8 (14.8%)	7 (12.9%)	7 (12.9%)	13 (24%)	19 (35.1%)	54
Regulatory	5 (1.88%)	8 (15%)	14 (26.4%)	18 (33.9%)	8 (15.1%)	53
Finance and industry	4 (19%)	3 (14.2%)	3 (14.2%)	4 (19%)	7 (33.3%)	21
Field	3 (3.5%)	8 (9.4%)	19 (22.3%)	25 (29.4%)	30 (35.2%)	85
Public sector	1 (9%)	2 (18%)	0	2 (18%)	6 (54%)	11
Development	1 (2.6%)	3 (7.6%)	10 (25.6%)	13 (33.3%)	12 (30.7%)	39

[1 = lowest level of satisfaction, 5 = highest]

female respondent's comments would suggest, a more likely reason for dissatisfaction with field postings is that conditions in the districts make it even more difficult for women to handle the strains of balancing career and family. Until recently the impact of this nature of stereotyping was that positions in finance and industry were the most coveted. However, as with most positions or jobs, as soon as a job becomes well paid or otherwise attractive, e.g. Women and Child, Education & Health Departments, it becomes "male" (for instance, cooking is considered "women's work", but when it comes to the lucrative job of being a chef in a restaurant, men predominate.)

With increasing interest and investment in the social sectors, today posts in these areas would begin to attract men because they have better perks etc. At this stage, the reason for exclusion of women may take the guise of breaking gender stereotypes and perhaps a better indicator would be the flow in the opposite direction especially in the central government. Bureaucratic practice can result in hidden biases of the roles and positions that men and women should/do hold.

The state reproduces stereotypes and reinforces them in the nature of postings for women. Although it is supposed to be a 'level playing field', women's access to posts is limited and, therefore, the choice is narrower. Thus for a variety of reasons which have been discussed, the effect of this is to entrench and perpetuate existing inequalities.

Interactions between Postings and Personal Life

Male and female officers alike cited the many ways in which practices related to postings impact on their personal lives. The issue mentioned with the greatest frequency by male respondents was dislocation of family life and the disruption of children's education due to frequent transfers. In more than one case, men said that while they were posted in a more remote district they had to leave their wives and children in an area where the schooling was adequate. Obviously, such forced separation is difficult both for the officer and for the family. The particular toll that such transfers take on the wife was recognised—in the words of one respondent: "Bad postings mean that the wife has to carry full burden. Unbearable tension for her during these times."

Clearly, at the heart of the problem is the need for security of tenure—an issue which has been dealt with extensively in the paper, "Reforms for the Indian Administrative Service", referred to earlier. Among the solutions suggested in that paper was the setting up of a State Selection Board.[13] Perhaps in certain areas where schooling is a problem, government should try and compensate officers for educating their children by providing some kind of allowance or facility.

In the case of IAS couples, another set of posting-related issues arises. When two IAS officers marry, there is the added stress of trying to arrange postings so that the couple can remain in close proximity. Often this forces a situation where either one member of the couple settles for a lesser posting, or both members settle for being apart. In several questionnaires instances were cited where women stated that they had to compromise on their postings (by taking lighter postings or opting out of field postings) for the sake of their children and husbands.

On the whole it is understood that the government is "accommodating" and "considerate" in keeping both husband and wife together except in field postings, but most wives usually give up postings, unlike their husbands. Another area which may require attention is the issue of long term training abroad. In this case, perhaps the government should consider the possibility of reducing hardship of separation for couples by sending the couples during the same year if both are otherwise eligible.

The problem of separation due to postings is even further exacerbated in the case of women whose spouses are outside the government or are officers from other services. One woman described the prospect of transfer as a "sword of Damocles".

Organisational Culture

The culture of the working environment sheds light on the inbuilt constructs regarding the relative roles of men and women in the workplace, and the manner in which an organisation deals with sexual harassment is a case in point.

Sexual Harassment

One of the landmark judgements of the Supreme Court in 1995 (AIR 1996 SC 309) was the case of Ms. Rupan Deol Bajaj vs. K.P.S. Gill, the former a Punjab cadre IAS officer and the latter the Director General of Police, Punjab, who had played a major role in guiding the state back to normalcy during the terrorist phase in Punjab politics. The judgement was the culmination of Rupan Deol Bajaj's long battle in the courts of justice to have her voice heard regarding sexual harassment. The case involved Ms. Bajaj's report of the DGP slapping her 'on the posterior' in the full presence of ladies and guests at a dinner party in 1988.

No court in Punjab (or administrative level) was willing to judge the case on its merits. The high court of Punjab quashed a first information report in which the officer had alleged outraging of modesty and lacunae in the procedures at the level of lower courts/police. The Supreme Court clearly opined that the matter was not 'trivial', the procedures adopted by the lower courts improper and remanded the case to the lower courts for adjudication.[14]

This case in a sense focused on an issue which tends to be invisibilised and we entered into this area a little diffidently, as we felt that men would react negatively if directly asked about this. Yet, when answering the question regarding gender as an advantage or disadvantage many women called attention to this issue, with some even referring to specific unpleasant experiences. Sexual harassment can take a vast number of forms and in the higher civil services when involving colleagues of the same/similar services does not take violent physical forms, but is concerned with the nature of behavioural or physical mannerisms that are adopted which threaten the woman verbally or physically.

From the sample, it seems that physical acts of sexual harassment are most likely to be perpetrated on single women. Some women would recognise a resounding familiarity in the case cited by one single woman officer: "I first faced sexual harassment in office from a very senior male colleague, who made it a habit to ask me to come to his office on petty pretexts after seven in the evening, suggested in an odd fashion that I accompany him on tours, and dropped in uninvited into my flat one evening."

What is most disquieting about this, perhaps, is the helplessness of the single woman officer, especially if she if fairly junior, in combination with the actual reactions and anticipated responses regarding the issue from senior, predominantly male colleagues. In the above case, when the female officer snubbed the male officer and informed the bosses she was "shifted out of a good desk to a bad one." In another case a woman officer attributed an adverse remark in her ACR to the fact that she had reported a certain incident of physical sexual harassment to the Chief Secretary. Complaints do not necessarily receive sympathy as sometimes the "K.P.S. Gill" syndrome operates, and normally the implicit idea is that it is the woman's fault. I have come across two cases of sexual harassment while training young officers. In one case, the trainee concerned was too worried to speak out since she had a wonderful reputation as an officer. As a woman, she felt her reputation would immediately be questioned—rather than that of the person accused of harassment. For this reason, many women remain silent. In the other case, after a young officer asked for a posting out of a particular subdivision on the grounds of sexual harassment she was posted back to the same subdivision after her training period was over! In the last case, where a woman openly came out with her experience of sexual harassment, which was even admitted to by the male officer and made the subject of an enquiry, it has not in any way impacted on the career of the male officer!

In view of the above responses from women, we tried to assess the point of view of men by soliciting opinions from those who were attending two in-service courses at the Academy. Of the twenty responses that we received not a single man thought this was a problem in the IAS!*

---

*However, since then there has been a major survey on gender and the Higher Civil Services—"Increasing Awareness for Change: A Survey of the Higher Civil Services"—which covers many services of the government.—This issue has been addressed directly and many instances of harassment openly cited.

Another level of consideration which has not been addressed in this paper but which requires further exploration, is sexual harassment by males of subordinate female staff. A case that has been highlighted recently is that of a senior DIG of police, from Rajasthan raping a constable's wife.

From the above it will be clear that there is an urgent need not only to increase awareness regarding the issue but also, more importantly, to put into place a redressal mechanism or forum within which women or men can address this issue without feeling that they are being judged, and where some action can be taken on the basis of their complaints. Its mere existence would perhaps deter male officers from indulging in these practices. This issue should also be addressed within the mandate of any forum set up to deal with issues of sexual harassment.

Having discussed the above, it needs to be clearly stated that it is difficult to ascertain the exact magnitude of the problem, and quite probable that these incidents are isolated and sporadic in nature. However, the fact that they exist at all is sufficient cause to take action to prevent their repetition and make the workplace more comfortable especially for women who are single/widowed or living away from their spouses.

There is another order of problems which has to do with so-called private matters such as changing one's religion in order to have more than one wife.

Informal Networks

Another career-related issue that needs to be addressed is the extent to which women have restricted access to informal networks linking officers of varying levels of seniority. Kantor calls this "homosociablity"—a more commonly used term is "the old boys network". Because men are more comfortable engaging in social and sport activities with other men, and because the networks developed around these activities can have a good deal of influence on career paths, women are at a disadvantage in this regard. Kantor discusses the manner in which the gender and social profile of an institution reproduces itself, as those in power choose others "like them" as replacements. In an organisation that is largely male, it is unlikely that a woman officer would fit the bill. Many female respondents noted their exclusion in such informal networks: a characteristic remark is that of a female officer who comments that when she is invited to dinner at a senior officer's home, "they [the seniors officers] converse only with my husband while I am implicitly expected to talk with the officer's wives." These networks are also related to the total number of men/women in the service.

Perks

The lack of perks was another concern mentioned by men in many contexts. Respondents noted that "unrealistic rules about the use of official cars and having class IV employees as domestic helpers" resulted in "moral compromises" and caused "unnecessary mental strain". The basic argument was that government perks should be similar to those in the private sector because it was not possible to live comfortably on a single salary. Of primary concern in this context was the problem of domestic help (for cleaning, looking after the children etc.) Some of the other issues that were raised in this category were (as far as working for the Government of India was concerned) the absence of clubs and recreation facilities, the "primitive working facilities", poor staff support, unproductive work.

Facilities

It is interesting that while issues regarding pay and perks did not come up in the women's responses, even at the level of IAS officers, the issue of inadequacy of toilets for female officers surfaced—an issue which is well known and has been taken up in various offices for the subordinate staff. An officer writes about the 'frustration' and 'anger' she felt at the lack of toilets and also how "tours and meetings had to be planned so as to ensure availability of ladies toilets without being able to openly ask about this". Another woman commented on the "loss of self esteem" that this problem creates—it is debilitating to realise that even the building where you work is insensitive to the most basic of needs. The absence of crèche facilities was cited by men and women alike.

Working Hours

A practice which *men* found disruptive to their personal and family life was the expectation of working long hours. The 'normal' working day almost always entails working far beyond the usual hours of 9–5.30. Moreover, there is also an implied accountability during weekends and holidays, all of which results in a situation where "family life is disturbed, children feel neglected, tense situations are created and health is also ruined."

This problem of long working hours is one that seems to be specific to men—while it was cited with some frequency by men, no woman listed it as a problem. The reason for this may stem from a public perception that because men do not *need* to be with their families (in the way that women do), that they can devote all their time to their jobs. It also seems to assume that such men, if they have a family, must have a wife managing things for them. Finally, it disregards the emotional need that men feel to be with their family. This is another instance of a reverse gender bias.

Women also cited the need for flexible office hours, so that more time could be spent with children on their return from school/college, etc. Additionally, both women and men mentioned the inadequacy of the period of maternity leave and the lack of paternity leave.

Personal Lives and Careers

While the above sections examined the manner in which career issues affect the personal lives of male and female officers, another area which the questionnaire sought to address was the extent to which the personal lives and other considerations impact upon the careers of men and women officers.

It is interesting to note, as the table below demonstrates, that a comparison of the overall percentages would indicate that whereas the majority of women (61 per cent) felt their careers have been affected by personal considerations, the majority of men (62 per cent) felt that their career goals had not been affected at all.

It is significant that even out of the 16 women who cited that their career goals had not been affected, at least four stated—with a sense of impending doom—that it had not happened "yet". One woman even said that the fact personal considerations had not affected her career goals "was achieved at a cost that very few male officers have had to pay"—a comment which suggests that her personal life must have suffered in some way or the other. At least two other women mentioned the fact that it was impossible for either male or female officers to have career goals because of "mixed up incentive structures, lobbying and compromises needed to get and keep 'meaty' positions."

Considerations of looking after the family, children or parents have been the chief factors affecting both men and women's careers, but in different ways. It is apparent that the

Table 7: When is Gender Sensitisation Necessary?

Stage	*Male*	*Female*
Induction	44 (80%)	33 (89%)
6–9 year	10 (18%)	2 (5.4%)
16–20 years	0	2 (5.4%)
17–20 years	0	0
20+	1 (1.8%)	0

Table 8: Interactions Between Personal Life and Career Goals

	No comment	*Parents, children, family*	*Health*	*Other*	*Total*
Men	52 (62.6%)	28 (33.7%)	1 (1.2%)	2 (2.4%)	83
Women	16 (39%)	25 (61%)			41

responsibilities of parenting and caring are not shared equally between husbands and wives, even in families where both may be working. It appears that in the early part of the career, the need to care for small children has impacted predominantly on women, often forcing them to choose between not being posted in the field at all, shortening their tenure, or being posted at a later stage than their batchmates. However, problems are not only confined to the early stages of a woman's career when she may also be trying to raise a family—the lack of field experience can mean that her later career is also adversely affected. In one case an officer felt (whether rightly or wrongly) that the cause for her non-empanelment was her dearth of field experience: "lack of experience in important field level postings is later cited as an additional reason for depriving women officers of important postings at senior levels." Additionally, several women cited the fact that they had to forego international assignments, long term courses abroad, deputations to Delhi when they wanted them, touring jobs, etc. because of family considerations.

Even in cases where there are no family considerations, women may be held back due to general perceptions regarding family responsibilities: in one case a woman noted that "it is presumed that I have family problems and hence, I have not been given a district charge." Furthermore, sometimes the simple fact of being a mother can have negative career consequences: one officer wrote that a "senior IAS officer cited having a child as a disqualification for holding the post of Additional Director Industries."

The tussle between career and family could also be felt in several answers where women said they are "happy", but feel that familial happiness has been achieved at the expense of career goals. Apart from postings women also felt in a few cases that they were not able to put in enough time to study, to socialise officially and to deal with sudden and urgent office work.

Family concerns were also cited as a major issue for men. In this context, the issues were primarily related to concerns about children's education, looking after parents and, in a more limited way, the career of their spouses (Four cases). The impact of these concerns on career goals was seen predominantly in terms of: not being able to go at the right point—or at all—on deputation to the Government of India (11 cases); the sacrifice of better career options within the state; and the inability to participate in foreign training (five cases). A consideration of another kind arose in two questionnaires (one man and one woman). Both stated that it was in deference to their parents' wishes that they had opted for a career in the IAS, but actually they would have preferred alternate careers. In fact, the man would have liked to have been an astrophysicist!

Conclusion and Recommendations

By way of conclusion, it is worth considering responses to the question:

> "At any stage in your career have you experienced your gender as an advantage or a disadvantage?"

This question raises not only the issue of how individual respondents perceive their gender, it also evokes the way in which the IAS as an institution imagines its officers.

While the majority of women experienced gender as at least partly a disadvantage, the majority of men did not consider it to be an issue at all—most replied "no" or "not relevant" to this question, and in fact one respondent suggested that "perhaps this question is only relevant to female officers." That all of the women (barring two) had a great deal to say on this issue shows the extent to which women are constantly reminded about their gender in what is supposedly a gender neutral service. This is something that at least one of the male respondents noted, commenting: "They say it's a man's world. True. As a male officer, gender has worked to my advantage as I have got good postings *in the normal course of events*. Whereas women colleagues have either not been given desired postings (e.g. District Magistrateships) or have had to fight for them, or have got what are perceived as 'soft' postings in 'inferior' sectors." (emphases added) What is noteworthy here is that the experience of the male officer is seen as following the "normal course of events", while that of the female officer is always somehow "exceptional".

Many representations on these issues were made to the Fifth Central Pay Commission and the Pay Commission, in the special chapter on "Women Employees in Government", recommended changes which reflected much greater gender awareness than earlier reports. One of its principal concerns was how women employees can combine the dual responsibilites of balancing work and family. In this context there were several innovative recommendations such as the introduction of flexi-time and flexi-place, leave storing between husband and wife, extending the duration of maternity leave and introducing paternity leave.

Other recommendations regarding the provision of adequate and appropriate amenties and facilities had been made earlier—such as the construction of toilets, special transportation, child care facilities etc. In the case of couples, the Pay Commission found that the present provision for House Building Advance and Leave Travel Concession were "adequate". The approach of the report has been primarily welfarist, addressing the level of "practical" gender needs—those that arise out of the socially accepted roles and responsibilites of women. While this is a beginning, to it could have been added a transformatory potential challenging the given gender division of roles and responsibilites; and the civil services could be viewed as leaders in the quest for greater gender equity in the workplace.

One of the general problems related to service practice which was raised by women concerned the general attitude displayed towards women officers within the government. As one officer said, this attitude is intended to make women officers feel small, ultimately resulting in "demoralisation".

As the above would suggest, there is a strong need for gender sensitisation in the service. Of the officers surveyed, 82 per cent of the men and 95 per cent of the women felt that gender sensitisation was needed in the service. A majority also felt, however, that this sensitisation would need to take place during either induction training or the 6-9 year in-service course (see table 7).

Furthermore, it is often difficult for the public imagination to accept a woman as an officer. As late as November 1966, the fact that West Bengal appointed its first woman as Home

Secretary (in charge of law and order) made front page news. One respondent says that her staff has difficulty following her orders because she is a woman: "thirty years ago the public perception of an IAS officer was as a demigod and people could not accept a woman in that position. A lot has changed in the last two decades, but still a woman has to constantly prove herself equal to a man." This issue never came up in any of the male responses, though one male respondent did note that after succeeding a female colleague he "could perceive a general change in the attitude of public representatives and officials towards the office. A few even commented that they could not be intimate and frank with female officers."

From the above it is clear that equality of opportunity has meant that women and men can both appear and take the examination for the civil services, and that for the most part the rules and conditions of service are based on similarity. However, such a view does not recognise the differences between men and women or take into account the nature of enabling conditions that would result in greater gender equity. As has been aptly stated: "Equalising agency requires recognition of different needs and requirements so as to ensure equity of outcomes." (Kabeer, 1995).

Finally, as the above implies, the very definition of power operates in a male idiom. While some theorists have argued that once a woman is in a position of power, gender is no longer an issue,[15] it is equally true that those jobs which are traditionally considered "women's" are viewed as insignificant for no reason other than that they are linked with women. Which is to say that in some cases the gender of the person holding the position defines the position. It is clear that while explicit biases may have been eliminated, implicit biases—assumptions about roles, unwritten rules—remain through which the IAS reproduces rather than challenges broader social inequalities.

Notes

[1] In 1995 there were only 5,047 officers in the IAS.

[2] For a fuller discussion of the administrative 'tradition' see Potter where he splits the tradition into the "content"—the structure norms and values constituting it and the "process"—the manner in which the con-

tent was reproduced through time by selection, training and the inculcation of certain values.

[3] The complete articles read as follows: Article 14 Constitution of India "The state shall not deny to any person equality before the law or the equal protection of the laws within the territory of India". Article 16, Constitution of India. The complete article reads 16(1) "There shall be equality of opportunity for all citizens in matters relating to employment or appointment to any office under the state." And 16(2) "No citizen shall, on grounds only of religion, race, caste, sex, descent, place of birth, residence or any of them, be ineligible for, or discriminated against in respect of, any employment or office under the State."

[4] Under the Constitution of India, certain castes and tribes have been identified and "scheduled" on account of being disadvantaged. These constitute some of the categories for which the state can, under Article 15 of the Constitution, make any special provision. Under Article 16, the state can make 'any provision for reservation of appointments or parts in favour of any backward class of citizens which, in the opinion of the State, is not adequately represented in the services of the State.

[5]Although the success rate of women taking the Civil Service Main Examination tends to be higher than that for men, the problem is the low number of women sitting the examination. However, as noted in the *Report of the Committee to Review the Scheme of the Civil Services Examination* (New Delhi, 1989) the percentage of women sitting the exam has steadily increased through the years. In 1995 there were 492 women out of 5,047 officers, or roughly 10 per cent. The annual intake fluctuates from 10–20 per cent.

[6]This study was published in 1989, but draws upon data collected in 1974–75.

[7]Rule 8 (2) of the IFS

[8]All the uncited quotations in this paper are from the questionnaires which were canvassed and in which we are maintaining strict anonymity and confidence.

[9]It is important to note that as all of the respondents pre-date the 1995 batch, none have entered into the service through reservation for OBC. In 1995 the government of India introduced quotas for a new category of persons—Other Backward Castes (OBCs). At the time of analysis, questionnaires from this batch were separated and not analysed.

[10]It is also worth mentioning in this context that this is an issue that the author first heard mentioned by Mr. Kaw in 1977, and it is still extant today. For all of the changes of the intervening years, the situation remains largely the same.

[11]Sex ratios (females per 1,000 males) of all the southern states are higher then the national average and than all northern states (barring

H.P.). Development indicators in terms of Infant Mortality Rate (IMR), literacy and Work Force Participation Rate (WFPR) are also higher than the northern states of Rajasthan and U.P.

[12]The category "Social Sector" encompasses posts related to health, education, women and child, welfare, tribal welfare, etc. "Field" postings are SDM (Sub-Divisional Magistrate), SDO (Sub-Divisional Officer), Chief Development Officer (or CEO), DRDA (District Rural Development Agency), DC, (Deputy Commissioner or DM (Depurty Magistrate). "Regulatory" indicates postings related to defence, personnel and training, civil supplies, excise, board of revenue, labour and planning. "Public Sector" indicates postings in corporations. "Development" encompasses agriculture, forestry, rural and urban development as well as culture and tourism. "Finance and Industry" postings are those related to heavy industry, finance, etc. "International organisations" means postings abroad.

[13]This has been recommended in the recent report of the Fifth Pay Commission to the government.

[14]At the level of the CJM, K.P.S. Gill was found guilty of the charge. While the case was sub-judice for a long time, Rupan Deol Bajaj's position was finally vindicated by the District and Sessions Judge. However the punishment for K.P.S. Gill was that the should pay monetary compensation of two lakh rupees to Mrs. Rupan Deol Bajaj.

[15]See Rosabeth Moss Kantor (*Women and Men in Bureaucracy*) for an explication of this argument. This is also an issue that came up in some of the questionnaires that make up the primary data for this study—some respondents felt that gender was not an issue as "power" emanated from positions of seniority, not gender. As this study will show, however, there is a distinct relationship between gender and the allottment of most significant postings.

References

Acker, J. 1990. "Hierarchies, Jobs, Bodies: A Theory of Gendered Organisations", *Gender and Society*, vol 2, no. 4, 139-58.

AIR 1979 SC 1968. V. Muthamma vs Government of India.

AIR 1996 SC 309. R.D. Bajaj vs Government of Punjab.

Davidson, M. J. and C.L. Cooper. 1992. *Shattering the Glass Ceiling: The Woman Manager* London: Paul Chapman Publishing Ltd.

de Rebello, D. M. 1995. "The Participation of Women in Government: Does It Make a Difference?" Draft Report Commissioned by the Overseas Development Administration.

Goetz, A.M. 1992. "Gender and Administration", *IDS Bulletin*. Vol. 23, No. 4.

Government of India. 1988. *The Constitution of India.*

———, 1989. *Report of the Committee to Review the Scheme of the Civil Services Examination* New Delhi: Union Public Service Commission.

———, 1989. "Women in the Civil Services: Study Report", Department of Administrative Reforms and Public Grievances New Delhi: Government of India.

———, 1994. *Union Public Service Commission: 44th Report (1993-94)* New Delhi: Union Public Service Commission.

Kabeer, N. 1995. *Reversed Realities: Gender Hierarchies in Development Thought* New Delhi: Kali for Women.

Kanter, R.M. 1977. *Men and Women of the Corporation* New York: Basic.

Kaw, M.K. 1993. *Bureaucrazy: IAS Unmasked* Delhi: Konark.

LBSNAA Faculty 1995. "Reforms for the Indian Administrative Service", *The Administrator*, Vol. XL, October–December.

Rosener, J.B. 1990. "Ways Women Lead", *Harvard Business Review*, November–December.

Sahai-Achuthan, N. 1989. "Women in the IAS (1948–74): A Study of Their Socio-economic cum Academic Background, and Attitude to Marriage and Career", *The Indian Journal of Social Science*, Vol. 2, No. 4. New Delhi: Sage Publications.

Savage, Mike and Anne Witz 1992. *Gender and Bureaucracy* Cambridge: Blackwell.

Thakur, Sarojini Ganju, 1998. *Increasing Awareness for Change: A Survey of Gender and the Civil Services* for the Department of Administrative Reforms, Government of India.

Potter, D., 1996. *India's Political Administrators* New Delhi: Oxford University Press.

Annexure 1

Questionnaire

1. General

1.1 Sex: [Male] [Female]

1.2 Date of birth: DD[ ] MM[ ] YY[ ]

1.3 Marital status: [Married] [Single] [Other]

1.4 Occupation of spouse: (if married)

1.5 Did you have an arranged marriage? [Yes] [No]

1.6 Kindly indicate: [SC] [ST] [OBC]

1.7 Year of entry into service: DD[ ] MM[ ] YY[ ]

1.8 Home state:

1.9 Allotted cadre:

1.10 Was the above cadre the one that was originally allotted to you? If not, then please indicate the reason for the change.

[Marriage] [Health] [Other (please explain)]

1.11 Level of education completed:

a) By your father
b) By your mother

1.12 Occupation:

a) Of your father
b) Of your mother

1.13 Number of siblings:

a) Brothers
b) Sisters

2. Education

2.1 Please give details of your education beginning with school leaving. Please list:

- The **Dates** of Attendance
- The **Name** and **Location** of the **School/ University** attended
- The **Subjects** studied
- Whether the school was **Co-Educational** or **Single Sex (CE, SS)**
- Whether the school was in a **Rural** or **Urban** Setting (**R, U**)
- The **Type** of school according to the following codes:

  G—Government School/College
  P—For Private School

- The **Medium of Instruction** according to the following codes:

  E—English
  H—Hindi
  O—Other

Dates	School/ University (Name and Location)	Subjects	Co-Ed/ Single sex		Rural/ Urban		Type		Med. of Instr.		
			CE	SS	R	U	G	P	E	H	R
			CE	SS	R	U	G	P	E	H	R
			CE	SS	R	U	G	P	E	H	R
			CE	SS	R	U	G	P	E	H	R
			CE	SS	R	U	G	P	E	H	R
			CE	SS	R	U	G	P	E	H	R

3. Services

3.1 Please give the details of your service. Please note:

- The **Major Posts Held** since entry into the service (only those posts held for one year or longer.)
- The **Dates** that the post was held
- The **Level of Satisfaction** with this post on a scale of 1–5 (**1** = Least Satisfied, **5** = Most Satisfied)

Post Held	Dates (Appro.)		Level of Satisfaction
	From	To	
			1 2 3 4 5
			1 2 3 4 5
			1 2 3 4 5
			1 2 3 4 5
			1 2 3 4 5
			1 2 3 4 5
			1 2 3 4 5
			1 2 3 4 5
			1 2 3 4 5
			1 2 3 4 5
			1 2 3 4 5

3.2 At any stage in your career have you experienced your gender as an advantage or a disadvantage? Please cite specific examples.
[Attach additional sheets if necessary]

3.3 Do you feel there is gender stereotyping in the nature of posts held by men/women?

a) In general? [Yes] [No]

For you personally? [Yes] [No]

b) What posts (please list) are typically given to men?

3.4 Have you worked with a female boss? How (if at all) was that experience different? Would you like to see more women as bosses?

3.5 Do you feel that there is a glass ceiling in job opportunities for men and women? (i.e. is there an invisible, but nonetheless very real barrier beyond which it is impossible to rise to a position of greater power?) If yes, what are the situations in which they operate?

[please list]

a) For men?

b) For women?

3.6 In your opinion, do you view gender sensitisation as necessary at the policy, planning and implementation level?

a) [Yes] [No]

b) If yes, at which stage in the service? (Please tick as many as you feel is appropriate):

Induction

In-Service Training:
6–9 years
10–16 years
17–20 years
20 years and above

3.7 At present, in a typical working day, how much time (in minutes/hours) would you estimate that you and your spouse spend on the following activities:

Activity	Time spent by you	Time spent by your spouse
a) Household chores		
b) Time with children		
c) Sports/leisure activity		
d) Personal/family affairs		
e) Socialising (for official reasons)		
f) Socialising (with family and friends)		
g) Office work		

3.8 a) Do you have domestic help? [Yes] [No]

b) Please list number of people you employ as domestic help:

Full time - [ ]
Part time - [ ]

3.9 If a child falls ill, who takes leave normally?:

[You] [Your spouse] [Other]

3.10 In what ways have the rules and practices of government service (i.e. leave, recruitment, facilities, etc.) been detrimental to your personal life? In the space below, please list the specific **Rule** or **Practice**, than explain the

effect (i.e. it kept you away from your family, etc.) [Use back of sheet if necessary]

Rule/Practice **Effect**

3.11 In what ways have personal/family considerations stood in the way of your career goals? Please list the **Personal/ Family Consideration** and the **Career Goal** effected.

Personal/Family Consideration **Career Goal**

Annexure 2

Distribution of Respondents by Cadre

Cadre	Number of	
	Men	Women
AGMUT	6	2
Andhra Pradesh	5	4
Assam	4	0
Bihar	7	4
Gujarat	2	1
Haryana	2	2
Himachal Pradesh	5	1
Jammu & Kashmir	3	0
Karnataka	2	2
Maharashtra	6	4
Manipur	2	0
Meghalaya	1	0
Mizoram	0	1
Madhya Pradesh	3	1
Orissa	4	2
Punjab	3	2
Rajasthan	8	1
Tamil Nadu	3	5
Uttar Pradesh	11	9
West Bengal	6	0
Total	83	41

Distribution of Respondents by Seniority

Batch	Number of Men	Number of Women
1961	1	0
1962	2	0
1963	2	0
1964	2	0
1965	1	0
1966	2	2
1967	3	0
1968	1	0
1969	2	1
1970	1	1
1971	3	2
1972	1	5
1973	2	1
1974	0	1
1975	6	1
1976	5	1
1977	2	1
1978	6	1
1979	7	3
1980	0	1
1981	2	1
1982	4	0
1983	4	1
1984	4	2
1985	4	1
1986	3	2
1987	0	1
1988	1	0
1989	1	1
1990	2	1
1991	0	2
1992	0	1
1993	2	0
1994	1	3
Total	83	41

5

"Brother, There are Only Two Jatis—Men and Women"

Section 125 Criminal Procedure Code and the Trial of Wifehood

MAITRAYEE MUKHOPADHYAY

Introduction

The general point that this paper addresses is that the processes by which gender inequalities are socially constructed are not confined purely to household and family relationships but are reproduced across a range of institutions (Kabeer & Subramaniam 1996). This includes institutions whose stated aim is to address inequalities within their societies. The state is one such institution which is seen as the just and final arbiter between the contending interests of groups in civil society. In fact the post-colonial state in India, which is the specific context of this essay, has proven ability in restructuring social relations and introducing social reform measures aimed at addressing class, caste and gender inequalities. Certainly the law is seen to be a neutral instrument which confers rights based not on the gender, class and caste identity of individuals but rather on the human essence that individuals are seen to enjoy.

However, legal activism by women's groups in India in the 1980s faced a specific set of constraints. Whereas new laws entered the statute book in this decade to redress gender inequalities particularly in the arena of family and household relations, the outcomes of legal battles seemed to point to the fact that legal processes articulate and reproduce gender and other forms of inequality which seemingly belong to the arena of family/kinship and community. It was very difficult, we found, to separate the identity of women litigants as wives, sisters, daughters and widows from that of their identity as subject/citizen imbued with rights. The case studies presented here of women litigants appealing for maintenance in the event of divorce or desertion by husbands, form part of a wider study which attempts to find a reason for this. In the process attention was shifted from the text of the law to an ethnography of litigation—the nature of disputes, the attitudes of lawyers, the experiences in court, the logic of judgements and so on—in order to scrutinise the unwritten rules, norms and practices which determine the way roles and responsibilities are allocated by gender and entitlement to resources made on the basis of these definitions. This analysis brings into play crucial factors about institutions—be they the state or the household—which are obscured in abstract discussions of 'rights'.

Section 125 of the Criminal Procedure Code (1973)

Section 125 of the Criminal Procedure Code (1973) was created for the specific purpose of providing maintenance to dependent wives, children and aged parents unable to maintain themselves. Its main purpose is to prevent destitution and vagrancy. The maximum amount that can be fixed as monthly maintenance under this Section is Rs 500. A wife is defined here as one whose marriage subsists as well as one who has been divorced. Until 1987 both Hindu and Muslim wives, whether divorced or not, could appeal under this section for maintenance. With the promulgation of the Muslim Women's (Protection of Rights on Divorce) Bill, 1987, Muslim wives who have been divorced have generally had to appeal to Section 3 of the new Act when seeking settlement of economic arrangements for extant marriages. Applications under Section 125 for maintenance can be made by Hindu women alongside their application for temporary alimony under the Hindu Marriage Act. In fact up until 1987 this Section of the Criminal Procedure Code (henceforth Cr.Pc.) was regarded as functioning in conjunction with the personal laws.

Section 125 stipulates conditions to be fulfilled before a decree for maintenance can be passed in favour of the applicant wife. The wife applicant must be able to prove that there was a valid marriage. It must be agreed that the husband-respondent has sufficient means to maintain the applicant. It should be established that the respondent-husband refused or neglected to maintain his wife. It must be determined in court that the wife is unable to maintain herself. A wife applicant loses the right to maintenance if she is found to be living in adultery. Remarriage also entails the loss of the right to maintenance. The court hearings, therefore, are woven around proving/disproving the fulfilment/non-fulfilment of these conditions.

The applications under Section 125 Cr.PC. are made in the criminal court. Non-payment of maintenance dues decreed by the court is therefore considered a criminal offence. The court can and often does authorise the police to arrest the husband for his failure to pay the maintenance dues. This Section has been very popular with wives seeking some kind of economic settlement of extant marriages. One of the reasons may be that it is not unusual for the applicant wife to get a decree in her favour from the court. Another reason is that the court can authorise the arrest of the husband to recover the maintenance dues. Since a wife is in most circumstances powerless to lay claim to her husband's property or income once the marriage ties are severed (either by desertion or divorce), this provision is a reassurance that the state at least is more powerful than the husband and will support her. Also, the proceedings under this Section, because it is held in the criminal court, are required to be disposed off quicker than in the civil court. Of the 16 women who comprised the sample of women appealing for marital property, 12 applied for maintenance under this Section. Eight of the 12 applicants were Muslim women and the remaining four were Hindu women. Table 1 lays out the status of each applicant's case for maintenance.

As can be seen from the Table, the outcomes of the maintenance cases have been varied and contradictory. They are contradictory because, on the one hand, almost all the applicants (barring those whose cases are still to be decided) have received favourable decrees. This gives the impression that

Table 1: Outcome of Section 125 cases

Respondent	*Case*	*Status*	*Recovery of dues*
Anjana (Hindu)	Sec. 125	Obtained decree	No recovery**
Ruma (Hindu)	Sec. 125	Case pending	No recovery****
Shanaz (Muslim)	Sec. 125 Sec. 3 MWDP	Obtained decree under Sec. 3	No recovery
Tahera (Muslim)	Sec. 125	Obtained decree	No recovery**
Marjina (Muslim)	Sec. 125	Obtained decree	No recovery*
Safia (Muslim)	Sec. 125	Obtained decree	No recovery** & ****
Taslima (Muslim)	Sec. 125 Sec. 3 MWDP	Obtained decree under Section 3	Recovered dues
Ohidenessa (Muslim)	Sec. 125	Obtained decree	Recovered part of dues
Asma (Muslim)	Sec. 125	Obtained decree	No recovery Remarried Withdrew claim***
Farzana (Muslim)	Sec. 125	Obtained decree	Recovered dues Remarried Withdrew claim
Arati (Hindu)	Sec. 125	Temporary order	Receiving payment
Aloka (Hindu)	Sec. 125	Temporary order	Receiving payment

Note:
MWDP: Muslim Women's (Protection on Divorce) Bill of 1987
* cases where husbands have been arrested for non-payment of maintenance dues.
** issue of Warrant of Arrest against husband by the court but failure of execution by the police.
*** issue of Distress Warrant by the court for attachment and sale of husband's property to recover maintenance dues.
**** refers to arrest of husband under Section 498A.

the judicial arm of the state works in women's interests. On the other hand, only a negligible percentage of women with favourable decrees have been able to secure maintenance payments. This gives the impression that the enforcement arm of the state—the police—works at cross-purposes with the decisions of the courts and is against women's interests. Since some women do get something through the courts, women persist in the belief that state intervention is useful. For the most part obtaining favourable decrees seems to validate a wife's claim to economic rights from her husband. However, most women appeal to the state for economic rights from their husbands from a position of great disadvantage. Women's actions in seeking state intervention to secure economic rights are to a large extent motivated by the belief that the state is, in contrast to kin and community level authorities, a just and final arbiter. It is assumed, therefore, that people are invested with rights irrespective of their gender, class, caste and communal differences. However, as the case studies will illustrate, men and women are constituted in law and in adjudication as different kinds of persons with differential rights. Further, the status of wife is invested with less power than that of husband and a wife's claim as dependent has less validity than claims by other dependent kin.

Section 125 is unequivocal in its positioning of wives as dependents. The underlying assumption of the provision for maintenance is that the male is the breadwinner and the wife is dependent on the breadwinner. The withdrawal of the breadwinner leads to loss of support resulting in the need for state intervention to prevent the dependent becoming destitute. However, in every single case this dependence has to be proved. In fact if the wife happens to have obtained a job while the case is still being examined in court, her right to maintenance is jeopardised. Further if it is proved in court that she has sufficient property from other sources to support herself, her claim to maintenance from her husband is weakened. The maintenance amount, although fixed at a maximum of Rs 500 per month, is determined on a case by case basis and the husband's income, his obligations to maintain other kin and the wife's own resources play a central role in determining the amount she will be awarded. In all the cases studied, the maintenance amount decreed by the court was less than the ceiling of Rs 500 per month. In each case the wife's entitlement to other resources (dependence on other male kin etc.) played an important role in fixing the amount of maintenance beside the husband's breadwinner status.

Furthermore, Section 125 does not pretend to give women equality with men because its ostensible aim is merely to award that much in maintenance that will save a wife from destitution. What needs sorting out in the trial is whether the wife is unable to maintain herself and whether the husband has the means to maintain her. However, the case proceedings reveal that a large part of the deliberations deal with the issue of whether the husband should maintain the estranged wife. Why this is so and how it positions women as subjects can best be examined through case studies.

The Trial of Wifehood

I will examine Aloka Sen's experience in applying for maintenance under Section 125.

Aloka instituted this case in 1989. In March 1990 she was awarded temporary maintenance of Rs 400 per month. (The general convention in such cases is to award temporary alimony while the case is being heard. The order of permanent alimony is made only after all witnesses on both sides have been examined, the husband's neglect of his wife has been proved, the wife's inability to maintain herself established etc. By awarding Aloka temporary alimony the court was thus not doing anything extraordinary in her favour). The present status of the case is that Aloka's evidence and that of her witnesses has been recorded and they have been cross-examined. Her husband's evidence was being heard in court till March 1992. At the time of writing, his witnesses' evidence and the cross-examination remained to be heard.

Aloka was married in 1977. She was educated up to the first stage of University at the time of marriage. She has five brothers and five sisters. Her mother is still alive. Aloka's husband, Anindo Sen, is a qualified engineer and a senior executive in the Calcutta Electric Supply Corporation. The couple have a son born in 1979. Aloka lived in her matrimonial home with her husband, son, parents-in-law and Anindo's youngest sister. According to Aloka, marital conflicts began within two years of the marriage and had mainly to do with the friction between her and the in-laws. However, Anindo always supported his relatives. In 1983 for the first time she was physically assaulted by her husband. Subsequent to that, quarrels in the family generally resulted in further physical attacks. In early May 1986, for the first time, Aloka retaliated by registering a case against her husband in the local police station. The versions of what happened subsequently vary according to the informants. Aloka claimed her husband was arrested. The husband's advocates stated in his petition that the police officer, aware of the domestic problems of the Sen household, called the husband to the police station to effect a compromise. In a sense this version is more plausible since as subsequent events indicate, Aloka's allegation of cruel treatment was at every juncture disbelieved by the police. This worked against her in court, because the police aided in the representation of Aloka as the unfit wife and mother.

On 13th June 1986 Aloka was evicted from her matrimonial home by Anindo and his relatives (the brother-in-law brought in specially for the purpose). There is considerable discrepancy between Aloka's account and the information contained in court documents and hearings regarding the description of the events which led up to her leaving. Also in contest was the question: was she actually evicted or had she left of her own accord? The importance of establishing events either way is in order to determine whether her husband wilfully neglected her and whether therefore she would be entitled to maintenance, or, whether Aloka wilfully left the house, refused to return and consequently would not be entitled to maintenance. What is critical here is which claims to truth received recognition and why.

Aloka's version was as follows (which is also more or less the version she gave in court). A quarrel had ensued between her and Anindo's mother on the morning of 11th June 1986 when she requested her mother-in-law to take out her ornaments. The mother-in-law complained to her son when he returned from work. Anindo did not ask her for an explanation. He called his married sisters and their husbands and together they locked the gate of the house to prevent Aloka leaving. They went to the police station and lodged a complaint against her. The sisters-in-law shouted at her and abused her and called in the neighbours to do the same. Her brother-in-law asked her for the keys to her cupboard which she refused to give. Aloka spent the night on a sofa in the living room. When she awoke she found that her cupboard had been broken into by the brother-in-law and he was checking every possession of hers. They confiscated her marksheets and certificates. They were looking for incriminating evidence (e.g. love letters). They went to Barrackpore court, registered a *vakalatnamma* (court document authorising appointment of an advocate) and forced her to sign it. They then took her to the police station, withdrew their complaint against her, and told the Officer-in-charge (O.C. henceforward) of the police station that Ashoka wanted to return to her mother's home. The O.C. dictated a statement which said that she was going to her parents' house for a few days and would return. She signed it. They then took her to the home of a distant relative of her husband. The following day the husband arrived and announced that he would not live with her. She was bundled into a taxi by her brother-in-law and deposited at her brother's house.

The institutional version is as follows. The account is taken from the ad verbatim recording of Anindo Sen's evidence dated 4th February 1992 in the court of the 9th ADJM, Criminal Court, Alipore.

ADVOCATE: When did your wife leave your house?

ANINDO: On 13th June 1986.

ADVOCATE: Did you and your family throw her out?

ANINDO: On 11th June my wife verbally abused and insulted my mother. My father tried to protect her (mother). After this my wife wanted to leave the house. I took her to the Officer-in-charge of the police station where she said that she would return in six months time.

ADVOCATE: This means that after the incident on 11th June your wife left your house of her own accord. Could you relate the incidents of that day?

ANINDO: That day my wife abused my mother in filthy language. She caught my mother by her hair, dragged her on to the road and continued to hurl abuses at her. The neighbours rushed to my mother's rescue. My father came forward to protect my mother and he was in turn assaulted by my wife, fell down and injured himself.

ADVOCATE: How old was your father at the time?

ANINDO: 82 years.

ADVOCATE: And your mother?

ANINDO: 70 years.

ADVOCATE: Did they need medical treatment as a result?

ANINDO: Yes, they were treated at the Barrackpore hospital. (Produces papers, prescriptions).

ADVOCATE: What was you wife's reaction after this incident?

ANINDO: She was extremely anxious to go back to her mother's house. The neighbours were extremely upset by my wife's behaviour. (Magistrate dictates to clerk—She was violent by nature).

ADVOCATE: Did you do anything else before she left the house?

ANINDO: I went to the police station.

ADVOCATE: Why?

ANINDO: I suspected that my wife would lie about the whole incident. Besides, the Officer-in-charge was well aware of the problems in our relationship—he had often mediated on my behalf before this.

ADVOCATE: What happened at the police station?

ANINDO: The O.C. Kabir Khan addressed my wife as 'sister' and tried to reason with her. He even reminded her of the story of Shakuntala.

ADVOCATE: Did your wife change her mind.as a result?

ANINDO: She gave in writing in the presence of the O.C. that she was leaving for home and would return.

ADVOCATE: (showing a piece of paper) Do you recognise your wife's writing?

ANINDO: Yes it is her writing. (The letter was filed as an exhibit in the court).

Anindo Sen's evidence establishes Aloka as a violent, irrational shrew, a woman given to fits of bad temper. She is reported as having committed the ultimate crime in Bengali society—assaulting her parents-in-law who are her superordinates because of their age and the relationship. The husband produced medical certificates as proof but even without this she would stand condemned under the circumstances. Note also the difference in the versions regarding the role of the O.C. Anindo's reporting of what transpired helped to present Aloka as the irrational woman whose versions could not be believed. The police officer's cajoling of Aloka and his mediation in earlier incidents clearly sets up Anindo Sen as the wronged husband who wanted to live with his wife except that the wife refused to oblige, despite intervention by the Officer-in-charge of the police station. Anindo Sen used the statement written by Aloka in the police station in his favour by showing that, although she had given in writing to the state authorities that she would return, she had not done so. It should be mentioned here that since the institution of the case Aloka's advocates had written numerous letters to the police station requesting a copy of the statement she signed, but had not received it. If Aloka had received this, or had the resources (of status/power) to obtain it from the police station, she could have argued that she had expressed in writing (sanctioned by the police station) that she wished to return but had not been taken back.

Had the husband attempted to bring her back thus expressing his willingness to maintain her? In his evidence in December 1991, February and March 1992 he showed documentary proof of letters written by him and his friends and relatives asking her to come back. Aloka, on the other hand, was unable to provide any documentary evidence to show her willingness to return.

Further evidence was given by Anindo Sen at the court hearing cited above to prove that Aloka was an unfit wife and mother.

ADVOCATE: How was your wife's behaviour towards the members of your family?

ANINDO: Her behaviour right from the time we were married was crude and uncivilised towards them.

ADVOCATE: You have a son?

ANINDO: Yes.

ADVOCATE: What was the attitude of the mother towards her own son?

ANINDO: She never fulfilled her maternal role, used to torture him mentally, did not love him.

ADVOCATE: She did not behave in a maternal fashion?

ANINDO: No.

ADVOCATE: What was the child's mental state?

ANINDO: He was so depressed that he became mentally ill.

ADVOCATE: Did you arrange for his treatment?

ANINDO: Yes, he had a number of sessions with the child psychiatrist Dr Debabrata Banerjee.

Aloka never mentions her child unless asked. Her pragmatic reply to queries about her son was that since she had no resources nor a roof over her head she had no option but to accept that he was being cared for by the father. Evidence regarding a woman's lack of maternal feelings features importantly in the determination of her worth as a person. The lack of paternal feeling does not, on the other hand, feature as evidence in court in the same way. This is demonstrated by the fact that paternal feeling or lack thereof was not made an issue in any of the cases studied, although many of the women who appealed under section 125 had children whose maintenance was also at stake in the cases.

Aloka was literally shelterless after her eviction from the matrimonial home. She initially lived at her brother's home and has since lived with friends, acquaintances and her sister. This too became evidence against her. She was so quarrelsome, it was alleged in court, that she could not live with anybody.

Between 1986, when she was evicted from her matrimonial home, and 1989, when the case for maintenance was instituted, Aloka attempted to seek the mediation of a number of welfare and counselling organisations to sort out her problems with her husband. Two of these welfare organisations actually conducted investigations and arrived at the conclusion that Aloka was at fault and ought to compromise with her husband. Her husband, the reports said, was a perfectly reasonable man, and was willing to take her back. Finally a third organisation (of lawyers) tried to bring about an out of court settlement. Aloka refused and asked for Rs 150,000 before signing a divorce document. She put this in writing. This letter now constitutes evidence in court. Her husband's lawyer produced as proof in court that she was not interested in keeping the marriage going. She was a greedy, opportunistic woman maligning her 'good' husband in order to get money out of him. On 11.3.92 when this letter was produced in court by Sen's advocate, it was followed up with the question about whether he had filed for divorce. He replied in the negative. His patience, tolerance and willingness to live with his wife despite everything was thus proved beyond a doubt. One of the key witnesses in Anindo Sen's favour is the counsellor of one of the welfare organisations which investigated the case when Aloka appealed for help.

Such was the intensity of feeling generated by this case that all the parties interviewed (Anindo Sen's lawyers, the counselling organisations, the police) were united in the effort to defeat Aloka's claim to maintenance. This intensity of feeling can only be explained by looking at the stakes involved. If failed wives like Aloka can have their claims to truth heard and accepted by state institutions, then the institution of marriage as understood by Bengalis with its clear demarcation of the roles and responsibilities of husband and wife, its hierarchisation of the status of the husband over that of the wife, is in jeopardy.

Although the case was not decided, it was evident by March 1992 that Aloka stood to lose her claim to permanent maintenance or at least have the amount reduced from that given her in temporary alimony. As Aloka's advocate wisely remarked after the final session of Anindo Sen's evidence in court, "The magistrate is a human being. He will be influenced by the portrayal of Sen as a good, responsible husband and a good man. He has done everything correctly and you have not. Who will believe your story?"

The question refers to what was happening in this trial. As I have said before, the court proceedings in a case under section 125 are supposed to decide on the eligibility of the woman/wife for maintenance by establishing that she is without means of support, that her husband does have the means to support her, and, that he has wilfully neglected to do so. Instead, as the above case illustrates, the court proceedings revolve around determining whether the husband should pay the maintenance. And the main criteria in determining whether he should or should not pay maintenance becomes whether he wilfully neglected her or not. Disproving the husband's 'wilful neglect' is then achieved via the elaboration of the woman's fitness/unfitness as wife. In other words the proceedings become a trial of wifehood. And what are the ideological ingredients that make up this 'wife'? At the core is the notion of the wife as 'sahadharmini' and as 'pativrata'. These concepts refer to the faithfulness of the wife to the husband and this as her primary duty and meaning in life. These were key concepts in the context of cultural nationalism in the late nineteenth century which reconstructed the Hindu male in the image of his glorious past and a similar Hindu woman whose faithfulness in her conjugal relationship was valorised and reified. As the legislative debates on Hindu law reform also show, divorce was, and continues to be, a contentious issue. The argument was that divorce was alien because it was premised on a notion of equality between the husband and wife which was western and modern. In the

Hindu conception of the conjugal relationship women were respected and a wife's interests were completely joined to those of her husband's. Add to this the nationalist resolution of the women's question whereby women's freedoms were assured within the contours of the culturally determinate codes of conduct which ensured their oneness with the home and the spiritual content of the national culture. These discourses about wifehood are now articulated through court proceedings and determine a woman's eligibility for maintenance from her husband. Aloka's case best illustrates the policing that goes into maintaining this notion of wifehood. The family, the neighbours, the police officer, the courts and the welfare organisations, share an ideology of wifehood.

Aloka was not alone in facing this trial of wifehood and it did not refer only to Hindu women. All the women who applied under Section 125 had to prove neglect by their husbands, and this generally meant proving their credentials as wives. Proving their credentials as good wives meant, for most applicants, providing evidence of having made every attempt to live in the marriage despite mental and physical cruelty; of leaving only because they were forced out of the matrimonial home under conditions of physical danger to them. In some instances the husband's failure to appear in court to disprove this was taken as testimony of his neglect. Thus in Safia's case she had to prove that she had lived in her matrimonial home despite physical torture for over four years, had returned to her matrimonial home on two occasions after being thrown out and had finally to leave because she was mercilessly beaten. At the time of her final eviction she went to the police station and complained. As a result a case under 498A was registered and the husband arrested. This served as proof of physical torture for the case under Section 125. It was not she who alleged cruelty and her inability to live in the matrimonial home as a result, but also that the law enforcement agency had recognised/legitimised her claim. Similarly for Shanaz, Asma, Taslima, Anjana and Ruma the ability to face physical and mental cruelty and yet remain steadfast, constant and devoted to their marriage and husbands was seen as a test of their wifehood.

The Two *Jatis:* Women and Men

The trial of wifehood on the terms described above is so central to the claims of maintenance under Section 125 that advocates often refuse to fight cases in court for women if they cannot provide instances of facing up to cruelty, and proof of the husband's violence. To authenticate their claim to violence and ill-treatment, say the advocates in the criminal courts, they should report the matter to the police. Farzana Begum, a Muslim woman, appealed for maintenance under Section 125 in 1984 and won the case. She was granted maintenance, received seven instalments of the dues and withdrew further claim to maintenance in 1990. Her husband divorced her at this stage. Farzana actually withdrew because she was remarrying (and would have had to give up her right to maintenance from her first husband under the circumstances).

Her second marriage, however, ran into trouble within two years because her husband's grown-up sons by his first wife resented Farzana laying claim to their father's income, and eventually, property. Unable to prevent his sons from breaking into his house, ill-treating Farzana and stealing his things, Farzana's husband removed her from his house and set her up in a rented house in a village on the outskirts of Calcutta. Initially he visited her, gave her money. When his visits became infrequent and stopped altogether, Farzana had nothing to subsist on. Furthermore, it was dangerous for her to live alone in this way. She went to the police station, made a report that she was leaving because her husband had stopped supporting her and returned to her mother's house. She then went to the advocate who had fought her first case to ask him to help her. At their meeting in February 1992, Farzana tried in vain to tell the lawyer, step by step, the whole story of what had happened to the second marriage. The lawyer behaved very badly with her. He kept interrupting her and saying that what she was recounting were mere stories, fabrications, and they were no use in a court of law. She should have come to him when the sons of Taher Ali (second husband) had stolen her things and were troubling her. He criticised her for not having stayed on in the house (in the husband's house). It would have been better if she had been assaulted there as then the case under Section 125 would have had some foundation. Farzana tried to explain that Taher Ali refused to complain against his own children to the police as he would have had to bail them out if they were arrested. As his wife, and keen to keep the marriage going, she was powerless to do anything against his wishes. She said that she had registered a complaint at Mahestola police station in which she said that he was not supporting her and that she was forced to leave the house because she had nothing to eat. The lawyer said that the complaint at the police station was of no use for the case. If she had complained of torture or of being beaten up then it would have served some purpose.

Under instructions from the lawyer Farzana and I went to Maheshtola police station to register a 'proper' complaint. At the police station Farzana's written complaint was much more elaborate than her first report but again did not mention physical violence by the husband. Farzana's explanation to me was that since Allah was her witness she could not lie that her husband had beaten her. He had neglected her and refused to maintain her.

An interesting sequel to Farzana's interaction with the lawyer is as follows. At the meeting in February 1992 the lawyer harangued Farzana about the ease with which Muslim men divorced their wives. She should have married the Hindu man who had shown interest in her when her first case was in court. The case for maintenance would have been easier because he could not have divorced her so easily. Farzana explained that she was afraid that she would have been ostracised by her community if she had married a Hindu. The lawyer expansively claimed that all *jatis* were the same, we were all Indians. Farzana, who hitherto had listened patiently to the lawyer's harangue, said quietly but firmly, "*No, dada* (elder brother). *There are two jatis—men and women.*"

Farzana's statement is in essence a recognition of the unequal status of women as compared to men, and wives as compared to husbands in their relationship to the state as also in civil society. Section 125 both in its intentions (protecting women from destitution) and in adjudication (protecting the ideal of the good and wronged wife) is embedded in a discourse of 'protection'. Pathak and Sunder Rajan point out in a discussion of the Shah Bano case and the promulgation of the Muslim Women's Bill, that all parties to the discourse shared the assumption that they were protecting Muslim women (Pathak and Sunder Rajan 1989). Similarly in cases under Section 125 the discourse of protection is ubiquitous. 'Protection' confers on the protector the right to intervene in arenas hitherto considered out of bounds and also to speak with authority for the victim. Thus in all the cases under Section 125 we find that state institutions, both the judiciary and law enforcement, intervene in family and conjugal relations hitherto out of bounds because of the private nature of the family. Women/wives are victims whom the state, in offering to protect, also defines by the authority invested in the role of the protector. In the process of offering and seeking protection an alliance is set up between the protector and protected. This in turn conceals the opposition between protector and protected which is a hierarchical one. Thus in a relationship of protector and protected, as between state and woman/wife, it is the first which bears more authority. By virtue of this relationship the state then defines what wifehood means, and what forms of violence by husbands will be construed as cruelty or neglect legitimising thereby her right to be maintained by him. As can be discerned, this discourse of protection shifts the discussion of women's right to maintenance from what women are entitled to, to a privilege conferred on women who fall within the parameters of victim status defined by the protector.

The apparent contradiction between the judiciary and the law enforcement agencies in implementing the maintenance rights of women can only be understood in the light of the problematic of protection. Despite the existence of Warrants of Arrest for husbands in six of the 12 cases in the study, only two were implemented and that, too, partially. For example, in Marjina's case the Warrant of Arrest resulted in arrest for a short period of 39 days (whereas the sentence was for 34 months) giving her husband enough time to appeal to the High Court against the judgement of the lower courts. He lost in the High Court, has not paid the maintenance dues and continues to have, since 1988, a Warrant of Arrest which has not been implemented. In order to understand the contradiction one needs to broaden the argument to encompass the relationship between the family, law and state. The family is a site and ideology which is protected by the state. Its right to autonomy and privacy is widely recognised and granted. The demarcation of the spheres of the family and the state as private and public enables these to work in a collaborative hegemony. This means that women's rights as individual citizens granted by the state can only be imperfectly enforced when its violation happens to be in the family. This is evidenced by the fact that when women appeal against victimisation in the family and where reports of violence by husbands do not result in arrests, the state agencies (read police) are more than reluctant to step in to prevent and punish the crime.

Does Section 125 serve the purpose for which it was created? The need to give women the right to maintenance arose out of a recognition of their dependent status in marriage both because they are unlikely to be independent income earners and also because most women do not have property. A principle tenet of Section 125 is to protect women becoming destitute in the event of withdrawal of the husband/breadwinner. However, as the experiences in the above twelve cases indicates, there is little to support the view that this is what is happening. The appalling record of outcome in these cases is that seven women out of the total 12 applicants have not recovered any maintenance dues at all despite the existence of favourable decrees. Only one woman, Ferzana, actually did recover her dues and withdrew the case when she remarried. Ohidenessa was able to recover part of the dues until her husband appealed to the High Court against the order. For the two women receiving temporary maintenance at present, the future is uncertain. Aloka's right to maintenance is jeopardised by her failure in the trial of wifehood. Arati's husband is paying at present because failure to do so might result in a Warrant of Arrest. Being a petty government functionary, arrest in a criminal offence would cost him his job.

If women were actually to receive the amounts granted in permanent maintenance it would still not save them from destitution. Marjina received a maintenance award of Rs 175 per month for herself and her two daughters. Ohidenessa's award was Rs 100 for herself and Rs 50 for her son per month. The ostensible reason for such small awards was that both these women live in rural areas where the cost of living is low. The real reason is that the court assumes that these women have natal homes willing to give them shelter, and natal families willing to bear the cost of maintaining them and their children. The urban women did not fare any better although the amounts awarded were higher than those of Marjina and Ohidenessa. On an average, most women living in urban areas were granted Rs 200–300, with the single exception of Aloka who received a temporary order for payment of Rs 400. Women with children were given on an average Rs 50–100 per child. The amounts granted are insufficient to meet the average woman's expenses on food alone. Other expenses like shelter cannot even be considered in these amounts. Women who have been divorced or deserted, therefore, have no alternative but to depend on natal families, kin and sometimes friends or fictive kin for shelter on whatever terms they may dictate.

The time taken to obtain a favourable decree also works to the disadvantage of women. Marjina instituted a case for maintenance in 1977 and was granted a decree in 1984. Discounting the fact that till 1992 she had not received any payment from her husband, Marjina spent a total of 12 years between 1977 and 1989 in and out of court. Ohidenessa applied in 1982, was granted a decree in 1983, waited till 1987 to file the execution order and till 1992 was in and out of court waiting for a settlement. Ruma applied under Section 125 in 1989 and till 1992 had not received even a temporary order of maintenance. Although the other women have waited for less time to obtain a decree, on an average it has taken three years for a case to go through court even in Calcutta city.

The inability to secure payment despite the existence of favourable decrees, the low amounts granted in maintenance, and the time that these cases take to be decided in court, all point to the fact that Section 125 does not serve its principal purpose which is to protect women from destitution. Agnes mentions that suggestions made by the Law Commission to overhaul this law by removing the ceiling of Rs 500, ensuring a woman's right to her matrimonial home, and introducing measures for enforcing payment have not received any attention from the legislature (Agnes 1992). Section 125 represents the state's unwillingness to restructure property relations in marriage. By denying women equal rights to marital property in the event of dissolution of marriage or desertion by the husband, women as wives are posited as lesser citizens than men as husbands. It is in this mode that Muslim and Hindu women share a common fate and are equally disadvantaged.

Note

The names of some of the litigants mentioned in the case studies have been changed at their request.

References

Agnes, F., 1992a. "Maintenance for Women; Rhetoric of Equality", *Economic and Political Weekly* Vol. XXVII; No. 19; Oct. 10.

Agnes, F., 1992b. "Protecting Women against Violence?", *Economic and Political Weekly* April 25.

Chakravarti, U., 1989. "Whatever Happened to the Vedic Dasi? Orientalism, Nationalism and a Script for the Past" in Sangari & Vaid (eds.) *Recasting Women* Delhi: Kali for Women.

Kabeer, N. and R. Subramaniam, 1996. "Institutions, Relations and Outcomes: Framework and Tools for Gender-Aware Planning", IDS Discussion Paper, 857.

Muzumdar, P.V., 1989. *The Law of Maintenance of Wives, Children and Parents* Allahabad: Malhotra Publishing House.

Parashar, A., 1992. *Women and Family Law Reform in India: Uniform Civil Code and Gender Equality* New Delhi/London: Sage Publications.

Pathak, Z. and Rajeswari Sunder Rajan, 1989. "Shahbano", in *Signs*, Vol. 14, No. 3.

Tharu, S. and T. Niranjana, 1994. "Problems of a Contemporary Theory of Gender" *Social Scientist*, March–April.

6

Gender, Poverty and Institutional Exclusion

Insights From Integrated Rural Development Programme (IRDP) and Development of Women and Children in Rural Areas (DWCRA)

NAILA KABEER AND RANJANI K. MURTHY

Conceptualising Poverty: Interlocking Forms of Institutional Exclusion

The conceptualisation of poverty is essential for grasping its causes and implications; for providing a basis for identifying the poor; and for designing programmes which address their constraints and release their productive potential. The poverty line has long been the dominant approach for conceptualising and measuring poverty in official planning circles in India and still underpins many poverty alleviation programmes. However, as a summary measure of household income/consumption, it is severely limited by its reliance on a dichotomous classification of the population between poor and non-poor households, and the resultant blurring of deprivational inequalities, both between as well as within, households below the poverty line. In terms of *inter*-household inequalities, it ignores the differences in income and productive capabilities of those just below the poverty line compared to those significantly below, as well as the socially ascribed forms of disadvantage which create distinctions along lines of caste and gender of headship between households who might appear equally deprived in income terms. It also ignores *intra*-

household inequalities in well-being and agency along lines of gender and age. Yet, as we shall see, these inequalities within and between households below the poverty line can mean that the delivery of benefits to the poor in general does not necessarily translate into their uniform realisation by all sections of the poor.

In this chapter we will be exploring how the institutional framework outlined in Chapter 1 can help provide an alternative approach to poverty and to the analysis of poverty-related interventions. Our starting point is the conceptualisation of poverty as a dually constituted deprivation in terms of both means and ends. 'Ends' in the context of poverty refers to the satisfaction of basic needs while 'means' refers to the resources neccesary to meet basic needs. Basic needs deprivation is manifested in some of the more visible and familiar characteristics of poverty, e.g. inadequate shelter, food, clothing, education and health, as well as its more intangible forms, such as social isolation, vulnerability and insecurity. Underlying these characteristics is a second order and deeper level of deprivation relating to the adequacy of means to meet these basic needs, which can be seen as constituting the causal mechanisms through which poverty is reproduced. While the poverty line implicitly privileges income as the key means and the market as the key institution for meeting basic needs, in reality, people meet their needs through a variety of resources, aside from income, and gain access to these resources through a variety of institutional relationships, aside from those of the market.

Sen's concept of entitlements, which draws attention to the different basis of claims on resources which prevail in a society has the merit of expanding the analysis of poverty from access to the market to this broader set of relationships and activities which enable people to meet their basic needs (1987). We can link up this concept of entitlements to the institutional framework developed in Chapter I which draws attention to the rules and practices which characterise different institutional arenas—market-based exchange; state provision; and the 'moral economy' of community and kinship—and which determine who gets what and on what terms.[1] Within this framework, poverty is manifested in shortfalls in the realised value of entitlements—as a result of inadequate endowments, of unfavourable terms of exchange or of 'unruly' practices[2] where official 'rules' of entitlement are subverted, ignored or imperfectly implemented—which lead in turn to a shortfall in basic needs satisfaction. In the Indian context, where vast sections of the population are dispossessed of land and other forms of material capital, poverty can be generally equated with the absence of any entitlements aside from those based on the use of bodies and labour.[3] Handing of control of their bodies, or aspects of their bodies, to others—as in bonded labour, prostitution, the use of one's children as collateral against loans, the sale of one's organs—are examples of some of the more extreme forms of self-exploitation which occurs as a result of this deprivation.

This broader notion of entitlement as extending beyond ownership and exchange to include social-ascribed definitions of who is entitled to what, the 'rules' (legal, contractual, customary or normative) as well as the actual practices which govern how successfully these entitlements are realised allows us to develop a framework for the analysis of poverty as the product of *multiple and frequently interlocking forms of institutional exclusion*. The powerlessness of the poor explains why they so often rely on relationships of dependency for survival and security. To deepen this account to encompass the caste and gender dimensions of poverty, we would need to explore how the relations of inequality encoded in the rules and practices of different institutional arenas 'entitle' women and men differently and unequally within different social groups within a population. The mutual constitution of caste, class and gender inequalities and the consequent production of diversity in the experiences and disadvantages of those who are regarded as poor, then becomes easier to comprehend.

Locating the analysis of entitlements within an institutional context also provides a framework for the design and evaluation of interventions for the reduction of poverty. Analysing poverty in terms of the different, frequently interlocking, forms of institutional exclusion which isolate poor people and confine them to a limited set of entitlements, focuses our attention on the *rules, norms, procedures and practices* of different institutional mechanisms in order to assess which are most likely to address the needs of the poor. In this chapter, we will be exploring the exclusion of the poor from mainstream banking institutions and the performance of two government programmes set up to compensate for this exclusion with a view to disentangling what could be regarded as class-based forms of institutional exclusion from those which might be related to gender. The first, the Integrated Rural Development Programme (IRDP), can be described as a gender-integrated intervention, in that it seeks to address the credit needs of both poor men and women. The second, Development of Women and Children in Rural Areas (DWCRA), is a women-specific project, set up largely in response to the recognised failure of IRDP to reach poor women. In our analysis of IRDP, we will review some of the general explanations given for its failure to achieve its intended goal of poverty alleviation and compare these with explanations which focus specifically on its failure to address the credit needs of poor women. In as much as DWCRA was set up explicitly for poor women, a survey of the existing literature on DWCRA will help to establish whether women-specific interventions help to overcome the gender biases of more generic interventions or whether they merely reproduce them in other forms. Thus the aim of this chapter is to establish the extent to which the failure of an intervention to reach poor women reflects its failure to reach the poor in general and to which it operates through gender-specific factors.

The Rationale for Credit Interventions for the Poor: The Emergence of IRDP

As a starting point for examining the impact of credit-related poverty interventions, it is necessary to link our earlier discussion of the shortfall in needs and resources associated with poverty with the kinds of credit needs they are likely to generate. The results of a participatory appraisal exercise conducted into the credit needs of groups of poor women and men in Bihar and Tamil Nadu (Murthy, 1994) highlight how closely such needs reflected the more general shortfalls and exclusions which characterise the lives of the poor. An analysis suggested three categories of need. The first related to production-related expenditures (e.g. working capital and purchase of productive assets) of the kind recognised by formal credit institutions. The second category related to consumption-related expenditures on health, education, marriages, funerals, house repair and entertainment of relatives. The third category could be seen as stemming from the social isolation and vulnerability of the poor: the release of bonded labour, repayment of previous debts with moneylenders, meeting the cost of bribes to avail of government services etc. The appraisal also highlighted the extent to which gender asymmetries in resources, responsibilities and opportunities shaped the credit needs and priorities of men and women. Women were, in general, more likely than men to report taking loans for feeding visiting relatives and for purchasing food during the lean season; men on the other hand were more likely to report borrowing in order to purchase larger productive assets such as a plough or a piece of land.

Gender differentials were also discernible in how poor people evaluated different sources of credit. Some criteria were common to both women and men. Thus both valued ease of access to credit sources, in terms of both procedures and proximity; timely availability of credit; fungibility of use of loans between different needs; the absence of restrictions on loan size; low interest rates; simple procedures; waiver of collateral requirements; absence of corruption; and flexibility of repayment schedules. However, divergences were evident in terms of other criteria. Women were more likely than men to value the feeling of 'ownership' over credit sources; they expressed greater need for information about how the credit system worked; and gave priority to the facility for saving along with borrowing. Men on the other hand were more likely to value flexibility in the size of repayment instalments; absence of group pressure in case of non-repayment; and the availability of credit irrespective of repayment by other group members. The apparently greater value attached to feeling 'ownership' over credit sources and the greater acceptance of co-operation by women is worth noting; it may reflect their greater sense of social 'disentitlement' as well as their greater awareness of their powerlessness as individuals. In addition, the greater value attached by women than men to facilities for saving has also emerged in a number of other studies and appears to reflect intra-household power relations; unless women were able to safeguard their savings, they are open to appropriation by husbands and can be spent on individual consumption (Sebstadt, 1982).

An examination of the rules and procedures of the formal banking system, in the light of the preceding analysis, readily reveals why it is unable to address the credit needs of the poor. Their rules and procedures tend to be inflexible, complex and opaque and do not easily accomodate to the range of needs for which poor people seek credit in the amounts in which they seek it, at the time at which they seek it or on the terms on which they seek it (Joshi, 1995). Indeed, the very culture of such institutions is premised on certain gender and class norms, making them inhospitable environments for the poor to come in search of financial assistance (Kabeer and Murthy, 1996). Exclusion from formal entitlements to credit has generally left poor people with little recourse in times of need or crisis except to informal sources of credit such as moneylenders, landlords and pawnbrokers. While such sources are generally more flexible than banks in terms of timing and conditions, they are also far more exploitative. Informal credit practices including usurious rates of interest, the requirement that loans be repaid as a lump sum, the mortgaging of assets till loan repayment and frequent recourse to threats and muscle power for loan recovery. Moneylenders have also been found to charge higher interest rates to women than men and there was evidence that where they did not charge interest rates, they recouped their payment in the form of sexual services (Everett and Savara, 1991).

Since the early 1950s, when the All India Rural Credit Survey (1954) revealed the high level of dependence of the rural poor on high-interest informal credit, the government has sought to promote their assured access to banking services. A major justification for the nationalisation of banks in 1969 was to force them to extend their lending to the rural areas in general and to the rural poor in particular (Pulley, 1989). The introduction of Differential Rate of Interest lending required banks to channel at least one per cent of their outstanding advances into productive ventures for poorer families at low (4 per cent) interest rates. The shift to 'social banking' was cemented by the 1981 report of the Committee to Review Arrangements for Institutional Credit for Agriculture and Rural Development which traced the basic cause of poverty to the low asset base of the rural poor, the low productivity of their enterprises, their exclusion from the formal banking system and consequently their heavy dependence on non-formal sources of credit.

The Integrated Rural Development Programme (IRDP) was conceived in this policy climate. Although fairly comprehensive in its early conceptualisation, envisaging the matching of local resources and local needs through various perspective plans, it was operationalised in much narrower terms to provide a capital subsidy and complementary credit at below market interest rates to households below the official poverty line in order to finance productive investments in income-generating assets (Pulley, 1989). Almost since its inception, there has been a wealth of studies, official and independent, examining the performance of the IRDP in achieving its stated goal of poverty alleviation. By and large, independent studies have tended to be extremely critical and we will be drawing on this literature to demonstrate how an analysis of the official rules and unofficial norms as well as the 'unruly practices' characterising the IRDP helps to explain some of these unplanned outcomes. Our analysis begins at the generic level with evidence of the 'anti-poor' bias of the IRDP before considering bias specifically related to gender. We then go on to explore the evidence of gender bias within DWCRA.

Reaching the Poor and Dealing with Diversity: The Politics of Beneficiary Identification in the IRDP

While IRDP laid considerable emphasis on the poverty line both to define who was eligible for assistance and to measure the effects of assistance in enabling beneficiaries to cross the poverty line, it acknowledged forms of diversity among those below the poverty line, not normally allowed for by this measure. The relevance of caste and gender as a basis of 'disentitlement' was built into the programme in the form of special quotas: 30 per cent of the assisted families had to be drawn from the scheduled castes or scheduled tribes (subsequently increased to 50 per cent in 1991) and 30 per cent of individuals assisted had to be women (subsequently increased to 40 per cent in 1991) with special priority to women-headed households. Moreover, IRDP rules also specified the selection of the poorest of eligible households first before moving on to the less poor.

Evaluations of IRDP note widespread targeting errors: of exclusion (of eligible beneficiaries) as well as of inclusion (of ineligible ones). While these estimates vary between states and sources, summaries suggest leakages of around 15–20 per cent to ineligible beneficiaries (Rath, 1985; Bagchee 1987; Kurian 1987). The programme has tended to reach the relatively better off within the poor at the expense of landless and women-headed families (Drèze, 1990) and eligible members of upper caste households at the expense of the scheduled castes (Joshi (1990). An important factor behind these targeting failures appears to be the reliance on the top-down identification of an internally heterogeneous category of poor people by officials serving in a massive, bureaucratised and target-driven structure. Errors of identification could occur with very little violation of the official 'rules': 'since the main criterion of eligibility is "income", and since incomes in rural India are extremely hard to observe, the door is wide open to abuse' (Drèze, 1990, p. A-98).

In UP, household surveys to identify potential beneficiaries were often dispensed with and the IRDP list was drawn up after loans had been allocated (Drèze, 1990). Although IRDP rules provided that the gram sabha should participate in the selection process to ensure accurate targeting, it was in fact never convened. Instead, the headman and the village level worker acted as intermediaries between villagers and the adminstration. However, identification performance also reflected local contexts. Drèze found it to be better in Gujarat possibly because the government administration was relatively more efficient but also, the rural population was more articulate and organised. In West Bengal, where targeting bias took a political rather than an economic form, the results still conformed to IRDP rules. Since panchayat elections were held on party lines, the implementation of schemes such as IRDP became the focus of party politics The dominance of the Communist Party (Marxist) in state politics accounted for the fact that the vast majority of beneficiaries in the West Bengal study were supporters of the communist parties; however, in as much as poor and disadvantaged sections of the population were a key political constituency of the CPM, the operation of party political bias in this context worked in favour of the IRDP's stated goals of reaching the poor.

Alleviating Poverty, Recovering Loans and Winning Votes: Goal Incoherence within IRDP

At least three different sets of institutional actors were involved in the implementation of IRDP—the government, the banking sector and politicians. The conflicting objectives and priorities of these differing sets of actors resulted in incoherence as to how the goals of the IRDP were to be achieved. For the central government who had formulated the programme, it was about the transfer of credit to poor households in the interests of poverty alleviation. For block development officers, responsible for implementation at the local level, the IRDP represented physical and financial targets which were centrally set and had to be met on an annual basis. For politicians at both national and local levels, the IRDP was an opportuntiy for making political capital out of the patronage potential inherent in subsidised credit delivery. For the banks themselves, the overall lending portfolio remained governed by the rules and procedures of commercial banking, which required that the interest on loans should cover the costs of administration and provision against default and that banks had to bear responsibility for capital losses which arose from inefficient loan policies. Government imposition of 'social banking' functions had not displaced these conventional concerns, but were simply an 'add-on' to their routine operations.

The results of this incoherence in the priorities and practices governing IRDP were manifested in a number of ways. Block development officers, who selected beneficiaries and approved their investments, were driven by the need to meet targets rather than assure viable investments. At the same time, the banks' ability to reject loan applications deemed non-viable was often constrained by political considerations and the need to ensure that they had met their 'priority sector' lending targets. This reliance on target-based indicators (e.g. amount of loans disbursed) rather than achievement-based ones (such as retention and profitability of assets purchased) tended to drive a wedge between immediate transfer functions of the programme and its long-term poverty alleviation goals. Although in principle, beneficiaries were supposed to decide on their own investments, in practice, a list of activities considered suitable for IRDP investment purportedly drawn up for purely 'illustrative' purposes, effectively narrowed the range of investments which qualified for consideration, leading to what Dandekar dubbed 'the IRDP cow' phenomenon: Rath estimated that around 5 million cattle were distributed under IRDP during the sixth plan period (1985).

One consequence of this was the failure to align the assets selected under IRDP with their availability (what Osmani termed the supply-side *'macro-mismatch'*, 1988). This was evident in the artificially inflated prices that occurred as a result of the IRDP-driven surge in purchase of assets such as cattle. The unavailability of good breeds resulted in large-scale purchase of poorer quality animals whose yields were lower, who were often less hardy and whose susceptibility to climatic variations led to high rates of mortality. The demand side 'macro-mismatch' meant that enterprises involving, for instance, cycle rickshaws or craft training which might have been profitable if they had involved a few new entrants failed to generate profitable employment because the markets for these goods and services were quickly saturated; demand did not keep pace with the expansion in supply. This tendency was exacerbated by the fact that such interventions were directed at a section of the population who had by virtue of their poverty been excluded from mainstream market opportunities and were confined to limited, and quickly saturated, segments of the labour and product markets. Drèze found in his UP study that the local bank responsible for IRDP lending had issued 12 out of its 26 loans solely for 'shopkeeping' and a further 8 non-IRDP loans for the same purpose over the same period. As Drèze observes, "... there is no scope for 20 shops in a village of 143 households, and only 4 of the IRDP participants who borrowed for this purpose actually had a 'shop' of any sort." The other officially stated use of bank loans was to purchase buffaloes, which Drèze suggests could easily have been described as the purchase of unicorns, 'since not a single one of these mythical animals was to be seen in the village two years later' (p. 48).

Further incoherence was introduced by the association of IRDP loans with government largesse, an attitude partly encouraged by the absence of attention to repayment criteria by government officials in their approval of enterprises but also exacerbated by the write-off of loans and loan *melas* during election times. The political capital gained out of generous loan disbursement encouraged politicans to lobby for ambitious targets, irrespective of actual investment opportunties, and made a whole area of banking practice vulnerable to political intervention. It also led to an attitude among borrowers that IRDP loans were government handouts and therefore did not have to be repaid. IRDP loan overdues tended to be 12–20 per cent higher than unsubsidised agricultural loans and would have been even higher if the capital subsidy were systematically excluded from repayment calculations. In addition, the effects of goal incoherence also showed up in various estimates documenting the economic ineffectiveness of IRDP lending. Osmani found that 24 per cent of assets purchased under IRDP had not generated any income at all. When loan repayment and inflation rates were allowed for, 50 per cent of assets had made little or no contribution to net disposable income. Adjusting income increments for loan repayments, Rath (1985) estimated the figure to be in the region of 10 per cent of beneficiaries or 3 per cent of baseline poor population over the Sixth Plan period. Swaminathan's study in Tamil Nadu (1988) found that after six years of IRDP lending, the upward mobility of assisted households in terms of assets was no better than that of unassisted households.

The Contractual Disadvantage of the Poor: Economies of Scale and Diseconomies of Isolation

Poverty, as construed by IRDP, was the product of two interrelated forms of institutional exclusion: from formal credit mechanisms and, consequently, from the market for productive assets. IRDP therefore sought to provide poor people with credit to purchase certain predetermined assets. However, the distinction maintained by formal lending institutions between the acceptable use of credit for production purposes and its unacceptable use in consumption, is not sustainable when the actual credit needs articulated by the poor are considered. Expenditures on food and health maintain the value of the primary productive asset of poor people, their bodies; expenditures on entertaining relatives and participating in social ceremonies also have this double aspect of consumption and production, given the significance of social networks in the crisis coping strategies of the poor; and finally the use of bank loans to pay off usurious forms of debt or to secure release of a family member from bonded labour can be seen as an investment in a family's future productivity.

Similarly, the tying of credit to the acquisition of subsidised assets does not necessarily translate into the *ability* to use such assets profitably. In particular, the ability to utilise an asset may be undermined by certain basic indivisibilities in production and power which constitute the basis of their institutional exclusion from the formal banking sector in the first place. First of all, there is what Osmani calls the '*micro-level mismatch*' between the income-generating assets provided under IRDP and the availability of the necessary complementary resources. Thus, the high mortality rates reported for livestock in some states were often due to inadequate protection for cattle from inclement weather among households who often lacked adequate shelter for themselves. It also reflected lack of access to grazing land, to sources of fodder and to veterinary services. Similarly indivisibilties in marketing costs and in insurance opportunties mean that poor people were least able to secure potential economies of scale and most likely to be trapped within isolated, marginal and highly risky segments of the informal market.

In addition to production-related diseconomies, the poor also suffered from the diseconomies of isolation which resulted in their inability to realise the full value of their 'official' entitlements to government loans and subsidies. Studies have pointed to the long delays, between application for a loan and its sanction, to costly procedures of application, to the high degree of corruption and to the large investments of money and time necessary to acquire an IRDP asset. The

IRDP practice of direct payment by the bank to the supplier of the asset served to undermine the bargaining power of the beneficiary purchasing the asset. Poor people were most likely to be defrauded by bank and government officials, animal brokers and veterinarians and were least well-placed to pay the bribes, fill in the complicated forms and influence village level intermediaries who determined the selection process. One estimate of the costs incurred by prospective beneficiaries—payment to intermediaries and bank officials, the search for suitable assets—amounted to 50–70 per cent of the subsidy component while in the Palanpur study, it was found the village level worker demanded Rs 200 from each beneficiary to cover the expenses connected with applying for loans (Drèze, 1988).

Some of these factors explain findings from studies of IRDP showing that households which started out from a position of relative strength showed the highest rates of asset retention and were most likely to cross the poverty line. Other studies have pointed to the importance of the broader context in mitigating the economic costs of social isolation. Thus impact has varied according to the level of development of an area and the availability of infrastructure. In addition, the political context may also play a role in minimising 'unruly' practices in the allocation of funds. Both Swaminathan and Drèze point to the superior performance of West Bengal, which had a left regime with a decentralised system of selection and implementation of IRDP. A survey by PEO found that the proportion of beneficiaries drawn from the poorest group was higher in West Bengal than in many other states. Swaminathan found that the the active mediation of panchayat councils in West Bengal also led to considerably lower costs of accessing loans for the poor compared to Tamil Nadu, where such democratic participation did not occur.

The Gender Dimensions of Institutional Exclusion: Insights from a Gender-integrated Programme

We have so far documented some of the norms, rules and practices which explain the exclusion of certain sections of the poor—those furthest from the poverty line, members of scheduled castes and tribes—from participating in or benefiting from IRDP. However, it is worth noting that there is persuasive evidence to suggest that the IRDP was even more ineffective in reaching poor women than in any other priority target group. The Mid-Term Review of IRDP conducted half way through the Fifth Five Year Plan found that of all its priority target groups, women were most likely to be excluded: it was estimated that less than 5 per cent of IRDP beneficiaries were women despite a quota of 30 per cent (Banerjee, 1990). Pulley estimated that in 1987–88, 43 per cent of assisted beneficiaries were SC/ST but only 17 per cent were women, while a number of researchers noted that the programme had been particularly unsuccessful in reaching out to women-headed households (Swaminathan, 1990; Drèze, 1990).

The manifest failure of IRDP in reaching poor women compared to the other disdvantaged groups that it had specially targeted, suggests the need to explore what it was about women's poverty that placed them in a position of greater disadvantage vis a vis poor men from similar backgrounds. Our review of the available literature suggests that gender inequalities among the poor in accessing government credit can be disaggregated into three distinct forms of exclusionary mechanisms:

- *gender-intensified disadvantage*: poor women suffered from similar disadvantages as men of an equivalent class or caste but in a more *intensified* form
- *gender-specific disadvantages* : they also suffered from certain additional disadvantages particular to women, which were not experienced by poor men
- *gender-imposed disadvantage*: finally, they were disadvantaged by the *gender biases and preconceptions* embedded in the bureacratic norms and practices of credit delivery.

The first mechanism related to the fact that whatever material and social disadvantages served to exclude or marginalise poor men in government credit distribution, they tended to apply in *an intensified form* to poor women. The problems posed by indivisibilities in the production process—and by the diseconomies of isolation—for poor women and women-headed households, were generally much greater than other sections of the poor because all the disadvantages associated with caste and class were further exacerbated by those of gender. Poor women were less likely than men to own any collateral of their own; to exercise power in local political structures or to afford the high costs of accessing loans. They were therefore least likely to be included in the identification process. They were also at a greater disadvantage vis-a-vis men in their ability to utilise IRDP loans: they were less likely than men to own the complementary resources to benefit from any productive assets; less likely to be literate or to possess marketable skills.

There were also certain *gender-specific* constraints on women's capacity to engage in entrepreneurial activities. Women in most states in India are burdened with primary responsibility for domestic work. As a consequence, their choice of income-earning activities tends to be curtailed and their enterprises are likely to be smaller, more dispersed and confined to even narrower segments of the market than men from an equivalent class. In many northern states, strong cultural norms of female seclusion further curtail their choice of livelihood. It is worth noting, for instance, that women are far more active in trade, commerce and agricultural wage labour in the southern states of India than in the north (Boserup, 1970; Agarwal, 1994). In order to illustrate why poor people are most likely to be trapped within isolated, marginal and highly risky segments of the informal market, Swaminathan cited the explanation offered by a poor woman in West Bengal for the poor returns to her labour: 'The price of paddy I buy is high because of the small quantity I purchase and the price of rice I sell is low because of the small quantity I sell' (p. A-20). It was not a coincidence that the woman in question happened to be earning her livelihood from parboiling rice since this was one of the few occupations traditionally open to women in this area. Consequently, her marginalised situation in the market can be seen as the product of gender inequality exacerbating inequalities of class.

Finally, a third mechanism responsible for gender inequalities in access to IRDP benefits was the product of gender biases either embedded within programme design or played out in bureaucratic practice. Thus gender-stereotyping of poor women led to the phenomenon of the 'IRDP sewing machine' to match the 'IRDP cow' as a result of dozens of sewing machines being distributed in single villages (Kurian, 1987). Bureacratic norms about 'the household' led, in some cases, to the acceptance of application forms from women only if they were co-signed by their husbands or fathers, thus excluding women who had been deserted or whose relations with their husbands were strained (Viswanath, 1989). In other cases, IRDP loans were denied to women whose husbands had defaulted. Since the problems that caused men to default were usually the same reasons for their failure to support their families, women were doubly penalised by this practice. The World Bank (1991) pointed out that even the low figures on the proportion of female IRDP beneficiaries were likely to be overestimates since officials often sought to fulfil their quota by first selecting a male borrower and asking him to bring his wife to sign loan papers. Mayoux noted that in Tamil Nadu, around a third of milch cattle loans were issued to women but as wives of eligible men rather than independently defined beneficiaries. In other cases what appeared to be joint activities within the household were in fact controlled by men so that loans for such activities issued in women's names ended up under male control. In Karnataka, for instance, Mayoux (1993) observed that while women's names appeared in the list of silk reelers receiving loans, silk reeling was a joint household activity involving both male and female labour, but men controlled the proceeds from production. In such cases, indicators on numbers of loans to women tell us very little about the extent to which women benefit from them.

It is also worth noting the evidence for region-based gender differences in IRDP practices. For instance, while women in Tamil Nadu, as in the rest of the country, received smaller loans than men, there were no clear-cut differences with respect to the *kinds* of activities funded for men and women: both received loans largely for milch cows and for bullock carts (Mayoux, 1993). In West Bengal, however, there were some clear gender differences in loan allocation practices. While women were better represented in the allocation process than in many other parts of the country, their loans were largely for household based industry, crafts and services, precisely the activities where women had been traditionally concentrated but also activities which tended to be the secondary occupations of the household with limited potential for generating high income. Mayoux also notes a concentration on home-based handicrafts in other government training and lending schemes, and the absence of any attempts to promote diversification in women's livelihoods. Men on the other hand were more likely to receive loans for establishing new or expanding existing high-income earning enterprises: fisheries, carpentry, lantern manufacture; welding and repairs businesses etc.

Such evidence of region-related gender differences in government lending practices can have a number of explanations. It may reflect, as government officials often averred, differential aspects of local socio-economic structure or it may reflect the biases and preconceptions of local bureaucrats. Mayoux offers persuasive arguments that, at least in the West Bengal context, the latter explanation had a part to play. She points out that the assumed universality and immutability of cultural norms of female propriety and seclusion appeared to be more a construct of a middle-class, upper-caste and primarily male bureaucracy than a reflection of a dynamic and changing reality. While such norms and constraints did indeed represent a powerful ideological backdrop against which all women had to live their lives, in practice, they were unevenly adhered to by women from different class, caste and religious backgrounds. Three main assumptions appeared to be at play in shaping programme delivery: that cultural norms of seclusion restricted *all* women's ability to undertake work outside the home; that the demand of domestic and child-care responsibilities applied uniformly to *all* women and necessitated home-based income-generating activities; and that *all* women were invariably secondary earners, dependent on a primary male breadwinner. These assumptions were not borne out in reality.

Cultural restrictions regarding women's ability to move outside the home have been undergoing rapid changes in West Bengal. Such restrictions have always been less stringent for women from scheduled caste, tribal and poorer households as well as for women from all social strata who have been widowed, abandoned or divorced. But in the past decades, the gradual increase in female education, the expansion of transport and communications and the catalytic effect of political mobilisation by Communist party cadres in the countryside have all led to a gathering momentum in the pace of change, making the old norms of female seclusion less of a constraint on women's mobility than before. As far as the constraint imposed by domestic labour responsibities, this varied considerably among women according to their life cycle and social status. Women who were unmarried or did not have young children did not have such pressing domestic responsiblities. While women in small cultivator families might be overworked because of their integral role in family production, landless women from these groups were most in need of full time work at adequate levels of remuneration. Finally, there were many women from all social strata who were the sole or main breadwinners of their families, either because they had no male breadwinner or because the male wage was not sufficient.

The lack of any serious attention to economic sustainability had its effects on programme outcomes. In her study of the West Bengal handicraft industry, Mayoux found that only 10 per cent of the 100 IRDP and DRI beneficiaries that she interviewed were repaying their loans and working in the industry for which the loan was received. This appeared to reflect the fact that the majority of beneficiaries for government handicraft training came from the upper castes although this group constituted only 34 per cent of the total population. They participated in the training as a way of acquiring useful 'female' skills while waiting to get married while others did it for the stipend. Landless women who had hoped to use their training to improve their earnings, on the other hand, found that the nature of the courses militated against this. The emphasis on training in the use of sewing machines was useless for women who had no hope of getting access to one. Bamboo and cane work was taught when there was no cane readily available in the area. It is worth noting the contrast between the social composition of government handicraft schemes described by Mayoux and privately run handicraft industries which were generally successful, profit-making enterprises: in the latter, the majority of women employed (78 per cent) were landless,

23 per cent were Muslims, 39 per cent scheduled castes and 12 per cent scheduled tribes. In other words, women who needed incomes and would have benefited from government assistance were more likely to be recruited by private enterprise than by government schemes.

To sum up, therefore, the IRDP's failure to reach poor women appeared to reflect the interplay of two sets of factors. The first related to gender differentials in the constraints experienced by women as a result of local workings of the structures of kinship, community and market and it is worth noting that these tend to be most unfavourable in precisely those states where IRDP failures are most marked: UP, MP, Bihar and Rajasthan. Indeed, Drèze found that in his village study in UP, not a *single* female beneficiary had been included in the whole IRDP list for that year. However, these institutionalised disadvantages appear to have been exacerbated by the lack of attention to the interplay of gender and poverty on the part of programme officials and their imposition of biases and preconceptions which were a reflection of their own social backgrounds and positions rather than a response to the ground reality.

The Gender Dimensions of Institutional Exclusion: Insights from a Women-specific Programme

The manifest failure of IRDP to reach credit to poorer women, as documented in the Mid-Term Review of IRDP, led to the setting up of DWCRA (Development of Women and Children in Rural Areas) with UNICEF assistance in 1982–83. Started as a pilot project in 50 selected districts, it has since been extended to other districts and by 1994/95 it was being implemented throughout India. Designed to address some of the exclusionary implications of IRDP, the goal of DWCRA was to bring about an overall improvement in the quality of life of women and children from households which qualified for IRDP assistance, by creating credit-based opportunities for self employment for poor women and by improving their access to and utilisation of services like child care, mother and child health care and adult education. Thus although DWCRA was intended as a sub-programme of IRDP, its objectives were wider and encompassed both economic and social aspects.

If the gender disadvantages that poor women faced made it difficult for them to compete for IRDP loans with poor men from similar backgrounds, then an assessment of a women-specific intervention like DWCRA can help to provide further insights into the interaction of gender and poverty in shaping women's access to and benefits from credit, in the context of a programme where they were *not* having to compete for available resources with poor men. Women's gender-intensified disadvantage would not therefore handicap them here. Furthermore, at least in its conceptualisation, DWCRA was designed to address precisely some of the gender-specific constraints which had hampered women's ability to participate in IRDP. This suggests, a priori at least, that to the extent that DWCRA failed to achieve its objectives, its failure was more likely to be a consequence of the third mechanism of exclusion we have identified viz. *gender biases and preconceptions* on the part of programme officials.

There are in fact very few studies of the impact of DWCRA but those that exist provide some insight into the gender ideologies, norms and practices embedded in the implementation process and help to explain various aspects of 'unruliness' in programme outcomes. A major evaluation by Mode (1990) carried out in 8 states in 11 districts along with a number of smaller scale studies, suggest fewer targeting errors compared to IRDP. The norm of minimum coverage of women from scheduled caste and tribal households was exceeded in most districts; beneficiaries tended to be from landless or land poor households and were generally not literate. Women-headed households made up around 10–20 per cent of beneficiaries while women-maintained households made up an additional 10–20 per cent.

However, DWCRA performed less satisfactorily when it came to improving the economic situation of poor women. Most the women interviewed in the Mode evaluation had joined DWCRA to earn extra income but very few of the DWCRA groups were economically active. Where women were active, it was on an individual or household rather than a group basis. A higher proportion of those who were economically active under DWCRA reported an increase in family income in the past three years compared to those who were not active, but average earnings were higher from non-DWCRA activities in six out of the 11 districts. Furthermore, the Mode study also suggested that the access of group members to IRDP loans had been low—less than 20 per cent of group members in seven of the eleven districts had utilised such loans—although this was one of the rationales for setting up a separate scheme for women.

The 'Gender' Subtext of DWCRA: Welfare and Welfarism

What factors might lie behind these outcomes? First of all, even a superficial comparison of IRDP and DWCRA throws up some of the stylised features of an ostensibly 'gender-neutral', but implicitly male-biased programme compared to one that is explicitly woman-specific. Bureaucratic interventions codify specific patterns of rules, resources and entitlement—who is eligible, in what capacity and on what terms—which signal the construction of particular categories of beneficiaries. Further insight on the significance attached by the government to the beneficiary in question is also communicated by how an intervention is funded and where it is located. The IRDP was funded from the outset by the central government from its mainstream poverty allevation programme written into the Fifth Five Year Plan. While women from poor households were explicitly 'named' as beneficiaries of IRDP, there was no further acknowledgement of the gendered dimensions of their institututional exclusion so that in practice, the goal of the programme to deliver subsidised assets to an individual *member* from a poor household was translated by programme implementors as the delivery of assets to an individual *male* member from poor households.

DWCRA, on the other hand, was set up as a pilot project largely funded by an outside donor agency, UNICEF. It exclusively targeted women from poor households for participation in a programme intended to enhance their welfare and thus precluded direct competition with poor men. However, the pervasiveness and deep-rootedness of gender ideologies and preconceptions within the government itself led to the introduction of inclusion and exclusion biases in selection procedures adopted by DWCRA. Whereas in the case of IRDP no relevance was attached to marital status and familial roles in defining eligible beneficiaries, the explicit link made between women and children in the 'naming' of DWCRA led to the implicit construction of eligible women primarily in terms of motherhood roles and, almost by corollary, of secondary earners. An official rationale for linking women and children under the rubric of DWCRA was to ensure that women's reproductive responsiblities were taken account of in the design of productive activities. Unofficially, and perhaps inevitably, this rationale was translated into procedures which had the effect of severely curtailing the scope of the programme in serving poor women. First of all, informal instructions were given to the gram sevikas to target only married women (Mode 1990) on the pretext that as women moved out of their natal villages at marriage, any investment in them was lost. However, a programme which explicitly links women and children together is in any case likely to militate in practice against the selection of unmarried women, particularly when family planning is a key component of the services that DWCRA groups are to be assisted in accessing. At the same time, while the programme had envisaged improving women's access to the child care programmes of the government, in reality this did not materialise so that the participation of poor women with children was also curtailed.

Although a significant proportion of group members studied by the Mode evaluation were the major or sole breadwinners of their households, the prevailing attitude among government officials remained the traditional welfarist one: DWCRA was described by one official as a 'spoon-feeding programme' for poor women. Such welfarism was reflected in the indifference to questions of financial viability in the recommendation of economic activities for DWCRA members. According to the DWCRA manual, the selection of economic activity should be left to group members with the sole qualification that the activity be viable and one for which forward and backward linkages (skill training, raw materials and marketing) were available locally. The manual did however provide an 'illustrative' list of activities which could be taken up under DWCRA. As with IRDP, the 'illustrative' list was intended merely for illustrative purposes but, as with the

IRDP, it tended to be closely adhered to in practice. The DWCRA list had certain predictable differences to the IRDP list. DWCRA activities, such as tailoring, knitting, embroidery, weaving, agarbatti making etc., tended to be more home-based, required lower levels of investment and generated lower incomes. Loans for land purchase and irrigation which could substantially increase the economic and social status of women, were conspicuous by their absence in the DWCRA list, though listed as potential activities under IRDP. Thus, while the illustrative activities listed under IRDP were generally determined by the existing pattern of self-employment among potential beneficiaries, resulting in the phenomenon of the 'IRDP cow', the list was even narrower in the case of DWCRA, because here the normative parameter of '*location*' of activity (was it home-based or not) further curtailed selection of activities.

The result, as a report by the National Institute of Public Cooperation and Child Development, (1988) suggests, was that DWCRA activities tended to be extremely narrow and highly stereotyped and officials frequently imposed the same activity for all group members without assessing its market potential (World Bank, 1991). In some cases, the market for raw materials had not been considered. The Mode evaluation notes a polythene bag scheme in Allahabad where the raw material had to be procured from Lucknow; detergent, papier mâché, dyeing and printing groups in Hazaribagh where women had to go to the cities for their raw materials; and even in the more traditonal activity of basket-making, women in one area had to walk several kilometres to obtain the necessary grass. In other cases, inadequate attention had been paid to the nature of demand for a product. Thus the Mode report notes that in Hazaribagh, where there was a local tradition of female involvement in papad-making, loans were made available to DWCRA groups for the promotion of papad-making schemes. The level of papad production in the area consequently increased but there was no commensurate increase in sales; the Mode evaluation noted that the problem lay in the fact that the DWCRA producers were from scheduled caste households, unlike those who had been involved traditionally, and that their papad could not be consumed by other castes.

The Dilution of Innovation in Women-specific Programmes

Dilution of the more innovative aspects of the programme occurred though a variety of (non-) practices. Based on her examination of available reports and evaluations as well as interviews conducted with officials in the Ministry of Rural Development, Ramachandran (1995) found that very little effort had been made to communicate its innovative rationale, concepts and strategies to the officials at state and district level who were responsible for actual implemention. In fact, her scrutiny of Government of India directives and government orders revealed that once the programme had been approved at the highest levels, the conceptual documents explaining the rationale of the programme were put to one side and only the financial and adminstrative guidelines were circulated to the implementing agencies lower down the bureaucratic hierarchy. Not surprisingly, this led 'to a major gap in the objectives of the programme and implementation on the ground' (Ramachandran, 1995, p. 8).

The dilution of objectives as DWCRA moved from design stage to implementation in Rajasthan is graphically illustrated in Ahuja and Jain's documentation of the varying descriptions of DWCRA offered by a series of institutional actors in the course of a state level workshop held to introduce and discuss the programme with the district and state level officials who would be responsible for programme implementation (Ahuja and Jain, 1986). The most comprehensive description of the programme's concepts and strategies was contained in the original report published by UNICEF: it stated that 'While women are encouraged to participate in the mainstream of the labour force, their role as mothers cannot be overlooked. And, since both roles are not incompatible, we should try to maintain a balance among our activities addressed to women so as not to overemphasise one at the expense of the other' (Lugo, 1983, cited in Ahuja and Jain (1986), p. 3). A training package in two parts was proposed, one of which would focus on family health and nutrition and the second on 'basic principles for income generation including building strength for overcoming intermediaries, getting better prices and better access to credit and skills to administer small shops or co-operatives' (p.4). Wage labour groups lobbying for better wages and the creation of child care facilities for women participating in state employment generation schemes, were also included. A capital fund was also to be made available to established groups to enable them to invest in child care support and the development of market linkages.

However, while the letter by the government of India sanctioning the scheme referred to its innovative methodology, it also described DWCRA as a sub-scheme under IRDP and the group organisers' role as one of liason between group, government agencies and banks. The dilution process was already underway. When it came to the briefing provided by Government of Rajasthan officers to participants at the Rajasthan workshop, it was very clear that they saw DWCRA purely as a sub-project of IRDP and the role of programme implementors as ensuring that 'women and children of families identified as below the poverty line as per IRDP criteria could be motivated, organised and benefited to existing government schemes' (Hooja, cited in Ahuja and Jain, p. 6). Thus, as Ahuja and Jain point out, by the time DWCRA reached those who were responsible for implementation, it was presented as neither new nor innovative but as providing an additionality to the existing IRDP programme: 'the message conveyed directly as well as implicitly was DWCRA is IRDP and TRYSEM for women'.

The absence of any attention to equipping staff at DRDA and BDO levels to deal with the social goals of the programme meant that the rationale for its more innovative aspects—such as processes of group formation—had not filtered into their consciousness. The target-driven mentality which characterised IRDP implementation resurfaced in DWCRA: Ramachandran found in her discussion with DWCRA officials that it led to the hasty formation of DWCRA groups with the main emphasis on the economic, rather than the social, components of the programme while a review of DWCRA in Rajasthan noted 'that the implementation of the programme is restricted to accomplishment of targets without concern for actual results' (PRADAN, p. 22). As a result there was very little group cohesiveness, and members joined DWCRA groups with the sole purpose of availing of loans (World Bank, 1991). Finding twenty women eligible in one village was often problematic, and thus women from different villages were brought together to form a group which made it difficult for them to meet periodically. In six out of the eleven districts where Mode conducted a survey of DWCRA groups, it was found that group members were not even familiar with each other.

Conclusion: Targeting Women or Transforming Practice?

We have suggested that government efforts can be seen as attempts to address the exclusion of poor people from mainstream sources of credit. Our analysis suggests that the government's strategy of creating 'add-on' schemes within mainstream banking institutions has not been particularly effective in compensating for the exclusion of the poor. Instead, it led to the creation of highly piecemeal and compartmentalised efforts to address some of their credit needs. The indivisibilities of production and power which characterise poverty, combined with the incoherence in the goals built into the design and implementation of IRDP, have led to the uneven distribution of its benefits among the eligible population.

Our analysis also suggests that attempts to address the additional gender-related constraints that poor women face in relation to poor men and which place them at a greater disadvantage in realising their entitlements cannot be reduced to 'quotas for women' as in IRDP or women-specific target groups as in DWCRA. Such narrowly formulated responses serve merely to institutionalise the marginal position given to women in official development. The analysis of both programmes and, in particular, of the process by which the more innovative aspects of DWCRA were transformed into yet another welfarist intervention for women, points to the silent and continuous interaction between the forces of gender discrimination in different institutional sites of society. The failure to communicate the rationale for these innovative aspects to those responsible for implementation, combined with the prejudices, biases and social orientation of the implementors, who in any case faced a multiplicity of 'rural development' programmes, meant that little was actually achieved within these programmes to percieve or challenge the gender-specific disadvantages of poor women. This does not mean of course that there are no examples of 'bureacratic activism' where local officials have taken the initiative to infuse anti-poverty programmes with a fresh and innovative spirit. Such positive examples suggest that where local conditions are right (see Thakur, 1995; Ramanchandran, 1995) or there is a powerful commitment on the part of an official (Mehendale, 1991), apparently moribund programmes can be given a whole new lease of life. However, the power of internal organisational imperatives of bureaucratic implementing agencies to dilute, dominate or subvert the rules, procedures and outcomes of a programme and the need for a comprehensive transformation of these organisations are key lessons that emerge from our analysis.

Notes

[1]Thus within labour and commodity markets, people can exchange what they own or control for a different bundle of resources; through selling their labour power in the production of goods and services for a wage in cash or kind, they can exchange the commodities they have produced. Within financial markets, people can use their assets as collateral to raise capital for their productive enterprises. Within the household and other kin-based organisations, entitlements are very often governed by implicit rather than explicit contractual arrangements, whose legitimacy rests on customary norms and practices rather than legally enforceable ones. Community-based entitlements for instance to the use of common property resources may also embody notions of entitlements that rest on accepted norms and customs rather than having a legalistic status.

[2]The phrase comes from (Fraser, 1989).

[3]It is worth noting for instance that among many non-governmental organisations, the poor are identified by occupational categories defined in relation to land e.g. small, marginal farmers or tenant farmers, landless labourers, rural artisans are generally targeted by such organisations as being among the poorest sections.

References

Ajuha, K. and S. Jain, 1986. 'An Evaluation of DWCRA: Banswara and Alwar districts', mimeo, Jaipur: Institute of Development Studies.

Bagchee, S., 1987. "Poverty Alleviation Programmes in the Seventh Plan: An Evaluation" *Economic and Political Weekly*, Vol. XXII (4).

Drèze J., 1988. "Social Insecurity in India: A Case Study", paper prepared for Workshop on Social Security in Developing Countries, London: London School of Economics.

Drèze J., 1990. "Poverty in India and the IRDP delusion", *Economic and Political Weekly* Vol. 25, (39), pp. A95–104.

Department of Rural Development, 1991. *Manual for IRDP and Allied Programmes of TRYSEM and DWCRA* Department of Rural Development, Ministry of Agriculture, New Delhi: Government of India.

Everett J. and M. Savara, 1991. "Institutional Credit as a Strategy Towards Self-reliance for Petty Commodity Producers in India: A Critical Evaluation' in H. Afshar (ed) *Women, Development and Survival in the Third World* London: Longman Publishers.

Fraser, N., 1989. *Unruly Practices. Power, Discourse and Gender in Contemporary Social Theory.* Cambridge: Polity Press.

Joshi, A., 1990. "Poverty Alleviation Programmes—Target Setting and Removal of Poverty: A Case Study of Villages in Maharashtra", *The Administrator*, Vol XXXVI No. 3.

Joshi, S., 1995. *Consumption Credit and Self-help Groups in India* mimeo, , Sussex: Institute of Development Studies.

Kabeer, N., 1994. *Reversed Realities: Gender Hierarchies in Development Thought* London-New York: Verso Press and Delhi, Kali for Women.

Kurian, N.J., 1987. "IRDP: How relevant is it?", *Economic and Political Weekly* Vol. XXII(52).

Mayoux, L., 1989. 'Income Generation for Women in India: Problems and Prospects", *Development Policy Review* Vol. 7, 5–28.

Mehendale, L., 1981. "The Integrated Rural Development Programme for Women in Developing Countries: What More Can be Done? A Case Study from India" in H. Afshar (ed) *Women, Development and Survival in the Third World* London: Longman Publishers.

MODE, 1990: *Development of Women and Children in Rural Areas: An Evaluation of DWCRA* report prepared for UNICEF, India.

Murthy, R. K., 1994. *Participatory Research on Credit Needs of Women: Lessons From Nari Nidhi* mimeo, Patna: Adithi.

Osmani, S.R., 1988. *"Social Security in South Asia"*, STICKERD Working Paper No. 18, London: London School of Economics.

Pulley, R.V., 1989. "Making The Poor Creditworthy: A Case Study of the Integrated Rural Development Programme in India", *World Bank Discussion Papers 58*, Washington: The World Bank.

Ramachandran, V., 1995. *The Making of Mahila Samakhya: A Personal Narrative* mimeo, Delhi.

Rath, N., 1985. "Garibi Hatao: Can IRDP Do It?", *Economic and Political Weekly*, Vol XX No. 6.

Rose, K., 1992. *Where Women Are Leaders: The SEWA Movement in India* London and New Jersey: Zed Books Ltd.

Swaminathan, M., 1990. "Village Level Implementation of IRDP. Comparison of West Bengal and Tamil Nadu", *Economic and Political Weekly*, March 31st, pp. a17–A27.

Thakur, S., 1995. "Women, Poverty and Empowerment—Field Notes on Nellore District, Andhra Pradesh and Raisen District Madhya Pradesh", mimeo, Mussoorie: Lal Bahadur Shastri Academy.

Thangamuthu, C. and N. Manimekalai, 1989. "Generation of Employment For Women Through DWCRA", *Journal of Rural Development*, Vol 8 (4).

Viswanath, V., 1989. "Extending Credit to Rural Women: NGO Models from South India", *World Bank Working Paper 184*, Washington: The World Bank.

World Bank, 1990. *World Development Report*. Oxford: Oxford University Press.

World Bank, 1991. *Gender and Poverty in India* Washington: The World Bank.

World Bank, 1989. *India: Poverty, Employment and Social Services* Washington: The World Bank.

Section 2

From Concepts to Practice

7

From Concepts to Practice

Gender-aware Planning through the Institutional Framework

NAILA KABEER AND RAMYA SUBRAHMANIAN

Introduction

The design, implementation and evaluation of policy and planning efforts do not occur in a social vacuum. Rather they are intended as responses to problems which are outcomes of specific institutional operations and they are designed, implemented and have consequences within specific institutional settings. In this chapter, we demonstrate the ways in which systematic gender analysis of a particular issue or 'problem' can be applied to subsequent stages of the planning process: the analysis of problems, the design of interventions and the evaluation of results. The chapters in this section illustrate the application of the institutional framework, outlined in the first section of this book, to a set of sectoral case-studies and provide the bases from which we lay out a methodology and a set of procedures and tools which can help to ensure that a gender-aware approach is used in the planning and design of interventions.

In order to address the ways in which the aims and strategies of public policy are planned, we start by articulating our understanding of policy. Firstly, we must emphasise that our concept of planning echoes the use of the term 'policy practice' (Gasper and Apthorpe 1996:6) as a way of overcoming false dichotomies between the formulation of policies and the processes by which they are made operational. Secondly, we acknowledge that, as Gasper notes, 'Public policy discourse is notably complex and further, has important distinctive features, including the need to incorporate value inputs, considerations of legitimacy, and assessments of the constraints on public action.' (1996:36). A statement of policy implicitly includes both a view of the world as well as a set of decisions embedded in a political and material context. Recognising both these integral and inter-related aspects of policy, we start with a very simple proposition which focuses our subsequent discussion.

Figure 1: Designing Inverventions: the technical relationship

INDIRECT MEANS	DIRECT MEANS	ENDS

Stripped to its essential elements, a policy statement can be conceptualised as a relationship between a desired end(s) and the range of means selected to achieve it (Figure 1). At the level of policy design itself, the first problem that arises is that for every chosen end, there are a number of possible means, while the finite means available to policy makers lend themselves to a variety of different ends. Thus, the basic dilemma for policy makers is how to go about selecting specific sets of means and ends over others. The second problem is that the selection procedure has been dominated by the most powerful interests within a community, who tend not only to be the most visible and audible to policy-makers, but often to be dominant within the policy-making process itself. Apthorpe uses the term 'framing' to describe the ways in which policies crucially determine or specify 'what and who is actually included, and what and who is ignored and excluded'; Kabeer (1994) uses the terms 'privileging' and 'suppressing' to further indicate that both conscious interest politics as well as unconscious bias may play a role in policy 'framing'. At the level of implementation or practice, too, the effects of policy framing in conjunction with institutional processes and management practices of implementing organisations further determine exclusionary and inclusive impacts.

To return to policy design, we can identify these issues in terms of two critical axes against which we frame, analyse or evaluate policy: *structural and ideological factors* shaping policy practice and *procedural aspects* of frameworks or methods of planning for policy practice. The first part of this chapter investigates some of the structural and ideological factors that shape the ways in which the ends and means of development are framed, and suggests an alternative framing based on the perspectives of the most disadvantaged. The second part presents a gender-aware methodology for problem analysis which can feed into the project or intervention management cycle, from design, to appraisal, execution, monitoring and evaluation. Our discussion in this section is loosely organised around the planning sequence embedded in goal-oriented project planning (GTZ n.d.) in order to illustrate how a gender analysis can be integrated into a widely utilised set of planning tools, and is illustrated with examples drawn from an overview of the Indian literature on the credit needs of the poor provided in Kabeer and Murthy (1996). The concluding section pulls together examples from the chapters that follow on the ways in which interventions can be designed to strengthen women's agency and participation in the articulation of their own priorities and interests.

Policy Formulation as the Relationship between Means and Ends

Rethinking 'ends'

The persistent conflation between development and economic growth is one product of the asymmetrical representation of interests in the policy-making domain. The voices of the poor, particularly poor women, who are most likely to remind policy-makers that economic growth is only a means to the desired goals of development are also least likely to be heard or listened to within the policy domain. The idea that the priorities of poor women should be the starting point for thinking about development policy should not be taken to imply that they are more knowledgeable than others but rather that they offer the viewpoint from below, a viewpoint of those who stand at the crossroads of various forms of inequality—class, gender and often race and caste as well. For the purposes of our planning exercise, therefore, we will begin with the priorities of the poor, and of poor women in particular.

If, as is generally accepted, human well-being is the desired 'end' of all development efforts, the first question must be what constitutes human well-being for those who have been largely excluded from the policy-making process? Whose priorities should count? There is a considerable body of research that suggests that as far as the poor are concerned, well-being is made up by the goals of survival, security and self-esteem (Chambers, 1988; Jodha, 1985). For most poor people—women as well as men—survival is an over-riding preoccupation because of the precariousness of their livelihoods and security is likely to be significant for the same reasons. Policy formulation for a human-centred development therefore requires that priority be given to interventions which meet the basic survival needs of the poor and that the means adopted also serve to strengthen security of livelihoods and reduce dependency relationships. In as much as gender equity is integral to a human-centered development project, it is necessary to ensure that these broad goals of survival, security and agency are met for women as well as men and we may then need to ask how the survival and security needs of poor women, as well as their ability to exercise agency and choice over their own lives, might differ from those of poor men. This approach would need to underpin interventions in all sectors, so that even, for example, an education intervention would need to evolve on the basis of understanding how access to education is shaped from the perspectives of poor households, and how education interventions can be designed in a way to enhance the survival, security and well-being of poor men and women (see for example Rajagopal's chapter in this volume).

The selection of ends is not a simple or uncontested process. The notion of well-being does not have a uniform meaning for all sections of society, and policies which aim to bring about the enhancement of human well-being must be informed by the definitions of those whose well-being is being planned for rather than by the definitions of those who are doing the planning. Several factors can result in the selective interpretation of what constitutes "well-being" in contexts of complex needs and conflicting interests. One is the strong possibility of personal, subjective bias entering the process of designing the goals of interventions, especially when a male-dominated institution is involved in evolving interventions to address issues that explicitly concern women, such as violence against women within the family. Chikarmane's chapter provides several examples of the ways in which interventions aimed at sensitive handling of intra-family violence against women often reflect the biases of the men who implement law and policy at the cutting-edge—the policemen—raising the question: "what does well-being mean?" There is thus a strong need for policy-makers and planners to constantly carry out 'reality checks' to ensure that their preconceptions and prejudices do not bias the design of their interventions. In the light of the power relations which permeate almost all institutional contexts, we would stress here the critical importance of participatory methodologies as a means of carrying out such reality checks informing even the selection of 'ends'.

A related problem concerns conflicts of interests between different actors, who are all the subjects of policy. Development interventions involve many actors, including those whose interests may conflict with the people the policy is ostensibly designed to help, raising the question: "whose well-being?" In the case of interventions in domestic violence against women, the interests of violent husbands and of battered wives are likely to conflict, particularly in the immediate aftermath of a violent incident. In such situations it is clearly the well-being of the battered woman with which policies should be concerned. However, as Chikarmane shows, the 'end' of family reconciliation is often interpreted to mean the husband's interest in saving face and reconciling his family, rather than the 'end' of not just enabling, but also securing, the woman's well-being.

Figure 2: Designing Interventions: the social content of 'ends'

RESOURCES AS INPUTS ⟶ RESOURCES AS OUTPUTS ⟶ BROADER GOALS
- Human well-being
- Survival, security, autonomy)

Figure 2 reformulates the 'ends' side of the policy equation as human well-being and suggests key dimensions to be taken into account to achieve the well-being of the poor.

The significance of means

If human well-being is the overall goal of development, what are the 'means'? The focus in much of mainstream planning in the past has been on material resources or 'things' as the 'means' of development: (land, assets, finance, equipment, infrastructure etc.). However, there are two additional categories of resources critical to an equitable development which are equally important and have sometimes been overlooked. The first category encompasses human resources. Human beings enter the policy process in two capacities: human well being is the final goal of development and human labour, energy, skills, creativity and imagination are the most important means.

In addition, along with material and human resources, one of the essential components in development activities are the intangible social resources which people create through their association with each other. In as much as poor people in general, and poor women in particular, are so often excluded from mainstream institutional allocations, these social resources are a critical element in their survival strategies. However, the disempowerment of the poor and marginalised often lies in the fact that the relationships they are able to mobilise to underwrite their survival and security tend to be based on patronage and dependency rather than on solidarity and reciprocity. Consequently, security has to be traded for autonomy in the interests of survival. For women who are generally most cut off from independent access to socially-valued resources, this trade-off takes a particularly intensified form in that their ability to define and act on their own priorities can often only be achieved by sacrificing the protection of hierarchical familial relationships. Unless the intangible aspects of human well-being (which powerful groups take for granted as their right and privilege) and the intangible resources which they frequently entail are integrated into the conceptualisation and design of policy, the poor will remain the objects of policy and the passive recipients of charity. Consequently, different 'means' for achieving policy goals have to be assessed not only in terms of their technical efficiency but also in terms of how well they contribute to the broader goals of survival, security and human dignity.

Intangible factors both enable social change to take place as well as inhibit processes of change. Rajagopal's chapter on education shows how fears about women's safety can be a major disincentive for parents to send girls to school. These fears are rooted both in the material reality of women's existence in the given context, as well as in ideological constructions, reinforced by traditional beliefs, about the appropriate sites of female participation (private rather than public). The 'means' of interventions need to build on those intangible factors that *enable* poor people, women in particular, to work towards their own security and survival with dignity, as well as remove those that *disable* women's participation. Thus we emphasise that recognising non-quantifiable yet qualitatively significant intangible processes, resources and support structures and making those the 'means' of interventions in the context of ends of 'well-being' will enhance the autonomy and self-reliance of those whom the intervention is designed to address. These we call the *'strategic means'* of development.

Here we would put forward a second rationale for the importance of participatory methodologies in gender-aware planning: enabling the participation of the excluded in the process of policy design is not only critical to ensure policy goals which respond to their priorities but is also a strategic means for overcoming social exclusion. We return to this point later when we identify some of the strategic means which contain within them the power to transform relationships of inequality between women and men. Figure 3 presents an expanded version of the means-ends relationships, stressing the multiplicity of resources which make up the means of development and the need to relate them to the broader goal of human well-being.

Finally, Figure 4 draws attention to the fact that all means-ends relationships exist within institutional contexts, that these institutions are sites of rules and resources, production and allocation/distribution and that the power relations within them determine the ability of different categories of people to achieve the goals of survival, security and

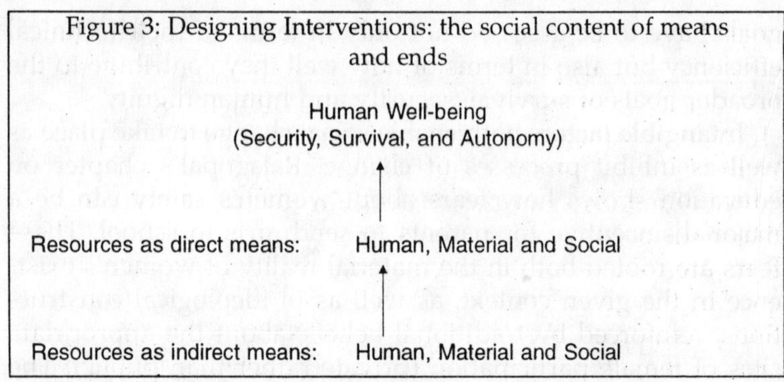

Figure 3: Designing Interventions: the social content of means and ends

Human Well-being
(Security, Survival, and Autonomy)
Resources as direct means:
Human, Material and Social
Resources as indirect means:
Human, Material and Social

Figure 4: Designing Interventions: the institutional content of means and ends

'Ends'
Whose?
Human Well-being
(Security, Surival, Autonomy)
Distribution Practices
(Institutional Locations)
Rules, Organisation, Allocation
Direct 'means'
Who owns what, who gets what, on what basis, who benefits, who decides?
Human, Material, Social Resources
Production Practices
(Institutional Locations)
Rules, Organisation + Allocation
Indirect 'means'
Who owns what, who does what (and how), who gets what, on what basis, who benefits, who decides?
Human, Material, Social Resources

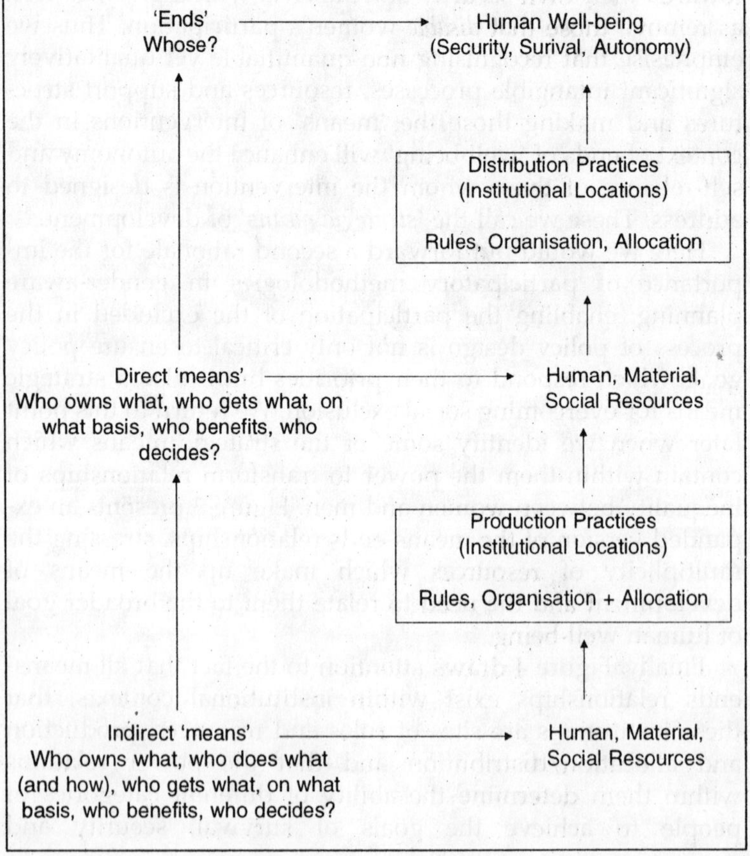

autonomy. Consequently, in order to understand why shortfalls in the achievement of well-being occur, we have to locate the observed shortfalls in the institutional sites in which they are produced and explore the structure of rules, norms and practices which characterise the relevant organisations, the constraints and possibilities which they generate and the causes and effects of the resulting shortfalls. This includes the institutional framework for households, markets, communities and state which we presented in the previous section. Here we also emphasise the importance of looking at the institutional sites of organisations which are involved in the management and delivery of services.

A key point underpinning all of this is the importance of participatory research methodologies and methods in providing the information through which problems can be identified, analysed and appropriate responses designed, in order to address what Gasper refers to as "the underdefinition of problems and criteria" in public policy (1996:36). Thinking through the relationship between the means and ends of development and ensuring that they are compatible and not in conflict is integral to the achievement of ends of well-being. Our emphasis on policy practice also leads us to reiterate the close interlinkages between analysis and response; the risks that derive from uncertainty, institutional variations, and the politics of interventionism are dealt with in the next section of the book.

From Analysis to Response: Designing Gender-aware Interventions

In this section we will be demonstrating the application of the institutional framework to the analysis of the causes and effects of problematic development outcomes in order to establish the means and ends through which the problem can be addressed. Our discussion is loosely organised around the planning sequence embedded in goal-oriented project planning (NORAD, n.d.; GTZ, n.d.) in order to illustrate how a gender analysis can be integrated into a widely utilised set of planning tools.

For the purposes of demonstrating this part of the gender relations framework, we will be drawing on the overview of the Indian literature on the credit needs of the poor provided in Kabeer and Murthy (1996; also this volume), as an example of how a gender-sensitive response (here credit) for a perceived or known problem (poverty) would be designed if taken through a gender-aware process of analysis as suggested in this book.

We suggest two levels or stages through which analysis of a problem can become the foundation for the design of interventions:

- **Identification of the problem (the rationale)**

⇒ Analysis of the causes of the problem
⇒ Analysis of the effects of the problem

- **Analysis of the objectives of intervention**

⇒ Identification of ends
⇒ Identification of the means

These two stages of analysis form the basis for the design of a gender-aware intervention, the outlines of which follow the analysis below.

a. Identifying the problem, its causes and effects

The relevance of credit to the poor will depend on how their poverty is conceptualised. Kabeer and Murthy (1996) suggest that one way of conceptualising poverty is as the product of multiple and frequently interlocking forms of exclusion with regard to the mainstream institutions through which people meet their basic needs in any given society. In the Indian context, there is considerable evidence to suggest the exclusion from reliable and non-exploitative sources of credit is one of the basic causes of poverty. The *core problem* that an intervention would need to address then is the *lack of access of poor men and women to institutional credit.*

Accepting this analysis for the purposes of exposition, a first step in our planning process will be to identify some of the causes and effects of the exclusion of the poor from access to credit. This includes identifying the organisations through which credit is distributed in rural areas in India in order to identify the barriers to access by the poor, and hence the reasons for the observed shortfalls in access to credit which we demonstrate in (a) below, as a generic, gender-blind analysis. However, the poor do not constitute a homogenous group. The significance of gender and caste as further axes of inclusion and exclusion in the Indian context suggest that the rules and practices of the credit delivery system 'entitle' women and men from different castes differently and unequally and must be factored into the account. In (b) we focus on the gender dimensions of exclusion, to demonstrate a gender-aware analysis of the identified problem. In both levels of analysis presented below, the demonstration of the framework is based on analysis drawn from Kabeer and Murthy (1996).

(a) The exclusion of the poor from formal credit: a gender-blind analysis

Formal financial organisations together with government-administered credit programmes, often in collaboration with the banking sector, constitute the mainstream of the credit system in India. At the community level, there are money-lenders and neighbourhood networks as well as a range of non-governmental efforts to meet the credit needs of the poor. An *institutional mapping* of credit organisations and their lending practices will immediately make clear that the poor are largely excluded from the mainstream banking system and even from much of the government's poverty-oriented lending and must rely largely on informal sources. However, the limitations associated with informal sources (e.g. usurious rates of interest charged by money-lenders; clientilist relations involved in borrowing from landlords; the insufficiency of funds from neighbourhood networks) mean that they are unlikely to constitute a long-term and sustainable solution to the problem of poverty.

In order to build regularised access, it is essential to understand the causes of institutional exclusion. This then becomes our analytical starting-point. In India, as elsewhere, the overarching goal of commercial banks is profit maximisation and corporate efficiency, leading to an institutionalised preference for dealing with local entrepreneurial elites who are perceived as 'people they can do business with'. From the point of view of bankers, lending to the poor is rife with problems: transaction costs are high (owing to the small amount of loan required by the poor and high cost of monitoring loans), recovery of loans is a problem (dispersed borrowers and their micro-enterprises, physical distance, wilful default and non-wilful crisis-led default), and there is low security for loans (collateral provided is often not easily disposable). While banks are clearly constrained institutionally from lending to the poor, the perspective from the borrowers' end is equally bleak. Not only are bank procedures fairly inflexible, they are also structured to reflect the kind of clientele that banks consider themselves best suited to serve: literate, knowledgeable, self-confident, urban and generally male entrepreneurs. From the point of view of the illiterate and largely rural poor, loan application procedures are lengthy, wordy and dense; bank staff have a limited and unsympathetic understanding of how their enterprises work and of the kinds of constraints poor borrowers are likely to face.

The various rules, norms and practices which lead to the exclusion of poor people from the formal banking sector can be organised as a hierarchy of causes and effects, distinguishing between different levels of causation—*immediate, underlying and structural*—and a corresponding hierarchy of effects. By precisely locating the identified problem's immediate effects and their causes, we stress that problem analysis often begins with that which is manifest or easy to observe, or commonly perceived to constitute evidence of the problem. By taking immediately perceived effects and causes as our first level, we are also suggesting that short-term impacts, because they have such an immediate effect on household well-being, are often needs to which responses are considered most urgently required. However, we also suggest that underpinning the short-term observable effects and causes of a problem, are intermediate and structural or medium-term and long-term effects and causes, which give rise to the immediate effects and causes identified. These levels are harder to pinpoint because they may be less visible, refer to power relations that lie outside of a specific context which is being studied or where an intervention is being designed, or can be made visible only through a different kind of methodology of research or analysis.

Figure 5.1: Gender-blind analysis

Analysing poor people's access to credit: causes and effects (gender-blind)

Long-term effects	Indebtedness; vulnerability; improverishment; disempowerment
Intermediate effects	Shortfalls in consumption; reduced capacity to recover from crisis
Immediate effects	Fluctuations in household income flows; resort to unreliable/exploitative forms of credit
The core problem	Lack of access to institutional credit
Immediate causes	
Household-based:	Lack of collateral; lack of self-confidence; uncertain repayment capacity
Bank-based:	Collateral requirements; complex and inflexible procedures; perception of poor as high-risk borrowers
Intermediate causes	
Household-based:	Low productivity enterprises; uncertainty of returns; illiteracy; ignorance about banking procedures; class distance from bank; personnel imperatives
Bank-based:	Risk-averse culture; perceived costs of lending to the poor; class distance from the poor
Structural causes:	Entrenched banking practices; unequal distribution of assets; imperfect financial markets; inadequate educational provision

Figure 5.1 presents the more conventional version of this analysis to be found in the general literature which tends to be couched in generic and gender-neutral terms. Such formulations suggest that poor women face the same problems as poor men in accessing credit, and suffer similar effects, so that there is no need for a gender-disaggregated analysis.

(b) The exclusion of the poor from formal credit: a gender-aware analysis

As we noted earlier, the routine use of non-gendered generic categories, such as 'the poor' and 'the landless', in the analysis of development problems has long helped to obscure the degree of internal differentiation and inequality within these groups. Ostensibly gender-neutral analysis is frequently extremely gender-biased in its assumptions and its implications and there is sufficient evidence now available to suggest that poor men and women in India do not have the same credit

> In Chapter 1 in this volume, Kabeer suggests three distinct, but obviously inter-related, categories of gender disadvantage:
>
> - ***Gender-intensified disadvantage*** refers to those disadvantages which women and men share, but which women suffer in a more intensified form. Thus illiteracy, lack of collateral, low self-confidence, social distance from banking staff are all problems which men experience in gaining access to bank credit but which women suffer in a more intensified form.
> - ***Gender-specific disadvantage*** refers to those constraints which women suffer by virtue of being women: the ideology of the male breadwinner, the constraints imposed by norms of female seclusion; the difficulties of combining domestic labour with entrepreneurial activity.
> - ***Bureaucratically-imposed gender disadvantage*** are forms of disadvantage which have little to do with the actual reality of women's lives but are the product of the biases, prejudices and sometimes straightforward ignorance of bankers as well as of the officials who are responsible for delivering development resources to the poor.

needs or face the same credit constraints. The question then is: what lies behind the disproportionate exclusion of poor women from both the formal banking sector as well as from the government lending programmes administered through these banks?

Figure 5.2 presents a level of analysis further disaggregated to allow some of the additional, more invisible constraints specific to poorer women in accessing credit to become visible.

Figure 5.2: Gender-aware analysis

Causes and effects of credit-based institutional failure: a gender-aware analysis

Long-term effects	Indebtedness; vulnerability; improverishment *Women's disempowerment vis à vis men* *Gender inequalities in physical wellbeing*
Intermediate effects	Shortfalls in consumption; reduced capacity to recover from crisis + *Gender inequalities in distribution of consumption shortfalls* *Increased dependence on male income*
Immediate effects	Fluctuations in hh income flows; resort to unreliable/exploitative forms of credit + *Sexually exploitative forms of credit*
The core problem:	Lack of access to institutional credit + *Gender inequalities in accessing institutional credit*
Immediate causes:	
Hh-based	Lack of collateral; Lack of self-confidence; Uncertain repayment capacity *Intensified gender disadvantage for women vis à vis collateral, self-confidence and repayment capacity* + *Women-specific disadvantage: constraints on social and physical mobility*
Bank based	Collateral requirements; complex and inflexible procedures; perceptions of poor as high-risk borrowers + *Discriminatory official and unofficial barriers against women; economic invisibility of women's enterprise*
Intermediate causes:	
Hh-based	Low productivity enterprises; uncertainty of returns; illiteracy; ignorance about banking procedures; class distance from bank personnel; survival imperatives

(*Contd*)

Figure 5.2: Gender-aware analysis (*Contd*)

	+ Intensified gender disadvantage in terms of low productivity and uncertainty of returns; illiteracy; ignorance about banking procedures; class distance from bank personnel; greater survival orientation of women's enterprises *+ Women-specific disadvantage: social isolation; gendered distance from bank personnel; uncertain control over loans/proceeds from loans.*
Bank based	Risk-averse culture; perceived costs of lending to the poor; class distance from the poor *Ideological norms about female dependency; greater perceived costs about lending to women; gendered distance from women borrowers*
Structural causes	Entrenched banking practices; unequal distribution of assets imperfect financial markets; Inadequate educational provision *Ideology of male breadwinner; gender segmented labour markets; gender biased institutional practice; intra-household power relations*

It is precisely these more invisible and submerged constraints which tend to be the basis of women's greater exclusion from mainstream allocational mechanisms. These also explain why planning credit interventions on the basis of some generic category of 'the poor' is likely to fail to meet the needs of poorer women.

While priorities and practices of banks generated by institutional rules dictate the kind of people they are best able to serve, discriminatory attitudes serve to close off any chances women might have. Bankers are as likely to subscribe to the ideology of the 'male breadwinner' as the rest of the population and not see any reason for lending to women. Studies point to the 'awkwardness' of dealing with women entrepreneurs and of engaging in follow-up activity for this more dispersed and less mobile section of borrowers (Kabeer and Murthy op cit.). Women's enterprises are generally perceived to be more risky than those of men. They often tend to be located in enterprises that are home-based, seasonal, with low capital-intensity and hence low returns. This, in turn, is partly linked to the gender division of labour and responsibilities within the household, such that women are burdened by domestic and child care responsibilities and their (women's) enterprises are more often geared to meet immediate survival and consumption needs. In addition, gender norms also constrain women to appropriate sectors, even if they themselves are willing to engage in a wider and more profitable array of enterprises. Unless a more disaggregated level of analysis is conducted, the specific constraints which women as a gender experience in accessing institutional credit, in addition to the more general ones of class, are likely to remain submerged.

The hierarchical organisation of causes and effects in Figure 5.2 helps to distinguish between the more immediate manifestations and causes of a problem—which may be possible to act upon in the short-run—and the more entrenched structural causes which entail a longer-term perspective. Our first step is to identify the different sites at which inequalities play out, leading to social exclusion from institutions, which in our chosen case are households and banks, emerging from which are the following levels entailed in gender-aware analysis:

- ***disaggregation of the problem*** into its immediate, underlying and longer-term causes and effects
- ***analysis*** of the extent to which these causes and effects are the same for men and women (but intensified for women) and the extent to which they are gender-specific (experienced only by women).

b. Components of gender-aware planning: moving from problem analysis to objectives analysis

The formats laid out above allow for the ordering of analysis into a framework for designing response, starting with *objectives analysis*. We suggest for instance that the identification of the core problem itself provides the rationale for intervention. Hence if the lack of access of poor women and men to institutional (reliable, non-exploitative) credit is identified as the key problem, the rationale for an intervention would be to *strengthen the access of poor women and men to institutional credit.* The existence of gender-specific effects of a problem can help to provide the rationale for a gender-sensitive response, pointing to effects that women specifically may experience on account of their gender, which would point to the need for gender-specific responses.

From causes and effects to means and ends

Just as causes and effects can be organised on a hierarchical basis into immediate, underlying and longer term, so too can the means and ends which they suggest. The identified effects of a problem tell us what needs to be mitigated or addressed—*the desired ends,* and the causes of the problem point in the direction of possible responses to it—*the possible means.* In mapping out causal relationships for our credit example, the hierarchy that emerges distinguishes between:

- *immediate disadvantages* causing the exclusion of the poor from formal credit sources
- the *underlying disadvantages* of class and gender which give rise to these disadvantages
- *the roots of these inequalities* in deeply-entrenched, structural arrangements.

The various levels of causes that we identified help to clarify the kind of needs and interests that have to be addressed by the policy response. Credit interventions which are designed around immediate causes may be responsive to immediate and practical needs but they are unlikely to contribute a great deal to changing the underlying causes of disadvantage which threw up these needs in the first place. Furthermore, even where interventions seek to go beyond the immediate to underlying causes, they may still confine themselves to addressing structural class disadvantage while ignoring underlying gender disadvantage. In terms of our gender analysis, they may address practical gender needs but leave unchallenged the strategic gender interests which gave rise to the gendered manifestation of the problem.

For instance, land reform may be one way of addressing the unequal distribution of wealth which underlies the exclusion of the poor from credit and commodity markets, but unless women and men are jointly entitled to redistributed land, such measures will leave a significant aspect of gender inequality intact. Our methodology suggests therefore that a gender-blind approach to the question of poverty and credit is likely to lead to one set of policy responses, based primarily on class-based disadvantage, while a gender-aware analysis is likely to lead to other or additional interventions which acknowledges the existence of gender inequalities among the poor. While some of the means we have identified—particularly those at the structural level—require changes in macro-level policy and are outside the remit of the lower-level interventions that are the focus of our discussion, spelling them out in the analysis in this way helps to make the argument that many of the class and gender constraints experienced by the poor derive from the broader environment. Unless attempts are made to tackle these broader sources of disadvantage, lower level, project-based interventions will remain limited in their achievements.

Moving from problem analysis to objectives analysis—or from the analysis of causes and effects to the analysis of means and ends—entails a reformulation of the 'negatives' of the situation into positive desirable conditions so that what were the causes of the problem now become the potential means for addressing it, while the effects of the problem are now reformulated as desired goals. This is done in the next figure which presents a comprehensive array of options for the design of interventions both gender-blind and gender-aware. Both these levels are collapsed into Figure 5.3. They help to illustrate what is entailed in the gender-aware analysis of possible responses to a problem:

- the immediate, underlying and structural causes of the problem point in the direction of the immediate practical needs and the longer term strategic interests which have to be addressed and a range of means through which this can be done.
- the existence of gender-specific causes points in the direction of the practical gender needs and strategic gender interests which have to be addressed and suggests a range of possible gender-neutral as well as gender-specific means through which this can be done.

Figure 5.3. Analysing poor people's access to credit—means and ends

Long-term ends	
Gender-blind	Self-reliance; security; accumulation; empowerment
Gender-aware	*Egalitarian intra-household relations; valued bodies; empowerment*
Intermediate ends	
Gender-blind	Smooth consumption streams; emergency funds; resilience in crisis
Gender-aware	*Equitable consumption; increased control over income*
Immediate ends	
Gender-blind	Reliable flow of income; reduced reliance on exploitative credit
Gender-aware	*Reduced reliance on sexually exploitative credit*
The core response	Assured access to non-exploitative credit + *Gender equality in access to non-exploitative credit*
Immediate means	
Household-based:	
Gender-blind	Strengthening collateral position; greater self-confidence; improved access to information, strengthened repayment capacity
Gender-aware	*Removal of gender disadvantage vis-à-vis collateral, self-confidence, repayment capacity and information; removal of women-specific disadvantages: leading to greater social and physical mobility*
Bank-based:	
Gender-blind	Altered collateral requirements; simple and flexible procedures; perceptions of poor as credit-worthy
Gender-aware	*Equal credit facilities for women borrowers; information on women's enterprise*

(*Contd*)

Figure 5.3. Analysing poor people's access to credit—means and ends (*Contd*)

Intermediate means	
Household-based:	
Gender-blind	Improved productivity of enterprise; certainty in returns; literacy; knowledge of banking procedures; affinity with bank personnel; accumulation-oriented enterprises
Gender-aware	*Removal of gender inequalities in productivity and certainty of return from enterprise; literacy; knowledge of banking procedures; affinity with bank staff; gender equality of responsibility for survival needs within the household; removal of women-specifi disadvantage in relation to social networks; control over loans/proceeds from loans*
Bank-based:	
Gender-blind	Risk-taking culture; realistic assessment of costs of lending to the poor
Gender-aware	*Removal of gender-specific stereotypes; realistic assessment of costs of lending to the poor; affinity with women borrowers*
Structural means	
Gender-blind	Transformed banking practices; redistribution of assets; improved financial assets; education provision for all
Gender-aware	*Egalitarian gender ideologies; gender-neutral labour markets;gender-neutral banking practice intra-household equity*

Building on the logical framework: prioritising means and ends

So far we have identified a problem, analysed its causes and effects from a gender perspective and identified the range of means and ends which were thrown up by our analysis. The gendered effects of the problem give us the rationale for a gender-sensitive policy response to the problem, lay out the immediate needs and longer term interests which are implicated in it and also sketch out the desired ends which will constitute the overall goals and objectives of the policy response. The next stage of the planning exercise is to select from the comprehensive array of means outlined in Figure 5.3, those elements which would constitute a feasible strategy to address the overall goal of building regularised access by poor women and men to mainstream credit institutions. As we have emphasised throughout our discussion, the specification of goals and objectives in terms of a generic category called 'the poor' is unlikely to signal the need to ensure that poor women are included along with poor men in the project design. It is essential that, until gender-awareness becomes an institutionalised and routine aspect of the planning process of an organisation, the goals and objectives of an intervention be stated in gender-specific terms from the outset, signalling the need to take account of gender-specific opportunities and constraints throughout the design of the intervention so that past exclusions and marginalisation experienced by women are not repeated and reinforced.

The core of this process is (a) the *immediate objectives* that have to be realised in order to achieve these goals, and (b) the *basic input-output relationship* through which these objectives can be met. What we have done so far, through rigorous analysis, is the identification of objectives for an intervention—a critical step in planning. In order to demonstrate how situation analysis and objectives analysis can give rise to the design of a gender-aware intervention, we will be using the different elements mentioned above to demonstrate the gender-aware application of the Logical Framework Analysis (LFA) now widely used in many development agencies. The Logical Framework Analysis, to quote Gasper:

> ... is an attempt to think in an integrated, systematic and precise way about:
>
> a) project objectives, distinguishing between various levels
> b) the causal linkages between these different levels
> c) the assumptions about the other factors that are needed for the connections between the different levels to be valid
> d) how to assess the degree of fulfilment of the various levels of targets and objectives
>
> (Gasper 1997: 5)

However, LFA has been critiqued for the narrow instrumentalist logic that it embodies, while the gender relations analysis we have suggested in the book so far, particularly in Chapter 1, is based on a broader and more political concern with issues of social justice. Consequently we have tried to incorporate a concern with the meta-level social goals which are missing from more conventional presentations of LFA, where the 'policyscape' encompassed goes as far as sectoral or national goals. This difference in approaches is to some extent captured by the following schema from Gasper (1996:45), comparing Fischer's policy evaluation model with the policy levels represented in USAID's version of LFA:

FISCHER			
	Higher principles		
	Predominant social ideals		
	Policy Goals	Goal	
	Programme objective	Purpose	
		Outputs	
		Inputs	USAID

The systematic analytical framework we have presented above provides the basis for addressing the higher level principles signalled by Fischer as we move into the design of interventions. These are the underlying principles of LFA that are to be found in the multiple versions of LFA in use by different development agencies.[1] Here we are not concerned with any particular LFA format, but rather with 'engendering' aspects of this widely-used tool to ensure that it reflects the complexities and diversity of a given planning context. The advantage of focusing on LFA, apart from its wide usage, lies in, among others, its potential "to force an integrated approach to project planning, ...[giving] a concise and clear overview...and [acting] as a basis for exchange of views between all involved in a project" (Gasper 1997:3), and its 'administrative viability' in that it provides clear principles which can be incorporated into administrative routine (op. cit.). However, like any tool, LFA will reflect the skills and commitment of its users. Clarity on what "objectives", "means" and "ends" are, and what indicators are relevant, are prerequisites for using

LFA well, emphasising our point that no set of tools can substitute for sound analysis. This is echoed by Gasper: "A logframe should be a product and summary of systematic analysis, and cannot substitute for that" (1997:1). Used inflexibly or apolitically, it can become a blueprint planning tool, wielded as a mechanism for enforcing conformity and control. However, used iteratively and interactively as a tool for participatory planning, in conjunction with a socially-attuned understanding of the institutional context in which planning is to be implemented, LFA can serve to promote transparency, accountability and participation among the various stakeholders in the planning process.

Bearing these caveats in mind, we focus on the 'informal logic' of LFA. The 'vertical' logic of the logical framework spells out the relationship between inputs and activities, the outputs which result, the objective which these outputs contribute to and the overall goal of the intervention. Its 'horizontal' logic spells out the indicators that have to be in place to ensure each relationship feeds into the next as planned, the assumptions that have to be valid for these relationships to materialise and the information that is necessary to construct the indicators. In Appendix A we present an adaptation of some aspects of this logic to illustrate the design of a gender-aware response to the problem of institutionalised exclusion of the poor from mainstream credit organisations. The overall goal adopted for the intervention is to build regularised access by women and men from low-income households to mainstream credit institutions. However, such access cannot be made to materialise overnight, given the existence of the major barriers identified to such access, which explained the exclusion of the poor from mainstream banking in the first place. Consequently, it has to be seen as the long-term objective of our hypothetical intervention, which will need a sequenced set of sub-objectives and activities which will help to build up this access over time.

Drawing once again on the analysis in Kabeer and Murthy (1996), we have identified the formation of self-help thrift-and-credit groups of the poor as an immediate objective of the intervention together with the provision of basic accountancy skills to group members. The savings accumulated by such groups serve to meet some of the more urgent survival and security needs until the longer term goal of the intervention can be realised.

The intermediate objective of the intervention would be to transform these thrift-oriented groups into credit management groups with the skills and resources to invest self-generated capital funds productively; means used include building group responsibility for repayment of loans and compliance with group-determined rules governing the rights and obligations of members. Such a process is intended also to give group members the self-confidence to negotiate with bank staff and to seek terms and conditions which suit the capacity of the membership. Thus the activities in the intermediary phase not only address certain aspects of poor people's productive needs but they also serve as the strategic means for establishing a secure route to more mainstream sources of credit, which is the long-term goal of the intervention.

Here we return to the concept of strategic means outlined earlier. While responses to immediate needs identified in the analysis may necessitate separate or specific interventions for women, a complementary focus from the outset would need to be placed on activities which start bringing women together to explore priorities and interests that they could address in the long-term. Activities which through training and exposure enable women to articulate their understanding of their worlds need to be integrated into activities which address short-term and immediate needs. Moving from practical needs to strategic gender interests is not a linear progression, but a mutually reinforcing process where moving between needs and interests is dynamic.

An important point to draw out of our presentation of goal-oriented planning is that gender-aware planning does not mean merely specifying women along with men in the goals and objectives of the intervention. Gender-aware planning entails an engagement with gender relationships far beyond just the language of equality, and analytical depth of the kind we suggest in this book. Our framework demonstrates that a gender-aware analysis of causes and effects of a problem will lead to a gender-aware specification of means and ends and this will have to be carried through into the design of the intervention. Our analysis has shown that women face gender-intensified disadvantages as well as gender-specific ones and that appropriate rules, practices and actors will have to be identified to ensure that the gender-specific opportunities and constraints of the poor are addressed along with more generic, class-based ones. The need to find innovative ways around rules and practices in the design of the intervention suggests that NGOs may be more suitable institutional actors, at least for this stage of the intervention, since they tend to be less rule-bound than government agencies and more closely attuned to local realities, although the longer term role of bank officials remains critical once the groups have developed their capacity to handle institutional credit.

Some aspects of an intervention that emerges from Kabeer and Murthy's analysis (1996; this volume) are presented below:

- *Separate group formation for women* as a need emerges from the views of poorer women who welcomed improved access to credit for both women and men but sought to form women-only groups to ensure that men did not dominate the proceedings and the resources. Group-based savings also address another gender-specific need expressed by women to safeguard their savings and the proceeds from their enterprises from appropriation by male members of the household. Women customarily save clandestinely in order to have some fall-back resource which cannot be appropriated by their men. Group-based savings not only ensure group protection but also allow such saving to take place more openly.
- *Organisational activity in close proximity to the homes of the poorest and most excluded women* both reflects the need to take account of constraints on women's time and mobility but simultaneously provides them with spaces outside their homes where they would be temporarily freed from the demands of their household chores as well as from the surveillance of senior members—their husbands or in-laws. Indeed, one of the attractions for women of joining such groups has been not necessarily the resources that

they might acquire but the possibility of having a 'space of one's own' where they can be temporarily freed from their domestic obligations. And given women's cultural exclusion from the community, such groups may be a first step to having a voice within that community.

- *Training* is a key element in the process of group formation both as a means of imparting the practical skills necessary to achieve the economic goals of the intervention as well as a way of developing the broader skills to analyse the nature of the constraints to which they are subjected, in order that solutions to these problems can be initiated on the basis of their self-analysis. Field workers also need to be trained in the gender-sensitive implementation of the intervention so that they are more aware of their own class and gender preconceptions and prejudices and do not unconsciously reproduce the biases and exclusions of the broader community. While issues of self-confidence, assertiveness and articulation should continue as part of the training begun in the first phase, these need to be backed up with training in enterprises that enable women to visibilise their economic productivity and enhance their own savings and contributions to household survival. Training along with market research is necessary if women who are willing to do so are to be assisted to break out of the traditionally 'feminine' confines of the market place; exposure to non-traditional occupations and enterprises will offer women a wider range of activities from which to choose, will enable them to engage in higher-return oriented activities, help them to build up productive assets in the long-term, enhance their savings capacity, while also enabling greater investment in the household standard of living. It also follows that continued training in leadership can help women ensure that they benefit equally, along with other family members, from the improved access to credit facilities and more strategically, it will help women break out of imposed social norms and expectations of what they can or cannot do, or who they can or cannot be.
- *Expanding vertical and horizontal linkages* will provide the means for achieving the longer term objective of the intervention. The positive experiences of organised groups

which mediate bank lending for their members illustrates the importance of group linkages that are horizontal and not just vertical. Such groups represent their members' interests with bank officials, provide support for each other, help to defray some of the transaction costs of lending to the poor, particularly to poorer women, and help to overcome some of the class and gender biases of bank officials.

Conclusion: Gender-aware Planning for Women's Empowerment

Our adaptation of the principles of the LFA to our methodology for uncovering complexity and its systematic use for the purposes of planning lays emphasis on the importance of participatory methods for analysing diverse situations and complex interrelations between people and their life-worlds. We used credit as an illustrative example drawing upon a review of secondary literature, to demonstrate how we see the process of moving from analysis to design. However, we emphasise repeatedly that without the rigorous prior analysis as suggested in Chapter 1 and without probing beyond the surface of standardised ideas about field realities, projects and plans are unlikely to come any closer to the world of disadvantaged women. Our adapted LFA-based framework presented above, moreover, is located within a perspective that is alert to the dangers of planning tools being used in rigid ways that reinforce unequal relations between planners and the "planned-for". As Chambers puts it:

> The question is "Whose reality counts?", "ours" or "theirs". As part of this we have to ask: Whose knowledge counts? Whose needs? Whose priorities/criteria? Whose appraisal? analysis? planning? Whose baseline? Whose action? Whose indicators? Whose monitoring? Whose evaluation? Is it ours, or theirs?
>
> (1996:7)

Ultimately both the means and ends we suggest are those that work towards emphasising the *transformatory potential* that exists within individual women, so that the development process involves women with self-identified and articulated priorities. Emphasising the importance of the transformatory potential of development strategies, involves making disadvantaged women in particular tap the power within themselves, by providing them with a wide range of vantage points from which to review their priorities. Experience from South Asia and elsewhere has shown that organised collectives and alliances of women can facilitate women's emergence from traditionally enclosed spaces. Kabeer suggests that for women to review their priorities and interests, there is a need to remove the culture of silence that surrounds them, through developing new forms of social and political consciousness, which she defines as:

> "the act of moving beyond acceptance of structures which are so pervasive" in order to unveil constructions of power, ... construct alternative visions, and to reflect on those strategies by which these visions might be brought closer"
>
> (1994b:251)

Moving from a welfarist perspective on women which views them as passive occupants of very specific social and cultural positions, to an empowerment perspective which acknowledges the agency and potential of every woman, and strives to remove existing constraints on women's agency

Figure 6: Evaluating the transformatory potential of projects

Transformed awareness

New economic resources	Building new and collective relationships
Participation in needs identification and Project design	Mobilizing around self-identified needs and priorities
Welfarism	Empowerment

Transformatory potential

APPENDIX A

Means, ends and indicators: a sequential analysis

Objectives	Activities	Evaluative Information
Long-term objective:		
Ensuring regularised access to institutional credit for women and men from low-income households	Meetings with bank officials by group representatives	Number of meetings; composition of group representation at meetings; group preparation and outcome of meetings
	Agreement of bank procedures for lending to group-guaranteed members	Extent, nature and composition of participation in the process of designing bank procedures; gender-awareness of new bank procedures
	Phasing out of agency support for groups	Institutional capacity of groups (e.g. management skills, democratic leadership structures; equity in participation at all levels; financial viability and sustainability)
	Expansion into wider range of enterprises by both men and women	Gender-disaggregated data on nature, viability and success of enterprises; women's participation in non-traditional activities
Intermediate objective		
Promotion of credit management groups of women and men to invest their self-generated capital funds productively	Training - members of older groups in leadership skills and more advanced forms of financial management - in enterprise development and management - women-specific groups in non-traditional skills and enterprises	Gender-disaggregated data on participation in training; impact of training on financial skills, awareness, confidence and management skills of women and men; impact on productivity; creation of new and non-traditional skills in women; expansion in range of enterprises undertaken by women

(*Contd*)

(*Contd*)

Objectives	Activities	Evaluative Information
	Knowledge dissemination about bank procedures	Outreach of information; gender-aware literature on banking procedures; use of different media and access of illiterate and neoliterate women and men to information
	Building group based approaches to overcome mobility constraints	Increased participation in distant markets; increased access and use of means of transport; direct interactions between group representatives and financial institutions
	Building access to other technical departments of government	Meetings between technical departments and groups; successful resolution of group demands
Immediate objectives		
Formation of separate self-help groups of poor women and men in order to promote savings and lending for self-identified needs	Recruitment of male and female organisation staff and fieldworkers	Numbers of men and women at all levels of the organisation; egalitarian/transformatory gender division of labour within organisation
	Training of staff and fieldworkers in group formation skills, gender-awareness and financial management	Numbers of training programmes conducted, extent of follow-up; participation of male and female staff in training; attention to gender content in training programmes; changes in practice as a result of training

(*Contd*)

(*Contd*)

Objectives	Activities	Evaluative Information
	Construction of centres close to target groups	Numbers of centres; satisfaction of group members with location of centres; increase in women members' participation in group activities
	Adoption of sensitive and flexible rules of group saving and lending	Consultation with poorer members in developing rules; satisfaction of group members with rules; increase in participation by poorer members particularly women in group saving and lending; reduced dependence on, or better terms from, money-lenders
Formation of separate self-help groups of poor women and men in order to promote savings and lending for self-identified needs	Training of group members in basic accounting skills	Numbers of women and men trained; application of accounting skills by members to relevant activities
	Use of literacy and numeracy for 'conscientisation' around class and gender issues for male and female groups	Use of examples with transformatory potential in training materials; full participation by women and men in the training; changed perceptions and practices attributable to the training
	Building group responsibility for loan recovery	adoption of processes/rules within group to manage default; improvements in repayment rates;

with the critical involvement of women themselves, involves making very specific investments in processes of consciousness-raising. Building on examples from projects which have concerned themselves with women's empowerment, Kabeer (1994a) suggests a range of ways in which "women can be provided resources to come together to analyse, to reflect, and to act to change the conditions of their lives". Figure 6 provides some examples.

The case-studies included in this section of the book are written to highlight examples of the ways in which interventions can either exclude women, or include them in a meaningful way, provided systematic gender-aware analysis of the situation and problems is carried out prior to planning. Chikarmane and Sarin provide examples of the former, while Rajagopal and Mathur present cases where sensitivity to the concerns and position of women has led to the design of initiatives that are explicitly concerned to ensure that women are not left behind in the achievement of project objectives. A reading of a number of chapters in this book will help to crystallize some of the policy points raised in this chapter. They illustrate how existing forms of gender disadvantage are often intensified or indeed added to by poor 'policy practice' and hopefully can be analysed from the perspectives raised in this chapter.

References

Chambers, R., 1988. "Poverty in India: Concepts, Research and Reality", IDS Discussion Paper 241, Brighton: IDS.

Gasper, D., 1997. "Logical Frameworks: A Critical Assessment", Working Paper 264, The Hague, Institute of Social Studies.

———, 1996. "Analysing Policy Arguments", *European Journal of Development Research*, Vol.8, no. 1, June.

———, and R. Apthorpe, 1996. "Introduction: Discourse Analysis and Policy Discourse", *European Journal of Development Research*, Vol.8, no. 1, June.

GTZ (n.d.) *ZOPP. An Introduction to the Method* Frankfurt

Jodha, N.S., 1985. "Social Science Research on Rural Change: Some Gaps", paper presented at the Conference on Rural Economic Change in South Asia: Differences in Approach and in Results between Large-Scale Surveys and Intensive Micro-Studies, Bangalore, India 5–8 August.

Kabeer, N., 1994a. "Gender-aware Policy and Planning: A Social Relations Perspective" in M. Macdonald (ed.) *Gender Planning in Development Agencies: Meeting the Challenges* UK: Oxfam

Kabeer, N., 1994b. *Reversed Realities: Gender Hierarchies in Development Thought* London and New York: Verso and New Delhi: Kali for Women.

Kabeer, N. and R.K. Murthy, 1996. "Poverty as Institutional Exclusion: Lessons from Indian Government and Non-government Credit Interventions", IDS Discussion Paper no. 356, Brighton: Institute of Development Studies.

Kabeer, N. and R. Subrahmanian, 1996. "Institutions, Relations and Outcomes: Framework and Tools for Gender-aware Planning", IDS Discussion Paper no. 357, Brighton: Institute of Development Studies.

NORAD (n.d.) *The Logical Framework Approach. Handbook for Objectives-Oriented Project Planning* Oslo.

8

"Should I Use My Hands as Fuel?"

Gender Conflicts in Joint Forest Management

MADHU SARIN

Historically, 'scientific' forest management in India has represented the usurpation by the state of forest dwellers' rights over their lands and forests. The resulting disempowerment and displacement of indigenous tribal and hill communities, and the devaluation and disintegration of their cultural and resource management traditions has been well documented (Guha, 1991; Gadgil and Guha, 1992; Kelkar and Nathan, 1991; Fernandes and Menon, 1987). In this context, the recent policy shift towards joint forest management is a belated, but welcome, first step towards reducing the gross inequities in access to forest resources embodied in past forest management policies.

Among its basic objectives, India's National Forest Policy of 1988 emphasises "meeting the requirements of fuelwood, fodder, minor forest produce and small timber of the rural and tribal populations" and "creating a massive *people's* movement, with the *involvement of women* for achieving these objectives" (GOI, 1988, emphasis added). On June 1, 1990, the Ministry of Environment and Forests issued a circular (No. 6.21/89-FP) to the forest secretaries of all states and union territories providing guidelines for the "Involvement of Village Communities & Voluntary Agencies in the Regeneration of Degraded Forests" (GOI, 1990). To date, 16 state governments have issued Joint Forest Management (JFM) resolutions specifying their basis for JFM partnerships with local communities. Between them, these 16 states have 81.5 per cent of the country's 75 million hectares of public forest land and over 90 per cent of the country's tribal population, whose symbiotic relationship with forests is well known (See Table 1). Even if extended to only the estimated 40 per cent of 'degraded' forest land in the above 16 states, JFM could embody a major re-empowerment of forest-dependent women and men to manage forest resources for greater livelihood, security and improvement in their quality of life.

JFM seeks to foster partnerships between state forest departments (FDs) and local institutions (LIs) of forest users and right holders on the basis of sharing benefits and forest management responsibilities.

In essence, the state JFM orders assure participating villagers free access to specified non-timber forest products and a 25 to 50 per cent (net or gross) share of poles/timber (in cash or in kind) on 'final felling'. In return, the villagers are expected to protect the forests after forming an organisation conforming to the membership and structure specified by the FDs.[1] Most states prescribe a forest officer as the LI's member secretary responsible for conducting all the LI's proceedings. Different state JFM orders prescribe varying organisational structures for local institutions which are variously called FPC (Forest Protection Committee) in West Bengal, VSS (Van Samrakshan Samiti) in Orissa, HRMS (Hill Resource Management Society) in Haryana and VFMPC (Village Forest Planning and Management Committee) in Karnataka and Himachal Pradesh.

However, current JFM policies continue to embody a number of contradictions. Firstly, there has been little change in the para-military organisational structure of state forest departments. Created over a century ago to enforce state control over forests, forest departments are highly centralised and rigidly hierarchical structures, with a culture of strict discipline for the execution of commands issued from above. The lowest functionaries of the department continue to be called forest 'guards', reflecting their primary role of protecting the forests from local people to prevent the theft of valuable timber. Till the late 1970s, when the elite Indian Forest Service was finally opened to women candidates, the forest departments were also exclusively male organisations. Many states still do not permit women to become forest guards as the work is considered too tough for them. It is these very forest departments, with little change in their hierarchical command-and-obey structure and their gender composition, which are now being called upon to implement 'participatory' forest management in a context where women are the major users of forests.

Limited questioning has recently begun on the incompatibility between the continuing use of technical and silvicultural prescriptions developed over decades to maximise state revenue from commercial timber even under JFM, meant to give priority to satisfying villagers' needs.

For forest-dependent women and men to initiate JFM, the first step needs to be the facilitation of viable alternatives to their existing dependence on unsustainable forest exploitation. Such dependence varies across regions and ecological contexts by class, caste and tribe and also between and within communities, and within households, by gender and age. Unless these varying dependencies are taken into account while implementing JFM, there is a danger that even under JFM, forest protection per se for regenerating valuable timber may get placed on a pedestal and 'people's participation' become equated with the more powerful and less forest-dependent villagers taking on the forest department's technical policing role against more dependent women and men.

Furthermore, most JFM resolutions provide for sharing income from timber between the State and local institutions or their individual members. JFM thus implies a new regime of property rights—rights that relate not to the forest, but to its management and produce. Issues of equity in JFM need to be given far greater attention in this respect. Both the nature of entitlements specified in JFM partnerships and the decision-making processes by which management priorities are defined will have far-reaching consequences in relation to who gets empowered or disempowered in the short and long term, between and within communities, and by gender and age within households.

This essay looks at how the JFM in its present form deals with the least addressed issue of gender equity. By treating the 'household' as the unit of participation at the community level, the JFM equates 'people's participation' with 'men's participation' on the assumption that as 'heads of households' men adequately represent the interests of all household members. However, as is widely recognised now, in different cultures women and men not only have different socially defined roles, but also have differential access to, and control over, resources. These roles are inextricably linked and complementary and vary across castes, classes and tribes, and change over time. Thus, within different communities, women and men perform different tasks for the household, earn income in varying ways, allocate time differently, have different legal and traditional rights and possess different types of knowledge. As a consequence, their priorities and goals may also differ, as would the impact of development interventions on them.

However, women are by no means a homogenous category. Groups of women within the same community may have differing, possibly conflicting forest management priorities, often for the same species, depending upon their class and socio-economic status (Sarin et al, 1996). There is a danger that by overlooking class and gender differences in the distribution of power, responsibilities and access to resources for survival within communities and households, JFM may end up further disempowering tribal and other poor women as has happened in many earlier 'development' interventions.

After a brief overview of the national context and the current patterns in both self-initiated forest protection and state-promoted JFM, this essay examines the field evidence of the gender differentiated impact of present 'community' forest protection.

The assumptions, norms and procedures implicit in state JFM orders do not recognise gender differences in survival dependence on forests. Due to this, the JFM may often transfer the Forest Departments' traditional policing role against the predominantly poor women gatherers of forest produce, to elite male members of their communities. In this essay I argue that this results in such women getting labelled 'offenders' within their own communities and homes. In such situations, women's 'involvement' in JFM gets reduced to policing 'out-

Table 1: Forest areas of the 16 states which have passed JFM orders and their Adivasi (tribal) population, 1980*

	State	Area controlled by forest dept. (million ha.)	Adivasi population ('000s)	Adivasi population as %age of total population
1.	Andhra Pradesh	6.41	2226	4.2
2.	Bihar	2.92	4933	7.1
3.	Gujarat	1.92	3757	11.1
4.	Haryana	0.16	–	–
5.	Himachal Pradesh	2.12	142	3.4
6.	Jammu & Kashmir	2.19	N.A.	N.A.
7.	Karnataka	3.79	2.62	0.7
8.	Madhya Pradesh	15.39	9815	18.8
9.	Maharashtra	6.41	3841	6.1
10.	Orissa	6.77	5057	19.3
11.	Punjab	0.24	–	–
12.	Rajasthan	3.49	3135	7.3
13.	Tamil Nadu	2.18	450	0.9
14.	Tripura	0.59	451	21.9
15.	Uttar Pradesh	5.14	199	0.2
16.	West Bengal	1.18	2603	4.8
A.	Subtotal	60.93	36871**	
B.	All India Total (area)	74.74		

A. **as %age of B = 81.52%**
C. Estimated area already under JFM or community protection by mid-1992 = 1.5 million ha. (Singh and Khare, 1993)
C. as %age of A = 2.46%
*Source: Commander, 1986, quoted in Kaur, 1991
**This represents over 90 per cent of the total Adivasi population of the country, excluding the tribal population of Nagaland and Kashmir.

side women offenders'—the needs and priorities of neither group of women are met, due to the lack of their participation in community institution decision-making. In the process, tribal women's already declining customary access to forest produce, and control over income earned from it, may be further undermined through 'benefit sharing' provisions which legitimise shares of income primarily from timber being transferred into male hands as they (males) are assumed to be 'heads of households'. Not only will such gender inequity in the distribution of costs and entitlements to a major public resource contravene the equal rights enshrined in the Constitution of India and the national goal of promoting gender equality, but it may also reduce the sustainability of forest regeneration being sought through 'community' participation.

In conclusion, this essay recommends that women's equal participation can be better integrated into practice through structuring women's independent identity, by entitlements into community institutions through the state JFM orders, and by designing procedural guidelines sensitive to gender equity concerns.

The Context: Forests and People in India

Forests in India are concentrated in the north east, the Himalayas, and Siwalik ranges, the Central belt, strips along the Western Ghats and other hill areas, and in patches of coastal mangroves. More than 50 per cent of forest land is located in five states: Madhya Pradesh, Arunachal Pradesh, Andhra Pradesh, Orissa and Maharashtra. Most forests are not large, contiguous blocks, but small patches interspersed by habitations.

State-owned forests account for 23 per cent of India's land area and represent the country's largest land-based common pool resource. Forests play an important role in village economies through conservation of environmental quality, provision of subsistence and income goods to the rural poor, and maintenance of productivity of agricultural lands. They are a major source of fuelwood, fodder and non-timber forest products (NTFP). According to one estimate, about 30 million people derive some part of their livelihood from forests (Kulkarni, 1983).

The 68 million scheduled tribe population representing eight per cent of the total population (1991 Census of India), primarily live in or near forest areas. The largest populations of tribal people are located in the states of Bihar, Gujarat, Rajasthan, Orissa, Madhya Pradesh and Maharashtra.

Only 6.2 per cent of the tribal people live in urban areas, 12 per cent of them practise shifting cultivation, 32.7 per cent are reported to be agricultural labourers and there has been a sharp increase in the number of landless tribals (Singh, K.S., 1993).

The most important problems of tribal people relate to their loss of control over resources—land, forests and water. This has occurred through forest nationalisation combined with curtailment of their traditional rights in forests, transfer of tribal lands to non-tribals, and through displacement for large 'development' projects. Although the tribal population is only eight per cent of the total, they comprise 40 per cent or more of those displaced by development projects (Fernandes, 1993). The mega-projects established in tribal areas have ruthlessly destroyed tribal economies. About ten million tribal people have already become victims of development, despite repeated assurances by the government about its belief in equity and justice, and its deep concern for their welfare (Sharma, 1993).

Due to their traditionally having subsisted on various combinations of gathering, hunting and agriculture, deforestation and ecological degradation has severely curtailed the traditional occupations of tribal communities resulting in their growing poverty and deprivation. While many have been absorbed in the organised sector as wage or plantation labour at the lowest rung of the socio-economic ladder, others are forced to migrate seasonally in search of wages.

Women and Forests

Rural, particularly tribal, women are major actors in India's forestry sector. Their interface with forests has traditionally included gathering a diverse range of NTFPs for both joint subsistence as well as income generation through processing and sale. In addition, they participate as wage labour in forestry works.

Women's role as gatherers includes collecting firewood for sale and self-consumption, fodder for livestock and other NTFPs including food, medicines, seeds, leaves, and building materials. NTFPs accounted for nearly two fifths of forest department revenue and three fourths of net export earnings from forest produce (Commander, 1986). (About 70 per cent of NTFP collection takes place in the central tribal belt in the five states of Maharashtra, M.P., Bihar, Orissa and Andhra Pradesh (World Bank, 1991)).

Women's employment in forest-based enterprises is estimated to be approximately 571.85 million womandays, of which 90 per cent is in the small-scale enterprises including activities such as rope-making, tassar silk cocoon rearing, lac cultivation, making products from bamboo and oil extraction. Two of the main cash earners among NTFPs—sal seeds and tendu leaves—are collected primarily by women. It is estimated that more than 350,000 tonnes of tendu leaves are harvested annually by 600,000 women and children (Kaur, 1991). Table 2 shows the diverse NTFPs collected by women in a village in West Bengal, as an illustration.

Since availability of NTFPs is seasonal, it does not provide employment through the year. The situation is made worse by the decreased availability of NTFPs because of deforestation. The combined result of these, and the lack of other employment opportunities over the years, has given rise to the harvesting of firewood for sale. Headloading, as this activity is called, has gained enormous importance as an occupation, also because firewood is available almost throughout the year. Dependence on firewood for income is particularly acute during the lean agricultural season when lack of wage employment creates conditions of semi-starvation among the poor (Mukherjee, 1995; Shramjeevi Unnayan, 1994). It has been estimated that two to three million people are engaged in headloading, making it the biggest source of employment in the energy sector in India (CSE, 1995). The majority of headloaders are tribal women.

Extensive field surveys, while confirming women's continuing dependence on NTFPs for income and subsistence, also indicate first, that the women receive abysmally low returns for their labour and second, between 20 to 60 per cent of such women are the sole earners of their households (GOI 1998a). Despite their statistical "invisibility", in the prevailing measures of labour force participation, women contribute heavily to the Indian economy. They represent one-third of the total labour force in India. About one-third of rural families

Table 2: Seasonal collection of major NTFPs by gender and their use
Village Karapara, Ranibandh Range, Bankura South Division, West Bengal[2]

Month	Name of NTFP
January	Amla, Harra, Behara, Bhiri Kumra, Sal patta
February	Sal patta
March	Mahua flower, Piyal fruit
April	Mahua flower, Kendu patta, Piyal fruit
May	Kendu patta, Mahua seed, Piyal fruit
June	Neem and Kusum seed, Mahua seed
July	Neem and Kusum seed, Chatu, Sal patta, Mahua seed
August	Chatu, Kalmegh, Anantomul, Ban-rasson, Sal patta
September	Chatu, Sal patta
October	Sal patta
November	Pania lata, Sal patta
December	Kalmegh, Anantomul, Ban-rasson, Bhuri Kumra, Sal patta

The majority of NTFPs are collected by women only. The exception is the mahua flower and seed which are collected by both men and women. Women keep the income from their gathering activities.

Mahua flower and seed: These are the two most important NTFPs for women. A portion of the collected mahua flower is consumed as food and liquor and the rest sold. The flower fetches Rs 6 per kg and, on an average, a household can collect three quintals per season.[3] Each household can collect upto one quintal of mahua seed per season which fetches Rs 8 eight per kilo. Mahua seed oil is partly sold and partly kept at home for consumption.

Sal patta: Sal leaf plates sell at Rs 2.50 per 100 plates. With protection, trees grow to great heights and sal leaf collection becomes difficult. However, fallen leaves are used as cooking fuel. A woman can earn upto Rs 10 for a full day's work. Demand for leaf plates is seasonal, mostly confined to the months of January to June.

Sal seeds: One kilo of sal seeds is exchanged for 1.50 kg of salt. usually women get 20 kg of salt in exchange for collecting about 13 kg of sal seeds in their spare time over ten days. Women can collect upto 4-5 kgs of sal seeds in about two hours. For eight hours work (collecting and threshing) women can earn Rs 15.

Contd.

Table 2: *Contd.*

Kendu patta: Kendu patta is collected from both private and forest land. It is sold at a rate of Rs 10 for 2000 leaves (i.e. Re 0.10 for a bundle of 20 leaves). When leaves are abundant, women can earn upto Rs 10 per day, which includes collection, sorting and tying the leaves into bundles. At other times, they earn about Rs 25-30 per day. During the short season (one and a half months) women can earn upto Rs 1000.

Medicinal plants: Kalmegh, anantomul, ban-rasson are used to treat cattle, bhuri kumra is good for treating blood sugar, amla, harra and behara are collected mostly for household consumption.

Neem and Kusum seeds: Oil is extracted from these seeds and used for domestic consumption.

Pania lata: This is a creeper sold at Re 1 per foot. It is used as a dye.

Chatu (mushrooms): These are collected for domestic consumption and also sold in the market. Women spend about an hour per day collecting chatu and, per season, collect a total of 8-10 kg. At Jhilmili, mushrooms

---

are headed by women (GOI, 1995). Women's economic productivity is particularly critical for the 60 million Indian households below the poverty line. The poorer the family, the more it depends for its survival on the earnings of its female members (World Bank, 1991). However, poor rural women

> are highly constrained by the limited (and declining) resources and means at their command—a constraint that stems not merely from their class position but also by gender. These gender inequities in access to resources take varying forms: necessities; women's systematically disadvantaged position in the labour market; their little access to the crucial means of production—land and associated production technology; and the growing deterioration and privatisation of the country's common property resources on which the poor in general, and women in particular, depend in substantial degree for sustenance. (Agarwal, 1989).

The nationalisation of large areas of common lands and their privatisation, primarily in male names, through land redistribution programmes, has further curtailed women's access to resources traditionally accessible to them. As JFM attempts to convert open access public forest lands into common property resources managed in partnership with local community institutions, it needs to develop institutional arrangements which ensure that women's traditional rights of access are not undermined and that they are equally empowered to participate in their management on the basis of clear rights of access and control over benefits.

The promotion of women's equal and active participation in community institution (CI) decision-making has to address the cultural constraints which have led to their exclusion from such forums by tradition. Although the status of tribal women differs from region to region, it is widely recognised that generally they enjoy a better status than women in mainstream Indian society. In the traditional forest-based tribal economies, women's important role as gatherers of forest foods and subsistence goods made them economically strong and valued members of the community. This is also reflected in the tradition of bride price instead of dowry, prevalent among most tribal communities. Till today, women's right to control their income from produce gathered from common lands, continues to be generally respected.

Even for tribal women, however, there have been two crucial areas of inequality—property rights and political participation. Among the Jharkhand tribes of Eastern India, for instance, property, particularly land, passes through the male lineage and under customary law, women do not have inheritance rights to land. The second important area of inequality is that of political participation. The traditional village assembly, the panchayat, is virtually an all-male institution. Membership is (normally) of the male head of the household and women are provided access only under highly exceptional circumstances (Kelkar and Nathan, 1991).

The degradation of the natural environment, deforestation and a rapidly shrinking resource base, has had its impact on the status of tribal women. Three generations back, Santhal women had a clear set of rights governing access to land and its produce, freedom of movement in forests and a valued status in the household (Singh, 1993). In contrast, income from privatised agricultural land, which passes through male lineages, is strictly considered the male owners' income even if women contribute substantial parts of the labour for its cultivation (Kelkar and Nathan, 1991).

Today, in Dumka district of Santhal Parganas in Bihar, male migration due to lack of employment is resulting in a preponderance of female-headed households in the area, either because the husband has migrated or because the wife has been abandoned due to the growing practice of bigamy or trigamy by the men. Increasing pauperisation, land alienation, indebtedness and abandonment has compelled large numbers of women in the area to resort to headloading as a prime source of income (Adhiti, quoted in Venkateswaran, 1992). As under customary law, Santhal women do not have inheritance rights to property, abandonment leaves them to fend for themselves without access to any other resources and headloading from public forests is one of the few viable income-earning options available locally (Adhiti, 1993).

JFM will inevitably overlap with such areas and must evolve viable, locally appropriate alternatives for women (and men) with such unsustainable forest dependence, to enable them to switch to sustainable forest management. Due to JFM's emphasis on participatory decision-making in reaching JFM partnerships with local communities, it should *in principle* be able to address such issues where they arise. In *practice,* however, gender differentiated concerns are often overlooked, not only further increasing women's hardship, but with possible implications for their oppression within the household.

Current Status of JFM

It is in the less developed forest regions, particularly in Central and Eastern India, that community forest protection is beginning to take place on a relatively large scale. By mid-1992, more than 1.5 million hectares of forest land were already being protected by villagers through more than 10,000 community institutions in ten states of India (Singh and Khare, 1993). Within this trend, there are two clearly discernible patterns. One consists of areas where the state government has actively encouraged local villagers to protect forests on the assurance of tangible benefits in return. West Bengal boasts the largest JFM programme of all states, with 2,423 forest protection committees (FPCs) registered by the West

Bengal forest department protecting approximately 3,90,919 hectares of regenerating public forest land (GOWB, 1994).

The other pattern consists of people initiating forest protection on their own, often with little or no involvement of the state forest department or the 'incentive' of a promised share of income from the regenerated timber. Such self-initiated forest protection is taking place on a significant scale in the states of Orissa and Bihar and to a lesser extent in Gujarat, Rajasthan, Karnataka, Madhya Pradesh, Andhra Pradesh and some other states. Many of these groups are gaining formal recognition under JFM.

Given the cultural tradition of women's exclusion from community affairs, most of the self-initiated 'community' organisations are essentially male organisations. Such groups perceive women's role as that of passive acceptors of male decisions. There has been little effort to change their exclusively male character where these have been formalised under JFM, even if the state JFM order prescribes one man and one woman per household to be eligible for the organisation's membership (Sundar, 1996). An indication of the attitude of such groups towards women's participation is evident from several case studies. In a study of two self-initiated forest protection groups in Orissa, it was found that in one, the Kudamanda Youth Association, women were not allowed to attend general body meetings even in cases where they were a party to the dispute being discussed. In the second case, that of the Dangarmunda Yuvak Sangh, women's participation was found to be non-existent (Pati et al., 1993). In another youth club protecting a forest in Orissa, although women were not eligible for membership, the men had decided that only women would collect NTFP from the protected forest as a means of regulating collection (Pattanaik, 1993).

Even in the case of FD promoted JFM groups, barring some recent initiatives to specifically increase women's participation, notably by the Haryana, West Bengal and Madhya Pradesh forest departments, it has tended to remain an all male affair. The almost 100 per cent male staffing of most forest departments, and the greater ease with which village men can be assembled, results in men interacting with men to take decisions on behalf of the 'community'. Even where some state JFM resolutions have specified the inclusion of women members in the general body of the executive committee of an FPC, theirs has been a token presence. Often it is only women's names that get entered on lists (sometimes even this is not done) with no active participation by them in decision-making or in articulating priorities.

Differential Impact of Forest Protection on Women: Evidence from the Field

One of the first and immediate costs of community forest closure for regenerating trees is the partial or total loss of access to firewood from the area. In all the country's forest regions, barring small exceptions, procuring firewood is culturally defined as women's responsibility. Firewood scarcity and women's increasing hardship in gathering it dominated forest policy discussions during the 1980s. Large social forestry projects were launched with the objective of increasing firewood availability, and macro level policy analysis continues to highlight the huge gaps in supply and demand. The hacking of trees and bushes, and even the digging out of their roots by desperate, predominantly female, headloaders in search of cooking fuel, continues to be viewed as a major cause of forest degradation. Stopping such extraction (whether by FD policing, or 'community' rules) on a sustainable basis can only be possible if a viable alternative is made available to them. Yet, there has been silence on how JFM is addressing the disturbing problem and how women members of forest protection groups are procuring cooking fuel after forest closure. The notable exceptions are Harda forest division in M.P. where firewood supplies are stated to have increased four-fold through management inputs (Singh and Khare, 1993) or the periodic 'lumpy' supplies through cut back or thinning operations on coppicing species in some areas.

While the majority of women collect firewood for domestic consumption, the very poorest often depend on selling it as a primary source of income. As a consequence, as discussed below, the nature and extent of impact on women varies from place to place and according to their socio-economic status, depending on alternatives available locally.

In the Santrampur taluka of Panchmahals district in Gujarat, 30 to 40 villages started protecting their forests entirely on their own initiative from the mid-1980s. The decision in each case was taken during traditional male gatherings to discuss community affairs. Elite male leaders discussed the non-availability of time for house construction and agricultural implements due to forest destruction. They proposed closing their forests to facilitate regeneration of teak from the surviving rootstock. Two to three men were assigned protection duties by each group and every household asked to contribute ten kilos of grain per year to compensate them.

Entry into protected areas with any kind of tools was totally banned. Only dry and fallen twigs and branches were allowed to be collected as cooking fuel. After three to five years of such total closure, some of the groups have started opening up their forests for cutting bushes for firewood for only one to five days per year. When asked from where they now obtained firewood from, the male leaders were dismissive and said that all households had private lands. Asked about the women's reactions to forest closure, they said that if any woman was caught violating their rules, the man of her household was reprimanded. The men's determination and discipline appeared an inspiring example of community forest protection.

A separate meeting with the women of some of the groups, however, revealed a different, rather disturbing picture. They said that now they had to walk between one to three extra hours (depending on the location of their village) for each headload of firewood which they obtained from forests at considerable distances that were still unprotected. The men had simply told the women about their decision to close the forest without consulting them. When asked why they hadn't protested or asked where they were to procure firewood from, the women said that if they did not comply, they would be "beaten with thick, heavy sticks" by their men.

While the men had ably taken care of the male responsibility for providing timber for the household, they had started policing the women from within the home, where they are most vulnerable and least able to fight back, to ensure that their resolve yielded the desired result. The women had come to terms with the dramatic increase in time and labour required for gathering firewood as a necessary evil, by rationalising that "every household needs timber for house construction and agricultural implements." But households also require fuel for eating cooked food. While timber is needed once every few years, cooking fuel is required with relentless regularity, every day.

Similar increases in labour and time required for procuring cooking fuel were revealed by the women of four FPCs visited in January 1994 in the south Bankura forest division of West Bengal (see table 2). The problem of cooking fuel scarcity resulting from forest protection was also evident during discussions with ten forest protection groups in south Bihar and has been mentioned in other studies (Raju et al, 1993, AKRSP, 1995). When a large number of villagers were motivated to start forest protection in the Hazaribagh East Division in south Bihar during 1990-91, the sudden scarcity of firewood in the area, particularly in villages with no forest area of their own, had created a near-riot situation. The Bihar Forest Division had to rush firewood suplies to its depots from outside to prevent the situation from getting out of hand.[4]

In the Malekpur tree growers' co-operative society (TGCS) participating in JFM in the Sabarkantha district of Gujarat, for two years after protection was initiated by the cooperative, women had to walk to the still unprotected forest of Vagheswari village 10 kms away to collect firewood. Their problem remained 'invisible' to village men, the Gujarat Forest Department (GFD) and even the supporting NGO until the NGO facilitated a separate meeting of village women. It was only then that one of the women pointed out that not only were the women now having to spend a whole day on collecting one headload of firewood from the distant forest, but that they were humiliated by the residents of Vagheswari who accused them of destroying Vagheswari's forest to save their own. This resulted in the co-operative's progressive chairman initiating annual cut-back operations in different forest patches which yield several quintals of firewood for each household. Not only did this alleviate the women's problem of firewood scarcity but it also led to a progressive change in the gendered division of responsibility for procuring firewood for the

Table 3: Impact of 'participatory' forest protection on women's responsibility for procuring cooking fuel

	Village	Time/Distance for gathering one headload		Frequency/other impacts of collection	
		Before protection	After protection		
	WEST BENGAL (Bankura Sth Div)				
1.	Kamardanga	1.5–2 hrs	4–5 hrs	5 days/ wk except monsoons	Partial switching to lantana, painful to collect.
2.	Bhadli	0.5 km	5–5 km	N.A.	Have to 'steal' from other's forest, hefty fines if caught.
3.	Barapaccha	1–2 hrs	3–4 hrs	Daily, except monsoons	Combine firewood collection with forest protection.
4.	Karapara	0.5 km	8–9 kms	N.A.	Partial switching to leaves, dung, husk, weeds
	GUJARAT				
1.	Vena (Panchmahals dist.)	0.5 hrs	3–4 hrs	1 week/ month	Harassment and abuse by FD staff and other villagers when they go to unprotected forest area further away.
2.	Chari (Panchmahals dist.)	1 hr.	2–3 km	Daily for one month/ year	Abuse by other villagers, fear of being beaten by own men.

(Contd)

Table 3: (*Contd*)

3. Malekpur (Sabarkantha dist.)	1–2 hrs	Whole day	N.A.	Abuse by residents of other village from whose forest collected firewood.
SOUTH BIHAR*				
1. Saraiya (Palamau dist.)	N.A.	N.A.	N.A.	Switching to leaves, dung, lantana, arhar sticks, some purchasing firewood.
2. Ramua (Hazaribagh dist.)	N.A.	N.A.	N.A.	Switched to leaves, lantana, dung, thorny bushes, some buying coal.
3. Banaso (Hazaribagh dist.)	N.A.	N.A.	N.A.	Switched to dung, weeds.

Source: Information collected by author during field visits (West Bengal Jan. 5-6, 1994; Gujarat December '93; Bihar Sept. '93).

*The poor quality of soil for agricultural production in the Chota Nagpur plateau of south Bihar is a major reason why villagers keep livestock to obtain dung for fertilising their fields. In such areas, switching to use of dung as fuel could have a negative impact on the already low agricultural yields.

household. Earlier, regular fetching of headloads from distant forests was only 'women's' work. Now, when multiple shoot cutting is done, men not only do the cutting but also help women carry large quantities of firewood to their homes.

However, for sustained availability of firewood even for Malekpur's women, the primary management objective of regenerating timber through JFM being promoted at present, needs to be changed. If the major objective of community forest protection is defined in terms of generating income from harvesting poles or timber, then, with time, firewood output from such forests is likely to decline. For example, regenerating sal forests managed according to standard silvicultural practices in West Bengal will generate some firewood in batches in the first, fourth and seventh years through coppicing, multiple shoot cutting and thinning operations. However, after that, the trees will not yield any firewood until the 'final' harvest. Villages endowed with large forest areas could maintain yearly flows of firewood by carrying out these operations on small patches in rotation. But this will not be feasible in villages with limited forest areas. In such situations, if JFM is to be genuinely responsive to meeting the needs of the most forest-dependent users, the forest may have to be managed only for firewood instead of timber or poles.

Similarly, it is generally assumed that poor women (and men) will enjoy the benefit of increased income due to increased availability of NTFPs from regenerating forests under protection. This assumption may often be misplaced. Monitoring of ecological change and relative changes in the composition of species under natural forest regeneration indicates that while some NTFPs increase, others decrease with protection. Maintaining steady flows of income or subsistence goods from the more useful species requires management interventions specifically designed for the purpose. Sal and tendu leaves are important sources of income primarily for poor women gatherers in Central and Eastern India. The yields of both may decrease rather than increase with protection. Tendu is intolerant of shade and its growth is adversely affected by the shade of other regenerating species. In the case of sal leaves, due to the increasing height of protected trees, leaf availability declines as they become inaccessible for gatherers. Recently increased interaction with village women by a Women's Coordinator appointed by the West Bengal Forest Department (WBFD) has made it evident that large numbers of them have suffered reduced incomes due to declining yields of tendu and sal leaves from JFM areas (Sarin et al, 1996).

Why Do Women Continue to be Major Forest 'Offenders' Even Under JFM ?

In different forums, be they of forest officers, NGOs or even of village women and men, the most frequently mentioned problem for JFM, as well as for self-initiated forest protection, is that of tackling 'women offenders'. At a workshop on JFM held in Calcutta in November 1993, an officer of West Bengal's FD stated that he would be happy to find ways of increasing women's 'participation' as 90 per cent of forest offenders in his division were women. Male chairmen of some tree growers' cooperative societies participating in JFM in Sabarkantha district of Gujarat talked proudly of how they had ruthlessly beaten women firewood gatherers from other villages to stop them from damaging their protected forests. A literate village woman (from an obviously well-off household), during a meeting in Ramua village in Hazaribagh district of Bihar in September 1993, demanded that women forest guards be deployed to stop other village women from damaging their protected forest. Even the dynamic women leaders of Nari Bikas Sangh, a grassroots women's organisation committed to women's empowerment in Bankura district of West Bengal, expressed the view that women FPC members could "snatch the axes" of outside women firewood gatherers and be more effective in forest protection than the men, who could be accused of molestation by the women. The fear of such accusations is repeatedly expressed by male forest department staff of different states as one of their major problems while dealing with women forest 'offenders'.

Ironically, many field initiatives of 'successful' women's 'involvement' in JFM have also emerged more as mechanisms for using local women to exclude outside women rather than to address the 'participating' women's forest-related needs more effectively. Many of the 'all women' FPCs constituted in some states also tend to be organised on these lines.

Such use of the protecting communities' women to exclude forest-dependent women of their own or other villages from the forests, without either group of women having a say in JFM or SIFPG priorities and decision making, is emerging as one of the major gender differentiated impacts of community forest protection in most states (Sarin, 1994 & 1995a; Sarin et al, 1996). The pertinent question this poses is: why do such large number of women continue to be forest 'offenders' even under 'participatory' forest management?

Women's Coping Strategies and Conflicts Over Denial of Access

The standard FD rule for meeting firewood requirements from forests is that 'dead, dry and fallen branches and twigs' may be collected. The same rule is being adopted by many of the self-initiated forest protection groups. The problem is that degraded forests do not have adequate dry and fallen twigs or branches. In the absence of any viable alternatives for cooking fuel accompanying forest closure through JFM, the women have to devise their own solutions to deal with the resulting scarcity.

While the better-off women are able to access firewood, coal or kerosene by starting to purchase them, the poorer majority are having to switch to much worse fuels—lantana, weeds, dung, husk, agricultural residues and leaves (see Table 2). All of them either worsen women's quality of life or are ecologically undesirable, or both. Lantana is painful to collect, and together with other weedy bushes, is smoky while burning. Dung being burnt instead of going into the fields affects agricultural productivity and leaf sweeping from forest floors is hardly desirable for improving the condition of the forest.

In addition, large numbers of women have to continue collecting firewood from other unprotected areas while their own forest is protected. Not only does this increase their work burden and time needed for firewood collection, it also transfers unsustainable exploitation elsewhere. In addition it makes women 'thieves' and 'offenders' not only in the eyes of those whose forests they cut but also within their own communities and homes—further reinforcing the stereotype image of the irresponsible and destructive tribal woman 'forest offender' needing to be controlled.

A less discussed facet of the continuing 'problem' of women forest 'offenders' is that desperate and impoverished women headloaders and other marginalised groups are not meekly acepting denial of forest access so critical to them for survival. The historical time lines of many 'community' forest protection groups indicate acute gender and class based conflicts with women commonly resorting to vicious abuses, accusations of attempted molestation, sometimes filing police cases against male guards or even physically attacking them on being prevented from collecting firewood (Poffenberger, M. et al, 1996; Sarin, M. and SARTHI, 1995; Sarin, M., 1995; Singhal, R., 1995).

> "Should I use my hands as fuel ?" asked Navliben of Kotha village when Bhagat Kaka, one of two watchmen appointed by the village men to protect the adjoining forest, stopped her from cutting firewood. When the similarly appointed watchmen of Mehndi phalia of Boria village snatched the tools and firewood of Maniben and her *jethani* (elder sister-in-law) when they were caught red-handed cutting wood, the humiliation made Maniben burst into tears and tell the guards bitterly that "they should use the confiscated wood for their own cremation".

Women's Entitlement to a Share of the Income : An Analysis of State JFM Orders

Under the present framework for JFM, women gatherers are incurring disproportionate costs of forest protection. What share of the income from the timber/pole harvests are they entitled to receive as reimbursement?

The state JFM orders provide for two types of arrangements for benefit sharing from final harvests between the FDs and CI's. Either the entire cash income or share of the produce goes to the CIs common fund or all or a part of it is to be distributed between individual 'members'. Thus, access to a share of the benefit is directly linked to membership. (Here, the term 'benefit' excludes NTFP collected individually). Even where there is no provision for distributing equal shares of cash income among members (as in Haryana's proposed JFM rules) by being a member of the CI, a person could be eligible for taking loans from the common fund (as is done by many co-operative society members in Gujarat) for investing in productive assets or for other emergency needs. However, in cases where distribution of shares of the income in cash has been provided for, it becomes a personal and inheritable property right of each 'member'.

In this respect, women's rights and entitlements have been almost totally overlooked by most state JFM orders (refer Appendix II). Five out of 16 state JFM orders (Bihar, Karnataka, Rajasthan, Uttar Pradesh and Tripura) provide for the membership of only one 'representative' per household. In the case of two other states (Gujarat and Maharashtra) the matter has been left open. Punjab's JFM order has no provision for a general body at all and in Jammu and Kashmir's case, it is unclear whether it is to be a man and a woman or a man or a woman representative from each household.

Thus, in eight out of the 16 states, there is no clear provision for women's membership of the CIs participating in JFM. As the one representative per household invariably ends up being a man (except in the case of widows with no adult sons), such a rule effectively excludes women from access to CI membership and the right to participate on their own behalf (Sarin et al, 1996).

Six states (Andhra Pradesh, Himachal Pradesh, Orissa, Tamil Nadu, Madhya Pradesh and West Bengal) have attempted to overcome this shortcoming by providing for one male and one female representative per household (in the first five cases) or for 'joint' membership of husband and wife (in West Bengal).

Although a substantial improvement over the one representative per household formula, such provisions still exclude a large number of both women and men (Sarin, 1993 & 1996; Sarin et al, 1996). For example, in the case of joint or extended families, such provisions can be grossly inequitable for the younger members within each larger household unit. They are particularly discriminatory towards second, third or abandoned wives living within households as the most disadvantaged and forest-dependent members who need to earn an income to support themselves.

However, as far as women are concerned, even in cases where membership has been opened to one man and one woman per household, in many instances the distribution of shares is still to be done using the household as a unit or it has been left vague or at the discretion of the MC or an FD officer (see Appendix II).

The question is, when it comes to distribution of cash, who will get the money ? As stated at the beginning of this paper, due to the provision for such distribution of shares of income, JFM implies a new regime of property rights to a vast public resource. This raises the question of equal rights of women and men and women *must* be provided such rights clearly in *all* the state JFM orders.

Two of the first cases of such benefit sharing to take place were Arabari in West Bengal and Soliya village in Gujarat. In Arabari, almost all the shares continue to be annually handed over to men, as West Bengal's retrospective amendment of making wives joint members with their husbands is still not applicable there (Chatterjee, A.P., 1995). Even in Soliya, as the CI had only male members, women remained out of the picture. From this year, the process of benefit sharing has begun with several hundred FPCs in West Bengal. In this context, the question of *who*, husband, or wife, or husband and wife jointly, should get the share was posed to the members of three FPCs in south Bankura Division. Both women and men were present in these meetings. Surprisingly, few of them seemed to have given the matter much thought. However, once the women understood the question, *in all the three villages, without any hesitation, all the women felt that the shares should be divided equally and given separately to both husband and wife.*

There was no vote for 'joint accounts' or the husband being more eligible as the 'head of the household'. In whispers, the women had pointed out that it is they who are responsible for household sustenance. They wanted control over their share of the income.

Empowering Women with Visibility and Equal Entitlements in JFM Resolutions

To effectively empower local communities to manage forest resources on principles of equity and sustainability, JFM **must** solicit the active participation of both **women and men**. Treating women as passive and presumed beneficiaries of decisions taken by (primarily) male 'representatives' of their communities and households will not only reinforce women's traditional subordination by continuing to deny them the right to take decisions on their own behalf but will also distribute disproportionate costs of forest protection by gender. While keeping JFM insensitive to gender differences in forest management priorities, it will also deprive JFM of the benefit of women's rich knowledge and experience as major users and managers of India's forest resources.

> Empowerment is a process of building capacities and confidence for taking decisions about one's own life at an individual and collective level and gaining control over productive resources. It is facilitated by creating awareness about one's rights and responsibilities and socio-economic, educational and political opportunities, by developing skills for utilising productive resources and by involving one in collective activities and community life. (Pandey, 1993 : 2)

While empowerment is equally necessary for both women and men of marginalised and impoverished communities, women face additional socio-cultural constraints of isolation, subordination and powerlessness. Unless women are empowered to question their subordination and assert their right to live as equals, their participation is likely to remain superficial (Sarin, 1991).

It would be unrealistic to expect FDs to promote such social change on their own, particularly while their organisational structures remain unchanged. However, as agencies of the state, they can facilitate the process of women's empowerment by making explicit provisions for women's equal rights in JFM orders and ensuring that women are aware of them by facilitating their attendance at village meetings and participation in decision making. They also need to ensure that gender differences in dependence on forests are taken into consideration while designing forest management interventions. Where the formation of new CIs is being promoted by FDs, or even where formal recognition to self-initiated groups is being granted as state agencies, the FDs are in the advantageous position of being able to insist that priority be given to gender equity in the organisation's structure and functioning as a requirement of state policy. As the majority of community groups have a high stake in gaining state recognition and legitimised access to forest benefits, there is surprisingly little resistance to acceptance of gender equality as a founding principle of community organisations (Sarin, 1993, 1996a).

A commitment to gender equity can be structured into the state JFM orders by making them incorporate the following generic principles:

1. *Make women's separate identity visible in the general body membership of community institutions by dispensing with the household as the unit of membership.* Using the household as the membership unit can be highly inequitable not only by gender but also by age, particularly in the case of extended or joint family households. As membership also ensures entitlement to benefits, the only satisfactory provision compatible with the equal rights guaranteed by the Constitution of India is keeping membership open for *all adult women and men.*

2. Similarly, *women's representation in the decision-making bodies of the CIs needs to be increased to at least a third of the total membership* (as provided for the Panchayati Raj institutions by the 73rd Constitutional Amendment) and preferably to 50 per cent, reflecting their proportion in the population. The present nominal provisions for one to three women out of nine to eighteen total MC members (refer Appendix I), are totally inadequate. They expect a tiny minority of women in a male majority forum to deal with their traditional handicap of exclusion from community decision making fora.

3. To ensure that the above provisions do not remain meaningless "names on lists" and to structure regular access to information and decision-making fora for women, *the quorums for both general body and MC meetings should include the requirement of 30 to 50 per cent of those present being women.* This simple procedural requirement will make it mandatory for both FD staff and CI male leaders to solicit women's participation in all CI meetings. This may also result in timings of the meetings being made more convenient for women to attend.

4. Wherever there is a provision for distribution of benefit shares in cash or kind among individual members, *the independent entitlements of women members' must be clearly specified.*

5. Commencement of any forest protection under JFM must be preceded by an analysis of existing dependence on forest produce by gender and socio-economic status combined

with clear short and long term alternatives for meeting the most essential of those needs following closure.

Although a vast range of additional inputs will be required to genuinely empower rural women to overcome their traditional and cultural subordination, inclusion of the above basic provisions in JFM orders will structure gender equity into JFM and at least ensure that women do not get designed out of even JFM by default.

Notes

[1]Most forest departments reserve the right to unilaterally cancel a JFM agreement (and in most cases, to even dissolve the LI itself) if the LI is considered to be violating any condition in the agreement. In such a situation, the LI has no right to any compensation for its investments of labour, time or capital during the validity of the agreement. If the FD fails to honour its commitments, the villagers have no reciprocal rights for penal action against the FD. Only Haryana's draft JFM rules, although awaiting approval from the state government for over four years, at least entitle the LIs to demand compensation from the state government in case the FD fails to honour its commitments.

[2]Information collected on 6.1.94 by the author.

[3]One quintal = 220 lbs or 100 kg.

[4]Personal communication, September 1993, Mr A. Kumar, who was Divisional Forest Officer of Hazaribagh East Division, Bihar Forest Department in 1990-91 when the above situation developed.

References

ADITHI, 1993. "Homage to Our Foremothers", Patna.

Agarwal, Bina, 1989. "Rural Women, Poverty and Natural Resources: Sustenance, Sustainability and Struggle for Change", *Economic and Political Weekly*, October 28, 1989.

AKRSP(I), 1995. *Soliya Harvesting—Gender Perspective*, mimeo, Ahmedabad.

Bihar Forest Department, 1993. Official note of Regional Chief Conservator of Forests, Ranchi, July 19.

Chatterji, A.P. 1995. *The Socio-economic Project at Arabari, West Bengal; Participatory Enquiry Toward an Understanding of Socio-cultural and Subsistence Issues*, mimeo. New Delhi: SPWD.

Chatterjee, Mitali, undated. "Women in Joint Forest Management: A Case Study from West Bengal", Technical Paper-4, Calcutta: IBRAD.

Commander, S., 1986. "Managing Indian Forests: A Case for the Reform of Property Rights".

CSE, 1985. *The State of India's Environment 1984-85: The Second Citizen's Report* New Delhi: Centre for Science and Environment.

Fernandes, Walter, 1993. "The Price of Development", *Seminar*, December.

Fernandes, Walter & Menon, Geeta, 1987. "Tribal Women and Forest Economy: Deforestation, Exploitation and Status Change", New Delhi: Indian Social Institute.

Gadgil, Madhav & Guha, Ramachandra, 1992. *This Fissured Land: An Ecological History of India* New Delhi: Oxford University Press.

Government of India, 1988. *National Forest Policy Resolution.*

———, 1988a. "Shramshakti Report of the National Commission on Self Employed Women and Women in the Informal Sector", New Delhi.

———, 1990. "Involvement of Village Communities and Voluntary Agencies in Regeneration of Degraded Forests", MOEF, No.6.21/89-F.P., June 1, 1990.

———, 1995. *Country Report, The Fourth World Conference on Women, Beijing* New Delhi: Department of Woman and Child Development, Ministry of Human Resource Development.

Government of West Bengal, 1994. *Role of Forest Protection Committee in West Bengal* Calcutta: Department of Forests.

Guha, Ramachandra, 1991. *The Unquiet Woods: Ecological Change and Peasant Resistance in the Himalaya* New Delhi: Oxford University Press.

Guhathakurta, P. & Bhatia, K.S., 1992. Case Study 1, "Gender and Forest Resources: Study in Three Villages of West Bengal".

Kaur, R, 1991. "Women in Forestry in India", Working Paper, Women in Development, Washington D.C.: World Bank.

Kelkar, Govind and Nathan, Dev, 1991. *Gender and Tribe: Women, Land and Forests in Jharkhand* New Delhi: Kali for Women.

Khare, Arvind, 1987. "Small Scale Forest Enterprises in India with Special Reference to the Roles of Women", National Review Paper, ISST.

Kulkarni, Sharad, 1983. "Towards a Social Forest Policy", *Economic and Political Weekly*, February 5.

Mukherjee, N., 1995. "Forest Management and Survival Needs: Community Experience in West Bengal", *Economic and Political Weekly*, Vol.XXX No.49, Dec.9, pp 3130-32.

Pandey, D., 1993. "Empowerment of Women for Environmentally Sustainable Development through Participatory Action Research", paper presented at the Workshop on Gender and the Rural Environment at IRMA, April 23-24, 1993.

Pati, S., R. Panda & A. Rai, 1993. "Comparative Assessment of Forest Protection by Communities", paper presented at JFM Workshop, Bhubaneswar, 28-29 May.

Pattnaik, A.K., 1993. "Five Years of JFM: Resource Users as Participatory Managers", paper presented at JFM Workshop, Bhubaneswar, 28-29 May.

Poffenberger,M., et al, 1996. *Grassroots Forest Protection: Eastern Indian Experiences* Berkeley: Asia Forest Research Network Report No.7.

Raju, G., R. Vaghela & M.S. Raju, 1993. "Development of People's Institutions for Management of Forests". Ahmedabad: VIKSAT.

Sarin, M., 1991. "The Potential Role of Rural Women's Organisations in Improved Natural Resource Management", paper prepared for FAO's Regional Expert Consultation on Local Organisations in Forestry Extension, Chiang Mai, October 7-11, 1991.

———, 1993. "From Conflict to Collaboration: Local Institutions in Joint Forest Management", JFM Working Paper No.14, New Delhi: SPWD & The Ford Foundation.

———, 1995. "Delving Beneath the Surface : Latent Gender-based Conflicts in Community Forestry Institutions", paper written for the FTPP, FAO, Rome.

———, 1995b. "Gender and Equity in JFM: Discussion and Emerging Issues", proceedings of the Gender & Equity sub-group meeting, November 27-28, 1995, New Delhi: SPWD.

———, 1996. Joint Forest Management: The Haryana Experience, Environment & Development Series, Ahmedabad: Centre for Environment Education.

Sarin, M., L. Ray, M.S. Raju, M. Chatterjee, N. Bannerjee and S. Hiremath, 1996. *Who is Gaining? Who is Losing? Gender & Equity Concerns in JFM*, New Delhi: SPWD.

Sarin, M. and SARTHI, 1995. "Process Documentation by a Self-Initiated Forest Protection Group in Gujarat", *in Wastelands News*, Feb-April, New Delhi: SPWD.

Sharma, B.D. (1993). "The Great Betrayal", *Seminar*, December.

Shramjeevi Unnayan, 1994. "*Sanyukt Van Prabandhan Mein Prashasnic Kamiyan evam Apekshayen*", paper presented at a workshop with Bihar Forest Department, Ranchi.

Singh, K.S. (1993). "The Problem", *Seminar*, December.

Singh, S. and Khare, A., 1993. "People's Participation in Forest Management", *Wasteland News*. Vol.VIII No.4, May-July.

Singhal, R, 1995. *Behavioural Factors in Institutional Effectiveness* JFM Study Series, Bhopal: IIFM.

SPWD, 1993. *Joint Forest Management Update*, New Delhi.

Sunder, N., 1996. Personal communication.

Venkateswaran, Sandhya, 1992. *Living on the Edge: Women, Environment and Development*, New Delhi: Friedrich Ebert Stiftung.

World Bank, 1991. *Gender and Poverty in India*, Washington.

APPENDIX I

Women's Access to Local Institution Membership in JFM rules.

State	Eligibility for General Body membership	Representation in Managing Committee (MC)
Andhra Pradesh	1 F, 1 M/per household	M. 3 women out of 9 to 13 members.
Bihar	1 rep/household	Min. 3, max. 5 women out of 15 to 18 total members. Quorum for MC meeting 10. (mandatory presence of any women members not specified).
Gujarat	'Any interested person' can become member	Min. 2 women. Total members not specfied.
Haryana	All F & M adults	Min. 2 women, proportionately higher numbers if women major forest users, could be all women.
Himachal Pradesh	1 F, 1 M/per household	Out of 9 to 12 total members, min. 5 to be from village. Out of village reps, 50 per cent to be women. Women's presence to complete quorum not specified.
Jammu & Kashmir	1 F or M/per household	Min. 2 women out of 11 total members.
Karnataka	1 rep/'interested' household	1 women out of 15 total members.
Madhya Pradesh	1 F, 1 M/per household	Min. 2 women.
Maharashtra	Unspecified	Min. 2 women out of 11 members.
Orissa (1993 order)	1 F. 1 M/per household	Min. 3 women out of 11 to 13 members.
Punjab	No provision for a general body.	1 woman out of unspecified total.
Rajasthan	1 rep/household	Not specified

(*Contd*)

APPENDIX I (*Contd*)

State	Eligibility for General Body membership	Representation in Managing Committee (MC)
Tripura	1 rep/household	Not specified
West Bengal	Joint membership of husband & wife	Not specified
Tamil Nadu	1 F. 1 M/per household	Min. 2, Max. 5 out of total of 5 to 11. Nominated members additional
Uttar Pradesh	1 rep/household (F or M). No min. presence of women specified.	One third out of elected members. 5 nominated members could be all male.

F = Female; M = Male.

APPENDIX II

Women's Access to 'Benefit sharing' in JFM rules

State	Eligibility for General Body membership	Entitlement to benefit-sharing
Andhra Pradesh	1 F, 1 M/per household	25 per cent of harvested timber/poles for distribution among members. Unspecified whether shares will be distributed on a household basis or separately to the M & F members.
Bihar	1 rep/household	MC to decide 'rightful owners' or harvested produce handed to it for distribution.
Gujarat	'Any interested person' can become member	LIs' 50 per cent share of benefit to be 'suitably distributed'.
Haryana	All F & M adults	No provision for distribution of share among individual members but women and men could equally access community fund for loans or influence priorities for its use.
Himachal Pradesh	1 F, 1 M/per household	"Entire quantity of usufructs to be distributed to villagers". 25 per cent of income from 'final felling' to go to LIs common fund. Existing rights to be protected.
Jammu & Kashmir	1 F or M/per household	CI to decide basis of sharing in consultation with all members.
Karnataka	1 rep/per 'interested' household	25 per cent sale proceeds to be distributed among "beneficiaries".
Madhya Pradesh	1 F, 1 M/per household	30 per cent of produce from 'final' harvest either in kind or as net sale proceeds to be distributed equally among all members.

(*Contd*)

APPENDIX II *(Contd)*

State	Eligibility for General Body membership	Entitlement to benefit-sharing
Maharashtra	Unspecified	50 per cent income to be distributed in cash to members.
Orissa (1993 order)	1 F, 1 M/per household	50 per cent produce or cash to be distributed equally using household as unit. Whether M or F member will get share unspecified.
Punjab	No provision for a general body.	Household as unit.
Rajasthan	1 rep/household	Equal shares for members.
Tripura	1 rep/household	50 per cent of net receipts to be distributed among members.
West Bengal	Joint membershipof husband & wife	25 per cent of net income from cashew & 'final fellings' to be distributed equally among all 'joint' members. Husband or wife can exercise household's right.
Tamil Nadu	1 F, 1 M/per household	Free firewood to headloaders and landless identified by MC. some free NTFPs and grasses to particular groups. All cash income to be distributed to individual members.
Uttar Pradesh	1 rep/household (F or M). No min. % of women members specified.	Only NTFPs. after meeting 'demands' (of members?), rest to be sold. 25 per cent to be shared among members based on their contribution.

F = Female; M = Male.

APPENDIX III

Women's Access to Local Institution Decision-making in JFM Orders

State	Eligibility for General Body membership	Structured access to information/decision-making forms
Andhra Pradesh	1 F, 1 M/per household	Separate meetings with women's groups and other disadvantaged groups to explain concept. Reps of 50 per cent households quorum for initial village meetings. No minimum percentage women's presence specified.
Bihar	1 rep/household	50 per cent adult population of village quorum for initial village meeting. No min. women's presence specified.
Gujarat	'Any interested person' can become member	Min. 60 per cent households must be CI members. Gujarat FD treating men as household reps. No mandatory presence of women specified.
Haryana	All F & M adults	Nothing specified.
Himachal Pradesh	1 F,. 1 M/per household	50 per cent members quorum for GB and MC meetings. Women's presence to complete quorum not specified.
Jammu & Kashmir	1 F or M/per household	No quorum or women's presence specified for GB or MC meeting.
Karnataka	1 rep/'interested' household	30 per cent members quorum for MC meetings.
Madhya Pradesh	1 F, 1 M/per household	50 per cent village adults required for initial village meeting.

(Contd)

APPENDIX III *(Contd)*

State	Eligibility for General Body membership	Structured access to information/decision-making forms
Maharashtra	Unspecified	Nothing specified.
Orissa (1993 order)	1 F, 1 M/per household	All adults to be present at initial village meeting. 66 per cent members quorum for MC meeting.
Punjab	No provision for a general body.	Nothing specified.
Rajasthan	1 rep/household	Nothing specified.
Tripura	1 rep/household	50 per cent quorum for GB meeting.
West Bengal	Joint membership of husband & wife	Nothing specified.
Tamil Nadu	1 F, 1 M/per household	Nothing specified.
Uttar Pradesh	1 rep/household (F or M). No min. presence of women specified	66 per cent quorum for GB meeting for MC election.

F = Female
M = Male
GB = General Body
MC = Managing Committee
CI = Community Institution
FD = Forest Department

9

Closing the Gender Gap in Education

The Shikshakarmi Programme

SHOBHITA RAJAGOPAL

Introduction

The goals of education for women and girls have been defined repeatedly over the years in different education policy documents in India and internationally.[1] Education has been perceived as an important social input and a long-term strategy for improving the status of women. The social benefits and returns from educating girls and women are seen in terms of a fall in the birth rate, reduced infant and maternal mortality, enhanced family health and welfare, improved children's education and increased economic productivity for women. The significance of education in creating awareness, gender equality and access to information has also been stressed.

Despite the recognition in policy documents "that a bold and determined effort [needs to] be made to close the existing gap between the education of men and women, in as short a time as possible,"[2] the ways in which, and the commitment with which this broad goal has been translated into strategies, have varied over the years. Early policy initiatives separated education for women and men into different streams, emphasising the social and familial roles of women as wives and mothers, and the roles of men as producers and economic actors. This segregative approach reinforced the ideological division between boys and girls. Education was seen as an instrument for the better performance by men and women of their roles as reflected in the existing gender division of labour in the country. It was not until the 1970s, when the Committee on the Status of Women in India published its landmark report *Towards Equality*, that these assumptions were explicitly challenged. The CSWI report clearly pointed to the urban, middle class and male biases of education planners which had resulted in the highly discriminatory and instrumentalist definition of women's roles, needs and priorities. For example, the CSWI pointed out that distinctions between men's worlds and women's worlds, the gender division of labour, and expectations of differential behaviour had a direct bearing on the process of socialisation, on opportunities provided for education, on the training of girls, the kinds of ideals projected before them, as well as on the kinds of expectations they come to have from life and the way they conduct their lives (CSWI 1974:85).

The CSWI emphasised that education should focus on equipping women to carry out their multiple roles as citizens, housewives, contributors to the family income and builders of a new society. Women's education was seen as a basic ingredient for the improvement of their status (ibid: 235). Around the mid-1980s, this approach blended in with the international shift in donor policy in which women were viewed as a critical human resource for enhancing the efficiency of national development efforts. Education, in this shift, was viewed as a tool for equipping women with skills and training for productive involvement (BRIDGE 1995:34).

The CSWI report and the concerns articulated within the country by a growing women's movement were influential in admitting into policy discourse the recognition that women required a special focus in planning, distinct from the neutrally-framed though male-biased approach in existence, in order to address the factors that impeded women's equitable participation in the education system. The Sixth Five Year Plan saw the introduction of a separate chapter on women's development for the first time in the history of Indian planning. In the mid-1980s, the emphasis in educational planning shifted from the provision of inputs and expansion of facilities, to a need to transform the system of education qualitatively in terms of its value, content, standards and relevance. Some of the resulting strategies focused on awareness-generation, conscientisation, empowerment and mobilisation efforts along with training women for economic activity and employment.

The most significant shift, however, is found in the National Policy on Education (NPE) formulated by the Government of India (GoI) in 1986, which recognised education for women as a means of ensuring gender equality, and also secured a central role for government in this process. In the NPE, this was sought to be achieved particularly through "...the development of new values through redesigned curricula, textbooks, the training of teachers, decision makers and administrators and the active involvement of educational institutions..." and "...through provision of special support services, setting of time targets and effective monitoring" (GoI 1986). The Programme of Action (PoA) which accompanied the NPE set firm time parameters for the implementation of elementary and adult education for women, and also recognised the need to expand women's access to vocational technical education and existing technologies. By shifting the focus on to education as a "means" to the broader goals of equality and empowerment, the NPE represented a fundamental rethinking of educational policies, particularly for women.

Conceptual shifts indicated in policy have not, however, been easy to put into practice. One of the major challenges in universalisation of primary education, for instance, continues to be ensuring girls' participation in the educational process. Although enrolment rates for children from all backgrounds are increasing, there are significant numbers who never enrol, and even more drop out soon after enrolment. The over-emphasis on numerical targets has often led to drives for enrolment, but the consequent neglect of attendance and achievement indicators suggests that the real reasons why children do not or cannot pursue education have neither been investigated nor addressed. This essay seeks to analyse some of these factors, and present how an analysis of the gender gap in education can be used to define parameters for intervention with the aim of meeting broader goals of education for equality as laid out in the NPE. The example of the Shikshakarmi Programme in Rajasthan will be used as an illustration of such a process.

Analysing the Gender Gap in Education

Reasons for the non-achievement of goals of universal elementary education can generally be divided into two categories which are thought to shape children's access to and participation in schooling: the *demand* for education, in terms of factors operating at the level of the household and community, and the *supply* of education in terms of the quality of state-provided services. While the opportunity costs[3] to poor parents of sending both boys and girls to school have been studied, the growing gender gap in educational access suggests that girls' participation continues to be affected by the existence of ideologies, norms and practices that define and reinforce distinct and "appropriate" roles for girls and boys. The education experience of Rajasthan in many ways exemplifies some of these issues. Statistics indicate that in Rajasthan, in spite of the huge leap in girls' enrolment which has increased threefold since the mid-1970s, girls' education still lags behind that of boys:[4]

- the percentage of girls to total children enrolled was 32.5 per cent at the primary level and 25.7 at the upper primary level
- the drop out rate in classes I–V was 48.93 per cent for all children, 45.70 per cent for boys and 52.16 per cent for girls
- the overall drop out rate for children in the state for elementary school (I–VIII) was 65.43 per cent; 62.34 for boys and 72.34 for girls.

Rajasthan ranks second lowest in overall literacy achievements in the country, with an overall literacy rate of 38.8 per cent recorded in the Census of 1991. Female literacy is the lowest in the country at 20.44 per cent. Some districts in Rajasthan have single digit female literacy rates. The overall gender gap in literacy has increased by four percentage points between 1981 and 1991, while the female literacy rate among Scheduled Castes is 8.31 per cent and 4.42 per cent among Scheduled Tribes (Census 1991).

Reasons for low educational attainment can be attributed to several factors. Palriwala presents an analysis of unequal gender differences in Rajasthan elsewhere in this volume. In particular, the burden of household chores, restrictions on mobility especially after puberty, early marriage, and increased vulnerability to violent attacks appears to shape unequal access to schooling for girls. The education of girls is also closely linked to the availability of water, fuel, fodder and child-care facilities in the rural areas—where there is a large distance to be covered, the chances of finding time for school are likely to be greatly reduced for girls. The education of girls is seen as unnecessary, unproductive, unaffordable, unfeasible and even threatening to social relations based on and reproduced through the subordination of women.

The provision of primary education services in Rajasthan is characterised by poor infrastructural facilities and unsatisfactory scholastic standards which affect both boys and girls. A large number of villages continue to be deprived of institutionalised access to services related to education and health. Approximately 6,200 revenue villages and about 20,000 small hamlets still do not have primary school facilities, despite the fact that there has been a 67.5 per cent increase in the number of primary schools between 1975–76 and 1993–94. Schools have also lacked sufficient teachers, particularly women teachers. The total number of teachers teaching in primary schools in 1993–94 was 83,388, of which the percentage of women teachers was about 27.1. Though this percentage has increased from the 1975–76 figure of 19.2 per cent, women teachers still constitute little more than of one fifth the total strength of teachers in the state in both primary and upper primary categories of the school system.

The Shikshakarmi Programme: Redefining Assumptions

The Shikshakarmi Programme (SKP) was started in 1987 by the Government of Rajasthan (GoR) with assistance from the Swedish International Development Authority (SIDA) as an innovative educational intervention to address the factors sustaining the educational backwardness of the state. Some of the assumptions of the programme were based on the analysis that (a) the problem of primary education was not so much caused by the undervaluing of education by users, but by their rejection of the way in which education was being delivered; (b) improving the delivery system was thus crucial for upgrading; the image of the school as an attractive place to send children (c) it was necessary to motivate people who did not have 'high qualifications' to become achievers if local human resources were to be developed and strengthened. The SKP design was based on the recognition that the mainstream educational institutions had provided neither the infrastructure nor the human resources and capacity for the education of children in remote areas of Rajasthan. The project thus sought to reach the 'unreached' by developing appropriate institutional responses. The various components of SKP aimed at ensuring effectiveness of the design at the field-level. The programme also recognised that educational services must get village-based support if they are to meet the needs of rural people in a significant way.

The concept and design of SKP emerged out the experience of the Social Work Research Centre (SWRC), an NGO based in Tilonia, Ajmer, working in the rural areas of Rajasthan since 1972. The central thrust in SWRC's educational projects has been the need to create awareness in the community on issues related to development. Some of the questions that they have been grappling with include: how children can be attracted to primary education; how a community can be involved in planning for itself; how there can be a sharing between the formally educated and the less educated; how primary education can be made more relevant to the village community. SWRC's programme of alternative education has focused on filling the gaps in formal education. The stress has been on building local potential and on developing the internal human resources of the village and long-term sustainability of development inputs (Jain 1994).

Following the SWRC experience, the design of the SKP was based on the merging of the goals of education with a solid community-based programme of internal capacity-building. Consistent with the aims laid down for primary education in the NPE and the Seventh Five Year Plan, SKP aims at:

- universalisation of education in remote, socio-economically backward villages in those blocks of Rajasthan state where the existing primary education system has proven particularly ineffective

- a qualitative improvement of primary education in such villages by adapting the form and content of education to local needs and conditions
- achievement of learning equivalent to the norm for class V to be achieved by all children in the project villages with primary attention given to girls.

Central to SKP's analysis of the strategies required to restructure the educational system in unserviced areas was the need for teachers who would run schools effectively and forge links between parents and the educational system. The experience of SWRC in eliciting community support for the selection of local teachers and in structuring regular and systematic training which could be assimilated by the young teachers, formed the base on which SKP strategies were formulated in 1986. A pilot project carried out by GoR in association with SWRC in thirteen remote villages of Silora block in Ajmer district had indicated that the attendance of children had increased substantially since the experiment with locally recruited and trained teachers began, as the teachers were regular in school (IDS-J, 1991). The positive feedback from the village communities involved and the increased participation particularly of girls and children from Scheduled Caste households indicated that the changed approach to education had been worthwhile.

Alternative Structures and Building Partnerships

The Silora pilot project indicated that to achieve universal primary education, it was necessary to have community involvement as well as the joining of hands by different agencies (Government and NGOs) in order to generate positive outcomes. Recognising this, the SKP structure was built around a partnership among different agencies. The main agency involved in delivering primary education in the state is the government with its different arms—the Directorate of Primary Education, the Directorate of Adult and Non-Formal Education, the Department of Rural Development and Panchayati Raj.[5] For the purposes of the SKP, NGOs like SANDHAN and the Institute of Development Studies, Jaipur (IDS-J) are involved at the state level. SANDHAN is the nodal

NGO responsible for the training and selection of Shikshakarmis in various blocks, the identification of supportive NGOs, and is involved in the development of curriculum and teaching materials. The research wing recently set up also provides research support to the project. IDS-J, a research organisation has been responsible for ongoing monitoring and evaluation, and research into aspects of the programme.

An important aspect of the organisational structure of SKP is that instead of making changes in the existing institutions delivering primary education, a new autonomous structure was created with its own rules and procedures for both entry and implementation. The Rajasthan Shikshakarmi Board (SKB), an autonomous body, is responsible for the planning, implementation, coordination and management of the programme, including the disbursement of funds. The SKB has an academic wing which is responsible for the development and implementation of the overall SKP strategy including training, curriculum development, and teacher selection. The shift in management has been from distanced planning and single agency management to a support structure comprising both government agencies and NGOs working directly at the local level. The block-level infrastructure of the government is also utilised in the SKP, with the BDO holding formal charge of SKI at the block-level. A Shikshakarmi Sahayog (SKS), an education extension officer, is responsible for the 10–15 Shikshakarmi schools in a given block, providing the Shikshakarmis (teachers) the necessary administrative and academic support.

Multiple Strategies for Schooling: Responding to "Felt" Needs

A significant aspect of the Shikshakarmi approach involved addressing the following issue: what types of schools are required to address the diversity of needs across gender and caste in relation to the education system. Many of the factors that constrained girls' access to education revolved around school-related issues, like the timing of classes, the distance of the school from the home and the sex of the teachers. Addressing the fact that in general, children were an intrinsic part of household livelihood strategies through the performance of diverse tasks, meant that a single type of school could not be considered sufficient to meet the diversity of needs in a given community, particularly at the early stages, where parents were yet to be convinced of the proper functioning of schools in their area.

In the initial phase the SKP took over dysfunctional schools in areas where the problem of teacher absenteeism was acute, and enrolment and retention of children in the age group 6–14 years was poor. These were regular primary schools, mostly managed by a single teacher. In its extended phase, SKP also started new primary schools in unserviced areas. In the process of upgrading the school, various measures were put in place. School equipment and teaching aids in schools have been made available by the SKB, and some have been provided under the Operation Blackboard programme of the Government of India. There has also been an emphasis on improving infrastructure facilities in the SKP schools, including repairing buildings, constructing boundary walls and improving water facilities. The provision of free textbooks, school bags and stationery, organisation of study tours, educational visits and tournaments are incentives that have helped in stimulating children's interest through exposure to a range of activities, and have improved enrolment and participation rates in SKP schools. To ensure that SKP school students are not isolated from the mainstream schooling system, the curriculum is the same as that of regular government primary schools, although some special textbooks in subjects like Mathematics and Hindi have been developed by the programme.

In addition to the main schools which function at regular hours, the SKP runs *Prehar Pathshalas* (PPs) or "schools of convenient timing" which function at night to enable children who work during the day, or even at night, to attend. PPs are the 'non-formal' component of the programme. They function for two hours, either in the premises of the day school or at a convenient place in the village. In some villages the space for the PP has been made available by the community. The curriculum of the day school is the same but in a condensed form in the PP. The PP largely addresses itself to the girls in the village as they are involved in household work during the day and their attendance in PPs has been much more than that of boys.

The concept of *Aanganpathshala* (AP) or "courtyard schools" was started by SKP more recently as an experimental initiative to address the issue of girl's access to formal primary schooling, by providing schools at a reasonable distance. APs have been functioning in three blocks since 1992. They were started in villages where there were no formal schools or other facilities for educating children. The main aim is to enrol girls in the age group of 6–14 years. A village woman is selected as teacher, and after a process of training, she runs a school in the courtyard or verandah of a home. The space for an aanganpathshala is usually provided by the community or it functions at the residence of the teacher. The physical facilities, however, differ from area to area. For instance, in Jhadol, the APs function from private homes and in spaces provided by the community, in Phalodi, rooms have been built with the initiative of the NGO, and in Karauli, the space has been provided by the community members (IDS Field Reports, 1996). As these APs are functioning in villages where there are no educational facilities, this model has facilitated a formal structure where children can come and participate in educational activities. Community responses have also been positive as many of these villages did not hope or expect the mainstream system to reach out and provide education to the children of these communities (ibid).

In addition to different kinds of schooling being made available to children with different familial circumstances, the SKP has also developed bridging strategies to account for other factors that impede girls' access to schooling. *Mahila Sahayogis* (women escorts) have been appointed to enable young girls to attend school, especially those who cannot attend day schools/night centres as they have to take care of their siblings. The Mahila Sahayogi is a local woman, who collects these children from their homes, and escorts them to the school and back. She also provides child care during class hours. At present there are 309 Mahila Sahayogis associated with SKP, in 35 blocks. The SKB reports indicate that about 1649 girls have started attending the Prehar Pathshala with this additional support. Most of these girls had been withdrawn from school by parents for various reasons like household work, puberty, and early marriage. The parents, however, agreed to send these girls to the night centres with a woman escort. Field-level feedback indicates that this support has facilitated the regular attendance of girls in the day schools and night centres in these blocks. there is also a demand within the programme to extend this initiative to all the blocks.

Building Community Capacity for Localised Education: The Shikshakarmis of SKP

An important aspect of the SKP has been to make communities feel responsible for education, through transferring the feeling of ownership of educational processes and institutions to the community-level in order to consolidate the notion of partnership between the state and communities. This was because workers realised that unless teachers were members of communities, lived within them, understood the contexts and circumstances of community members, and were there to respond flexibly to emerging needs in respect of schooling, the education system would continue to remain an outside intervention which the community had little stake in participating in and shaping.

The creation of cadres of local teachers is one of the fundamental aspects of the SKP. SKP schools are identified on the basis of initial requests from the block. A list of 'problem' villages is provided by the block officials to the SKB, often villages where the school teacher does not attend work regularly owing to the inaccessibility of the villages, where the drop-out and/or non-attendance rate of eligible children is very high, and where consequently, the process of education lacks momentum. These villages are visited by a selection team comprising the different state and non-state actors of SKP. During these visits, ideas and information about SKP are disseminated through meetings conducted by the gram sabha.

The qualification for men and women willing to join the project is Class VIII and Class V respectively, which is considerably lower than the standards for regular primary teachers who need a one-year teaching degree, after completing 12 years of formal schooling. Candidates (both men and women) with the required qualifications are then interviewed by the selection team. The opinion of the community is central to the identification and selection of suitable candidates. The acceptability of the person is also important and at the time of selections of Shikshakarmis, the community members also verify details about where the person lives and what his or her qualifications are. The community therefore double-checks the information provided by those identified/selected. Most of the women and men identified are either involved in subsistence farming, wage labour or are unemployed.

In a state in which the segregation of men and women is strictly imposed and 'purdah' for women is enforced, one of the major constraints in low enrolment of girls in schools has been the absence of women teachers in schools in remote areas. Though there were no women teachers identified in the pilot project of SKP (1986), the concept of *Mahila Shikshakarmi* (MSK) or woman teacher was seen as a priority within the project, despite the difficulty of finding educated women in the rural areas of Rajasthan. The initial document clearly states the principle of two SKs, one man and one woman in each village, and it was felt that the presence of MSKs in the SKP could help create an environment which would be more conducive and encouraging to girls who were expected to enrol in the schools. But identifying women and retraining them continues to be socially challenging and requires sensitive handling.

The women selected as MSKs are in most cases the bahus (daughters-in-law) of the village (as in the Indian context, the daughters generally leave their natal homes on marriage). The presence of a woman member in the selection team therefore becomes necessary because in many instances, it is the mother-in-law and sister-in-law who have to be convinced to release the bahu from household obligations. Some of the common problems that have emerged in identifying women include:

- Low literacy levels among women in remote villages. This is particularly true of many villages in the desert districts which have single digit literacy rates for women.
- Household and familial responsibilities barely leave any time and energy for women to participate in such

programmes. The severe conditions in many parts of Rajasthan make it difficult to meet the survival needs which are largely the responsibility of women.

- The restrictions imposed by family members on mobility, control exercised by the husbands, and purdah, inhibit women's participation. This specifically comes into play when identified MSKs have to go out of the village for the initial training which is always viewed with suspicion.
- Most often women who have received some education belong to upper caste/class families which are economically self-sufficient. These women do not feel the need to go out to work and earn a salary and working outside the home is viewed with disapproval.
- Even when qualified women are available, their low self-image inhibits them from taking on roles of authority, knowledge and assertiveness which are accepted only in men.

In order to boost the numbers of women teachers in areas where there are few, the SKP set up *Mahila Prashikshan Kendras* (MPKs) or training centres for women. The main objective of the MPK is to identify and train women to become teachers in SK schools. Rural women are identified for the MPKs from the villages where SKP schools are already functioning. There is no formal qualification for admission to these courses. Women are trained and educated up to a level corresponding to standard V. These training centres are managed by NGOs working in different regions. At present, there are 9 MPKs functioning in SKP in different areas of the state and about 200 women are enrolled. The training is residential: all the women live together and share the various responsibilities of the centre. The period of stay ranges from a minimum of six months to two years.

The women who join the MPKs have varied backgrounds. The identified women are either minimally literate, having left their studies early due to marriage, or illiterate. The selection is done with the agreement and consent of the husband and other family members. This is to ensure support during and after the training period. Some of the women who have joined the centres are wives of SKs already working in SKP. In such cases the resistance has been minimal, and the men have been more positive to women taking on these roles. Resistance to women's participation in the training programmes ranges from outright resistance that is overcome only through the persuasion of external agencies like NGOs, to non-opposition, for example, in the case of a woman widowed in childhood. Field reports of IDS-J, the evaluating agency, indicate that for some women the doubts are largely internal, including concern about their ability to live away from the family (Rajan and Sharma 1995).

The impact of the experiences of stepping out of tradition-bound roles on both their self-confidence as well as the perceptions of members of their families and communities has been significant in many cases. Lalita of Upargamiya, Bichiwada, stated, "My husband was against my joining the MPK, but I stayed on. Now he is proud of me, and my community members give me more respect." Damodar Kanwar of Lunkarunsar said "I have gained a lot of self-confidence after becoming a Shikshakarmi. Now I do not feel awkward about travelling alone or staying away from my family during training." The SKP trainings have provided an opportunity for women who are not highly qualified, to express themselves through their work. Clearly, the personal circumstances of each woman are likely to play a significant role in determining their motivation and ability to participate in the training programme.

The women who are trained at the MPKs, are identified from villages where SKP schools function. Since women have to stay at the centre for a minimum period till they complete their course, their absence from home is not easily accepted, and family members constantly need to be convinced and reassured. It has often been found that there is a gap between the number of women identified and those that eventually come to the MPK. Between April 1994 and March 1995, 150 women were identified, from different SK villages of which only 80 women finally joined the MPKs (SKB 1995). There have also been instances of male members (usually husbands) coming to the MPK and forcibly withdrawing women from the centres. Even when the woman trainee is keen on studying, she has to leave under pressure of the husband or other family members.

Recognising that married women with young children are likely to be the most difficult women to recruit, given their responsibilities to their marital homes, child-care facilities have been provided at most MPKs. Trained women helpers look after the smaller children in the crèche. Special nutrition is also provided for children. However, despite the alternative strategies created to fill the gaps between women and men teachers, the numbers of MSKs has not increased significantly in comparison to their male counterparts. SKP interventions also have to build bonds of trust between the programme actors and the community so that an overall, supportive environment is created. Such an environment, it is hoped, will enable recognition of the value and importance of allowing women to work and participate in the education system at all levels.

Eliciting Community Participation

The role of community members has been seen as crucial at different stages of the programme implementation and selection of SKs, as one of support and participation in all school activities. The SKs are responsible for constituting the Village Education Committees (VECs) whose membership comprises different people in the village, with a particular emphasis on having representation of deprived groups in the committee. SKs strive to involve parents and other community members in the activities of the school, using a variety of entry-points to establish contact. One of the more innovative methods used by the SKs is to work through traditional groups in the village, as for example the Bhajan Mandali, where groups of people come together to sing devotional songs. The VEC often plays the role of a pressure group in the village. Many SKs have also elicited the help of the VEC members in the initial survey work, increasing enrolment in schools by persuading the parents to send their children, especially girls, to school. Though both men and women are members of the VECs, in most cases, men actively participate in the various meetings and women take a back seat, particularly as the norms of purdah or female seclusion, remain strong.

An indicator of the extent of community involvement in the programme is also the size and type of contributions made by community members to various initiatives of SKP. In many of the villages, community members have also contributed, both financially as well as through physical labour, towards the building of rooms, the construction of boundary walls, making arrangements for drinking water and planting trees in the school permises. Donation of materials such as bricks, clocks, windows and doors have also formed a significant category of contributions, including the donation of land, as in the village Raimalvada of Osiana district (SANDHAN 1995).

Training: Learning Together

The training of Shikshakarmis has a central place in the entire strategy of the SKP. Since the Shikshakarmi concept involves substituting formally qualified teachers with Shikshakarmis, who have fewer educational qualifications and no teaching experience, their training is an extremely important aspect of the programme. In SKP training is not a one-time activity, but a continuous process leading to the enhancement of skills, teaching techniques and innovations at every level. After being selected, each identified SK goes through an intensive initial training of 37 days, which is followed by two refresher courses of 10 days and 30 days each, every year. Two-day meetings are also held every month for problem solving and individual coaching in every block. Both men and women SKs are trained together in the programme, and the trainings are organised mostly at the block level.

The initial training is in-house and residential, and focuses on equipping the SK to teach the primary school curriculum. This includes understanding basic concepts as well as the curriculum content of different subjects for Classes I–V. The emphasis is on the use of locally available materials and adapting the course to suit local conditions. Clearly the training is a challenge both in terms of building the confidence of the teachers as well as helping them to relearn teaching techniques in a totally different way from that which they were taught in school. As Shakuntala Devi of Ajmer put it, "There were 35 men and two women in the training camp. I was not very confident as I was resuming my studies after a gap of six years, and I was also inhibited by the presence of so many men. The training method was different to what I had been taught in school. We learnt songs, stories and games which we now use with the children in the school." (Rajan and Sharma, 1995). In the initial trainings, the number of men exceeds the number of women. The uneven gender balance inhibits women from participating fully as it is often the first time that they are interacting with men *other* than their family members. Recognising this as an immediate need for women, the MSKs have requested that either separate trainings be organised for women or that there should be at least two-third women participants in the training programme so that women can participate more freely. Recently separate camps for women have also been organised.

Evaluation as Process: The Tests of Participation

The purpose of participatory evaluation in SKP was to get regular access to fresh knowledge generated through the specific activities within the programme and to see how this could be used to reinforce the subsequent activities within the programme. This reflection was woven into each facet of the engagement constituting a continuous reaffirmation of the central values of the SKP.

In the initial years of the project, participatory evaluation processes found a strong reinforcement through a simple and effective intervention: the creation of a forum for review, dialogue, problem solving and planning which met every month, if possible, or at least after each major training. The information generated through these exercises acted as feedback ensuring and facilitating effective monitoring. As the programme expanded and the number of trainings increased, this participatory forum could not be maintained on a regular basis. A decision was then taken to decentralise these review forums, by handing them over to NGOs. However, it was found that the NGOs, for which SKP was only one activity, were unable to sustain the participatory ethos of the decentralised evaluation system owing to lack of time, as well as the human and material resources required for such a complex process.

As of January 1996, the SKP is being implemented in 85 blocks of 27 districts. There are 1,410 day schools and 2,944 night centres being managed by SKP. There are 1,22,112 children (72,544 boys and 49,568 girls) attending SKP schools. There are 3,476 SKs (3,073 men and 403 women) in the project (SKB 1996). Facilitating a review process that is ongoing and covers such a wide range of project participants is clearly a difficult task. Overcoming this "numbers" constraint has meant that the goals of evaluation have been modified to reflect an ethos of self-reflection and continuous learning on the part of all the participants. This has led to the inclusion of the teachers as 'evaluators' and 'researchers', where they are involved in the exercise of collaborating with the state-level bodies in the area of testing achievement levels of children, and other activities of the project. Learning is also emphasised at the level of the individuals as well as institutions, and as project partners are involved in the process, the stakes of the process are uniformly distributed among partners. Thus evaluation is not used as a means to apportion blame, but as a way of enhancing the total learning output of the SKP as a whole. The coordination of this review process has been decentralised to eight NGOs which operate as regional centres and organise quarterly review and planning meetings.

Lessons Learned

Although the enrolment of girls has increased in SKP schools since 1987, the gap between the enrolment of boys and girls continues to be a vulnerable area. A recent study carried out on achievement and retention of children in 50 schools out of 10 blocks (where SKP was implemented before 1989), shows that drop-out rates of girls continues to be high. In grade I the drop-out rate was as high as 26.3 per cent as compared to 17.1 per cent for the boys in 1989 but it declined to 17.9 per cent by 1993 for girls and 9.0 for boys. Similarly, for other grades, girls' drop-out rates have declined, but not as sharply as they have for boys. Results of retention rates also show that the retention rate for girls was much lower than that for boys (SANDHAN 1995). It is obvious that forms of patriarchal and economic control, multiple traditional roles and cultural norms which have been barriers to girls'/women's learning have to be addressed in a sustained manner to bring about visible changes.

When the SKP was implemented, gender issues were noted but were not a priority. The focus was on getting *all children* to the school, including girls. As the programme gradually expanded, it was evident that girls were marginalised and their access to primary education was considerably less than that of boys. The enrolment of girls, their attendance and retention were therefore recognised as a serious issue. Appointing women teachers, enabling the functioning of PPs and training rural women to become teachers were the main inputs visualised for improving the enrolment of girls. As the programme expanded it was evident that ensuring equality of access required a constant review of processes not only within the education system but also in the general social milieu. The awareness that many of the existing inequalities are rooted in gender relations in wider society has made the programme conscious of the depth and breadth of the strategies that are required to address gender inequalities. Later interventions like women escorts evolved out of this process of learning.

The selection and appointment of women teachers in SKP is indicative both of how the dominant patterns within households are reflected in community interactions and pull back women, as well as of the need for gender sensitive planning to transform given realities. The number of MSKs has not increased significantly in comparison to their male counterparts. The fact that for most MSKs it is the first time they have started "working" (in a "naukri" or proper job), maintaining a balance between the household and school responsibilities has not been easy. This also reflects the lives of many women in rural and urban Rajasthan.

Gaining the approval of the community has also been crucial for the MSKs. The initial resistance was articulated in "how can women with low qualifications and lack of training teach in schools?" or "how can village 'bahus', daughters-in-law, teach in school without purdah and along with male teachers?" The fear that women would become independent and 'go out of control' has also been constantly expressed. The shift in responses has, however, come gradually and now MSKs are being accepted as 'competent' teachers within the community. The experience of the women teachers also reflects that the unequal access to resources in the early years continues to influence women's activities and participation in 'public' spheres and they enter these spheres with a cumulative disadvantage.

At the institutional level, the entry of women has been facilitated by making flexible the institutional rules for entry, reflected in the lowering of qualifications for women. But the number of women at all levels is still limited. Till recently there was only one woman at the SKB level, and fewer in the training group. A small number of Master Trainers/Resource Persons are women. The block level functionaries are mostly male. The women in the project are in a minority compared to their male counterparts. The need for representation at every level—preparation, planning, implementation and evaluation—seems necessary.

The SKP experience indicates that a gender dimension to understanding existing inequalities is essential. An initiative with the best of intentions can have a negative impact if the activities of women and men as well as the resources they use are not taken into account. The SKP has also demonstrated that it is important to progressively integrate the specific needs of girls/women into overall programme goals, targets, activities and budget.

Conclusion

The SKP represents a design and implementation strategy for providing quality education in distant areas of Rajasthan and achieving quantitative goals of universal access to education. The implementation process at the field level has ensured that schools which were functioning irregularly are now regular. By and large the verdict from the villages is that the schools 'function' and the teaching and learning transaction has the approval of parents. It has taken into account the problems of out-of-school children, especially girls in the rural areas and devised appropriate mechanisms for their enrolment and retention. While retaining the textbooks and the curriculum of the regular educational system, Shikshakarmis have been provided with sufficient flexibility for adapting to local conditions and making the teaching process creative for the children. The programme is not aimed at creating a parallel system, but can be seen as a step forward in non-formalisation of formal education with the active involvement of the community.

Given the intensity of the problems in universalising primary education in Rajasthan, the Shikshakarmi represents a "sensitively" designed strategy for bringing about change in a bleak scenario. Phase II of SKP further envisages the increased participation of women as teachers and the improved enrolment and retention of girls in the day schools and night centres. A further need would be to create circumstances within SKP whereby girls and women can analyse their life situations which would help them to reach out to new skills and knowledge systems and weaken the ideological beliefs that impede women's participation in education. The goal of gender integration in education is not only to increase the participation of girls and women in the education process but to contribute to the transformation of gender relations at both community and institutional levels and thereby bring about equity within the social fabric.

Notes

[1]See King and Hill (1993) and Nayyar (1991) for detailed discussions of the policy focus on women's education.

[2]Government of India (1995: 38).

[3]"Opportunity costs" refer to the costs of labour foregone in terms of children's contribution to paid and unpaid segments of household economy.

[4]All statistics are for the years 1993–94. These figures are from Mahajan et al. 1994: 15.

[5]Panchayati Raj refers to the three-tiered system of local government in place all over India.

References

Baden, Sally and Cathy Green, 1994. *Gender and Education in Asia and the Pacific Bridge* Sussex: Institute of Development Studies.

Bellew R. and E.M. King, 1991. "Promoting Girls and Women's Education: Lessons from the Past", IBRD, WP 715, Washington: World Bank.

Colclough C. and K. Lewin, 1994. *Educating All the Children: Strategies for Primary Schooling in the South* Oxford: The Clarendon Press.

Department of Education, 1986. "National Policy of Education", New Delhi: Government of India.

———, 1992. "National Policy of Education 1986: Programme of Action", New Delhi: Government of India.

Department of Women and Child Development, 1994. "Draft Country Paper for Beijing 1995", New Delhi: Government of India.

Desai, Neera, 1995. "Women's Education in India" in Conway, J.K. and S. Bourque, [ed] *Politics of Women's Education: Perspective from Asia, Africa and Latin America* Ann Arbor: University of Michigan Press.

Government of India, 1959. *Report of the National Committee on Women's Education*, New Delhi: Government of India Press.

———, 1991. *Census* (Directorate of Census Operations).

Government of Rajasthan, 1987. *Shiksha Karmi Project, Rajasthan, India, Draft Project Document Phase I.*

———, 1993. "Elementary Education in Rajasthan", Jaipur.

———, 1994. *Shiksha Karmi Project, Rajasthan India, Draft Project Document Phase II* Jaipur.

Herz, B., Subbarao, M. Habib and H. Raney, 1991. "Letting Girls Learn: Promising Approaches to Primary and Secondary Education", Washington: World Bank Discussion Paper 133.

Institute of Development Studies, 1991a. *The Shiksha Karmi Project* Jaipur.

———, 1991b. "Situational Analysis of Women and Children in Rajasthan", Jaipur.

Jain, S., 1994. *SWRC: A Journey through a Decade—Education of Out-of-School Children: Case Studies from India* London: Commonwealth Secretariat.

Jain, S., 1992. "Participatory Processes in Shiksha Karmi Project: Rationale and Modality", Jaipur: IDS.

King, E.M. and M. Hill [eds], 1993. *Women's Education in Developing Countries: Barriers, Benefits and Politicies* IBRD: John Hopkins University Press.

Mahajan, B., R.S. Tyagi and S. Agarwal, 1996. "Educational Administration in Rajasthan: Structures, Processes and Future Prospects", New Delhi: NIEPA.

Nayar Usha, 1993. *Universal Primary Education of Rural Girls in India* New Delhi: NCERT.

Rajan, S. and R. Sharma, 1995. "Mahila Shiksha Karmis in SKP", IDS Jaipur.

Srinivasan, S., 1987. "The Kumbalgarh Experience", Jaipur: Institute of Development Studies.

Study of Retention and Achievement in Shiksha Karmi Schools, 1994. SANDHAN Research Centre, Jaipur.

UNESCO. "Basic Education for Girls and Women", Paris: International Consultative Forum on Education for All.

World Bank, 1995. "Levelling the Playing Field: Giving Girls an Equal Chance for Basic Education: Three Countries Efforts", Economic Develeopment Institute.

10

From Private to Public

The Emergence of Violence Against Women as an Issue in the Women's Development Programme, Rajasthan

KANCHAN MATHUR

Introduction

Although the degree and form of gender-related violence may vary from society to society, its practice appears to constitute a relatively universal aspect of the subordination of women. In some societies, the threat and practice of violence is used to ensure women remain within socially-defined boundaries of behaviour and space; in others, their status as 'property' of male family members deprives them of rights over their bodies and sexuality within the familial sphere; in yet others, violence against women may constitute a legitimised and routinised aspect of prevailing cultural definitions of gender. In Rajasthan, all these three forms of violence are in evidence and reflect the historically low value attached to women in this extremely feudal society. The devaluation of women in this region of India is manifested in the documentation of historically high rates of female infanticide, restriction of widows, worship of sati, adherence to purdah and more recently of female foeticide and of dowry deaths, along with the more conventional developmental indicators of some of the lowest rates of female education and life expectancy in the country. It also has an alarmingly high and rising ratio of men to women in the population: there were 919 females to 1,000 males in 1981, a figure which, by 1991, had fallen to 913. Underpinning, and reinforcing these assaults on women's bodies is their material powerlessness: ownership of property and assets are traditionally vested in men, women's ability to seek any form of economic resources is ruled out by the strict controls on their mobility while the norms and values which are internalised by both women and men in the course of growing up ensures that this is seen as a pre-ordained set of inequalities.

Some attempts have been made by the state to address some of the more extreme or visible casualties of violence and discrimination against women. State-run homes have been set up to support destitute, outcaste, delinquent and mentally disturbed women as well as victims of assault, but they have not always been shown the necessary level of commitment by the state. The Mahila Sadan in Jaipur accommodates women who are mentally unbalanced, women who have been convicted for crimes, deserted women and girls from remand homes. In 1989–90 an official enquiry of a case of death by burning of a 15-year old inmate brought to light many inadequacies in the organisation. By contrast, Shakti Stambh, a short stay home for women in distress, presents a viable alternative to women with problems. Established in 1987, it is financially aided by the Government of India and run by RUWA (Rajasthan University Women's Association). The home offers shelter, vocational training, free legal aid and rehabilitation to women during the course of their stay. Similar services are also provided at Kota by the Sri Karni Nagar Vikas Samiti. Other examples of state effort include the Voluntary Action Bureau of the State Social Welfare Board, established in 1983 and the affiliated Family Counselling Centre (Asara), established in 1989, run with the assistance of RUWA. The Family Court set up in Jaipur in 1986, and the first of its kind in the country, was followed by two more in 1988 in Ajmer and Jodhpur. The Directorate of Women, Children and Nutrition in Rajasthan has its own cell to look into cases of atrocities against women. Since it has no authority to investigate the registered cases, it functions as a referral agency, from where cases are forwarded to the appropriate departments. Also as a part of the law enforcement facility in the state, the first Mahila Thana was established in 1989 in Jaipur. The Mahila Thana facilitates women victims of exploitation and violence in registering their cases. The cooperation of women's groups is also sought in many cases.

While NGOs/women's groups have strongly vocalised the need for support services in the state, they also feel that a systematic review and reform of the existing services is an essential first step before further interventions are designed and implemented. Evaluations carried out suggest that "the existing services very often exploit the very people they are meant to save". The facilities provided are grossly inadequate, the living conditions appalling and official attitudes have often been to put the blame on the women for inviting 'trouble'. Most of the state's efforts in the past have been clearly welfarist in design, attempting to act on behalf of women as victims without involving them in either articulating the problem or designing the solution. Moreover, most of these efforts have been directed at some of the more visible manifestations of violence against women; the more hidden or unacknowledged problems of domestic violence or culturally sanctioned violence against women have taken longer to come into the public domain of politics and collective resistance. To some extent, this can be attributed to the cultural construction of womanhood itself which entails suffering in silence and keeping private what occurs within the four walls of the home so as not to bring shame and dishonour on the family, regardless of the emotional and physical costs this imposes.

The Women's Development Programme (WDP), Rajasthan

This essay deals with the process by which this silence was broken by a group of women in Rajasthan. These were women working with a government intervention designed for women's development and some village women that they worked with. Although the WDP began as an innovative programme in 1984 to facilitate the 'empowerment of rural women', the issue of violence against women was not initially on its agenda. Its emphasis was instead on training, information dissemination, and formation of women's groups at the village level so as to provide a microlevel compensation for the failure of the more centralised development efforts to significantly alter women's marginalised status in society and the economy.

The WDP was launched by the Government of Rajasthan in August 1984 with financial assistance from UNICEF for the initial years of the project and in a context where a number of development schemes were already in place but were recognised to have bypassed women. WDP differed from previous government efforts in a number of significant ways. First, it shifted away from the notion of an intervention as a 'delivery mechanism' in which women were positioned as passive recipients, to a concern with strengthening women's ability to act on their own behalf. Its basic premise was that women had the capacity for equal participation with men in the process of development and its stated goal was the realisation of this capacity through the removal of various mechanisms which curtailed it. Noting that men had hitherto been entrusted with the responsibility for women's welfare within the family and community with little sign of success, WDP also gave women responsibility for all levels of the programme. Its strategy was to empower women through a process of education and training, communication of information, and collective action so as to allow them to act on their own behalf in bringing about change in their social and economic status (IDS 1986).

The initial formulation of the project began with the pooling of experiences and lessons from the existing NGOs and women's groups. In particular, attention was paid to the leadership training programme of rural women conducted by an NGO, Social Work and Research Centre (SWRC Tilonia, Ajmer district, Rajasthan) in the year 1980, which testified to the leadership potential of rural women. A series of discussions were simultaneously initiated with administrators, researchers and activists. This sharing process took place over a period of two years, leading finally to the drawing up of the project document in 1983.

Given the poor record so far of 'blueprint' approaches to programme implementation, which allowed little scope for lessons from the field to be incorporated into programme design, a far more flexible approach was considered necessary. In the case of WDP, it was decided that rather than working out a detailed programme, the guiding principles of the programme would be agreed and a relevant set of activities then allowed to evolve through practice-based learning. The willingness to recognise that all planning is done on the basis of incomplete knowledge and is hence neccessarily provisional was the hallmark of the WDP's special methodology in which 'participation' and 'revisability' constituted the central principles. In other words, it was a methodology of discovery by 'doing' [IDS(J)1986] rather than of mechanistic implementation in accordance with a predetermined set of operations. The rationale running throughout the entire programme was to create the conditions which would allow networks of communication to emerge amongst rural women, giving them the necessary 'space' to discover their priorities and act upon them. In the spirit of 'learning by doing', monitoring and evaluation were interpreted as 'shared reflection' which would be woven into each of its processes, be it a training programme or a village meeting or a workshop for subsequent planning. This approach lent itself to the process of constantly 'revising' programme strategies in view of information and knowledge acquired through group-based reflection.

However, a predictable support structure for change—both administrative and emotional—was considered essential from the very beginning of the project to both support the village worker and to provide checks and balances at all levels. The structure encompassed different levels of state adminstration and a range of different institutional actors in order to draw on the comparative strengths of each. At the village level, each selected gram panchayat (village council) appointed a sathin (village worker) who belonged to one of the villages of the gram panchayat. She was responsible for the formation of women's forums at the village level and for facilitating discussion issues related to development. She was expected to work in close coordination with sathins of neighbouring gram panchayats. She was to be paid an honorarium of Rs 200 per month (increased to Rs 250 in 1992). A cluster of 10 gram panchayats with 10 sathins was coordinated by a pracheta, the block level government functionary, whose role was to provide support and guidance to the sathin. The pracheta was also the link between the village and the district level.

Two different organisations were charged with district level responsibilities: the District Women's Development Agency (DWDA) under the chairmanship of the District Collector and the Information Development and Resource Agency (IDARA) which provided technical support. IDARAs were part of a local voluntary agency working in the field of adult education and women, within a district. The concept of IDARA was based on the fact that a substantial portion of the work at the grassroot level was related to the information needs of women which had to be responded to through appropriate training and communication methodologies. The State IDARA was responsible for overall co-ordination of these activities. The Director WDP (a government officer from the Indian Administrative Service) was the overall in-charge of the programme. The monitoring and evaluation of the programme was to be facilitated by the Institute of Development Studies (IDS), Jaipur. All the state level agencies worked as 'partners' and in close collaboration with each other.

WDP was initially implemented in six districts of the state. These were Ajmer, Jaipur, Jodhpur, Bhilwara, Udaipur and Banswara. Training activities played a key role in the evolution of the WDP's activities and goals, particularly the trainings conducted to induct sathins and prachetas into the programme. Resource persons who had been actively working on women's issues were invited to participate in these efforts which were aimed at bringing about a revised perception among women workers of their identity and self image as a first step in a larger process of social change. Its rationale and methods were consequently very different to trainings imparted in schemes like DWCRA and TRYSEM, which focused on imparting skills rather than bringing about a shift in attitudes. It did not resort to the usual lectures on cleanliness, nutrition and child development. Instead it sought to break down or minimise hierarchies among women so as build their sense of collectivity and to create a climate of questioning, reflecting, sharing, choosing, seeking and discovering, through listening and talking as the most fruitful medium for this shared learning. The emphasis was primarily on exploring and assimilating new ideas through different modes of expression—songs, puppetry, drawing and dancing—which came easily and naturally to the women involved.

With the programme still awaiting a full-fledged take-off, a beginning was made with the first sathin training in August 1984 at Bada Padampura (Jaipur district). In the absence of any district personnel to look into the selection, the Rajasthan Adult Education Association (Jaipur and Ajmer) assisted in identifying villages and sathins for the programme. The first lot of sathins, selected at random, was heterogeneous in terms of age, caste and literacy. They were between 16 to 55 years old, from different castes, with educational levels ranging from illiteracy to a matric pass (standard X). They were selected on the basis of two clearly stated criteria: openness to new ideas and willingness to participate in a process of social change. The induction process was intended to provide new recruits with a space to share their experiences. The first step, almost always was an exercise in 'coming out of oneself', i.e. looking at one's own being and actions as an 'outsider', asking oneself, 'What is it that I do?' 'What is it that I think?' In a climate of togetherness, these questions slowly melt into a deeper perception of, 'What are the things we do?' and, 'What are the kinds of experiences that we go through?' This move from the private world to a 'shared' world generates an experience of strength. Suffering in privacy, recognising one's lot as god-given or 'destined', is always an experience of powerlessness. Sharing, listening and reflecting lent a distance from oneself and facilitated a balanced perspective (IDS J 1988).

Although violence against women had not been formally foregrounded in the training processes, it very quickly emerged as a common theme running through the lives of women from different social backgrounds. As poor rural women began sharing incidents of violence suffered at the hands of fathers, husbands, sons, mothers or mothers-in-law, what had hitherto been concealed behind a wall of silence began to be articulated in public. Middle class and semi-urban women were also forced through this process to look at violence in their own lives and, abandoning 'respectability', came out with stories of violence they had encountered. This sharing of experiences brought home to women that what they perceived as 'destiny' or 'fate' or their own isolated experience was, in fact, a socially constructed way of controlling them. Commonly held beliefs to which they had also subscribed and on which they had invariably placed the blame for any form of violence that they suffered, whether at home or outside, began to be seen for what they were: the legitimation of the cultural devaluation of women, their bodies and their sense of self.

The spontaneity which marked the training process was evident from the early days. In the first pracheta training in Jaipur district, two of the participants who were returning to the training quarters from the agricultural college in the early evening faced harassment at the hands of some students. They depicted this incident later to their colleagues in the form of a role play, in which they acted out the utter indifference of some of the onlookers to the incident, including some professors and students. The roleplay evoked an immediate response among the other participants and many told similar stories from their own lives, drawing from experiences of harrassment and humiliation within the family and at work. Thus violence against women came onto the WDP agenda from its first moment of implementation, despite never having been articulated at the planning stage, precisely because of the 'learning by doing' flexibility upon which it was premised.

Responses to Violence

As the programme evolved, it became increasingly clear that the issue of violence had to be given priority within the programme, whether the violence concerned the sathins themselves or the village women. If WDP's goal of altering women's self images was to be realised, it was imperative to free them from the fear of violence, starting with domestic violence: unless women were respected in the domestic realm, they would be unable to emerge as self-confident actors in the public domain. As the magnitude and pervasiveness of the problem became apparent through the WDP trainings, it provided a platform of solidarity as the women began to realise that change would not come about unless they were prepared to make the 'private' public and the 'personal' political. Women had initially been extremely hesitant to talk about their personal problems, particularly because they had also internalised the belief that whatever the problem, "*ghar ki baat ghar mein hi rahni chahiye*" (family matters should remain within the family). Thus, it became necessary for the sathins and prachetas to create 'safe spaces' at the village level where women could come together and talk about themselves as individuals. The jajams and shivirs proved to be a successful forum for this purpose. Over time, a large number of women started attending the jajams. Though initially it was difficult to create an atmosphere in which personal issues could be discussed without inhibition, gradually the jajams enabled the women to overcome their deep rooted inhibitions and to talk at length on various issues including domestic violence. Soon no group meeting passed without a story of violence from one of the participants which would invariably lead to narration of other stories of violence.

The feeling in the early days was euphoric because the movement gathered momentum at a great pace. Networks of women across villages were set up through the sathins and then across different blocks via the prachetas and then brought together at the district level. Women who had previously not moved beyond their homes, or their villages, were now part of a state-wide network. Thus, almost from the outset, a recognition emerged within the WDP that there was a close link between women's subordinated status and the violence they faced within the household and the community. The functionaries used different communication skills to create awareness and inform the villagers about gender violence and gender discrimination. For this purpose, songs, puppetry, role plays, nukkad nataks (street plays), posters using the local idiom, proved to be a powerful medium of expression. The WDP functionaries believed that these would help women to evolve suitable mechanisms to fight their subordinated status. They also disseminated legal information regarding child marriages, dowry, rape etc. in village level meetings.

At the same time, many cases of violence pertaining to wife battering, deserted wives, molestation, sexual harassment and rape were being reported in various districts so that discussions and sharing began to give way to strategies for dealing with the problem. The sharing process had given rise to the belief that resistance to the problem of violence against women had to be handled publicly. At the same time, and in contrast to more conventional development issues, like famine relief works, the drinking water problem or smokeless chulahs, the approach was to deal with each individual case as it arose rather than a generalised campaign. It was clearly understood that any step taken would affect the life of the concerned individual. Moreover the approach taken by the group would set a precedent for the rest of the community. Thus, it was not an issue in which WDP could indulge in blunt, random or trial-and-error methods. The ground rule followed was that the intervention should not increase the victim's vulnerability but rather should aim to empower her and build her support networks with other women associated with various levels of the programmes i.e. sathins, village women, prachetas, IDARAS, DWDA functionaries etc.

The case of Vimla Rana of Jaipur district is illustrative of this collective approach to an individual incident. Vimla Rana is a young woman of the dholi caste. While bathing at the village well, she was assaulted by Gangaram Meena of the same village. Vimla was able to thwart his attempt and forcefully resisted his attack. Sathin Bhanwari discussed the incident in the jajam and the sathins and prachetas decided to take up the case with immediate effect. They reached Bhateri and met Vimla Rana who was willing to talk about the incident and insisted that Gangaram ought to be punished. The sathins and prachetas decided to confront Gangaram. They found him bathing at the village well. The group surrounded him and cursed him, "Gangaram *doob mar*!" (Gangaram, drown and die). "Gangaram hai! hai!" Gangaram managed to escape with grave difficulty, by running into a nearby field leaving behind his bicycle. The women chased him for a kilometre and a half.

The prachetas and sathins then decided on strategies for further action. On making enquiries they learnt that Gangaram had already raped four women in the past. Vimla and her husband did not want to approach the police. They said that they were very poor and would not be able to afford the expense. However, they were willing to take up the issue at the community level. Vimla's mother-in-law was not supportive for she felt that making 'private'/family matters public would only lead to losing the family honour. The sathins, Bhanwari and Godavari, tried to convince Vimla's mother-in-law that taking up the issue would ensure that no other woman would be subjected to such humiliation. Since Gangaram had committed similar deeds in the past it was extremely important that he be punished. When this case was discussed in the jati panchayat, the members decided to punish Gangaram in the traditional way by placing a heap of shoes (tied in a cloth) on his head and more formally by imposing a penalty of Rs 1100. They then declared that justice had been done and a 'suitable' punishment given to the culprit.

However, when Vimla heard about the judgement of the jati panchayat she felt that gross injustice had been done because she did not agree with the decision and the punishment had been meted out at night without public knowledge. The sathin was also threatened by the men in the village with dire consequences, if she raised her voice. As a strategy the WDP group decided to hold a large 'show of strength' meeting at village Bhateri. This meeting was attended by the entire district WDP personnel, by the Additional Director, Department of Women and Child, as well as by concerned women activitists and academics. Some sathins and prachetas from neighbouring districts also participated in the meeting.

The sarpanch was asked to call Gangaram. But Gangaram (being the sarpanch's nephew) had been hidden by some of the villagers. He was afraid that his face would be painted black and he would be put to shame in the presence of the entire village community. Vimla (though in purdah) spoke openly in the meeting and insisted that justice for her entailed hitting Gangaram publicly with shoes five times on the head. However, Gangaram did not come before the gathering. After a long wait the sarpanch assured the gathering that he would bring Gangaram to the panchayat meeting within a week. The meeting was called off once this assurance was given. This was the first time a village woman had articulated in a public forum that she had been the victim of an attempted rape. The meeting succeeded in bringing forth some basic issues, i.e., the onus of guilt should be borne by the culprit, not by the woman who is raped. It also helped the WDP functionaries in putting forward a woman's perspective on rape and the notion of justice in relation to rape. The meeting helped to highlight the fact that the notion of justice for the jati panchayat and for the woman who has been raped vary considerably.

As reports of violence were discussed in greater detail, it was found that in a majority of the cases, women were subjected to violence by members of their own family. The first such cases of the so-called 'suicide' of Haryana Brahmin women (village Tholai and Khawha Rani) in Jaipur district were reported during the Panchayati Raj camp at village Bhateri in 1987. It was brought to the notice of the WDP group that women of this caste are forced to have sexual relations with their husband's brothers and father. In cases where they refused to suffer this humiliation, they were murdered and thrown into village wells. These had been reported as cases of suicide but it had now become clear that they were linked to sexual exploitation within the family; also that cases reported as suicide by women needed to be investigated thoroughly as they could also be murders. Such cases also helped in creating a deeper understanding of the wide range of forms of violence against women. As a strategy the sathins felt that since cases were mostly related to familial/domestic violence, they should attempt to hold extensive discussions with the concerned family members. If such an initiative proved to be unsuccessful, it would be taken up in a larger forum within the village.

Every case of violence, and the process followed, was thoroughly discussed, reviewed and evaluated at every step of the way. For instance, in cases such as the above or in most instances of dowry deaths where the mothers-in-law or sisters-in-law clearly emerged as the perpetrators of violence, women often saw it as a vindication of the clichéd belief that women were women's worst oppressors and went on to narrate instances of similar harassment in their own lives. This led to sustained dialogues with the WDP functionaries and trainers in order to analyse why women so often appeared to collude in their own oppression—in a world where women and men have both internalised partriarchal values, and where women are excluded from most forms of self-expression, the only way open to them to exercise power is through the oppression of other women.

Involving the Jati Panchayats at the village level in resolving cases of violence against women was seen as a necessary step. The effort has been to resolve cases at the village level as far as possible. However, though the Jati Panchayats have been involved in resolving cases of violence against women since 1987, women have not always been able to participate in them and often the decisions have gone against them. Since 1993 the women have begun to raise their voices against this. For example a landmark case of September 1995 in Jodhpur district is indicative of the shift where women have been able to assert their rights and create their own spaces in public spheres like the Jati Panchayat. Durgaram of village Raimalwara, Osian P.S., a Meghwal by caste, mercilessly beat up his aunt. A village panchayat was called by Khiyaram and his wife (Durgaram's aunt). Panchayat members did not ask Khiyaram's wife to attend. A decision was taken in her absence that Durgaram would pay Rs 10 as penalty and one sack of jowar (grain) would be fed by him to pigeons. When the women got to know about this decision they contacted sathin Dhapu Bai and informed her. Dhapu and several other women decided that they would refuse to accept such a decision because justice had not been meted out. Dhapu then called a meeting of the women's panchayat. An alternative decision was taken that Durgaram would pay a sum of Rs 100 to his aunt, as well as 4 kgs of ghee. He would also pay her Rs 1200 towards her medical treatment. The women's group argued with the men in the village that they had to be objective and just when making important decisions. Moreover any decision involving women ought to include the women's perspective. The men finally agreed to the decision of the women's group.

Quite often it was only through a strategic approach that the WDP functionaries were able to call the panchayat meetings and ensure a discussion on women's issues. Usually the pracheta or the Project Director was instrumental in achieving this after a sustained dialogue with village elders/panchs. Initially it was not easy for the WDP functionaries to involve the entire village community on issues relating to violence against women. However, the experience of the functionaries showed that village bodies were consistently involved in solving the issues and in most cases their decisions were taken as final. A large number of cases relating to rape and sexual harassment were resolved at the panchayat level. The victim's family was given the choice of approaching the legal structure or village-level bodies. In a large number of cases, specially those of rape, the family preferred village-level settlements. For, according to the villagers, "approaching the formal structure and registering it as a police case would lead to loss of honour for the family as well as the village." Taking private matters outside village boundaries was seen as bringing adverse publicity to the village and the villagers did not want to risk this. Usually most of the cases could not be solved in one single meeting and a series of meetings were needed before a resolution could be reached.

Punishments at the panchayats generally took traditional forms of social humiliation (*jati-bahar*) of the culprits: for example, blackening the face of the accused and riding him around the village on a donkey or requiring him to gather the footwear of the villagers into a cloth bundle and put it on his head. However, in some districts the emphasis was also on monetary punishments. For instance in Bidmani's case (Jodhpur district) the sathin received information that Bidmani was being forced by her mother-in-law into sexual relationships with strangers. She immediately called a panchayat meeting of the 84 Jati Panchayat villages. In this village panchayat it was decided that the men who had forced Bidmani into sexual encounters would be punished. The offenders were made to pay Rs 1500–2500 and her in-laws were also made to pay Rs 2500. Apart from this, as a form of social humiliation, the family members were told to collect the shoes of all those who were present in a basket and carry them on their heads.

Experience also showed how deeply embedded the notion of men's prerogative to use violence against women was and hence how difficult was the struggle to change attitudes. In cases of domestic violence, even where the family member had asked forgiveness, it was easy to resort to violence once again. Therefore, as a strategy, WDP functionaries insisted on taking written apologies where applicable. These written statements were taken in the presence of the village community, especially the village elders. This usually acted as a deterrent not only for the perpetrator of the crime/violence, but also for others.

Though a common pattern was discernible in the programme's response to violence, individual district functionaries also evolved their own strategies in handling cases of violence. In Jodhpur district, for instance, a decision was taken that in any case of violence the nature of counselling should be such that the victim should herself be able to decide what course of action should be resorted to by her and by the group. It was also decided that women whose issues had been taken up and resolved should join in dealing with subsequent cases of violence against any other woman in the district. This helped serve as an example for other women in distress. It helped them to understand their own situation better and gain greater confidence in the working of the programme.

Rehabilitating the women was seen as a priority. The WDP (Jodhpur) group felt that in cases taken up by them, it was important that some form of relief should be made available to the woman. Identifying the specific problem of each woman therefore became a necessary step. In cases pertaining to single women whose husbands had either deserted them, or remarried/migrated, or were dead, and the woman needed financial assistance (besides other help), an effort was made to provide them with employment in famine relief works or in government schemes. Later, loans were also provided through the Sambal Project. In some cases, as in the case of Ghevri Bai who was raped and gave birth to a son, the unwanted child was given for adoption by the district functionaries.

The Roop Kanwar Sati: Gender, Religion and Cultural Identity

The history of the WDP was punctuated by two episodes of violence against women in Rajasthan which caught the nation's attention and had major ramifications for the way in which the programme evolved: the Roop Kanwar Sati (Sept 4, 1987) and the Bhanwari Devi rape case (Sept 22, 1992). These two events shaped and influenced the course of WDP, bringing home to its members, in very different ways, both the deep-rooted legitimation of violence against women within the culture as well as its ramifications in terms of national and state-level politics. Roop Kanwar, an 18-year old Rajput girl of village Deorala in Sikar district, was forced to immolate herself on the funeral pyre of her husband on September 4, 1987. The incident shocked women's groups in Rajasthan and throughout the country, because a living Roop Kanwar was set on fire in broad daylight, in the presence of thousands of people, without a single protest being voiced. The incident generated a serious debate within the WDP forums.

Interviews with a cross section of people, both urban and rural, educated and uneducated, women and men, revealed an alarmingly large number of people who felt that if Roop Kanwar had committed sati of her own free will, she deserved respect but if she had been forced into it, it constituted a crime. Few sought to ask what factors might lead to, or justify, the public burning of a woman, whether self-inflicted or forced. The sathins, however, who had in the short space of three years learnt to question the 'sanctity of culture' on issues where it so clearly violated women's rights, gave very different responses:

> "*Jeev to sabko pyara lagta hai*" (everybody loves life). No woman gives her life away happily, even those who have committed sati. The thought of leading the life of a widow, which appears hopeless, makes her take this decision."

> "Every year so many women jump into wells and die. Why don't we call them satis ? But then that will mean recognising the fact that women kill themselves because of *dukh* (unhappiness). This is what society does not want to see."

> "Roop Kanwar could have been saved if her family members and villagers had wanted her to live."

> "I don't believe in the power of Sat or Sati Mata (sati goddess). People of our community go to worship Sati Mata after the birth of a child and for marriages. When my two year old child was ill we took him to the temple, the child died and we came back crying. If Sati Mata had Sat due to her miraculous powers, my child would have survived."

The issue was recognised by the sathins as an issue of women's identity and dignity rather than an issue of "dharma". The slogan "*sawal hai naari ki pehchan ka, nari ke samman ka*" (the question is one of knowing women, of respecting them) reflected this concern and became instrumental in mobilising a large number of women who not only questioned this practice but also the way in which society exercised control over women through its interpretation of religious ideology. The WDP group and all the women and men who rallied around this incident strongly felt that Roop Kanwar had been burnt to death at Deorala under the garb of a 'holy' act, following the death of her husband Maal Singh. They clearly stated that it was not a case of individual or familial violence but a case of institutionalised violence, committed with the sympathetic support of a whole community as well as the district administration, who not only witnessed the enactment of the gruesome spectacle but made no attempt to stop it. Women in Deorala were terrorised into silence when approached by women from outside the village; they were surrounded by groups of men who dictated their reponses.

The Roop Kanwar case became an important turning point for understanding and countering gender violence both within the WDP and other forums. The subsequent anti-sati rally organised in October 1987 in Jaipur by women's groups (state and national level) attracted an unprecedented number of rural women and men besides WDP functionaries and urban groups. The event linked WDP with numerous women's organisations all over the country. The isolation that women experienced in facing violence was hence further broken. Solidarity now moved from the village block, district, state, to the national level, and women's long-repressed emotions were aired in a variety of different forums.

The Roop Kanwar widow immolation brought home to many women how easily religious discourses could be deployed to transform what could be regarded as the murder of a widow into a sacred event, one which brought honour, rather than punishment, for the widow's family. Any attempt at dispassionate debate between opposing views was further dispelled as the issue was transformed into one of religious and cultural identity for Rajputs. Time and again the debates would shift from the right to life to the right to practise religion, from constitutional and legal issues to the realm of dharma to which there could be no challenge. Rajput youths came out in a large procession through the streets of Jaipur with swords in their hands, in support of sati and ostensibly as an assertion of their cultural identity but also as a show of strength.

However, the unprecedented outrage and anger, nationwide, especially among the women's groups, against the murder of Roop Kanwar in the name of sati, led to the promulgation of the Rajasthan Sati (Prevention Ordinance), 1987. Ultimately, a Federal Legislation—the Commission of Sati (Prevention) Act, 1987 (Act No.4 of 1988) providing for stringent punishment, including the death sentence, for abetment of sati was passed and made applicable throughout the country. As key activists in the movement, the WDP sathins could feel a sense of achievement and also recognise that they had moved from the sphere of local community politics to an appreciation of how gender politics was played out at the level of the state.

The Rape of Bhanwari Devi: Gender, Caste and the Practice of Law

The interconnections between gender politics at local and state level were spelt out again but rather differently for the WDP sathins as a result of their involvement in another incidence of violence against women—the Bhanwari Devi rape case (September 22, 1992). The case also brought together the interplay between caste and gender in a particularly graphic way. Bhanwari, a 40 year old Kumhar woman from the village of Bhateri was selected and trained as a sathin in 1985 in the WDP. Her sensitivity to women's issues as well as an overall commitment to ensure justice on various occasions made her especially respected in the WDP group. She had taken up issues related to land, water, the public distribution system, literacy, health and payment of minimum wages at famine relief works, and had received the support of the men and women of her village on all these issues. In 1987 she took up a major issue of attempted rape of a woman from a neighbouring village and elicited substantial support. Till then, Bhanwari had no history of enmity over land, money or caste issues with the village community. Bhanwari's isolation in Bhateri began specifically on the issue of child marriage just before the festival of Akha Teej in 1992. This year the State Government had decided to observe the fortnight preceding Akha Teej as an anti-child marriage fortnight. A public appeal was issued by the Chief Minister, and the Chief Secretary wrote to all the District Collectors to conduct a campaign in this regard.

The stopping of child marriages became a 'target' of the programme. This was substantially different from the soft-line approach WDP functionaries had been taking, treating it as a matter of discussion and persuasion. Together with the pracheta, the Project Director and the District Women's Development Agency (DWDA) tried to persuade the people in the area to not go in for child marriage. It was clear that, along with others, some of the influential upper caste Gujar families were planning child marriages and were determined to perform them. When Bhanwari visited Ram Karan Gujar of Bhateri and tried to convince him not to get his year-old daughter married, she met with hostility and aggression. The Vidhayak (MLA) of the area also strongly opposed Bhanwari, possibly because 40 of the 100 households in the village belonged to Gujar caste and many of them were both wealthy and had powerful political connections.

In response to the appeal of the District Collector, a list was prepared by all the sathins in the district, and the SDO and the Deputy Superintendent of Police (DSP) began to make rounds of the villages to prevent child marriages. On May 5, 1992 the SDO and the DSP came to Bhateri to stop the marriage of a one-year old girl in Ram Karan Gujar's family. As was the case with all the other marriages in the area, the state machinery only succeeded in preventing the marriage from taking place on the day of Akha Teej. It took place, instead, at 2 a.m. the next morning and no police action was taken against the family. People in the village, however, linked Bhanwari's efforts to persuade the families not to marry their children with the police action.

Once the marriage was over, the Gujar community became aggressive in registering its anger at the "temerity" of this low-caste woman in seeking to advise them. Harassment of Bhanwari took various forms. Fodder was taken away from her field and she was boycotted socially. The entire Gujar community in the village was instructed not to sell milk to her family and not to buy the earthen pots made by her and her husband. Similar harassment continued all through the summer of 1992 culminating in September 1992 with an assault by five prominent men of the village on Bhanwari and her husband, Mohan, while they were working on their field. Bhanwari was then gang-raped.

Then followed her long quest for justice, in which she was fully supported by the entire WDP machinery in various ways, as well as by local and national women's groups. From the moment Bhanwari went to lodge a First Information Report (FIR) to the time the medical examination was conducted, the police treated her with a singular lack of respect. The local MLA made a public announcement in the State Legislative Assembly that she was lying. The political and financial clout of the Gujars was clearly in evidence. However, Bhanwari decided not to succumb to pressure. The newly set-up National Commission of Women was asked by women's groups to intervene on her behalf. It conducted an independent enquiry and reached the conclusion that she had been raped.They published this report and circulated it widely in the media. Medical experts in Delhi were particularly critical of the 52-hour delay in getting Bhanwari medically examined. However, the local police remained unmoved. Bhanwari's supporters organised a massive rally on the streets of Jaipur on 22 October, 1992. Sathins from all over the state and women's groups from Rajasthan and the rest of the country, participated. The women demanded that the accused be arrested and the investigations be transferred to the Central Bureau of Investigations (CBI).

While this demand was met, the CBI's investigation was initially no different from that of the state. They harried Bhanwari into giving her statements nine times. It was only the continuous pressure of women's groups in Delhi and Jaipur that led to an intervention by some top officials of the CBI. Bhanwari and her husband's statements were finally recorded by a magistrate under Section 164 and became the basis for the CBI to charge-sheet the accused after a full year. Following the charge-sheet in September 1993 it took the police five months to arrest the five accused—seventeen months after the crime had been committed. In April 1994, the High Court divided the accused into co-accused and main accused and granted bail to the three co-accused who had assisted the two main accused to perform the act of rape. Women's groups in Jaipur closely followed the happenings in all three courts regarding this case. More than 180 hearings were attended by them. Bhanwari was continuously pressurised to withdraw the court case. In August 1994, the three accused were released on bail and they called a meeting of the village elders in which they begged Bhanwari to withdraw the court case. The Gujars even appealed to Bhanwari's supporters. Bhanwari made a public confession of their guilt a pre-condition of any withdrawal. The result was an impasse.

The trial in the lower courts started in the month of October 1994. It entailed five changes of judges so that the judge who heard Bhanwari and Mohan was not the one who finally delivered judgement. Consequently, each judge was able to have only a piecemeal perspective on the case. Bhanwari's statements in court were ostensibly recorded *in camera* but the privacy was only in name. She had to narrate her story in the presence of seventeen men, she was continuously cross-examined about the position of her body during her alleged rape and who held her arms and legs during the act etc., and since Bhanwari described the act of rape explicitly in the presence of the three accused who were on bail, her testimony was made public knowledge in her village and was used to taunt her when she returned. In November 1995, the Sessions and District Court (Rural) in Jaipur acquitted all five accused against the charge of gang rape although they were sentenced to six months imprisonment on other minor charges such as conspiring against and beating up Mohan and manhandling Bhanwari. Since the two had already spent about two years in jail, they were exempted from imprisonment. The remaining three carried out their sentences.

The arguments which led up to this judgement are starkly revealing of the biases of gender, caste and class which permeated the court proceedings. The defense counsel argued that "the case itself was against Indian culture and human psychology". The rationale for this statement was that the alleged rapists were middle-aged and as such were 'respected persons' in their communities. It was further observed that rape was "usually committed by teenagers". Finally, it was argued in the judgement that "since the offenders were upper caste men and included a Brahmin, the rape could not have taken place because Bhanwari was from a lower caste". Even a cursory scrutiny of various rape cases would indicate that such crimes are have little to do with barriers of caste, community and religion. The judge endorsed the insinuations made by the defence counsel about Bhanwari having committed adultery with a man who was not one of those accused. Finally, questions about the reliability of the evidence given by Bhanwari's husband Mohan were raised on the most extraordinary grounds—"In our society how can an Indian husband, whose role is to protect his wife, stand by and watch his wife being raped?" While these aspects of male gender identity were raised to cast doubt on Mohan as a witness, no explanation was offered about why Bhanwari would have fabricated the story of being raped, given that it would put her and her family's honour at stake, and why Mohan would bear it out, given the aspersions it cast on his ability to protect his wife. Kirti Singh, an advocate of Delhi High Court, associated with the All India Democratic Women's Association summed up the defence counsel's strategy: "It raise(d) the issue of Bhanwari's credibility as a witness. Her own evidence was there, her husband was there but she was completely discredited as a witness by the judge."

The acquittal came as no surprise given the low rate of conviction in rape cases in India. For Bhanwari, for her supporters and for the sathins of the WDP, however, the judgement was a bitter blow. The strength of support behind her and her own personal courage in seeking judgement on the powerful members of her community who had raped her had engendered a spirit of optimism. The verdict was also certain to discourage thousands of victims of sexual assault from speaking out, let alone fighting a court case, given the failure by Bhanwari to receive justice despite the massive support she had behind her. Within her own community also, the verdict was received with anger. People felt that Bhanwari, who had begun to symbolise the fight for rights, had been denied justice by the court. The Ballais, Kumhars and the Bairwas with whom Bhanwari had worked intensively over the past year (1994–95) on issues of land-grabbing by the Gujars have lent their support to Bhanwari. Support is currently being mobilised in favour of Bhanwari on other fronts as well. The WDP officials have officially reinstated their support to Bhanwari. The director of the state programme and the DWDA have both written to the District Collector regarding Bhanwari's safety and security. A national rally was organised to express solidarity towards Bhanwari on December 15, 1995. Bhanwari herself remains undaunted: "I have not accepted this decision of the judge. I am going to fight this. I will fight against this *faisala* [decision] and the rape that is inflicted on me". WDP and other supporters are with her and a senior advocate has agreed to be the special Public Prosecutor in the case. They plan to ask the CBI to go and appeal before the High Court.

Conclusion

The verdict on the rape of Bhanwari has served as a stark reminder to many women across the country of the price they may be asked to pay if they agree to act as agents of change on behalf of the government, in a society which remains male-dominated and caste-riven. However, important lessons have also been learnt. Old hierarchies cannot be challenged without releasing violence. The WDP project did not envisage this and hence, at its inception, did not take sufficient measures to protect its workers from the backlash they have had to face from the privileged sections of society. Bhanwari's case was an extreme example; other functionaries too have faced social ostracism and taunts within their communities.

In a short span of ten years the workers in WDP have experienced both highs and lows. If after Roop Kanwar's sati, and the resulting campaign, the programme functionaries experienced a feeling of achievement, the rape of Bhanwari and its aftermath have brought home to them how limited their power is. The WDP programme could not have existed in isolation. For it to function efficiently it needed the support of the state machinery. But this machinery was not prepared to handle the forces of change and provide meaningful support to the women. This has resulted in creating a force of enlightened individuals who have been rendered ineffective as agents of change. For instance, in the Bhanwari case the obvious expectation was that the state would come down heavily on the perpetrators of a crime comitted against one of their functionaries as a result of her carrying out her duties. The reality has not borne this out. On the contrary, the whole state apparatus appeared to have gone into motion to "prove" that she was a liar.

The uniqueness and effectiveness of WDP was to a great extent, the outcome of its ideology, approach and methodology. A non-hierarchical approach, creation of solidarity, non-target-oriented work (in terms of numbers), equality and social justice for women were the key factors in providing a texture to the programme. Today the WDP has, to a large extent, been enveloped in the fold of government hierarchies, power structures and targets, the very notions that WDP tried to reinterpret through the participatory processes that it instituted.

References

Jain, Sharada and Anita Dighe, 1986. "Some Insights in Participatory Evaluation: Women's Development Programme", Working Paper No. 2, Jaipur: Institute of Development Studies.

Roy, A., S. Jain, 1986. "Training for Women's Development Programme", Working Papers, Training Report, Jaipur: Institute of Development Studies.

"Exploring Possibilities: A Review of the Women's Development Programme (Rajasthan), 1988, Research Report No. 16, Jaipur: Institute of Development Studies.

"Rural Women Speak", *Seminar*, February 1988.

"Situation of Women and Children in Rajasthan", 1991. New Delhi: UNICEF.

"Women's Development Programme: Emerging Challenges", 1991, WSU, Research Report No. 43.

"Violence Against Women: The WDP Perspective", 1996, Jaipur: IDS Research Report 1996, Jaipur.

11

Too Big For Their Boots?

Women and the Policing of Violence Against Women

POORNIMA CHIKARMANE

Introduction

This essay reviews the institutional initiatives taken by the police to address the issue of violence against women. In the first part I contrast the experiences of violence among women who approach the police, with the ideological construction of violence by the police, particularly in cases of domestic violence and rape. Following on this, the contrasting construction of gender needs and interests in response to violence against women are examined through an analysis of the police system, its dominant ideologies, rules and the division of roles and responsibilities. The final section reviews different approaches being tried out by the police force in different states to respond to incidences of crimes against women.

The essay draws upon a study of Special Cells and All Women Police Stations carried out by S. Chakravarti (Additional Commissioner (Crime), Bombay), P. Chikarmane and A. Dave (Lecturer, Tata Institute of Social Sciences, Bombay), who have been involved with training of police officers in Maharashtra. During the course of training, it emerged that we needed to review different initiatives to deal with violence, by locating them within the overall police framework in order to gauge their efficiency. The study was concerned with the institutional responses of the state to violence against women. The key questions asked were: what led to the setting up of the initiative, where is it located within the system, what kinds of powers and resources does it have, what do victims of violence seek from the police, to what extent is this need met, who are the key functionaries, what are the factors that enhance or reduce their effectiveness, and what are the comparative advantages and disadvantages of the different approaches? The Crime Against Women Cell, New Delhi, the Women's Police Station, Hyderabad and the All Women's Police Station, Bhopal were covered. Interviews were carried out with Senior Police Officers, Inspectors, Sub-Inspectors, women complainants and representatives of women's organisations.

The Eye of the Storm

The issue of violence against women came came into the public arena in the early eighties, when the judgement in what came to be known as the Mathura rape case, was denounced as anti-women, by four legal academic luminaries.

Mathura, a 16-year old tribal girl was raped by two policemen in a police compound in 1972. The Sessions Court acquitted the policemen on the grounds that she had eloped with her boyfriend and was habituated to sexual intercourse and, hence, she could not have been raped. The court also ruled that Mathura was a liar and that the sexual intercourse had been with her consent. The High Court convicted the policemen and held that passive surrender in the face of threat, did not constitute consent. The Supreme Court set aside the High Court judgement, and acquitted the policemen in 1979, contrary to established precedence in such cases.

This judgement led to a spirited public outcry, spearheaded by newly emerging women's organisations across the country. While the issue of rape and violence had featured in the women's movement prior to this, it was somewhat localised in scale. Following the judgement in the Mathura case, violence against women became a rallying point, and the campaign for reform in rape laws, acquired a national character.

Almost simultaneously, the increasing spate of dowry deaths or murders was also taken up in a big way, in the form of the Anti-Dowry campaign. This was followed by the Campaign Against Sex Determination tests in the late eighties.

Violence against women has been a constant preoccupation of the women's movement in India. Women's groups have relied on street plays, songs, protest marches, demonstrations and signature campaigns to keep the issue alive. The media have also played a significant role in taking the issue to the public arena for discussion and debate. Apart from this, women's organisations also set up crisis centres, counselling centres and refuges for victims of violence.

High on the agenda have been the demands for legal reforms; a more responsive and sensitive criminal justice system, including the police and the judiciary; the increase in the involvement of women police in cases of violence against women; and the treatment of violence against women as a crime.

Under mounting pressure, the state was forced to respond, and the first Anti-Dowry Cell was set up by the Delhi Police in 1983, headed by a woman officer of the rank of Deputy Commissioner of Police. Subsequently police organisations in other states also initiated measures to address the issue. Tamil Nadu, Uttar Pradesh and Madhya Pradesh started all-women police stations, special cells in the crime branch were set up in Andhra Pradesh and Maharashtra and a Cell for Women in Distress was set up by the Tata Institute of Social Sciences in Bombay. In the last three years, Maharashtra has also been pursuing the integration of women police into the mainstream.

Crimes Against Women or...? Police Perceptions of Violence Against Women

> A poor ragpicker, ran to the local police station, kerosene dripping from her saree, demanding to register a complaint against her husband who was threatening to burn her alive. The officer on duty smirked, stubbed out his cigarette and remarked, "Why are you making such a racket, at least he didn't set you ablaze! You must have done something to provoke him. Do you think the police are sitting here to solve your family problems?" Distraught and feeling powerless, the ragpicker telephoned her trade union.
>
> — *Kagad Kach Patra Kashtakari Panchayat, Pune*

What was the officer really saying? That women are hysterical, that violence against women is always provoked by women themselves, that violence is a private family issue and therefore not within the purview of police action? This episode encapsulates the attitude of the police towards incidences of violence against women.

The aim of policing is the maintenance of law, order and public peace and the prevention of crime. Official discourses on crime relate to injury to the person, property and the state, insofar as there are violations of the law in the public sphere. The interpretation and the application of the law, however, is subjective. It is influenced by the class, caste, age and gender of the perpetrators and the victims.

Intrafamilial, interpersonal assault on women is not considered a crime by the police. The dichotomous conceptual distinctions made between 'public' and 'private', serve to decriminalise acts of violence on women. Deeply entrenched beliefs about the sanctity of the family, the superiority of the male, the forbearance of women and the preservation of family unity at all costs are key determinants in the perception of crime. The reluctance of the police to intervene in familial violence amounts to a legitimisation of the use of violence as a form of social control. There seems to be an expectation that there are parallel systems of justice, which are determined by gender, civil for women and criminal for men. Consequently, the use of violence as a tool for 'punishment' in the face of 'provocation', is often condoned. Some policemen even refer to the use of 'punishment within limits', with no explanation of what those limits might be or who should determine them. The differential application of the law constitutes the unofficial discourse on what is considered to be a 'crime'. A senior Superintendent of Police (Maharashtra) once remarked to the author that she could not remember crimes against women featuring in the weekly crime conferences.

According to a male Police Inspector at the Special Cell for Crime against Women, New Delhi, "Girls have become too big for their boots. They are ready to fight over the smallest matter, like being woken up early by the mother-in-law. Their sense of tolerance has reduced considerably. No one is willing to adjust, neither the boy nor the girl. I sometimes feel men are getting a raw deal because of our intervention. There is no law to protect men whose wives trouble them. In most cases the woman tries to frame the man. A very small percentage of cases is genuine."

Similar sentiments were voiced by a male Deputy Commissioner of Police, Women Police Station, at Hyderabad. He said, "Couples fight for silly reasons. If a woman does not get privacy in a joint family she alleges dowry harassment."

Implicit in the above comments are the stereotypical images that the police carry about women, among which are that the onus of "adjustment in a relationship" is on the woman, that women are "silly", "petty", "vengeful" and "scheming" and that the law is loaded in favour of women.

In sharp contrast are the statements of a woman Sub-Inspector of Police,

> For Indian women, the husband is everything. Nothing can be dismissed as a silly reason. A woman has every right to seek redressal, even if I think the reason is flimsy. Men think that the law is one-sided and interferes in marriage and the family. I do not think so. A complaint is registered only after enquiry. Men are given an opportunity to present their side. Evidence is collected to substantiate the case. Wife beating cannot be justified. About 97 per cent of the cases are genuine.

It is interesting to note that within the police system, perceptions are likely to vary about ways in which the police should respond to violence against women. While it would appear that differences in perceptions can be divided by gender, this is not always the case, as will be seen later in this essay. The point emerging from the above quotes is that the response of the police is not unconditional, but is likely to be influenced by the structures of individual experiences, as well as the internalisation of gender ideologies prevalent in society. By and large, responses to violent crimes against women are influenced by notions of "deservedness", "goodness", "morality", social status and demeanour, which are categories infused with assumptions about what is appropriate for men and women. To many police officers, as witnessed also in law courts, a sex worker or scantily clad woman out alone at night would be classified as a "woman of loose morals" and therefore someone who is "inviting rape".

At a gender sensitivity workshop for the police, we asked the participants why rape occurred. Pat came the answers, "women go out alone at night, dress provocatively, the influence of films on youth, declining morals and unbridled male sexuality". They were then asked whether most victims were young, attractive, unaccompanied, unknown to the perpetrators and whether most rapes took place in public places at night. They replied in the negative. They however, found it difficult, to reconcile the contradictions between their firmly held beliefs and the real evidence of their experience.

The reaction of the police is also based on the visibility and extent of the physical injury. The absence of bruises and burns, often elicits the response, "He slapped you and you ran to the police?" The definition of violence emphasises the visible and the quantifiable to the exclusion of the individual and the diffuse (Hatty, 1986).

Frequently, male violence is attributed to substance abuse or mental instability, thereby placing it outside and beyond the control of the perpetrator. In such cases, the victim is admonished, told to placate the spouse and advised not to aggravate the situation.

Frameworks within which the police could act to intervene in cases of violence against women, do exist, despite claims to the contrary. For example, the absence of a single law on domestic violence is often cited as a reason for police inaction. However, existing laws on rape, manslaughter, grievous injury and murder, can be applied to the domestic situation, if the police choose to do so. Other alternatives also exist, but they require a more proactive role from the police which may be hard to expect given the existing levels of apathy and inertia on their part. Expecting the police to play a role in prevention is far-fetched given that police officers often believe that the responsibility of protecting women rests with male members of the family, and those that are not under such protection are not deserving of it, anyway. This creates a double bind for women: the marital family is the norm that the police accept, but based on the assumption that the male is the protector; and violence against single women within relationships does not even count. So women within and outside of marital relationships are considered not to merit police protection, albeit for different reasons.

What emerges from the foregoing observations is that the police are often constrained by their own individual perceptions, as well as the institutional culture in which they operate, which is further located in a gendered social canvas. The ensuing quote summarises it effectively.

> The disjuncture between masculinist conceptions of policing and feminist analysis of violence against women, which recognise men's violence as reflecting and securing women's subordinate status in heteropatriarchal societies, is immense. Because men hold greater social power, the largely male police and judiciary reflect their gendered knowledge and understanding of definitions of violence, and the actions that flow from them. The police are engaging in a world inhabited by gendered subjects in unequal power relations. Further, the police are also gendered and constitute a part of, they are not above or outside, struggles around gendered relations.
>
> [Hammer, 1989]

Protectors, Conspirators or Perpetrators? Women's Perceptions of the Police

The police force represents the law enforcement arm of state power. Historically, it was associated with being a repressive agent of the colonial administration. Though the administration is now Indian, the elements of repression, violence and power continue to be associated with the police. The image of the friendly, helpful neighbourhood cop, the protector of life and property, is mythical. More commonly, the police are feared for the power they wield, ridiculed for their inefficiency, hated for their brutality and corruption. The image of the police in India is not very good and this is established by the responses of a cross-section of society. Seventy six per cent of the respondents of a study (Aleem, 1991) were of the opinion that the image of the police in India ranged between okay and poor.

Given this image, most citizens are wary of approaching the police for assistance, more so women victims of violence. The first step adopted by women in violent circumstances is to attempt to defuse the situation and pacify the spouse through compliance, passivity or coaxing. Women often report that the violence perpetrated on them is unprovoked. When the abuse continues unabated, relatives, friends and neighbours are called upon to intervene. The failure of this intervention sometimes leads women to seek police intervention—an indication of the fact that they have reached the limits of their endurance.

What women victims frequently seek from the police is the immediate cessation of violence and protection against further harassment. At this stage they experience feelings of betrayal, conflicting loyalties and ambivalence. There are strong social sanctions about the "public airing" of "family secrets". The sense of powerlessness, filial loyalties and the lack of options available to them also contribute to these feelings. At this stage, women are often not sure of what they want to do and are subject to tremendous pressure, both from within themselves as well as from the spouse, relatives and neighbours and also from the reception they receive from the police. The feeling that following police intervention, she must return to the violent situation, is often a strong deterrent for a woman. In the face of such odds, the number of women who are driven to self-immolation and suicide, to escape the situation, also shows a marked increase. The most common request to the police is that the perpetrator should be apprehended and kept in custody overnight, in order to be taught a lesson.

> Ms Patil was married for 20 years, to an officer working in a public sector defence establishment in Pune city. All through her married life, she suffered harassment from her husband, including demands for money from her brothers. Physical violence took the form of beating her and locking her up in the house. Whenever the situation became intolerable, Ms Patil complained to the local police. Invariably, the police called the husband and advised him to take his wife home. A case was never registered, despite her repeated requests to do so.
>
> (Janwadi Mahila Sanghatana, 1993)

Such cases only serve to heighten the woman's fear of reprisal and escalation of violence, and to erode her confidence.

The police are often unable to comprehend the feelings of ambivalence that women experience particularly in the case of repeated complaints. They perceive the woman's demand to lock up the offender and her attempts to get him released the next day, as indicative of the "contrary", "whimsical" and impulsive nature of women generally.

By and large, women's needs vary from mediation to formal registration of a complaint. This calls for a range of responses on the part of the police, based on the expressed wishes of the victim.

Women's lives are often controlled by the threat and reality of men's violence. The treatment received by abused women is always mediated through experiences with men, those who inflict violence, and those who make up the state machinery that has the mandate to intervene through the use of criminal law. The divergence between the construction of violence by abused women, based on their real experiences, and by the police, based on their gendered perceptions, causes a mismatch that further disadvantages women.

Apart from the reception given to women complainants at the police station, investigation and action following registration of a complaint are crucial elements of the redressal process. Most often, the perpetrator is called to present his case and the police advise the sparring parties to maintain peace.

> Seema Mahadik was about 50 years old when her husband, after a lifetime of abusing her, thrashed her so badly that she became a paraplegic as a result of a spinal injury. A case of simple assault was registered, when the victim and her neighbours demanded that the husband be apprehended for attempted murder. As she languished in the public hospital, the husband carried on his life with his second wife. Seema threatened that she would see him hung from the gallows and he laughed in her face. Six months later, she died of infections brought on by neglect. In the interim, the neighbours who had been supportive of her were threatened by the husband and forced to change their statements, all with connivance of the local police. Her death was registered as a natural death, notwithstanding the fact that it had been caused as a result of the husband actions.
>
> (*Kagad Kach Patra Kashtakari Panchayat, Pune*)

The 'court worthiness' of the case rests largely on the registration of the first information reports, the recording of statements, the collection of evidence, the framing of the charge-sheet and the willingness of the witnesses to appear in court. All except the last are within the total control of the police. Cases are often dismissed by the courts on grounds of lack of sufficient evidence. Perpetrators of crimes against women go scot-free because of the failure of the police to build a convincing case.

The Abuse of Authority: Custodial Violence Against Women

The issue of the police as perpetrators of violence against women is significant in that the very agents of protection, abuse the trust and confidence placed in them. The issue of custodial rape, has featured with disturbing regularity over the years.

The 1993 amendment to the rape law tried to address the issue of custodial rape by shifting the burden of proof. But rapes by police and people in authority have continued, and as a rule, the courts have refrained from going away from the established norm whereby the burden of proving the offence is on the prosecution. Even in well-publicised cases like the Suman Rani rape case, the discussion has been more on the conduct and character of the girl rather than the issue of custodial rape (Agnes 1995).

Gender and Service Delivery

In the eighties, women's organisations considered the gender of the police officer to be a significant variable. This led to demands for induction of more women into the police force and assignment of women's cases to women officers and women judges. However, the renewed understanding that in a gendered society, entrenched thinking about femininity, masculinity, the roles of men and women, and behaviours appropriate to men and women, is common to both sexes, has led to a reconsideration of these demands. That merely being a women does not make an individual more sensitive to gender issues, is now accepted within the women's movement. Nevertheless, the shared experiences of being women, do account for some identification and common meeting points.

Some of the women complainants interviewed during the course of a study of police initiatives, did believe that they found it easier to relate their experiences to women officers. This was particularly true in the case of Bhopal and Hyderabad, where the practice of female seclusion is prevalent.

Public Perception of Women Police (Andhra Pradesh)

		Yes
1	Women police should be entrusted with independent powers in investigation of cases of victimisation of women	78 per cent
2	Women can implement laws pertaining to women more sincerely and effectively than men police	76 per cent
3	Women should be interrogated by women police only	46 per cent

(Source: *Women Police and Social Change*, 1991)

A woman complainant viewed the Mahila Police Thana (All Women Police Station), Bhopal, as a "specially created physical, temporal and emotional space". This to her was a significant and welcome departure from the regular police station. Many women thus experience a greater degree of comfort in talking to women officers.

Some of the respondents interviewed, expressed doubts with regard to the extent to which "women police could be effective on male aggressors, since women are seen as secondary citizens". Interestingly, some other respondents said that "time, attention, interest and sensitivity were more crucial variables, than gender, in family-related matters. When the power and authority of the law is vested in an individual, gender becomes irrelevant. If a male police officers exhibits the above attributes we will not hesitate to approach him."

As part of this study, women police were asked about the significance of gender in dealing with violence against women. They were unaminous in suggesting that abused women were more comfortable with women police officers. According to one Police Sub-Inspector, "Women police deal better with women's complaints. Male police are less sensitive, not only to women, but also to people in general. Men by nature have less sensitivity. The social structure is such that it promotes the male, his ego and his pride. Women on the other hand, are more cloistered. They feel free to approach a woman officer, as a police officer and as a woman." Adds another woman officer, "Men have no foresight. They act regardless of the consequences. They have the attitude: file a case and be done with it."

Another PSI observed, "Especially with respect to section 498A of the Indian Penal Code, which deals with domestic violence, male police while not negligent, would not bother with the case details, while a woman officer would. The most common way of handling the situation would be to effect an informal compromise at the police station, between husbands and wives, even if such an understanding was not very much in the women's interests." This, she said, "obviated the need for lengthy litigation, preserved the family and thus, in a way social stability." The propensity of the police to effect informal compromises is evident in the above quote. It is reflective of the efforts of the police to deal with domestic issues outside the legal framework. What emerges from the voices of both women complainants and women police officers, with respect to the issue of violence against women is that what abused women seek from the police is a set of responses ranging from sympathetic hearing, mediation and compromise to formal registration, investigation of a complaint, and penal action. While the victims seek allies, regardless of gender, the police respond as judges or, at best, arbitrators.

The problem lies in the gendered ideological framework within which the police operate and the practices that flow from it. It is also located in the organisation of police services and the place given to crimes against women, in the hierarchy of crimes.

The limitations of the police system to address other related issues such as short-stay homes, counselling services, legal aid, medical assistance and means of survival for victims, also need to be recognised and acknowledged. The existence of alternatives would relieve the pressure on both the victims and the police to resort to mediation and compromise.

The Police Organisation: A View Through the Gender Lens

The police organisation in India, is an almost exclusively male preserve. Women first entered the police force as early as 1938, but they were the exception rather than the rule. Even after independence, no significant progress was made in this regard.

Today, women constitute between one to two per cent of the total police strength in most states, as the table below indicates.

Proportion of Women Police in the States

	State	Total police strength	No. of women police	Percentage of women police to men police
1	Andhra Pradesh (1987)	58340	500	0.86
2	Assam (1987)	46455	258	0.55
3	Delhi (1987)	38065	580	1.52
4	Himachal Pradesh (1987)	10190	91	0.89
5	Karnataka (1987)	47111	330	0.7
6	Kerala (1987)	33722	348	1.0
7	Madhya Pradesh (1991)	87246	1053	1.0

(Source: States)

Women were first inducted into the police force, primarily to help in dealing with women. According to an Inspector General of Police, Madhya Pradesh, "Women would protest about being manhandled by male police officers during house searches, arrests and mob situations. It therefore became necessary to recruit women."

Recruitment into the police force takes place through three channels, the central civil services for the higher echelons, the state civil services for the officer cadre and general recruitment for the constabulary. Up until 1971, women were not recruited into the Indian Police Service (IPS), even if they passed the entrance tests.

Recruitment into the police force is not open in most states, but limited to the number of posts available for women police. In Madhya Pradesh, for example there were only 135 women officers (1994), the last recruitment being in 1990. The recruitment rules, therefore serve as an exclusionary device to keep women from entering the system.

The dominant ideology in policing relies heavily on the rough and tough masculine image and a command and control profile. Added to this are connections to the underworld, sleaze, crime, nefarious activities and the seamier side of life, which are considered unsuitable for women. Entrenched thinking based on biological imperatives such as the "physical powers of men", "commanding nature of the male", "protective instinct of the male" are powerful determinants in the rules for entry into the service, the position within the hierarchy and the duties assigned to men and women.

Promotional avenues for women are limited to the number of posts available for them. One woman sub-inspector I met, claimed she was tired, frustrated and lacked any intellectual stimulus. She had spent twenty years in airport security. According to an Inspector General of Police, Madhya Pradesh, promotional avenues for women in the police force are the same as those for men. But since these are restricted posts, they compete among themselves. Furthermore, postings are limited to urban centres or at most, district headquarters. Women are not posted in rural areas or in special branches, the reasons for this were: problems relating to the security of women officers, inadequate housing in rural areas, the vulnerability of women to harassment, including sexual harassment, distances and community problems. It was also mentioned that women could not be posted alone or travel unaccompanied, which meant deployment of additional manpower and the consequent wastage of time.

When the issue was raised with women officers, they did say there was some truth in their seniors' statement. However, they expressed a willingness to undertake rural postings, given the chance.

Within the police organisation as a rule, duties assigned to women include airport security, frisking of female passengers, escorting female prisoners, assistance to juveniles and women, police welfare, and law and order problems involving women. These areas are referred to as the "soft sector" which implies that it is for "softees" (women/feminine) or duties that require the "soft touch" (read woman's touch), as opposed to hard core mainstream policing.

The Commissioner of Police, Hyderabad (vide GR 4/505/85/4544), has laid down the following functions to be performed by women police

1. Protection of women criminals kept in custody.
2. Assisting local police in interrogation and investigation cases wherein women are involved.
3. Escort of women criminals to court, prisons etc.
4. *Bandobast* (mob control) duties in places where women gather in large numbers.
5. *Bandobast* and security duties at the Andhra Pradesh Legislative Assembly when in session.
6. Security and anti-hijacking duty at the Hyderabad airport.
7. Security during visits of VVIPs to the city.
8. Regulation of queues at cinema halls.
9. Verification and enquiries in connection with passport applications etc. of *purdahnashin* (secluded) ladies, family investigations.
10. Coverage of meetings exclusively held by ladies.
11. Assisting traffic police in laying traps against refusal for plying vehicles.
12. Assisting local police in laying traps for eve-teasers.
13. Assisting Anti-Corruption Bureau authorities during raids.
14. Interrogation of juveniles and producing them in courts.
15. Assisting local police in eviction in Rent Control cases.
16. Executing warrants, assisting local police.
17. Regulation of queues during elections.

The long list of functions relates exclusively to women. This is the situation in most states. Aspects like riot control, gathering of intelligence, crime prevention, investigation and detection are assigned only to male officers.

In some states, there have been attempts to remedy the situation, in order to provide equal opportunities to women within the organisation. In Madhya Pradesh and Maharashtra, women have been posted at regular police stations. This, in itself, does not mean that they are engaging in mainstream duties. Very often they continue handling cases of women and children at the local police station. However, on an experimental basis women at police stations are being assigned the same duties as their male counterparts, in these states.

According to the women officers interviewed, "... the pressure upon women to prove themselves is very strong at regular police stations." One PSI recalled being told by her commanding officer, "Why have they sent you here? You are useless to me! I will believe in your competence only after you demonstrate your prowess with the *lathi* (baton)." Initially, she was a mass of nerves, until she controlled a mob situation, single-handed, and received an award.

Another officer reported with great feeling, "Men have developed their psyche to think women are incapable. At my last posting, assignments were limited to women's cases. Assignments depend largely on the attitude of the senior officer. We have had the same training as the men, we have been taught to handle arms. They why should we have a limited role?" This resentment was echoed by her colleague, who explained that women were exempt from night patrolling (by order) and were not given a beat to patrol. She said, "A lot of police work gets done at night. Why should we be left out of it?"

Since most women are not involved in mainstream policing and their promotional channels are limited, their influence in the decision-making process is negligible, be it at the local police station or in the determination of policy.

The officers of the IPS cadre who enter the system via the civil services examination, are slightly better placed. They share the same responsibility as their male counterparts and promotion is based on seniority within the cadre. One of the IPS officers interviewed, has been in service for 12 years. She held both urban and rural postings, including areas with a high crime rate. She is one of four women police officers of the rank in Maharashtra. According to her, "The low representation of women in the higher ranks, put greater pressure on them to perform, in order to establish credibility within the organisation and with the public." Within the force, she is perceived as being "softer" towards women's issues, an image that she herself is not comfortable with. She says, "Women offenders are not looked on with greater sympathy than male offenders, but I am more responsive to women victims. I acknowledge mental cruelty as a form of violence despite the fact that my seniors have gone on record to state otherwise and I take action in cases of custodial rape. The person responsible in the incident was suspended to facilitate investigation."

Some senior officials interviewed, subscribed to the view that the number of women in the police force should be increased in proportion to their presence in the population. In the words of an Inspector General of Police, Madhya Pradesh, "Women constitute 48 per cent of the general population, [yet] crimes against women account for only 10 per cent of all the crimes reported. Women should therefore have equal representation in the police and be given mainstream duties. Corruption and the abuse of power are prevalent in society. To use these as excuses for excluding women from the force, is retrograde. Society needs policing by both men and women. Every police station should have women officers whose duties are concurrent i.e. crimes against women and regular policing."

Policing is a high risk, high pressure occupation. Unionisation is not permitted within the police force. Duty hours are irregular, weekly off-days and public holidays are not assured. In extraordinary situations, the police are required to be on continuous duty. Transport and rest rooms are inadequate. Jobs are transferable. Consequently, the police work in a stressful environment and have an erratic family life. These factors affect women even more than men, given the reality that women have to shoulder the dual burdens of a taxing career and domestic responsibilities. Those married to policemen find it a little easier, since their husbands are more conversant with the demands of the job. Said an Inspector, "The long duty hours, absence of a weekly holiday and the demanding nature of the work make it impossible to fulfil family and social obligations. Those whose husbands are willing to adjust manage to take mainstream postings. Those who find it difficult, seek transfers to desk postings where there are regular hours. In a male-dominated society, policewomen are powerful at work, but at home that power is greatly reduced. They have to manage the home and the workplace, resulting in tension." The respondents were however, unanimous in asserting that this was not an insurmountable problem. This is another reason why policing is not considered suitable for women and sometimes parents actively discourage their daughters from entering the system.

The above evidence reveals that the police organisation is a gendered system. It does not provide equal opportunities to women both at points of entry and within the police system. If the organisation is serious on this count, a certain amount of restructuring will be required, which will reflect commitment to equal opportunities, going beyond mere rhetoric. Ideally, the spouses should share equally the responsibility of home making and child rearing. This is easier said than done. In order to facilitate recruitment and retention of women police, the organisation would at the very least, have to provide facilities such as rest-rooms, toilets, conveyance, child-care centres, sabbatical leave and long-term postings.

Policing Violence Against Women: Institutional Initiatives

Gender Specific Interventions in Service Delivery

This section will detail and review the initiatives taken by the police organisation in three states, the Crime against Women Cell (CAWC) New Delhi, the Women Police Station (WPS) Hyderabad and the Mahila Police Thana (MPT), Bhopal. All three are urban initiatives located in the state capitals. The tables below provide comparative status of the three initiatives.

Tables 1 and 2, indicate that the MPT, by virtue of being a notified police station has relatively higher powers than the CAWC and the WPS, despite the fact that the latter are headed by persons of higher rank. In the CAWC and the WPS, cases are required to be registered at the local police stations. These serve as referral centres and centres for monitoring investigations. The limited mandate (crimes against women) is similar for all the three initiatives.

Table 3 reflects that the volume of complaints handled by the CAWC is much higher than the MPT. It needs to be mentioned however, that the CAWC receives complaints from police stations across the city, while for the MPT, the data

Table 1

Initiative	Year of establishment	Source of order	Jurisdiction	Nature
Anti-dowry Cell later expanded to CAWC	1983	Ministry of Home Affairs 1985	New Delhi	Special Cell
WPS	1992	Police Commissioner	Hyderabad	Special Notified Cell in Crime Branch
MPT	1987	Governor's Ordinance	Bhopal	Notified Police Station

reflects only those cases registered at the MPT. Cases are also registered in the local police stations, the details of which are not reflected in this table.

It was reported that on average the MPT receives five complaints per day, of which only about six per cent are actually registered. The WPS also receives about five complaints per day, of which 10–20 per cent are registered. This supports the submission, made earlier in this chapter, that women complainants seek a variety of responses. This is partly because they have few options if they leave the marital home. For this very reason, the police also advise the complainants not to book the perpetrators.

"In the hierarchy of crimes against women, rape receives the highest priority, followed by dowry violence, eve-teasing and wife beating in that order. The last is particularly seen as low status work." (Senior IPS officer, Maharashtra). The data show that the highest number of complaints relate to the section on domestic violence i.e. 498 A.

While a couple of respondents opined that counselling was not the job of the police, most reported that they were called upon to 'counsel' complainants. The ACP, WPS, Hyderabad illustrated a case where counselling had been used.

Table 2

Initiative	Powers	Mandate	Head	Staff strength
CAWC	Cannot register; cannot effect arrest; can issue summons; can investigate 498A	Crimes against dowry, rape, eve teasing harassment kidnapping murder	Deputy Commissioner of Police	DCP 1 F ACP 3 M 1 F PI 3 M 5 F PSI 6 M 6 F ASI 1 M 6 F HC
WPS	Cannot register "Non grave cases cannot effect arrest, can issue summons, can investigate offences of atrocities against women", i.e. Dowry, 498A		Asst. Commissioner of Police	PI 1 M PSI 2 F ASI 2 F
MPT	Can issue summons; can register cases; can arrest; can investigate Section 294, 302–309, 312–332, 341–348, 363–377, 493–498A, 509 of IPC		Police Inspector	

Source: CAWC, MPT, WPS, 1993–94

Case: Joint family. Wife wants to live separately. Husband was the eldest son. Wife was a working woman. She left home to live with her parents, with support from her brothers.

Counselling intervention:

Advice to the wife: If you live apart from your husband, society will not respect you. It will insult you and look down upon you. Living with your husband will give you status. Your brothers talk nonsense. You must adjust and understand your husband's responsibility.

The wife reports that the husband assaults and ill-treats her.

Table 3

Nature of crime	Cases registered at MPT - 1993	Complaints received CAWC - 1993
Murder	1	–
Attempt to murder	–	–
Rape	20	376
498A (IPC)	42	792
Kidnapping/Abduction	6	580
354 IPC	7	–
Dowry Prevention Act	–	–
406 IPC	1	308
501 IPC	1	–
509 IPC	1	–
304 B	1	–
Total	80	2056

Source: MPT, Bhopal
Source: Delhi Police

Advice to the husband: Your wife does not ask you for money, she is also earning. You carry out the responsibility to your family. Give them financial support. But live separately with your wife.

The husband says the wife is influenced by her brothers and parents. The police officer instructed the girl's parents to visit only in the husband's presence.

Conclusion: The concerned officer felt the case had been amicably settled.

Comment: The wife's subsequent isolation from her natal family would, to some extent, deny her the support required to cope with the situation and any recurrent problems. Further, for the police, "successful cases" are those where the estranged couples live together as a unit, regardless of what the woman wants and whether it is in her best interests to do so.

While the CAWC has both male and female officers, the WPS and the MPT are staffed by female officers. Most expressed satisfaction with the job because they were able to help women by virtue of being women. However, when asked their preference, they opted for mainstream policing. They also felt sidelined because they dealt with only certain sections of the Indian Penal Code, for which they were subject to ridicule by their batch-mates.

Training

Training of functionaries is an important part of capacity building in any organisation. Within the police system, IPS (Indian Police Service) officers receive training at the National Police Academy, officers are trained at the State Training Academies and constables are trained at the Police Training Schools. Gender issues do not feature in the induction training. In some states there are a couple of sessions devoted to violence against women, as part of social issues. In this case again, violence against women is relegated to the secondary position of "social issues", in relation to "real crime".

In-service training is not mandatory. There have been sporadic attempts by women's organisations to impart training on gender issues and violence against women. The major attempt to institutionalise training on gender-related violence has been a collaboration between the Department of Personnel and Training, Government of India and the British Council Division which commenced in 1993. Training modules on "Violence against Women", and master trainers consisting of representatives of Administrative Training Institutes, Police Organisations and NGOs, have been the major outcome. Regular in-service training programmes have been organised in some states. However, the training is yet to be institutionalised at induction level.

Women's Organisations and the Police

All the three initiatives associate themselves with women's organisations in their respective cities. At the CAWC and the MPT, representatives of women's organisations are actually present on the premises, on a rotational basis. They were also interviewed. The CAWC was seen as a "toothless tiger" because of its lack of powers of case registration and arrest. The team work and camaraderie were perceived as being greater in the WPS and MPT where only women were posted. This difference was evident even to the interviewers. The police women at MPT particularly, were more relaxed and friendly, hierarchy was not so much in evidence and there was a separate room available for private conversations.

The interventions of women's organisations were seen to have had two advantages over the local police stations: first, they made victims feel more secure and second, their existence sent out the message that women's problems were being taken seriously. Most organisations intervened at the pre-registration stage.

The issue of partnership with the police was also brought up with the women's organisations. A Hyderabad-based organisation said the police do not see their intervention as a partnership but as an audit. Other organisations saw partnership as dangerous because it allied them with the police rather than with the victims.

To the extent that the police are viewed as agents of state repression and women's organisations are committed to struggle against injustice, there is bound to be inherent conflict in the relationship between them. On the other hand, association and cooperation is perhaps necessary, while respecting the other's autonomy in order to ensure justice to victims of violence.

There is a popular saying in Maharashtra, "*Navryane marle ani pavsane zhodle, sangayche kunala*". (The whiplash of the rain, and the battering by the husband, whom do we tell?) This saying assumes significance in relation to the three interventions covered here. Institutional interventions to address the issue of violence against women can be an empowering tool in the hands of victims of violence, who have little recourse to other means of redressal. The efficacy of the intervention hinges on the extent to which the police are viewed as allies of victims rather than as co-conspirators of the perpetrators.

Composite Policing vs. Gender-specific Initiatives

The interventions covered in this chapter are gender-specific, in that they specifically seek to address the issue of violence against women, exclusively and separately, in relation to general crimes. That they serve to meet the immediate needs of women victims today, is an important consideration. They however, do not challenge the isolation of crimes against women from other crimes, the belief that women are best equipped to handle women's cases, or that crimes against women do not come within the ambit of mainstream policing. Though they may actually benefit women in the short term, it is necessary to take a long term perspective on the desirable changes.

Ideally, women victims should feel free to approach any local police station and be assured of assistance regardless of the gender of the officer, for the intervention to be empowering. Secondly, there is also the issue of provision of equal opportunities to women within the police force.

It would be interesting at this point, to go into the experience of Maharashtra state, where some attempts have been made to address these twin issues. The provision in the chapter on "Violence against Women, Maharashtra State Policy for Women 1994", indicates a movement towards a more redistributive policy.

The policy recognises fear of physical and emotional violence as a major constraint in women's development. It provides for:

1. Gender orientation courses to be introduced in police training centres with at least 20 per cent of the training time allotted to issues relating to the social sectors.
2. A separate cadre for correctional administration and counselling.
3. Restructuring of police cadre and cadre unification for men and women with identical recruitment and training.
4. Induction of more women into the police force (30 per cent reservation for women).
5. Mainstreaming of women police and ensuring that they are given equal and interchangeable responsibilities with male colleagues.
6. The separate identity of "women police" to be dropped from the next recruitment itself.
7. Women-headed police stations.
8. Mobile security units with women police for night patrolling.
9. Separate recording of atrocities against women.
10. Short-stay homes and refuges.
11. Institutions for women.
12. Legal aid.

Unfortunately, the subsequent changes in the political scenario in Maharashtra, have considerably slowed down the process of operationalising the policy.

Gender redistributive policies are bound to generate some resistance from those who are privileged by the existing system. While pursuing redistributive policies, it may be necessary to place on the ground effective mechanisms for addressing the issue of violence against women. To begin with trained teams of men and women police personnel could be posted at the zonal level in urban areas and at district headquarters in rural areas to handle cases of crimes against women.

References

Agnes, Flavia, 1995. *The State Gender and Law Reform* RCWS, SNDT, Bombay: Women's University.

Aleem, Shamim, 1991. *Women Police and Social Change* New Delhi: Ashish Publishing House.

Chakravarti, S., P. Chikarmane, A. Dave, 1995. *Composite Policing vs. Gender Specific Initiatives: A Review* (unpublished research project).

Hanmer, Jalna, Jill Radford and Elizabeth Stanko (eds), 1989. *Women, Policing and Male Violence* London: Routledge.

Hanmer, Jalna, 1983. *The Changing Experience of Women* Milton Keynes: Open University Press.

Joshi, G.P., N.P. Gupta, T. Chakrabarty, 1993. *Functioning of the Crime Against Women Cells in the Police Forces in States/UTS* New Delhi: Bureau of Police Research and Development, GOI.

Policy for Women, Maharashtra, 1994.

Section 3

Following Through the Process

12

Following through the Process

Implementation, Monitoring and Evaluation

NAILA KABEER AND RAMYA SUBRAHMANIAN

Introduction

Development interventions emerge and take form in a variety of contexts—socio-political, cultural and economic—and within a range of institutions and organisations, as seen in the previous chapters of this book. Mediating the interplay between institutions, organisations and planning processes are people at different levels and their interrelationships—between policy makers, implementing officials, clients and project beneficiaries, and external constituencies of stakeholders such as funders, local community members, politicians, husbands and wives. Relational fluxes and the politics of power thus impose 'unruliness' on the development process, reminding us of the uncertainties and risks entailed in planning and managing development interventions.

In this essay, we look at the different ways in which people's interrelationships with structures of gender and power, their internal values and external commitments and their personal ideologies can determine the ways in which gender redistribution is addressed by development organisations. How projects learn about their context is mediated through the way in which project goals are expressed, the extent to which values and commitments are shared across organisations, and the way in which commitments are supported by sufficient resources and time. Where there is resistance to gender redistribution—and the sources of resistance are many—how can organisations identify internal constraints to the achievement of gender-redistributive goals and commitments? In the first part of this essay we review some of the ways in which intra-organisational politics can affect the translation of commitment to outcome, and suggest some adapted tools for analysing the extent to which such intra-organisational resistance exists.

Following on this, we look at the relationship between development interventions and their programme contexts, focusing particularly on developing gender-sensitive monitoring and evaluation tools that can alert organisations to the needs, priorities and preferences of women and men. These tools are conceptual rather than routine, and require a clear analytical framework as suggested earlier in the book, if they are to be used to best effect. The chapter concludes with a review of the importance, and limitations, of participatory methodology in forging the relationship between organisations and their constituencies but suggests critically that organisations should take their cue from the voices of the most disadvantaged, particularly disadvantaged women, in ensuring that their goals reflect real concerns and that these goals translate into suitable organisational structures and management processes, to ensure the minimisation of conflicts over interpretations and values about the means and ends of development.

Risks, Assumptions and the Politics of Implementation

Most interventions are premised on a hypothesised relationship between outputs and intended goals and, in an uncertain and imperfectly known world, most will entail both unanticipated risks and invalid assumptions which can lead to unintended outcomes, including the collapse of the project. However, the analysis of implementation failures when some form of gender-redistributive policy is entailed also reveals that a particular source of failure results from the ways in which policies are often perceived, both in the communities in which they are implemented as well as by those responsible for designing and implementing them. Within the community, gender redistributive polices run into the same problems of resistance that any policy aimed at altering pre-existing power

Fig. 1: Forcefield analysis through the institutional framework

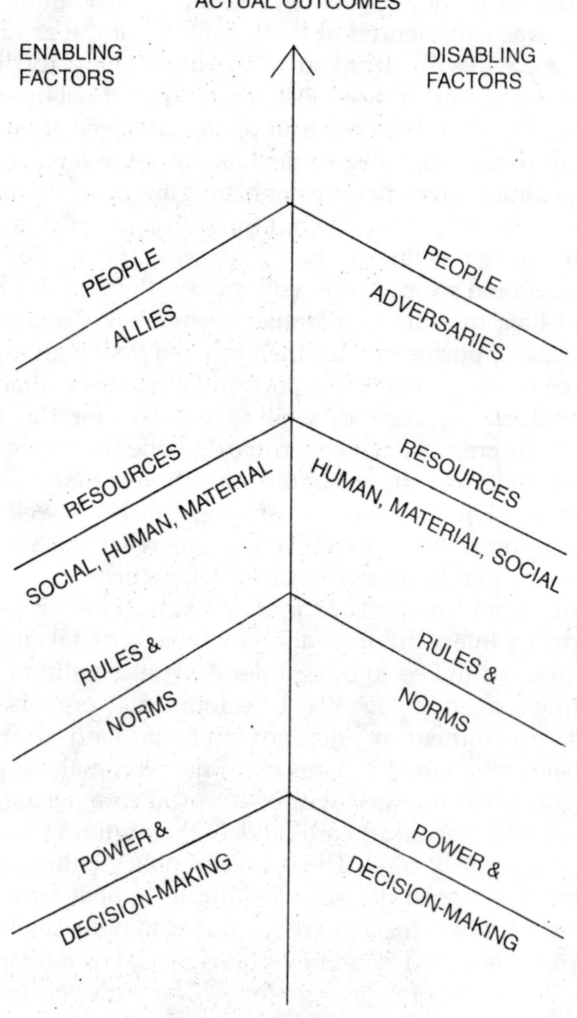

relations is likely to encounter. The resistance may reflect hostility to the idea of going against taken-for-granted cultural norms and practices governing local gender relations or it may reflect a more material concern with the possible loss of prior resources or denial of access to new ones. In the case of the Tamil Nadu Women's Development Programme,[1] which sought to lend money to women's groups, considerable male resistance was experienced at the beginning of the group formation process, with drunken husbands seeking to disrupt meetings. However, it was also found that resistance from family members tends to occur in the early stages of an intervention; in the Tamil Nadu context, most of the men reduced their antagonism over time, recognising the possible benefits to the family and there was a shift from discomfort about their wives attending meetings to positive encouragement of attendance. Rajagopal's essay (this volume) on the Shiksha Karmi Project in Rajasthan notes a similar phenomenon: male resistance to new opportunities for their women finally giving way to positive acceptance and support. In Bangladesh, attacks on Grameen Bank workers, as well as workers for the BRAC education programme which primarily benefits girls, can be seen as attacks on organisations which threaten both the power of local money-lenders and landlords as well as of religious figures, by seeking to change what such groups regard as acceptable gender norms and practices.

The other, and major source of 'misbehaviour' in gender-related policy interventions—and one which has taken longer to recognise—is linked to the gender dynamics within the implementing agency itself. Development organisations, whether government or non-government, tend to be organised along hierarchical lines, with decision-making power most densely concentrated within a central core, what Staudt (1985) calls the 'technical core' and Lotherington et al (1991) call the 'deep policy core'. The source of policy failure may be located at this central decision-making level or it may be located further down the hierarchy; and it may be manifested through a variety of different decisions or, just as damagingly, through a variety of 'non-decisions'. The experience of the past decades suggests that while considerable progress has been made in winning policy commitment to gender issues by those in the central decision-making core, this has not necessarily resulted in gender-equitable outcomes lower down the policy process.

Figure 2: The composite forcefield analysis of WID programmes in six Commonwealth Caribbean countries

Disabling Factors	Enabling Factors
No budget or inadequate funds	Support from National Commission
Lack of staff in bureaux	Commitment of women attached to agency
Inadequately trained staff	Supportive international bodies
Bureaux unable to meet demands	Availability of international aid
No cooperation/understanding from Ministries	Cadre of trained/committed women
No national advisory body	Pool of volunteers available
Unclear policy	Realistic role & programme emerging
Bureaucratisation of the bureaux	Achievement of income generating projects
Unclear status of bureaux	Emphasis on socio-economic development of women
Competitive forces	Regular contact with PS and cooperating ministries
Political pressure	Link with official regional policy
Dependence on international finance	Specialised sub-committees valuable
Funding agency pressure	Government commitment to WID
No/few support staff	
Inadequate transportation	

Source: *Ladies in Limbo: The Fate of Women's Bureau*, Women and Development Programme, Commonwealth Secretariat, London 1984.

Sarin's and Chikarmane's essays in this volume also indicate how organisations like the Forestry Department and the police force in India, construct 'masculine' identities which obstruct their ability to respond to the situations and experiences of women, and often result in deep resistance to the recruitment of women. Organisational cultures and rules can have significant impact on the way in which personnel construct and follow through their 'roles', shaping their responses and strategies which can run counter to goals, as in Chikarmane's case of the police force, where police preferred to reconcile husbands and wives in conflict rather than follow official legal and policy routes. In Sarin's case of the Forestry Department, institutional blindness to women and the very specific model of the altruistic household, has led to rules in Joint Forest Management that allow for only one member of the household—invariably male—to be represented on village committees, further silencing women, with the result that women's specific relationship to natural resources is never taken into account. This results in the restriction of women's access to vital resources and makes them vulnerable to punishment as 'offenders' rather than as legitimate users.

To the extent that this failure often lies within the implementing agency, *force field analysis,*[2] which promotes reflection on the 'enabling' and 'disabling' features of the institutional environment in which the implementation takes place, can be a useful tool in the planning process for anticipating the risks and resistance likely to be encountered within the implementing agency as well as to potential areas of weakness. Figure 1, which links the idea of force field analysis to our overall institutional framework, draws attention to the significance of the prevailing structure of rules, resources, practices, people and power within an agency as the basic elements which determine the translation of an intended policy goal into a practical outcome. It reminds us that a major reason why gender-aware policy goals do not always translate into gender-aware policy outcomes lies in management failure to rethink the pre-existing rules, resources, people and practices of the organisation in order to meet the requirements of these new goals. Figure 2 synthesises the results of a force field analysis undertaken by Gordon (1984) on women's bureaus in six Caribbean countries and provides empirical evidence for some of the points we are making here. Gordon concludes:

> Evidence suggests that the major impediments confronting the operation of the Caribbean women's bureaus lies in the administrative arrangements in which they are embedded. Presumably, such arrangements emanate from existing policy directives, but the current level and style of operations suggest that if real policy lies in bureaucratic practice then policy in this area of women's affairs can be said to be non-existent. *It is true that policy statements exist, but they contain no clear definitions of goals and priorities and the associated arrangements for the provision of proper levels of resources and imaginative management support structures which can transform those statements into creative and dynamic action programmes.* Rather the bureaus have emerged as weakly structured, ill-defined units whose ability to function as the sole implementing agency for the government's policy on Women in Development is seriously compromised by the absence of appropriate support and resource provisions.
>
> (p. 115, our emphasis)

There are examples of similar kinds of implementation failure from the experience of international agencies as well. In their study of the ILO and the FAO, Lotherington et al (1991) indicate that failure to carry out the realignment between goals, on the one hand, and rules and practices, on the other, considerably slowed down the ability of these organisations to implement their commitment to integrating gender concerns into their activities. The pre-existing rules, values and norms within these organisations reflected a sector-oriented, technical expertise and were adapted to serving sector-oriented technical policy; by contrast, the adoption of a gender-mainstreaming agenda required a new, human-oriented approach and socio-economic expertise. Rather than seeking to mainstream this new approach and the expertise it required, the organisations relied instead on a strategy of ad hoc 'adding on' of gender considerations. In an earlier study, Maguire (1984) had pointed to an example of this ad hoc approach in a UNDP report on a $120 million joint multilateral agency project on river blindness in West Africa for which the FAO had included 'a woman consultant sociologist' to review the programme in order to ensure that 'the concerns of the rural family and women would be included in the programme'. As Maguire suggests, the implication was that but for this lone female sociologist, the concerns of women in Benin, Ghana, Ivory Coast, Mali, Niger, Togo and Upper Volta would be overlooked.

The case study of an FAO fish farming project in Zambia by Harrison (1995) suggests that the ad hoc and piecemeal attention to gender issues remains an aspect of FAO practice. The fisheries department in the FAO office in Rome was made up of expert staff with a technical background in biology or fisheries management; gender policy has remained little more than the collection of information and calls for more information and the implementation of unsystematic and ad hoc measures which frequently lead to the marginalisation of gender issues. In fact, Harrison suggests, the lack of clarity on what constituted a 'gender-aware' perspective in the planning process led to the translation of gender concerns at implementation level in ways which reflected the priorities and preferences of local project workers and interest groups. The result was, for all the concerns expressed at policy level about 'gender', the promotion of a fish farming technology which was primarily adopted by men and was 'a dawn-to-midnight grind for some rural women' (ALCOM, 1992, p. 9 cited in Harrison, 1995, p. 43).

These examples from the agency context illustrate the point made earlier: that the language of 'mainstreaming' can often conceal very limited integrationist goals. A genuine concern with mainstreaming gender issues would have required the incorporation of socio-economic knowledge into the existing body of technical expertise and entailed rethinking of old rules and procedures. It would also have required the allocation of adequate and appropriate material, human and financial resources within the organisation in order to ensure that policy goals can be translated into practical outcomes. As Staudt's case study of USAID in the seventies showed graphically, organisations that adopt gender-related policy goals very frequently sabotage their own chances of success by allocating completely inadequate resources for implementing the policy. Assessing the poor performance of the USAID WID office in the seventies to carry out its mandate, she notes that its annual budget was limited to $1 million (out of $4 billion) and a staff of four (in an agency of around six thousand), precluding the WID office from achieving little beyond an exhorting role. The UN agencies allocated around 0.2 per cent of their overall budget to projects which benefited women while less than one per cent of FAO projects specify strategies to reach women farmers (Staudt, 1990).

However, even where appropriate rules and adequate resources are in place, this will not necessarily guarantee the success of gender-related policy. What is critical is also the beliefs and values of the people responsible for implementation. Power may be officially concentrated within the central policy-making core of an organisation but staff located at mid and lower levels can ignore, dilute or alter the spirit of its policies and systematically make or break implementation. Clearly all policies with redistributive intentions are likely to come up against resistance at some stage in the policy-making process. What is specific to the resistance to gender-redistributive policies is the fact that both policy makers and implementers in these organisations tend to be predominantly men who live intimately with the group who stands to benefit from such policies, and individual aspects of these relationships carry over into the workplace in potentially distorting ways (Staudt, p. 1985, p. 7). Gender-redistributive policies thus impinge directly on the personal beliefs and values, relationships and identities of those who formulate and implement policies to a degree that no other transformatory strategy does. Such organisational actors do not generally live in intimate and highly personal relationships with the poor, with members of minority groups or those whose environments are threatened. The fact that they often live with women leads them to believe that they can generalise from their own experiences; it also gives them a very personal stake in defending the existing ideas and practices through which they have acquired their gender identities and therefore in the outcomes of policies which threaten these ideas and practices. Indeed persistent references to some idealised set of family relations and the sexual stereotypes this entails appears to be a feature of a great deal of the articulated resistance to gender redistributive policies, as seen in Chikarmane's essay, on attitudes within the police force to domestic violence.

When policies which seek to redress culturally-sanctioned inequalities have to be implemented by individuals who themselves have been beneficiaries of these inequalities, then implementers are critical stakeholders in the policy process along with members of the community that will be affected. An important aspect of gender-aware planning therefore must be an analysis of the various institutional actors responsible for various aspects of implementation and the kind of stake that they are likely to have in the success or failure of gender-related policy goals. In this context, a useful classification provided in Lotherington et al 1991 can be used to further disaggregate the category of 'people' in the institutional force field analysis outlined in Figure 1 into :

- *Innovators:* Those who have been active in getting gender-aware policy onto the organisational agenda and would seek to assure its implementation as the innovators. For successful implementation, a minimum critical mass of an organisation's staff need to be innovators in this sense.
- *Loyal Bureaucrats:* This is a category of staff within an organisation who may not be personally convinced of the need for integrating gender concerns into their agency's policies and plans but will not allow this to affect their professional commitment to ensure such integration if that is what is indicated by organisational goals. They can prove effective allies for gender advocates, even if they are not privately enthusiastic about the promotion of gender equity goals, provided they are given the analysis, concepts and tools to guide them in carrying out their duties.
- *Hesitators* consist of those who may subscribe to gender-oriented goals in principle but find it difficult to support their practical implementation. There are a number of reasons why this may be so: the experience of resistance from the community in which implementation will take place; a felt loss of prestige in working on gender issues; or the inability to grasp how policy reformulated from a gender perspective might differ from a more traditional welfarist approach to women. In addition, as development agencies add gender on to their existing priority goals, the

complexities, contradictions and trade-offs between these various goals can have a paralysing effect on those responsible for implementation. Here again, analytical tools and technical expertise can help to convert ineffective hesitators into effective allies for the implementation of gender-oriented policies.

- *Hardliners* are those who are fundamentally opposed to the adoption of gender-oriented goals within their organisation. They are likely to deploy various tactics to ignore or block the implementation of these goals, silently and tacitly if such goals are espoused by those at the top, vociferously and actively if support at the top is perceived to be purely rhetorical or a response to donor pressure. They resist because they are either actively opposed to such policy or because they see it as a lesser priority to other development issues. In addition, they resist because they feel threatened; professionally threatened by the redistributive connotations of such policies and personally threatened because of the perceived challenge to long-internalised notions of what constitutes proper gender roles.

An analysis of the beliefs and practices of hardliners within an organisation at the evaluation stage has often helped in the past to cast light on why organisations apparently committed to gender equity fail to deliver on their policy goals. Various researchers have sought to compile what we might call an inventory of resistance tactics deployed at the implementation stage (Longwe, 1995; Buvinic, 1983; Staudt, 1985). Kabeer and Subrahmanian (1996) also document an inventory of biases and errors that are frequently the product of deeply internalised, and often unconscious biases. However, resistance to the implementation of gender-related policy goals is less easy to explain in terms of ignorance and thoughtlessness and is more often consciously adopted by men, as well as women, who feel uneasy or threatened by the redistributive connotations or ideological changes represented by the goals they are being asked to implement. Among the various resistance tactics utilised by implementing officials, the most frequently documented appear to be:

- *Trivialisation:* attempting to reduce the significance of the gender-related policy goal by personalised attacks on gender advocates within the organisation or trivialising jokes about gender issues. Almost all those who are engaged in such work have experienced this treatment and it has been widely reported in the literature. Staudt points out that the level of personalisation and trivialisation of gender-related issues within an organisation provides a good barometer of the depth of resistance and notes its incidence within USAID in the early seventies in the form of tedious jokes about 'developing a woman' and 'what about men in development' and the persistent tendency to discuss gender issues with reference to their own wives. According to Moser (1993), when a Gender and Development Unit was first set up in OXFAM, it was met with some amount of hilarity and a tendency to refer to its members as lesbians and dykes.

- *Dilution:* or the process by which an innovative policy is watered down into a weak and routine set of actions. Kabeer and Murthy (1996; this volume) trace how DWCRA (Development of Women and Children in Rural Areas) in India was initially conceptualised as an innovative credit programme for women, based on a long-term group formation process and a recognition of women's productive potential as well as their domestic roles and responsibilities. By the time it was implemented, it had been transformed into yet another 'spoon-feeding programme' for poor women. The main reason for this dilution lay in the lack of effort to communicate the rationale and philosophy which underpinned the innovative aspects of the programme so that by the time it reached the field level, the entrenched rules, norms and practices of the implementing apparatus together with the gender biases and preconceptions of field level officers were powerful enough to submerge the programme's innovative aspects.
- *Subversion:* when the transformatory goals of a policy are reinterpreted as welfarist ones. Buvinic (1986) pointed out early how even when projects for poor women were initially designed with explicitly production-related goals, they were frequently transformed into welfare-oriented programmes in the course of implementation, because welfare programmes were seen both as promoting

'appropriate' roles for women and, more importantly, as not taking away resources from men. She quotes a high-level official in a planning ministry who expressed willingness to support income-generating projects for women as long as they did not lead to women earning more than men since he perceived this as having undesirable effects on family stability.

- *Outright resistance:* Agarwal (1994) cites several examples of the reluctance and often downright refusal of state officials to carry out government policy on land rights in India which allows women to use common property resources and inherit land on the grounds that the transformatory potential of such policies could jeopardise the stability of the family through its challenge to male authority. Such attitudes often start at the top and Agarwal notes the response of the Indian Minister of Agriculture to her advocacy of land rights for women at a seminar for the Indian Planning Commission in 1989: 'Are you suggesting that women should be given rights in land? What do women want? To break up the family?' (cited in Agarwal, 1994, p.12).

Monitoring, Evaluation and Gender Aware Indicators

The above discussion on the resistance to and risks inherent in managing gender-redistributive interventions helps to highlight both the importance of having indicators of achievement in place at the outset of the implementation process as well as certain additional ones related specifically to gender redistributive goals. Conventionally, indicators are necessary for most interventions to ensure that there is baseline information and data from which the impact of the intervention can be evaluated at a later stage. Furthermore, when collected on a periodic basis, they can provide a mechanism for feeding back information on the conversion of inputs into outputs and the contribution of outputs to the immediate objectives and longer term goals of an intervention. It thus ensures that the planning framework is treated as a dynamic rather than static tool and the implementing organisation has the capacity to be able to respond to unanticipated opportunities and constraints thrown up in the course of its life in the field.

Less conventionally, from a more specifically gender perspective,. indicators of achievement serve to signal to all actors involved in planning and implementing an intervention, the need to ensure that gender concerns are integrated at every stage of the process and to measure how successfully this integration has occurred. The long history of gender blindness in the planning process, combined with the present tendency to 'add women on' as a form of symbolic politics, makes the attention to gender-aware indicators which relate to inputs, outputs, objectives and goals of critical importance as statement of intent, as: *signal* to all actors involved in the intervention, as *constant reminder* during the life of the intervention, as *measure of performance* in the achievement of gender-aware goals and objectives and as a *tool* for analysing shortfalls.

There is a salutary example of a consultant hired by DANIDA in Bangladesh to design an aquaculture project for landless and poor farmers. Given DANIDA's commitment to gender equity, his initial report was returned because no mention had been made of its possible relevance to landless and poor women. The consultant responded by adding the term 'and women' wherever reference had been made to intended beneficiaries in the Logical Framework. It is highly unlikely that an intervention designed in this way is likely to promote a great deal of attention to the needs and interests of women and to their social relationships with men since it confines women purely to the goals and objectives stages of the project design and totally ignores the kinds of constraints that women specifically might suffer and that might require different or additional features in the inputs, outputs, activities and indicators of the project.

It is precisely in order to avoid such token efforts to incorporate gender perspectives into the planning process that indicators for monitoring achievements of the stated gender-related goals and objectives of the intervention have to be in place at the outset of a project. They provide an important precautionary measure to ensure that a gender-transformatory inverven-tion does not get diluted, subverted or derailed by unofficial norms and actual behaviour in the implementation stages. For indicators of achievement to be operationalised, the requisite information has to be available, either in the form of existing surveys, reports and studies or else by commissioning the necessary research. Here it becomes important to decide from the outset 'whose reality', and hence whose indicators, should inform how achievements are to be assessed since, as we pointed out earlier, certain interests are better represented or heard within the policy domain than others. Information can be acquired through conventional, top-down and generally quantitative methodologies or else through alternative, participatory and more qualitative methodologies. As Schaffer (1996) points out, each set of approaches posits a particular relationship between those who ask questions and those to whom the questions are addressed and will have particular implications for the transformatory potential of the intervention in question.

An attempt to take account of the different, and possibly divergent, 'realities' is to be found in Greeley, Kabeer, Davies and Hussain (1992) where three different categories of indicators were suggested, each offering a different window into the reality in which an intervention was located, and representing the perspectives of different sets of actors relevant to the intervention. These are presented in Box 1 below:

Taking account of intersecting realities in evaluation

The 'outsider's' indicators: these are indicators which have gained wide acceptance in a particular field of development, arising from a substantial body of research.

The agency's indicators: these tell us how an agency perceives and measures its own objectives.

Beneficiaries' indicators These express how those who are expected to benefit from a particular intervention would themselves assess their own well being and experiences as a result of the intervention.

In addition, and to some extent echoing the distinction we made earlier between different levels of causality underlying a problematic outcome, Greeley et al (1992) suggest a number of dimensions of information to be collected on this 'beneficiary-identified' set of indicators:

- *what the change has been*
- *the immediate causes to which the change is attributed*
- *the underlying causes to which the change is attributed.*

This sequence of information allows changes in the well-being of the intended beneficiaries to be traced through to the institution or actors responsible since a reported change does not by itself constitute evidence of an organisation's performance if there is no way of interpreting and attributing the change. Some examples from the literature will illustrate the point. An evaluation of Nari Nidhi's credit programme for poor rural women in Bihar found that the majority of women loanees interviewed reported increases in their incomes while a significant majority also reported an increase in the share they contributed to household income (see Kabeer and Murthy 1996). However, such an increase did not necessarily constitute evidence of Nari Nidhi's success in improving the economic situation of women since it could have reflected some other factor unrelated to Nari Nidhi's efforts. A further level of information was clearly needed for the change to be attributed to Nari Nidhi. Further information from the loanees revealed that they attributed the immediate cause of their improvement earnings to their expansion into a new economic activity or expansion of the scale of existing economic activities and that the underlying cause of this ability to expand was in turn attributed to the fact that they had been able to switch their source of loans from local moneylenders who charged interest rates of 10 per cent monthly to Nari Nidhi who charged 12 per cent interest annually. Consequently, the economic improvements reported by these women were in fact attributable to Nari Nidhi's efforts. On the negative side, women from one particular district reported a fall in returns from their main activity which was fish vending. The immediate cause of this was found to be a shortfall in the supply of fish to meet the needs of women traders which in turn reflected the fact that Nari Nidhi had provided a large batch of loans for investment in fish vending activities simultaneously—in one village alone, 60 women received such loans—which led to a sudden upsurge in the demand for fish and an increase in its price.

Changes in income may be considered to have a relatively straightforward interpretation in terms of well-being but there are areas of change where there is a danger that 'our' assumptions may translate into misleading interpretations of 'their' priorities. For instance, a number of poverty-related credit interventions in the Indian context, where indebtedness to moneylenders has long been analysed as a key cause of poverty, have identified the reduction or elimination of reliance on moneylenders as a long-term goal. Consequently, the finding that women borrowers with the Madras-based Working Women's Forum (WWF) continued to rely on moneylenders, despite receiving yearly loans at increasing amounts, might be taken to signal that the intervention had failed to achieve its stated objectives. However, a study by Noponen (1990) also found that women who routinely combined loans from moneylenders and subsidised credit had statistically higher overall earning levels than women who did not. She suggested that women resorted to moneylenders in times of consumption crisis, for which WWF loans were not forthcoming. As a result of this strategy, their working capital was not eroded by family needs. Reliance on moneylenders need not therefore in itself represent a problem, as long as it did not lead to debilitating debt.

Finally, mainstream gender-blind interventions have often erred in attributing altruistic and harmonious interpretations to intra-household distributive outcomes, feminist assumptions may lead to a different kind of interpretative bias, the tendency to attribute passivity and victimhood where there may be agency and negotiation. The issue of interpretative bias is particularly evident in cases where evaluations of the same programme come up with very conflicting findings. There are some striking examples of this from the Bangladesh context. One set of evaluations of poverty-related lending programmes came to the conclusion that lending to women had led to increases in their decision-making power, reduced male violence, increased their consumption levels and security assets, enhanced their mobility outside the home, led to greater independence in purchasing activities and enhanced their political participation (Hashemi and Schuler; Pitt and Khandker). Yet another set of evaluations of the same set of programmes concluded that most women lost control over their loans to male family members, violence against women increased, subsistence resources were depleted to pay for loans and, by and large, women were left worse off than before (Goetz and Sen Gupta, 1996; Montgomery, Bhattacharya and Hulme, 1996). However, neither set of evaluations actually consulted women themselves about their views on programme impact.

Conflicting interpretations of empirical phenomena are also evident in two separate assessments of the Tamil Nadu Women's Development Programme cited earlier. The programme offers credit to members of poor women's groups on the condition that they accumulate a minimum amount as savings in order to ensure that they had learn to manage their funds effectively. One evaluation was carried out in a workshop with the project organisers while the other was specifically commissioned by the project funders. Both evaluations noted that it was often men's savings that were being used in order to meet the qualification. However, the first suggested that men were using the women in order to access the credit while the second suggested it was the women who were using men's savings in order to expedite their access to programme credit. As in the Bangladesh context, neither interpretation appeared to be based on the accounts provided by the women in question.

Evaluations are intended to judge the intended and unintended effects of an intervention and to make recommendations about its future. Yet the question of whose vantage point, whose priorities, should inform the assessment of project outcomes, remains a problematic one. In relation to the conflicting evaluations of the Bangladesh credit programmes, Kabeer (1998) found that they reflected the very different models of gender power which informed those who were conducting the evaluation rather than conflicting empirical findings. Furthermore, she also found that the women who received the credit themselves subscribed to a very different view of its empowerment impact than did those who evaluated them. Clearly, very different programme implications will flow from evaluations which suggest that men appropriated women's loans from those which suggest that women both controlled and benefited from their own loans. Similarly, in the Tamil Nadu example also, programme responses are likely to be very different if 'men were using women' to get access to government credit and if 'women were using men' to expedite their own access to government loans. Evaluation is essentially about making value-judgements about what constitutes a desirable outcome (and what does not), and we should be aware of whose 'values' a project is being judged on. Allowing women to speak on their own behalf about their own priorities and lives will not only help to rescue them from the position of eternal and muted victims, but will also help to separate very clearly whose values can, and should, count in an evaluation.

Power, Participation and the Political Sub-text of Gender-aware Planning

The policy process is seldom a neutral one. It is imbued at all stages by the power relations which govern the contexts in which policy is formulated and implemented, and it is characterised by struggles over meanings as well as over resources. For women, particularly poorer women, who have tended to be marginalised in these struggles, their needs and priorities have always been defined on their behalf and often in terms which help to contain them within pre-existing roles and relationships. A planning process in which causes, effects, means and ends are analysed and evaluated in collaboration with those whose voices have been traditionally excluded has the advantage not only of allowing hitherto submerged needs and constraints to emerge but also of acknowledging the incompleteness of a development process in which such groups have not been given the space to participate. Participatory techniques are a means of ensuring that local interpretations, particularly by those whose lives are affected by an intervention, are given priority in the design and assessment of the intervention. This is not an entirely unproblematic process.

For women in particular, in societies where deeply-entrenched and internalised cultural rules, norms and values not only tend to devalue their worth and well-being but also to militate against recognition by women themselves of what Sen describes as a 'spectacular lack of equity in the ruling arrangements' (1990, p.149). The power of social conditioning in shaping the 'choices' that women make to the extent that they may be resigned to, and indeed actively promote, the distribution of resources which discriminate against themselves and their daughters, cannot be underestimated. It is this concern which underlies Jackson's critique (1995) of the populist claims made for PRA as 'giving voice' to the perceptions of local people. Noting the 'mutedness' that goes with political and economic disenfranchisement within a community, she challenges the implicit assumption of many PRA practitioners that the perceptions and priorities that women articulate are necessarily complete truths. Sarin's case-study of Joint Forest Management in this volume, shows that if this assumption remains unchallenged in the course of using PRA methods, it can result in exercises privileging the priorities and preferences of a particular group of women in a community, setting up different groups of women in opposition to each other.

What is important to realise is that *gender-awareness relates more to the theoretical perspectives and political stance of the analyst than it does to the superiority of one set of methodological tools over another.* Participatory methodologies can only be as gender-blind or as gender-aware as their practitioners. At present, the gender biases of many PRA practitioners are disguised by the populist rhetoric of PRA discourse, a disguise not easily available to researchers using more conventional quantitative techniques. Nevertheless, to deny a role to participatory methodologies in the processes by which needs and opportunities are identified, prioritised and responded to, carries the danger of reinforcing the exclusion of women from the policy process and denying them a voice a second time around. Participatory approaches which require 'us' to listen to 'them', and are informed by sensitivity to the different forms that gender power and inequality takes in different contexts, are critical in challenging the assumptions, preconceptions and biases which are part of all our cultural and disciplinary baggage, whether the 'we' in question is the feminist researcher or the neoclassical economist. They allow us to analyse the 'choices' that women make, the meaning of these choices and the extent to which they are a product of agency or the denial of agency to women within their households and communities. And when denial of agency is entailed in the choices women make, they allow us to explore the extent to which such denial is the product of internalised ideologies or external constraints and hence what the priorities of policy intervention should be. 'Listening for change' is an essential part of the process by which poor women can be given 'voice' in shaping the interventions that are intended to address their poverty and by which they can take their place as central actors in deciding both the ends and means of development.

Notes

[1]This is an example drawn from N.Kabeer and R.Murthy (1996).

[2]Force field analysis is popular analytical tool used to understand organisational dynamics.

[3]The sheepish response of some of the development officials we have trained suggests that this is not an isolated response.

References

Agarwal, B., 1994. *A Field of One's Own: Gender and Land Rights in South Asia* Cambridge: Cambridge University Press.

Buvinic, M., 1983. 'Women's Issues in Third World Poverty: A Policy Analysis' in M.Buvinic, M.Lycette and W.P.McGreevey (eds) *Women and Poverty in the Third World* Baltimore: John Hopkins University Press.

———, 1986. 'Projects for Women in the Third World: Explaining their Misbehaviour' *World Development*, Vol. 14, no.5.

Goetz, A.M., and R. Sengupta. 1996. 'Who Takes the Credit? Gender, Power and Control Over Loan Use in Rural Programmes in Bangladesh.' *World Development*, Vol. 24, no. 1.

Gordon, S., 1984. *Ladies in Limbo: The Fate of Women's Bureaux. Case studies from the Caribbean*. London: Commonwealth Secretariat.

Greeley, M., N. Kabeer, S. Davies and K. Hussein, 1992. 'Measuring the Poverty Reduction Impact of Development Interventions', Report prepared for the ODA, Brighton: IDS.

Harrison, E., 1995. 'Fish and Feminists', *IDS Bulletin*, Vol. 26, no. 3, Brighton: IDS.

Hashemi, S.M. Shuler, S.R., and A.P. Riley. 1996. 'Rural Credit Programs and Women's Empowerment in Bangladesh.' *World Development*. Vol. 24, no. 4.

Jackson, C., 1995. 'Rescuing Gender from the Poverty Trap', *Gender Analysis in Development* series, East Anglia: University of East Anglia.

Kabeer, N. and R.K. Murthy, 1996. 'Poverty as Institutional Exclusion: Lessons from Indian Government and Non-government Credit Interventions', IDS Discussion Paper no. 356, Brighton: Institute of Development Studies.

———, and R. Subrahmanian, 1996. 'Institutions, Relations and Outcomes: Framework and Tools for Gender-aware Planning', IDS Discussion Paper no. 357, Brighton: Institute of Development Studies.

Longwe, S. 1995. 'Opposition to Gender-sensitive Development: Learning to Answer Back.' *Gender and Development*, 3, no. 1, Oxford: Oxfam.

Lotherington, A.T., M. Haug and A.B. Flemmen, 1991. *Implementation of Women-in-Development Policy* Oslo: Centre for Development and Environment, University of Oslo.

Maguire, P., 1984. *Women in Development: An Alternative Analysis*. Amherst, Massachusetts: Centre for International Education.

Montogomery, R., Bhattacharya, D. and D. Hulme. 1996. 'Credit for the Poor in Bangladesh.' in D. Hulme and P. Mosley (eds) *Finance Against Poverty* Routledge, London.

Moser, C.O.N., 1993. *Gender Planning and Development: Theory, Practice and Training* London: Routledge.

Noponen, H., 1990. 'Loans to the Working Poor: A Longitudinal Study of Credit, Gender, and the Household Economy', Project on Regional and Industrial Economies, Working Paper no. 6, New Jersey: Rutgers University.

Pitt, M., and S. Khandekar. 1995. 'Household and Intra-Household Impact of the Grameen Bank and Similar Targeted Credit Programs in Bangladesh', paper presented at a workshop on Credit Programs for the Poor held at Dhaka and organised by the Education and Social Policy Department of the World Bank in Washington in collaboration with the Bangladesh Institute of Development Studies.

Staudt, K., 1985. *Women, Foreign Assistance, and Advocacy Administration* New York: Praeger.

———, 1990. 'Gender Politics in Bureaucracy: Theoretical Issues in Comparative Perspective' in K. Staudt (ed.) *Women, International Development and Politics: The Bureaucratic Mire* Temple Philadelphia: University Press.

13

Gender Training Experiences with Indian NGOs

RANJANI K. MURTHY*

Introduction

Indian women occupy a subordinate position relative to Indian men due to the deeply entrenched gender hierarchies in Indian society. These hierarchies are played out in, and perpetuated through, different institutions of Indian society: the household, the community, the market and the state, and are always intertwined with inequalities based on social relations of caste, class, religion and ethnicity. However, these institutions are not monolithic. They take different organisational forms, some of which are committed to, and have been effective in, reducing gender disparities in society.

Here the concern is with 'Non-governmental Organisations' (NGOs) which work directly at the grassroots, which can be viewed as a specific organisational form of the institution of community. Since the 1980s, Indian NGOs have been espousing their official concern to promote a gender equitable society. In theory, they have a comparative advantage over government in bringing about gender aware societal change, as they have greater flexibility than the government to define their rules and practices, recruit people

*I would like to acknowledge the contribution of the participants and organisers of different gender training programmes facilitated by me in shaping some of the thoughts articulated in this paper. The responsibility for any shortcomings is, however, mine.

and distribute resources in favour of women. Some NGOs[1] have realised this potential advantage and have been fairly effective in promoting gender-aware change at the community and policy level. A significant number of Indian NGOs, however, have failed to capitalise on this potential advantage. They have, in fact, reflected and perpetuated gender hierarchies in the institutional environment through their goals, programme policies and activities, policies and practices governing internal functioning, attitudes of personnel and allocation of resources (Murthy 1995; Subrahmanian 1993). Gender training has emerged since the 1980s as an important strategy to make Indian NGOs gender aware, as well as to empower women and humanise men working in them. There has been a mushrooming of gender training efforts, with a variety of actors—donor agencies, support NGOs, academic institutions and the Indian government—organising gender training programmes for NGOs. The target group has ranged from policy makers to implementing officials of NGOs, and at times included marginalised sections of the community as well. These gender training programmes vary widely in terms of their goals, understanding of gender and operational objectives. The gender training strategies, methodologies, content of training and follow up measures vary accordingly. Given this diversity, the effectiveness of gender training programmes in bringing gender-aware change at the personal, organisational and/or institutional level in the region has varied widely, and enhancing the effectiveness of gender training in this regard has emerged as a key concern of gender trainers, policy makers and practitioners associated with NGOs. Another concern has been the mainstreaming of gender within all development training programmes for NGOs. Though gender training has gained legitimacy in the 1990s, it is largely compartmentalised. The majority of development training programmes continue to be gender-blind. This essay seeks to point out strategies for addressing these concerns, through a critical reflection on experiences of the author and other gender trainers in India.

The first section begins by examining different ways in which gender may be present or absent within development training of NGOs, and distinguishes between *gender-blind training, gender-neutral training, gender-ameliorative training and gender-transformative training*. It argues the case for moving away from gender-blind training, towards gender-aware training (the last three categories) in the short run, and ultimately towards gender-transformative training. The second section illustrates two experiences of the author in gender-transformative training of NGO personnel in India. The first is an example of an inter-NGO training of gender trainers workshop (TOGT), and the second is an example of a follow up workshop with one of the organisations which participated in the TOGT workshop. The criterion for choosing these two examples is the number of lessons which they have to offer, and not because they are examples of success. The last section summarises lessons from these two experiences, as well as from the experience of other gender trainers, on the factors crucial to effectiveness; covering areas such as goals and objectives, entry points in training, training strategies, selection and agency of participants, choice of facilitators and facilitation strategies, and impact assessment and accountability of trainers. The concluding section points to the lessons on the potential and limitations of gender training, and suggests complementary non-training strategies which may be required.

The Absence (or Presence) of Gender in Training

All training programmes privilege certain categories of analysis, and suppress others. Gender is one such key aspect. Extending and building upon Kabeer's (1994) framework for analysing development policies from a gender perspective to analysing development training, it is possible to distinguish between four different ways in which gender has been absent or present in development training in India, leading to *gender-blind, gender-neutral, gender-ameliorative and gender-transformative training*.[2] A directory of 217 training programmes offered by 36 support NGOs and academic institutions in the country to grassroots NGOs (compiled by GTZ/SHF in India in 1996) reveals that 84 per cent of these training programmes are gender-blind i.e. they deal with objectives and content which appear gender-neutral (development perspective, planning, monitoring and evaluation, leadership and human resource development, agriculture, environment etc.), but are implicitly male biased as they do not delve into gender biases within mainstream thinking on these themes, and are premised on the notion of a male actor and men's roles, needs and interests (Mathew et al. 1996). A review of a few other reports on development training for NGOs and government functionaries also reveals similar tendencies (Murthy 1991).

Greater gender-awareness since the late 1980s has led to three alternative ways in which gender has been incorporated into training in India. These are elaborated in detail in Murthy (forthcoming), and summarised briefly below.

Gender-neutral Training

Gender-neutral training seeks to provide accurate information on the existing gender-based division of labour and resources, and strengthen skills to incorporate this information into the design, implementation and evaluation of projects with pre-determined (but gender-blind) objectives, so that these objectives are met in the most efficient way possible.[3] The primary goal of such training programmes is thus to increase project efficiency. This approach to training was popular amongst some of the donor agencies, government departments and NGOs in the late 1980s, and its influence is apparent even in the mid 1990s. The descriptive category of gender roles, rather than the analytical category of gender relations is used within such training programmes. The former emphasises the *roles and behavioural differences* of and between men and women, while the latter places emphasis on the *power relations* between them which lead to these differences and gender inequalities. The Gender Analysis Framework developed by Overholt et al. (1985) has often been used as the chief training methodology, but frequently only the efficiency rather than equity concerns within the framework have been emphasised.

Gender-ameliorative Training

Gender-ameliorative training seeks to provide an understanding of the gender-based division of labour and access to skills and resources, not for their instrumental use in increasing the efficiency of development interventions, but to highlight women's secondary status in society and to strengthen strategies to improve their condition in society. However, women's secondary status is seen as arising out of their lack of skills, confidence, motivation and unity, rather than gender hierarchies in society. The primary weakness of NGOs is seen as their lack of management expertise to enhance the economic independence of women, and meet their day-to-day needs through a group approach. Gender-ameliorative training aims at addressing these weaknesses, and may be directed at NGO/government personnel or members of the community. This approach is popular amongst NGOs, government departments and donor agencies pursuing gender specific policies, i.e. policies enhancing women's access to resources and skills, but leaving issues of control and division of labour intact (Kabeer 1994a). Such training programmes and policies address and highlight the practical gender needs of women in the area of enterprises, health and education, rather than their strategic gender interests. As in the case of gender-neutral training, the concept of gender is discussed at a descriptive, rather than an analytical level. The Gender Analysis Framework developed by Overholt et al. (1985) is quite popular within such training programmes, and so is the Gender Analysis Matrix developed by Rani Parker (1991).

Gender-transformative Training

Gender-transformative training encompasses a variety of approaches (see Section 3). At the bare minimum, these approaches seek to provide an understanding of gender at an analytical, rather than descriptive, level, emphasising the political point that women occupy a subordinate position in society not because they are the problem, but because of the socially constituted power relations between men and women played out within different institutions of society. The emphasis is on gender relations, rather than gender roles, and these are seen as leading to the unequal distribution of resources, responsibilities and power between men and women. Gender relations are seen as intertwined with relations of caste, class, religion etc., leading, in particular, to the marginalisation of poor dalit, tribal, minority groups and single women. While gender-transformative training programmes seek to contribute to the process of transforming gender relations, they differ in terms of whether they aim to bring about changes in gender relations at the personal, organisational or/and (societal) institutional levels. The nature of gender training needs and interests which they seek to address, therefore, varies, but they are of a strategic rather than practical nature.

Given the fact that gender has been absent within most development training programmes for NGOs, any move towards gender-neutral and gender-ameliorative training may be a step forward. But such steps may not be adequate to change the gender hierarchies perpetuated through many of the Indian NGOs (especially those headed by men), and internalised by their staff. Gender-transformative training may be essential. Whether transformative goals should be couched in gender neutral or ameliorative language in pre-training communication is another issue, discussed in the third section.

Experiences in Gender Training of NGO Personnel

This section shares two experiences of the author in facilitating/co-facilitating gender training programmes for NGO personnel. The first experience is that of an *inter-NGO* 'training of gender trainers workshop' (TOGT) which sought to bring about gender-transformative changes at the personal and organisational level in a few NGOs in Eastern India. This workshop had a mixed impact. The objectives, content and methodology adopted in this workshop, and the reasons due to which the impact of the workshop was poor in the case of one of the participating NGOs is elaborated in this example.[4] The second experience is that of an *intra-NGO* gender and development workshop with this particular NGO. The attempts made in this workshop to incorporate some of the lessons from the TOGT workshop and the outcome of these efforts at the organisational and personal levels are outlined in this example.

Training of Gender Trainers Workshop

Workshop content and methodology

In 1994, a five day 'Training of gender trainers (TOGT) workshop' was organised by one of the international funding

NGOs for its partners in the eastern region workshop was primarily targeted at senior-level gender-focal persons[5] of NGOs, and was preceded tional level workshop for chief functionaries of NGO gender concepts. Of the 11 partners invited by the funding agency, only six responded by sending participants to the TOGT workshop. One or two of these organisations sent their field-level functionaries, rather those at a senior level. The TOGT workshop had six objectives: i) to trace the historical evolution of women as a category in development in India, and develop a critique of WID approaches; ii) to provide an overview of a gender approach to development, and draw out the main elements of an institutional framework to understand gender relations in the Indian context; iii) to review gender issues within key concerns, and the effectiveness of government and participating NGOs in responding to these; iv) to create spaces for personal reflection on gender issues and strategising for change; v) to strengthen skills in mainstreaming gender within participating organisations goals and perspectives, programmes, systems and internal functioning; and vi) to strengthen skills in training from a gender perspective. The author was the main facilitator for the TOGT workshop, but was not involved in the earlier one for chief functionaries. As she felt ill-equipped to deal with the issue of 'gender and self' the funding agency invited a male resource person with expertise in behavioural area, who unfortunately could not take part in the preceding or subsequent sessions.

The workshop began with an introduction by the funding agency representative in India on the need for such a workshop. The participants then shared their expectations from the workshop, as well as the happiest and unhappiest moments experienced by them due to their gender identity. The latter discussion paved the way for understanding that gender issues do not just affect members of the community, but also people as individuals. Subsequent to clarification on what expectations could be fulfilled in the workshop, and what would have to be dealt with in other settings (e.g. management training for women), the workshop content was finalised. The workshop content planned by the funding agency and the facilitator had to be slightly reworked to accommodate the needs of the participants.[6] The substantive part of the workshop commenced with an introduction and critique of Women in Development (WID) approaches and structuralist perspectives on women and development, and then moved over to a session on gender relations and gender approaches to women's development; using the institutional and social relations framework. From this perspective gender concerns in the sectors/issues of health, education, poverty, agriculture and violence were examined, and the institutional framework was used to understand how ideologies, practices and structures of institutions lead to gender differentiated outcomes in different sectors. Practical gender needs and strategic gender interests in each sector were then explored; and the programmes of the Indian government and participating NGOs were reviewed to see what needs and interests were being addressed by them. Most of the participating NGOs were addressing practical gender needs. Hence, discussions followed on how these could be used as starting points to achieve strategic concerns, either through adoption of strategic 'means' (e.g. mobilisation of women to demand their rights to water from the government) or reconstituting the 'ends' (e.g. promoting not just access to water, but equal responsibility for fetching water). From a narrow focus on specific sectors, the deliberations proceeded to looking at NGOs as a whole; and brainstorming on what we mean by a gender sensitive NGO, a vision of a gender sensitive society, criteria for evaluation programmes, planning, monitoring and evaluation systems and criteria for reviewing internal organisational aspects from a gender perspective. Based on this criteria the participants from each organisation carried out an assessment of their organisation. This was not shared with the larger group, though some shared their analysis with the author in private. The sensitive topic of 'gender and self' was then approached by the external male resource person, through a discussion on stereotypes associated with men and women, how far they applied to themselves as individuals, the positive and negative qualities which women and men were socialised into and the need for alternative definitions of personhood which combined these positive attributes. Contradictions and dilemmas arising out of their gendered identity at the personal and work fronts could only be briefly discussed due to shortage of time. The workshop then concluded with a session on designing training programmes for middle/field-level functionaries of NGOs and community members on gender concerns.

The concepts were shared primarily through lectures or reading materials, followed by group discussions to link them with the experiences of the participants. On most of the other topics the methodology was reversed. Group discussions or individual experiences were used as starting points, and inputs then followed.

Workshop feedback and actual impact

Feedback sheets from individual participants administered at the end of the workshop, revealed that the workshop was found to be extremely useful by the participants, and they listed ambitious plans of how they would practise what they had learnt in their personal lives, and in the context of their organisations. The short duration of the workshop, the complex language of some of the reading materials and the differences in levels and understanding of the participants were expressed as some of the factors which reduced the effectiveness of the workshop. Reading the feedback sheets the author felt that perhaps the objectives of the workshop had been largely achieved. But visits to one of the organisations whose representatives had participated in the workshop and discussions with chief functionaries of three others revealed that the extent to which the objectives were achieved varied. In the case of the organisations whose chief functionaries were gender sensitive (one woman-headed, and another headed by a man), the senior-level representatives who were sent were already aware that women occupied a subordinate position. They, however, needed conceptual clarity to root their understanding, and to try to translate it in the context of their organisation; they also needed space to reflect upon strategies in order to bend institutional rules and achieve their personal goals. The workshop helped them to a significant extent. But in the case of two other organisations (both small, and headed by men), the workshop resulted in few visible gains in terms of gender-aware changes in the organisation's goals, programmes or internal functioning, or personal attitudes on gender issues.

Reasons for shortcomings

A visit to one of the two NGOs falling in the second category for a follow-up workshop revealed several underlying factors leading to the poor impact of the TOGT workshop at the organisational and personal levels. Though the chief functionary espoused an official commitment to gender issues, in reality he was not particularly sensitive to gender concerns. In spite of being invited, he had not taken part in the national level workshop on gender and development, or other gender training workshops. He did, however, attend workshops organised by the funding agency on issues such as environment, the impact of structural adjustment, project planning, monitoring and evaluation etc. It seemed that he sent participants to the TOGT workshop and organised the follow-up gender training workshop partly to keep the funding agency personnel happy. Both the participants from this organisation sent to the TOGT workshop were from the middle, rather than senior levels. They had little say in decision making within the organisation, and were not in a position to use their learning in the workshop to influence its policies. In contrast participants from the senior level were sent for workshops around environment and structural adjustment. Further, many decisions were taken by the Board members, and sensitisation of this group has received little attention from support organisations and funding agencies.

Starting directly with a critique of macro-policies and concepts was also perhaps not the right training method for middle level participants of this small NGO. This was apparent when the author went to the NGO for an intra-NGO follow-up on gender training, thinking that she could draw upon the two staff (one male, and one female) who attended the TOGT workshop as co-facilitators. Preparatory discussions with them revealed that in spite of attending the TOGT workshop they held the belief that women's subordination partly arises out of their biology: less physical strength, body constitution as a result of which women can be raped and they alone can give birth and breast feed children. Starting with personal beliefs and attitudes, and building concepts and planning frameworks around them would perhaps have been a better methodology for this group, as was revealed and attempted in the intra-NGO workshop (see below). Though discussions on beliefs and attitudes were woven into the session within the TOGT workshop on 'gender and self', the male resource person was not adequately equipped to pull out or re-inforce key concepts. Thus, both the participants from this NGO not only lacked access to decision making, but were also not clear on the analytical category of gender relations.

Another factor leading to the 'translation gap', was the limitation of the content of the TOGT workshop. The session on integrating gender concerns within NGOs dealt with 'what' organisational features were required (for example, the goals need to be sensitive to gender issues, programmes need to address institutional barriers at the community level, women staff need to be represented at decision-making levels within NGOs etc.), and not in-depth on 'how' they were to be achieved in the context of each participating organisation. Little attention was given to incorporating in detail a session on *political strategies* to deal with resistance to alter gender-blind goals, planning, monitoring and evaluation systems, allocation of resources, decision-making processes of the organisation, funding agency policies which do not facilitate gender-transformative goals (e.g. short term funding) or institutional barriers at the community level. Another lacuna, was that some sessions facilitated compartmentalisation, rather than mainstreaming of gender concerns. For example, while gender planning frameworks like Molyneux/Moser and the institutional/social relations framework were discussed, how to mainstream gender within SWOT analysis and goal oriented project planning received little attention, which was used by this NGO for strategic planning. As a result gender issues were poorly integrated into organisational level plans evolved by this NGO using this methodology. Some of the shortcomings in terms of the content were due to the short duration. It was very ambitious to think that five days were adequate to familiarise the participants with all the key concepts, issues and skills and to change attitudes. But some part of the problem was also due to the lack of adequate time, space and methodologies for the facilitator (at that juncture) to reflect critically on what she was doing, and how to enhance the effectiveness of their efforts.

Intra-NGO Gender and Development Workshop

Attempts to address shortcomings in the follow-up workshop

Many of these shortcomings became apparent only during the preparation for the follow-up workshop with the concerned NGO (a day before the workshop), and could not all be incorporated into the workshop design. Further, as shall soon become apparent, addressing some of these shortcomings requires strategies beyond the purview of gender training. Nevertheless, the attempts made to incorporate few of the lessons outlined above, and their impact at the personal and organisational levels are outlined below.

As a first step, the funding agency personnel insisted that the chief functionary be present throughout the workshop. Though his physical presence could be ensured throughout the workshop, his attention could not always be secured. In between discussions, he was seen doodling pictures and names of the latest commercial film heroines. But his presence did help in two ways. It, firstly, lent greater credibility to the programme. Secondly, due to the presence of funding agency personnel, he was compelled to support gender concerns in public, whatever his private opinion.

Next, the methodology adopted in this workshop was reversed when compared to the TOGT workshop to take into account the background and experiences of the participants. With the exception of the chief functionary and a few other senior staff, a majority of the participants were from the field and the middle level. Instead of starting with macro polices and concepts, the workshop began with gender preference of the participants; and concepts on gender relations were built through an analysis of the reason for their preference. A simple exercise (which CHETNA, an NGO based in Ahmedabad had used to raise gender awareness on health) was used: the participants were asked whether they would like to be born as a male or a female in the next birth if they had a choice, and the reasons for their preference. This was followed by a discussion on differences between men and women in terms of their roles and responsibilities, qualities and behaviour, and the reasons for these differences. A majority felt that these differences arose out of variation in the biological or physiological constitution of men and women. An in-depth analysis of whether this belief was well-founded or not led to the understanding that the body constitution of women, per se, was not the problem; rather, the problem lay with the social reality of male violence. The ability to give birth was again not a problem but the societal view point, that by nature, women alone can bring up children, was. Thus the difference between socially constructed gender relations and biological sex was clarified. At the end of the session the woman participant who took part in the TOGT workshop walked upto me and said "Didi, I can now understand what we mean by gender". The discussion then moved on to a gender approach to women's development, differences with earlier WID strands, different institutions through which gender relations were constituted, gender issues within key sectors in which the particular NGO was involved and strategies for mainstreaming gender within the goals, programmes and internal functioning of the organisation. The ways through which gender relations impacted on individuals and strategies for negotiating spaces to work towards one's personal goals were also discussed.

Being an intra-NGO workshop, the changes required at the organisational level to mainstream gender concerns were discussed more concretely than was possible in the TOGT workshop. Further, greater space was created for discussion on 'how' to bring about change, though it was far from adequate. It was felt that the objectives of the organisation in working with women should shift from "promoting family welfare and communal harmony" to working with women so "as to enhance consciousness over gender issues, control over resources and their lives, and community level decision making processes". In the process the former objective, also the goal of the organisation, would be achieved. This gender-blind goal itself came into question in the workshop; especially from the militant field-level women staff. It was considered that promoting equity based on gender, religion, caste, and class identity, also needed to be added on to these goals. Programme policies and activities were also reviewed critically from this perspective, and required changes were identified. It was decided that the chief functionary would place some of these changes before the Board[7] for approval, as the Board was more powerful than the functionary himself. Changes required in the internal functioning of the organisation was discussed less openly—through informal discussions with militant women (all middle level, and who constituted the majority at this level). The idea of a women's forum within the organisation was mooted in this informal setting. It was decided to hold a separate workshop with the author to brainstorm on mainstreaming gender concerns into internal functioning, and review progress made in carrying forward the collective suggestions from the workshop.

Impact of the follow-up workshop

The review workshop never took place, and neither were separate spaces created to discuss mainstreaming of gender into internal functioning. Instead, after five months, another gender training workshop was organised at the behest of another funding agency supporting the organisation. The resource person, well known to the author, was informed about the earlier workshop only on reaching there. After finding out what topics were covered in the earlier workshop, she concentrated on strengthening concepts and strategies on 'women and violence', which was a new programme funded by this particular funding agency. Subsequent conversations with her revealed that ideas from the follow-up workshop on mainstreaming gender into implementation and monitoring (e.g. who controls credit, who bears the cost of savings) were more effectively carried forward, than those which required policy level changes (goals of the organisation). Though the importance for placing the need for policy level changes before the Board was discussed in the follow-up workshop, what steps to take in case the chief functionary failed to do so was never discussed informally with the militant women in the organisation. The idea of a women's forum within the organisation was operationalised, though functioning as a nascent group. Though the impact of the workshop was never gauged formally, this feedback indicates that the workshop *seems* to have had a limited, but positive, impact.

The actual impact of the follow-up workshop at the personal level could not be gauged by the author through her visit. But the workshop report points to the mixed impact at the personal level. Three of the women participants in this workshop were planning to get married soon, and the discussions revolved around the importance of strategies for negotiating conjugal contracts before marriage and the division of responsibilities of motherhood (not because the author felt that marriage and motherhood are the only options for women), but because of the reality of their lives. One woman participant said, "What can I do... I do not have a choice. If I object to an alliance because he does not agree to my working, my brother and parents will throw me out. Where will I go?" An elderly, militant, woman participant suggested that she move in with her family if she wanted to; in a way compensating for the loss of security which her family had to offer in spite of its gendered norms.

The challenges of bringing about transformative changes at the personal level through gender training are greater in the case of male participants. One participant (field level), who did not wish to lose the material benefits of the present distribution of power, denied totally that women occupied a subordinate status. Firstly, he pointed out "How can women be subordinate, when we men worship them as goddesses?" Then he added, "What is wrong with the division of labour? Women and men complement each other and this is based on comparative advantage." Practical strategies (training and non-training related) used by the author and other gender trainers to deal with these and others forms of male resistance are discussed in the next section. Fortunately, not all men participants in the follow up intra-NGO workshop were hardliners. One male participant (middle level) was an advocate of women's rights. He said that the workshop helped him to better understand the underlying causes of women's subordination, as well as areas for bringing gender aware change within his family.

Enhancing the Effectiveness of Gender Training of NGO Personnel: Some Lessons

Some of the main reasons for the mixed impact of these two training programmes have already been highlighted in the above two cases. This section moves beyond these two particular examples. It focuses on drawing out from them the broader lessons on factors which need to be taken into account to enhance the effectiveness of gender training efforts directed at NGO personnel. These lessons are summarised below, supplemented where necessary with lessons from experiences of other gender trainers (Rao and Jain 1986; Almadia 1990; Bhasin 1990; Vasudevan 1990; Bhasin and Kannabiran 1992; Subrahmanian 1992; Bhatia and Prasad 1992; Rangaswami 1993; Kabeer 1994b) and other experiences of the author (Murthy 1993a, 1993b, 1995, forthcoming).

The importance of strategic communication of transformative goals

Wherever NGOs are headed by gender-blind persons, there may be a need to couch gender-transformative goals of training programmes in gender-neutral and gender-ameliorative language. Pre-training communication with such NGOs may need to emphasise not just the equity gains of incorporating gender concerns, but also the efficiency and welfare gains. Failure to do this in the case of the TOGT workshop, as well as the earlier workshop with chief functionaries, resulted in poor representation of NGOs which really needed such training. That such strategic thinking may yield results is illustrated in the case of the 'Gender and Health' workshop organised by ADITHI, a nodal NGO based in Bihar, for heads of NGOs (predominantly men) in the state and those in-charge of health programmes. The invitation letter stressed the need for understanding gender issues to improve the health condition of the family and women, as well as the position of women. The participation rate was over 70 per cent.

Need for clear and realistic objectives

The specific objectives of gender-transformative training programmes directed at NGO personnel may vary: i) sensitisation on gender issues, ii) mainstreaming of gender into all/specific aspects of NGOs, iii) gender-transformative personal change. While the first objective is a pre-requisite for the other two, the second and third objective may demand different training strategies. It may be necessary to be clear at the outset on the specific objectives, and not mix objectives which require different training strategies; or spread them over separate modules. Further, the objectives have to be realistically achievable given the feasible duration of the training programme. The objectives of the TOGT and the follow up workshop encompassed all these three aspects at one shot, and were ambitious given their short duration. Some of the shortcomings of the workshop were also a consequence of this.

The importance of choice of appropriate entry points in training

Different entry points may be appropriate for different audiences,[8] and different objectives. There is a need to avoid standardisation, and choose the right entry point for each gender-transformative training programme. It is possible to distinguish between five broad approaches to initiating debates on gender within training programmes: *conceptual approach, policy analysis approach, empirical approach, action-reflection approach and experiential approach.* These approaches are elaborated in detail in Murthy (forthcoming), but their salient features and the kind of audience and objective for which they may be relevant are outlined here. Under the 'conceptual approach' one starts directly with relevant concepts. This approach may be appropriate for women and men at the senior level in NGOs with radical agendas who are already gender aware (in the transformative sense), but need to root their understanding in relevant concepts. The policy analysis approach, which begins with a critique of WID policies and the need for integrating gender within development policy, may again be useful for those at policy-making levels, but who work with NGOs involved in concrete development activities. It may be relevant for those who are already gender aware, as well as those who are semi-converted. Both these approaches may not be appropriate for hard-liners, who are fundamentally opposed to the adoption of gender-oriented goals within their organisation or in their personal lives. Converting them requires provision of concrete evidence of women's secondary status or efficiency and the welfare gains of taking gender into account—the empirical approach. Hard-liners may belong to any level of the organisation: senior to field level. But even for non hard-liners from middle and field level (of small NGOs) starting directly with concepts or a critique of policies may not be appropriate. These inputs may simply fly over their heads. Beginning with the development experiences of the participants, building gender-related concepts, attitudes and skills from them, developing and implementing concrete action plans and learning lessons from their implementation may be the right strategy. This approach is often referred to as the 'action-reflection' approach to training. All these four approaches may be appropriate for sensitisation on gender issues and mainstreaming of gender concerns within NGOs, but may not be appropriate for bringing about transformative changes at the personal level. For bringing about such changes, starting with the personal experiences of the participants, locating these experiences within hierarchical structures of society, reflecting on what sort of a person one wants to be (identity) and exploring ways of moving towards this, may be the right approach. This approach is referred to here as the experiential approach.

The participants of the TOGT workshop on gender and development belonged to different levels, came from NGOs with different ideological orientations and held different attitudes towards gender issues. Thus no one approach would have been appropriate for all the participants. Further, the workshops sought to achieve changes at the organisational, as well as the personal levels; both these objectives perhaps require different entry points. This diverse and incompatible mix of participants and objectives may partially explain the mixed impact of the TOGT workshop. This observation also holds good for the follow-up workshop, but at least here all the participants worked with the same NGO which strengthened efforts towards building skills to mainstream gender within the organisation.

This brings us to another issue in terms of entry points to gender training. *Should one start with inter-NGO gender and development workshops, or intra-NGO efforts*? Inter-NGO gender training programmes may be appropriate if the objective is limited to sensitisation,[9] but if the objective is mainstreaming of gender within NGOs, intra-NGO gender training programmes may be more effective. With regard to the objective of personal transformation, inter-NGO efforts offer greater anonymity, but lesser room than intra-NGO programmes for strengthening mutual support systems. Inter-NGO programmes may be necessary where the objectives go beyond the personal or organisational, for example, forming regional gender training teams, advocacy groups etc. The reach of inter-NGO gender training programmes is wider and the costs in terms of time and resources are lower. On the whole, the choice between the two entry point strategies would depend on the objectives, the time and resources available and the desired reach.

The importance of choice of content which matches the goals and objectives

For ensuring effectiveness, there has to be a match between the content of gender training programmes and their goals and objectives. In the case of programmes with transformative goals, the content should bring out the political dimensions of gender issues. Further, if the objectives include mainstreaming of gender within NGOs, the content should actually facilitate mainstreaming, rather than lead to compartmentalisation of gender concerns. Some of the shortcomings of the TOGT and the follow-up workshop were a consequence of overlooking these aspects. The goals of these two workshops were transformative in nature and one of the key objectives of the workshops was to strengthen skills to mainstream gender in a redistributive manner within participating NGOs/the particular NGO. But the content in some areas was either *depoliticising* or led to *compartmentalisation* of gender concerns. An example of depoliticisation is the session on mainstreaming gender within NGOs, which dealt more with 'what' changes were required; and ignored the political question of 'how' these were to be brought about (see section: "*Reasons for Shortcomings*", p. 370). An example of compartmentalisation is the introduction of separate gender planning frameworks in the session on gender planning, and overlooking of methodologies to incorporate gender within mainstream planning tools like SWOT and GOPP (see section: "*Reasons for Shortcomings*", p. 370). Similarly, the session on gender training methodologies and strategies dealt with skill building to facilitate separate gender training programmes, and ignored the question of how to mainstream gender within all development training programmes.

Who participates, and who does not? The match between objectives and choice of participants

A careful selection of participants for a particular objective may be essential to ensure effectiveness of gender training programmes. If the objective is to mainstream gender within NGOs policies, it may be important to ensure that chief functionaries and other staff involved in decision-making, as well as Board members, are represented within training programmes. The last category of participants may be particularly important in the case of NGOs where the Board members play a key role in shaping policies. In the case of the follow-up workshop which sought to mainstream gender within the particular NGO, the Board members were excluded. As a result many of the policy recommendations arrived at in the workshop were followed through less effectively than the operational ones. Other constituencies who may need to be sensitised for effective mainstreaming of gender within NGOs are representatives of funding agencies, support and network NGOs, functionaries of relevant government departments and quasi-government organisations which interact with, support or fund NGOs. In the case of gender training programmes which seek to bring about personal transformation, it may be important to sensitise not just the NGO personnel, but also their family members. This was highlighted in the follow-up workshop, where it was clear that unless other family members were sensitive to gender issues, the young woman participant would not be in a position to negotiate conjugal contracts in her favour. A beginning in this regard was made in Bihar, where a gender sensitisation workshop was organised for selected staff of three NGOs along with their spouses so that gender aware changes could be better fostered at the personal level.

The importance of appropriate participation

It is possible to distinguish between different degrees of participation (of participants) within gender training programmes: a mere presence, active listening, contribution to discussions, consultation in design and equal agency in design. If the goal of training is transforming consciousness and practices at the personal or organisational level, it is important to move from lower levels of participation to higher levels. While ideally the participants should exercise equal agency in the design of the programme and modifying the programme as one goes along, a necessary precursor to this is the clear understanding on their part of their learning needs and interests. Wherever such an understanding is not there, it may be appropriate to consult participants while designing the workshop. In both the TOGT and the follow-up workshop the level of participation encouraged by the author was the 'consultation level', given the pre-training awareness of the participants. But the actual level of participation ranged from being merely present at the workshop to actual contribution to its design. The poor degree of involvement on the part of some participants reduced the effectiveness of the programme. Some of the barriers to effective participation were language,[10] differences in terms of levels of participants, differences in pre-training consciousness, skills of the author/other resource persons in eliciting participation, presence of funding agency personnel and the timing[11] of the workshop. The gender of the facilitator/resource person and the mixed gender composition of the participants were also other constraints in the session on personal sharing. Care must be taken to surmount/reduce these barriers to enhance participation and effectiveness of gender training efforts.

The importance of evolving strategies to deal with resistance from hardliners

Hardliners (predominantly men) adopt different forms of resistance within gender training programmes. Some, as we saw in the follow-up workshop, deny that women occupy a subordinate position in the first place.[12] Others accept women's subordinate status but see it as arising out of a lack of interest among women to avail equal opportunities in society. A few admit that individual men may oppress individual women, but do not accept the existence of patriarchal structures. In fact, they argue that instances of women oppressing women are more common than men oppressing women. The ultimate from of resistance is to deny the insights of the resource person, by labelling them as urban, western and middle class feminists with no belief in religion. If the resource person is single the charges levelled against her are even more. For combating the first form of resistance—denial of women's secondary status—it may be essential to provide hard empirical evidence of women's secondary situation in every sphere of life. Raising questions which help them to come to the same conclusion may be an even better strategy.[13] To deal with the viewpoint that women occupy a secondary status because they do not avail of equal opportunities in society or because women oppress women, there are several strategies that can be adopted. One is to promote debates on the reasons for women's secondary status by asking the participants to choose between different viewpoints on this issue: biological/physical differences, lack of motivation/interest to avail opportunities, women oppressing other women, societal structures with men at the top etc. The arguments between gender aware persons and the hardliners could help change attitudes. The other is to draw parallels with the reasons for the secondary status of the poor, dalits or/and tribal people. Very few hardliners will admit that these groups are the cause of their own oppression. (For other strategies refer Kanabiran et al. 1992 and Murthy 1993.) To counter the denial of the insights of the women facilitators, it may be useful for them or the organisers to lay emphasis on their general development credentials, as well as their gender-related experience. Further, sharing their educational qualifications, years of experience, and their marital status (if married) may also help. It is also essential not to lose one's temper or show one's vulnerability when faced with different forms of resistance from the hardliners.

The importance of preparatory measures and follow-up action

Higher levels of participation require certain preparatory measures before the training programme. Pre-training visits to the participating organisations may be essential in order to ascertain their commitment to gender issues, identify training needs in a participatory manner and select appropriate participants. This process also enhances the sense of ownership of the workshop. In the TOGT workshop such preparatory measures were not carried out. Instead letters were written to the chief functionaries informing them about the workshop and the audience for whom the workshop was designed, exploring their interest in sending participants. The training needs were also explored through correspondence. Some of the shortcomings of the workshop in terms of the nature of participants, the level of participation, the workshop objectives, content and methodology can be attributed to overlooking this aspect. Similarly, subsequent to the gender training programme, systematic follow-up efforts are required to ascertain back-home implementation of learning, to identify constraints in carrying forward new ideas and strategies to address these, to ascertain additional training needs and to organise follow-up workshops to meet these needs. In the case of the TOGT workshop, the follow-up efforts straightaway took the form of intra-NGO gender training programmes. A visit before such training programmes to judge the impact of the TOGT workshop and the national workshop on gender concepts was never carried out. Some of the limitations of the follow-up workshop arose out of overlooking this aspect.

Who facilitates? And how? The importance of appropriate choice and dealing with hierarchy

The appropriate choice of facilitators for a given objective and audience is crucial to the effectiveness of gender training programmes, as well as to the nature and quality of facilitation. Most facilitators of gender training programmes for NGOs are women. They range from radical to liberal feminists, those who are in their mid 20s to late 50s, and those who work in autonomous women's organisations around issues of violence to support organisations working on mainstream socio-economic issues. For facilitating gender-transformative training programmes it is important to choose facilitators who share a socialist feminist perspective. Gray hair helps in training programmes, especially where participants are 'hard-liners'. Male gender trainers who share the appropriate political perspective are particularly helpful when the participants include men. It is also useful to bring in gender sensitive leaders of people's organisations, if the audience includes armchair NGO leaders with little time to listen to the voices of the people. The choice of facilitators who know the right language for a particular audience is also crucial. The criteria for selection should be determined by the objectives. If the objective is to mainstream gender within development NGOs, it may be useful to choose resource persons with experience in integrating gender within concrete socio-economic programmes. Facilitators from autonomous women's organisations, on the other hand, may be useful if the target audience is NGOs working around issues of violence, reproductive rights and sexuality. Persons with behavioural skills, who are competent to link personal experiences with structural issues, may be the most relevant for bringing about change at the personal level. Wherever the objectives are multiple, it may be important to set up a multi-skilled 'facilitation team' which is preferably present through the workshop. If this is not possible, at least a pool of resource persons should be drawn upon with one or two facilitators who provide the link through the workshop. In the TOGT, and the follow-up workshop, the choice of facilitator(s) was appropriate in terms of the ideological orientation of participating NGOs and the objective of mainstreaming gender within NGOs, but not for the objective of gender aware personal transformation; in which the author had little expertise. Though a male resource person with expertise in behavioural issues was drawn upon, he was not able to link the personal with structural issues. Further, women participants needed private space to discuss personal issues. This space could not be provided by him due to his gender, as well as the perception of the workshop as a public arena. His presence, however, did help enhance the legitimacy of the workshop in the eyes of male hard-liners. The facilitator's lack of familiarity with the regional language was a constraint in the follow-up workshop, as a result of which valuable time was lost and the workshop suffered.

There is normally a hierarchy between the facilitators and the participants on the basis of class, caste, language and authority. Being conscious of this hierarchy and dealing with it may be important. In both the workshops a conscious attempt was made by the facilitator to sit on the floor together with the participants, eat with them and sing common songs and allow them to chair discussions. In spite of this, the hierarchy still remained; as she occupied a privileged position in terms of class, caste, fluency in English and educational background. This hierarchy reduced the authenticity of some of the discussions. Further, the funding agency personnel, present throughout both the workshop and acting at an informal level as a co-facilitator, occupied a position of authority vis-á-vis the participants. Their presence reduced the factual validity of some of the discussions; especially the session in which the participating NGOs were reviewed from a gender perspective.

The need for impact assessment methodologies, and mechanisms for mutual accountability

Effective evaluation of any intervention is central to learning. But very little effort has gone into evolving indicators and methodologies for systematic evaluation of the impact of gender training efforts.[14] At the end of the TOGT workshop, feedback sheets were administered which assessed the perceptions of the participants on the overall usefulness of the workshop, and the appropriateness of the content, methodology, facilitation, duration and materials used. Open-ended questions on what they liked and did not like about the workshop, and suggestions for improvement were also included. Another content area included their plans to incorporate their learning from the workshop at the personal, organisational and target group level. However, the feedback sheet did little to gauge the change in their attitudes, knowledge and skills as a result of the workshop, and the actual impact of the workshop in bringing about gender-transformative changes at the personal and organisational level. Even the extent to which commitments made at the end of the workshop were operationalised, was not gauged. Overlooking these aspects led to inappropriate preparation for the follow-up intra-NGO workshop. The facilitator thus assumed that more or less the same training strategy could be used. Last minute discussions with the two participants from this NGO revealed the mixed impact of the TOGT workshop, and the need for changing the training strategy. However, mere indicators and methodologies for impact assessment are not enough. The mechanisms for enhancing mutual accountability of gender trainers, and creating spaces for their interaction and learning are essential.

Need to mainstream gender within development training

One of the key lessons from the two examples above is the need to combine separate gender training programmes with efforts to incorporate gender concerns within general development training programmes—not just within areas allocated to women staff of NGOs such as health and education, but also within spheres allocated to male staff such as agriculture, environment, structural adjustment and its impact, planning, monitoring and evaluation, organisation development etc. This is important from the point of view of mainstreaming gender within organisations, as well as from the viewpoint of sensitising those hard-liners (predominantly men) at leadership levels, who will not attend exclusive gender training programmes. As was apparent from the case studies, such chief functionaries tend to attend the latter workshops, rather than exclusive gender training programmes.

Conclusion: Lessons on the Potential and Limitations of Gender Training

Many of the Indian NGOs reflect gender hierarchies in societal institutions. It is in this context that this essay has argued the case for moving away from gender-blind trainings, towards gender-transformative ones. Though there has been a mushrooming of gender training efforts since the late 1980s, very few of them fall in this category. The impact of these few efforts at gender-transformative training has perhaps been mixed, as illustrated by the two experiences of the author in facilitating such training programmes. These two cases, as well as experiences of other trainers, show that the effectiveness of such training programmes depends on how far their goals are transformative and how they are communicated, the extent to which there is clarity on their specific objectives and how far the objectives are realistic, the match between the entry strategy, the content, the audience and objectives, the appropriateness of the choice and agency of participants, the appropriateness of the choice of facilitator and facilitation strategies (especially those adopted to counter resistance from hard-liners), the attention paid to preparation, follow-up and impact assessment, and the extent to which such efforts are combined with measures to mainstream gender within development training.

The two cases also point to the potential and limitations of gender training as a strategy, by itself, to bring about transformative changes at the personal and organisational levels, as well as some of the complementary strategies required. These lessons are summarised below. Looking at personal change first, it is possible to distinguish between three different categories of participants based on their pre-training gender consciousness: the converted, semi-converted and hard-liners. Gender training can help the converted to a large extent in bringing about changes in their lives, by enabling them to reflect upon their experiences using relevant concepts and identifying strategies for personal transformation. The semi-converted can be helped only partially. Though they may be motivated to change their personal goals, they are often scared of losing the resources and security which patriarchal structures have to offer.[15] The gains often seem less certain and visible, compared to the losses. Such people may require lateral support systems (collectives of gender aware women or/and men etc.) which will provide them the security to take the risk, and secure the gains. This was apparent in the case of the young woman participant, who said that she could not change the conjugal contract of her arranged marriage in her favour as she had nowhere to go if she was thrown out by her parents and brothers. The elderly woman participant who suggested that she move in with her family if she wanted to, was in a way compensating for the loss of security which the young woman's family had to offer in spite of its gendered norms. The hard-liners (predominantly men) can rarely be helped through gender training programmes. They do not see any gains out of personal transformation, and envisage severe loss of power and resources. Power based on authority,[16] financial resources,[17] or/and collective strength[18] may be essential to bring about change at the personal level, though its impact may still be limited (Murthy 1995).

The experience of the TOGT and follow-up workshops reveals that much of the impact of gender training programmes on mainstreaming gender within NGOs as organisations depends on the commitment of the chief functionary towards gender issues. The higher the commitment, the more favourable the impact; and vice-versa. Even where the chief functionaries are committed, it may be essential to combine training with non-training strategies to mainstream gender within NGOs. Such strategies, in the order of complexity involved in execution, include: identifying key persons or setting up structures accountable for mainstreaming; identifying and strategically using allies within the organisation; evolving systems for integrating gender into planning; monitoring; evaluation and HRD systems of the organisation; formulating an organisational level gender policy and designing an organisation development strategy to carry forward the gender policy. These non-training strategies can also be helpful in the case of NGOs headed by hard-liners; as they create spaces for expression of dissent. In such cases, they would have to be initiated by funding agencies or Board members through the exercise of power based on financial resources or authority. Threats on the part of funding agencies to withdraw funds or on the part of the Board to change the chief functionary have also worked in the case of such NGOs.

Notes

[1] Like SEWA and Mahila Samakhya (women's NGOs) and SUTRA (a male-headed NGO).

[2] Earlier attempts at extending Kabeer's policy analysis framework to gender training can be found in Murthy, forthcoming.

[3] Through targeting resources at the actors appropriate for realisation of pre-determined goals.

[4] This case study was also cited in Murthy (1995), but not in as much detail as in this paper. Further, the reasons for the shortcomings were not analysed in detail, as the objectives of the paper were different.

[5] Those in charge of co-ordinating efforts to mainstream gender within the organisation.

[6] For example, discussions on gender differentiated impact of the structural adjustment programme were included as part of the critique of the efficiency approach to women's development.

[7] The Chairperson, in particular, played a key role in framing the policies of the organisation.

[8] In terms of levels (senior, middle and field level), personal attitudes (converted or gender aware, semi-converted and hard-liners) and ideological orientation of the NGOs (empowerment NGOs and development NGOs).

[9] As there is more space for sharing of experiences and cross fertilisation of ideas.

[10] The TOGT workshop was conducted in English. Not all the participants were familiar with this language. The follow-up workshop was carried out in the regional language. As the author was not familiar with the language, she had to communicate indirectly—through the mediation of a translator.

[11] The timings of the follow-up workshop (9 a.m. to 6 p.m.) did not suit some of the women participants who had dual responsibilities. As the duration of the workshop could not be altered, the timings could not be altered/reduced significantly to suit their convenience.

[12] Apart from the two concrete forms which such denial took in the follow-up workshop, denial of women's subordinate position takes other forms as well. Generalising from personal experiences is one such form. In another workshop, one participant pointed out: "In my extended family, we give equal amount of food, health care and education to girls and boys. Things have changed in society."

[13] For example, how many hours of work do men and women do? What resources do men and women possess?

[14] For a good effort at assessing the impact of a gender training programme directed at women from the community, refer to Zuijlen and Mahajan, 1994.

[15] They have struck, what Kandiyoti (1988) refers to as bargains with patriarchal structures.

[16] Code of conduct evolved by their superiors, enquiry by Chief Functionary or Board of Directors.

[17] Enquiry from funding agencies on sexual harassment.

[18] For example, women's collectives at organisational or inter-organisational level which take up cases of gender-based harassment by men in the organisation.

References

Almedia, L., 1990. "My Conflicts as a Woman Trainer" in *Search News*, Vol. V Issue No. 3 (Special Focus on Training in Women in Development)

Bhasin, K., 1990. "Participatory Development Demands Participatory Training," mimeo, New Delhi: FAO.

Bhasin, K. and V. Kannabiran, 1992. "A Dialogue on Feminism: A Workshop With Men in NGOs on Women's Issues" in *Link, Vol. 11*, Madras: Achan.

Bhatia, K. and A. Prasad, 1992. *Gender Training in Development: Workshop Report*, Noida: National Labour Institute.

Kandiyoti, D., 1988. "Bargaining with Patriarchy" in *Gender and Society*, Vol. 2 No. 3.

Kabeer N., 1994a. "Gender-Aware Policy and Planning a Social-relation Perspective" in Macdonald, ed. *Gender Planning in Development Agencies, Meeting the Challenges*, UK and Ireland: Oxfam.

Kabeer, N., 1994b. "Triple Role, Gender Roles, Social Relations: The Political Sub-text of Gender Training Frameworks" in *Reversed Realities: Gender Hierarchies in Development Thought*, London and New York: Verso, Delhi: Kali for Women.

Mathew, M., R.K. Murthy and M. Singh, 1996. *Draft Directory of Training and Organisation Development Support Extended by Organisations. Covered as Part of the Study "Enhancing Effectiveness of Indian NGOs in the Context of the 1990s: Training, Organisation Development and Sectoral Strengthening Strategies*. New Delhi: GTZ/SHF.

Murthy, R.K., 1991. "Review of Training of Development Functionaries in India from a Gender Perspective," M. Phil. Thesis, Sussex: Institute of Development Studies.

———, 1993a. "Gender Concepts in Training and Planning", paper presented in the Tools for Trainers Workshop organised by the Population Council and Royal Tropical Institute, Amsterdam, 6–12 June, 1993.

———, 1993b. "Issues and Strategies in Gender Training of NGOs in India", paper presented in the Tools for Trainers Workshop organised by the Population Council and Royal Tropical Institute, Amsterdam, 6–12 June, 1993.

———, 1995. "Power, Institutions and Gender Relations: Can Gender Training Alter the Equation?" in *Madhyam, Vol. X No. 1.*

———, 1998. "Towards Gender-transformative Training: Lessons From South Asian Experiences", in *Gender Training: A Source Book, Gender, Society and Development* Series No. 2, Amsterdam: Royal Tropical Institute.

Overholt et al., 1985. "Women in Development: A Framework for Project Analysis", chapter in Overholt et al., *Gender Roles in Development Project: Cases for Planners* Kumarian Press.

Parker, R., 1991. "Gender Analysis Matrix" in *Gender Analysis Training: A Manual for Community Based Development Practitioners* Publisher unknown.

Rangaswami, et al., 1994. *Report on the Workshop: Strengthening Gender Training Through Conceptual Clarity*. Madras: Initiatives: Women in Development.

Rao, A. and S. Jain, 1986. *Training for Women's Development* Jaipur: Institute of Development Studies.

Sharma, A., 1990. "Experiences of a Male Facilitator in a Woman's Group" in *Search News*, Volume V Issue No. 3 (Special Focus on Training in Women in Development).

Subrahmanian, R., 1992. *Report on the Workshop on Gender Training for Men and Women in NGOs: Issues and Strategies*. Madras: Initiatives: Women in Development.

Vasudevan, B., 1990. *Gender Related Learning Experiences with Government and NGOs*, paper presented in the workshop on "Gender Training in Development" organised by the National Labour Institute in December, 1990, Bangalore.

Zuijlen, V.M. and A. Mahajan, 1994. "Exposure with Perspectives: Evaluation and Explorative study of a Project of Awareness Generation and Organisations for Young Women by a NGO in Himachal Pradesh, India", *VENA Working Paper*, No. 94/1.

14

Lessons Learned

Gender Training Experiences with the Indian Government

RAMYA SUBRAHMANIAN WITH NAILA KABEER, KANCHAN MATHUR, SHOBITA RAJAGOPAL AND SAROJINI GANJU THAKUR

Introduction

In this chapter we weave together the documented experiences of five people involved in different ways in the Gender Planning Training Project in the context of which many of the papers included in this book were written. Sarojini Thakur has recorded her reflections and experiences as a senior civil servant who was first a participant in the project, and then managed and co-ordinated the gender training programmes generated by the project at the apex national administrative training institution, the Lal Bahadur Shastri National Academy of Administration (LBSNAA).[1] Kanchan Mathur and Shobhita Rajagopal, also participants in the project in their capacity as researchers from IDS, Jaipur and working actively with NGOs in their state, reflect on their subsequent experiences of training different agencies on the basis of the framework presented in this book.[2] Naila Kabeer (1994, mimeo) reflects on her experience as the key trainer in the project, particularly on the adaptation of her previous international gender training experience to a very specific country and work context. As a person involved in the research, management and training aspects of the project, Ramya Subrahmanian has also recorded some of her reflections on gender training of bureaucrats.[3]

There is a fairly long history of gender training in the Indian context but a great deal of it has been done within NGOs and donor agencies. The focus on training government planners and policy makers has been more recent and, as Thakur notes, what gender training had been done within the government has not been part of a concerted effort to reach policy-makers, but has focused on single training programmes, aimed at "sensitising" government officials to gender inequalities:

> The systematic conversion of gender training into a policy concern, and the definition of a project directed at mainstreaming gender training for civil servants through a focus on policy and programme formulation and implementation has only begun to take place in the early 1990s (1996:3).

In 1993, the Gender Planning Training Project was initiated as a joint collaboration between the governments of India and the UK with the aim of developing such a training resource capacity by drawing on trainers and potential trainers from diverse agencies: government training institutions and departments, academic institutions and NGOs (see introduction, this volume). In terms of its approach, strategy, content and process, this project constitutes a landmark of sorts in the whole experience of gender training in India, and possibly elsewhere. In each of these areas, the project attempted to ensure that gender training was not used just to sensitise people, but to develop an integrated gender focus on both the personal as well as professional fronts for individuals from diverse agencies—NGOs, government officials, researchers and trainers. Focusing on training potential trainers brought its own challenges, as it meant that the project "had to leave behind it not only a change of attitudes and practices among those it had worked with, but also had to transfer the capacity to effect such changes in others" (Kabeer 1994).

The project, which spanned the years 1993–96 in its initial phase, spawned numerous other processes. The participants as well as the trainers on the project brought with them many years of experience of working in the development sector. Several of the participants continued their engagement with gender training outside of their involvement with project-specific training, and went on to provide training to a wide range of agencies in India and outside. In this chapter we attempt to capture some of the richness of this body of experience as a way of reflecting on the ways in which gender training can become a useful and strategic tool for addressing institutional and policy change in government.

The reflections and experiences of a number of different actors from the project have been synthesised here in order to select lessons that can provide some basis for future efforts in gender training of government. Their diverse voices point to one common conclusion: that effective gender training requires that approach, content and process be tailored to the needs of particular constituencies. Some of the needs specific to the bureaucracy are highlighted in this essay. The first section presents some of the challenges faced in training personnel within a specific institutional context, the Indian government, in relation particularly to the content and process of training. The second section presents some of the ways in which the project sought to take on these challenges. The last section pulls together some of the pitfalls as well as forms of resistance that gender training of bureaucrats brings with it.

Challenges to Gender Training of Bureaucrats

Reflecting on the genesis of gender training in the body of feminist development scholarship and activism, Kabeer (1994) notes that for many feminists, it has represented the decision to move "from being a critical voice outside the mainstream of development to becoming a critical voice inside, seeking to influence how development practice is thought about and done." However, this has entailed rethinking the language in which feminist insights are communicated: "The language we speak as trainers has to be accessible to people who do not generally spend their days immersed in abstract theory, revelling in the complexity of ideas. It has to be accessible to people who are intervening in the development process in a purposive way on an everyday basis."

Simplifying concepts, and communicating them in terms which a diverse group of men and women of different ages, experience and life histories can apply to their lives and hence absorb, has to be the central approach of gender training, since "the most profound and sophisticated analyses of gender are likely to have little impact if they are communicated in ways which do not make sense to people." (ibid.). Further, as Thakur notes, for most of the civil servants who attended the project, 'gender' was entirely a new concept and area, and for effective impact it was important to present the issues, debates and concepts in terms that communicated both the point of gender training as well as highlighted the adaptability of the training content to their specific departments, and geographical areas of work. Kabeer's experience of working with state officials and donor agencies from different parts of the world, a constituency not known for an interest in Theory, suggested that gender trainers sometimes underestimated the receptiveness of such professionals to learning about new ideas: "One of the best ways of communicating why there has been a focus on women's issues in development, what the shift from 'women in development' to 'gender and development' is about, and indeed what 'gender' itself means is to take participants through the history of these ideas. Nothing serves to illuminate the meaning of a new concept than knowing about its origins."

This point is also made by Mathur and Rajagopal who note a very important, and widely experienced, challenge: the issue of translating the term 'gender' into different Indian contexts. Given the relative novelty of the term 'gender' in development for many of the participants, the difficulty of finding a suitable word in Indian languages was further compounded. This exacerbated resistance to the concept.

> An important aspect of gender training unlike other training is that the process is interactive and the participants have the space to choose and reject what they like and don't like. The initial resistance, in many instances, has been to the term 'gender' since it has been imbibed by most as a grammatical term, and there remains a problem of finding an equivalent term in other languages—in [our] case Hindi.

Mathur and Rajagopal also found that an understanding of the international as well as Indian context of gender issues helped to facilitate an understanding of the way in which shifts in ideas have been linked to shifts in practice. By working through some of the different ways in which gender norms and practices were manifest in their own daily lives, participants came to understand that the word was simply a conceptual shorthand for a complex reality which they recognised—and if the concept was clear in their own heads, then it became clear why a grammatical term signifying the difference between 'masculine' and 'feminine' should have become invested with larger meanings about gender difference. However, until the group as a whole attempted to translate these ideas into their respective local languages, this issue did not surface. The feedback component of the training programme thus played an important role in drawing attention to some of the problems trainers new to this field would have to learn to deal with.

Murthy's essay in this volume raises many of the complexities entailed in developing a gender perspective with different levels of staff within voluntary organisations. In the context of the bureaucracy, however, these challenges take on specific forms. Government officials in India are responsible for service delivery on vital issues relating to the survival and well-being of men and women, covering the entire country, and delivering the largest share of resources that reach poor people in India. Within government departments and organisations, the huge scale of personnel and operations have been regulated by a fairly entrenched system of governance by hierarchy, and a complex set of rules and procedures which are not transparent to those who constitute the clientele of bureaucrats, the public (Subrahmanian 1995). For gender training to be effective for such a constituency, it is important to tailor the approach and the process to ensure that the content of training is meaningful.

One of the key challenges has been created by the culture of training which exists within government. Subrahmanian (1995) notes that in government "training is not generally used as a creative process of interaction and discussion, but more as a process through which information is transmitted within the bureaucracy. Much of the training within the bureaucracy appears to be routine . . .. there is little emphasis on social analysis or interactions between bureaucrats and their 'clients'." Thakur endorses this point:

> Training in the bureaucracy, per se, is generally not viewed as an important activity—there has not been an overwhelming recognition of its important potential as a contribution to both human resource development and to the achievement of improved performance. As a result this not only influences the kind of nominations that are made, but it also means that the training infrastructure in some of the sectoral institutions is very limited. In general since training is not seen as a priority, the funds that are allocated for it are rather limited.

Because most of the participants had been sent by their institutions, rather than having vountarily opted to participate in the Gender Planning Training Project, "we had to persuade them that gender training was a serious enterprise which had implications for their work before they were prepared to put their minds to thinking through what these implications might be" (Kabeer 1994). Not only was it crucial to sustain their motivation and continually make links with both their personal and organisational contexts, but to translate this new information and perspective into a framework that they could carry with them into their work and future training. Kabeer reflects on the development of the framework used in the GPTP training and presented in this book:

> One of the things that became clear very early on in our 'training-of-trainer' efforts was that we had to develop a framework. I had tried to avoid doing this so far because of my fears that gender training frameworks often acted as intellectual straitjackets, offering the answers before asking the questions or at least prescribing the kinds of answers that could be given. However, it was clear that a 'training of trainers' project needed some kind of analytical framework. The development of gender training frameworks in the international arena has created a demand for more frameworks as gender training becomes identified with the idea of a framework. But from the point of view of the participants on the project, who were almost all new to the field, a framework was something that gave them something concrete to hold on to, something to refer back to.

Over the period of a year, participants were taken through three stages of training: a pre-course workshop where they were introduced to each other, to the course and the project; the actual training course which was initially for eight weeks but reduced to five by the end of the project and at the end of which they had developed their own training modules; and a post-course workshop where participants gave feedback on their experiences as trainers and clarified any problems they may have encountered. Gender Planning Training Project (GPTP) participants hence made the transition in the course of one year from not knowing what "gender" is to being gender trainers themselves. Developing consensus and clarity on gender equality in the span of a year, in the midst of which participants returned to their own institutional environments, was clearly a big challenge. The framework developed and used thus had to be flexible enough to encompass multiple goals: it had to

> retain the power of social analysis but make it more accessible; ... to retain the politics of gender but without ending up with polarised positions; ... to relate the analysis to what people did. Also there are different strategic entry points through which an introduction to gender analysis can occur: we have tried to opt for one which appeals to the 'head' rather than the 'heart', which tries to get people to analyse for themselves the nature of the problem rather than seeking to appeal to their emotions; the emotions can come later. (Kabeer 1994).

Despite the concern that a framework would create an "intellectual straitjacket", the development of the framework and its use actually proved otherwise: it helped to foster, in participants, a feeling of ownership of the ideas. While it helped to systematise the process of absorption of new ideas and a reference point for return at any stage of the training course, the subsequent use of the framework by participants in their own training courses, their additions and innovations helped each participant feel ownership of the ideas and the analysis. The transfer of a feeling of analytical ownership is critical for the success of training efforts, and was essential to the success of the Gender Planning Training Project.

Because GPTP was a training of trainers, there was a further challenge—how to monitor the 'second generation' training programmes run by participants, and how to ensure the building of support structures to replenish and refresh the ideas and training methods of the participant trainers. The quality of training programmes depend heavily on the clarity, skills and abilities of the trainer, and importantly, their commitment. Thakur notes the difficulty of sustaining effective monitoring of training programmes held at the state level:

> Lack of monitoring and quality control are a problem. Although at the level of the transfer of the course there was strict quality review, this aspect has not permeated down to the courses conducted at the level of the state training institutions.

The challenge of monitoring lies not just in the development of an effective process and system for ongoing constructive feedback, but also in the generation of indicators that capture, for participants, the dynamic impact of training on the personal as well as professional fronts.

Rising to the Challenge: GPTP's Innovations

Building on the collective experience of trainers involved in the project, but principally on the experiences of the Institute of Development Studies at Sussex University, which has for several years successfully run 3-month training programmes on 'Women, Men and Development', the GPTP was carefully designed to take on some of the challenges discussed above, as well as to avoid some of the pitfalls otherwise experienced. As a strategic measure, GPTP was committed to securing a gender balance among the participants, for a range of reasons: to signal commitment to equal opportunities by gender, to ensure that the participating institutions did not fall into the trap of assuming a conflation of interests between programmes on gender and women officers, and to ensure that there would be fair and equitable interaction within the training programmes, merging the insights, views and experiences of both women and men. Strikingly, as Mathur and Rajagopal note, this balance has been sought in all subsequent state-level training programmes that have emerged out of the project.

Kabeer reflects on the impact that a mixed gender group has on the trainer's style and methodology:

> Gender training is usually received differently by groups with different balances of women and men; training with a group that is largely women does allow one's own assumptions and biases about gender to go unchallenged. When there is a substantial proportion of

men, or even a majority, assumptions that one took for granted have to be rethought.

Ensuring an equitable gender balance enabled a fairly healthy set of dynamics to develop, reducing the possibilities of any one majority drowning out the voices and ideas of another minority. Another strategic innovation within GPTP was to mix the target audience—so government officials, trainers from both state and non-state institutions, activists and researchers were made to work together. This had two effects: it increased the scope for multi-actor dialogues—and disagreements!—but also over a period of time fostered healthy mutual respect between institutions which may otherwise have viewed each other with suspicion. It also meant that the modules developed were multi-dimensional, drawing on experiences from both voluntary and state sectors, as well as building on the insights and skills of a wide range of development actors. The success of this particular feature of GPTP is evident in the enduring collaboration between different individuals in the project, reinforcing one of the key features of the training methodology—that it views the training session as a means and not an end in itself:

> The political content of gender training can often lead trainers to treat the training process as an end in itself, expecting it to result in a complete transfer of certain values. It is much more strategic and useful to create an environment which emphasises the sharing of perspectives, so that trainers and participants may agree, or agree to disagree at the end of the process. Training should ideally offer an environment where participants feel free to express contrary views, minimising judgement and allowing for personal experience. (Subrahmanian 1995)

Respect for the diversity of experience and viewpoints was necessary in order to enable participants grappling with new ideas and perspectives to absorb the process in their own time and at a comfortable pace. In order to create this enabling environment, the trainers themselves had to be able to look at their own positions from the point of view of the participants. Kabeer reflects on how she realised the political sub-text of the training environment:

> Those who have the power to make policies within these bureaucracies, mainly men, live in intimate relations with the members of the group about whom [gender] policy is made, and the individual dynamics of their personal relationship carries over into their professional relationships in ways that are potentially distorting. ... But what I also learned is the extent to which we as feminists also have to be aware that we have a very personal stake in the process of addressing gender politics within, in this case, bureaucracies. Sometimes the comments that one encounters in the course of gender training, not personally directed, but implicating all women in some unfounded stereotype, touch on personal emotions, that no computer trainer, for example, is likely to experience and therefore have to learn to deal with.

Both trainers and participants enter the training environment with their own sets of fears and expectations. Although all GPTP training courses started with a session levelling off these fears and expectations and talking them through, there are assumptions as well as expectations that only get aired after a certain amount of trust has been built up. GPTP's design was developed to ensure that such a process of trust-building did take place—all courses were residential, and the main course was no shorter than five weeks at its minimum. This was essential to allow all participants and trainers to be aware of, and let go of, stereotypes they might otherwise be carrying about others involved:

> One of the greatest problems inherent in a gender training environment is the existence of stereotypes that trainers and participants often hold about each other. Gender trainers are easily typecast as westernised and urban, only theoretically concerned with gender issues, too overtly feminist, removed from the realities of grassroots women (which bureaucrats often feel they are better equipped to understand) or simply people with a one-point agenda to destroy social institutions and the moral fabric of society. However, gender trainers often have stereotypes of bureaucrats which are equally negative—disinterested, disengaged from reality, bound by red-tapism, corrupt, hierarchical, incapable of innovation or creativity, etc. ... Both sets of stereotypes contribute significantly to the resistance experienced within a training environment and need to be addressed. ... It is important for trainers to interact formally and directly with participants during breaks and during sessions to deconstruct stereotypes and point out the implications. (Subrahmanian 1995)

Kabeer endorses this point, and describes the training process as "an encounter between two kinds of stereotypes: the bureaucrats' stereotypes about feminists as humourless, dogmatic, bent on being right and our own stereotypes about bureaucrats as humourless, officious and bent on being right." In such a context then, how did GPTP manage to break the stereotypes and foster such diverse partnerships? Thakur vividly recreates the feeling of camaraderie that permeated the training courses on the project:

> Consciousness of peer group pressure does not exist [in the groups]. A subsidiary result of this whole process has been the cementing of very strong friendships which have stretched beyond the course and which represent cross-sectoral bonds. At the same time, a healthy competition was generated for developing a good module. One sign of participants' commitment to the outputs of the course was that, in all four years of the course, teams have voluntarily worked on the modules until the early hours of the morning.

Both Thakur and Kabeer attribute this in part to the structure of the course but significantly, to the methodology of the training. Both note that the training sought to involve people at two levels: critically at the level of their personal lives and relationships, but also crucially linking the personal to their organisational and professional lives. Thakur elaborates on this:

> The high level of personal involvement on the part of the team members distinguishes this course from other trainings, and the explanation for this lies in the fact that the course appeals at two levels—it increases individual skills and specialisation, and also enhances the ability of the individual to contribute to the department or organisation in a specialised capacity. In fact in some cases if the officer is located strategically he/she becomes the spokesperson for gender issues in the department.

Thakur cites the example of a senior police officer from Maharashtra state who not only organised training within his department on gender issues, but has also played a crucial advocacy role in influencing policy for the promotion of equal opportunities for women within the police force. Similarly, a woman officer from the Department of Education in Karnataka state who has systematically worked at promoting gender awareness within her department, has developed many innovative ways of enhancing girls' education apart from training. The focus on the two levels of people's lives and the demonstration of some of the links between how they think and experience gender in their personal lives and how gender structures their organisational lives has clearly had an impact, according to Thakur:

> The impact of the gender training imparted through this programme has not been assessed formally, but can be broken into two separate components: the gains at the individual level in terms of sensitisation, and the gains at the level of institutionalisation and mainstreaming. In so far as gender sensitisation is concerned, the training of trainers definitely does open a totally new perception of reality both at the personal level and in the work situation. Of course it is difficult to gauge, especially in the case of the men, the extent to which this training translates itself into attitudinal change. However, for men it does represent one more string or variety of training that they are equipped to offer and so while there is intuitive male resistance, the ability for men to distinguish themselves in an area which is currently quite a buzz-word, is appealing.

The development of skills alongside the building of perspective creates incentives for individuals to participate more effectively because they can see the link between what they are learning and how it can be used within their organisations effectively. Further, it provides individuals with an extra set of credentials that they can use to carve out specialised niches for themselves at the workplace. For the project there was an enhanced value to the development of a cadre of male gender trainers, which is picked up by Mathur and Rajagopal:

> [A] strategy which has been particularly effective is networking with 'men' gender trainers and working with them as a team. This has been very useful since women trainers, more often than not, are branded as 'feminists' trying to push down concepts alien to 'our culture'. It is interesting to note that in many trainings we find male participants giving more attention when a man is talking about gender. The need then is also to identify more men as gender trainers, though it would require both time, energy and networking.

Building up commitment and motivation was an essential part of the project strategy, and influenced the design. As noted earlier, the project had a cycle of events over the period of a year, building in time for reflection and feedback. Follow-up mechanisms were designed to reflect the project's philosophy, somewhat captured in Subrahmanian's reflections:

> Gender training needs to be part of an institutional strategy, building linkages and creating supportive networks. Time and resources are always a constraint, but as far as possible, gender training programmes need to end with some plan for follow-up, even if it is just to discuss participant responses and learning. This will help interested participants to examine ways of moving from the 'why' of gender training to the more concrete areas of 'how to'.

As Thakur notes, the process of reiteration was achieved through the post-course workshops as well as through other opportunities generated within the project for upgradation of skills and for sharing experiences. The constant loop between design and feedback meant that *flexibility* was essential within the project. Thakur gives some examples of how the project design was constantly reviewed and adapted to incorporate lessons learned:

> The entire process of the project as mentioned above has been characterised by an openness of approach on the part of all the key actors at each stage of the project. There has been constant review at the end of each cycle which has fed into the planning of the following cycle of events. This has resulted in changes and deviations from the original project, both major and minor, from the outset. The inclusion of the field visit as an essential part of the course, the identification of the LBSNAA as a major player mid-project, and the modification of the teams to include the subject-related national level institution (as well as the state-level sectoral institution wherever possible) are examples of changes made as a result of review. Similarly, due recognition was given to the fact that whereas state training institutions often had the mandate to conduct trainings for specific development departments (such as rural development, health, Panchayati Raj), quite often development sectors had their own training institutions, and it was necessary to bring them in if gender training was to be mainstreamed.

Using gender training as a means to institutional change and mainstreaming of gender within policy-making bodies and implementing departments was essentially the core goal of GPTP, and its design was aimed at helping to achieve this through targeting carefully selected institutions, and reviewing the project's strategy at all times. It became apparent to participants that advocacy was critically linked to the training process: advocacy not just in terms of creating a greater profile and awareness about gender training itself, but also about the organisational changes that would be required to sustain mainstreaming and gender-sensitivity at all levels. As mentioned earlier, it was strategic to locate the training methodology within an understanding of the kinds of organisations that participants were coming from, and tailoring the content of training to the reality of their work contexts. Mathur and Rajagopal summarise the strategic value of a 'realistic' set of entry-points and approaches:

> Gender is a strategic issue and gender-based interventions in institutions need to be carefully planned. If gender training has a negative outcome because it is pitched at the wrong-level/ group and if it is seen as patronising because it is pitched low, the process of mainstreaming can be set back. Furthermore, these trainings will have little impact without follow up, which needs to be woven into the original training programme itself.

Ultimately, gender training has to be able to reach out to each individual participant and enable them to see themselves as actors in a wider world, with the power within to change structures immediately around them. Subrahmanian sees this as part of the strategic agenda of gender training:

> Middle-level officials and field-level officials in particular can often feel paralysed by the hierarchy that characterises bureaucratic organisations, and often cannot see a role for themselves in initiating change. The training environment can positively reinforce the capacity of bureaucrats to act as agents of change.

Ultimately, she cautions against viewing training as the only means of creating change:

> Training is often seen as an end in itself, with the potential to transform people and institutions. This is clearly not possible, particularly in programmes of short duration and such expectations place unrealistic and unnecessary pressure on trainers to achieve 'success'. In fact training must be viewed as a part of a broader strategy seeking to offer alternative values. However, a training process can also con-

tribute significantly to the exchange of skills, tools and methods for research and analysis that can help bureaucrats translate awareness into skills.

Disagreements in the Gender Training Environment: Some Common Experiences

Finally, we present Mathur and Rajagopal's reflections on the disagreements (from participants) that they encountered in the course of their training programmes. We choose to end with this selection of examples of conflict as a reminder that gender training, as part of the social transformation project, is likely to surface people's deepest fears and most intimate notions of their identity and relationships with those immediately around them. Gender trainers thus need an enormous amount of patience and conceptual clarity to enable participants to cross the bridge of fear and taboo over into a new world of insights and perspectives.

> It must be kept in mind that gender issues are complex and sensitive. The trainings aim at breaking new ground for people and tackling old entrenched habits of thought and action. Thus training can be seen as both a threat and challenge by different participants and strong reactions, therefore, are to be expected.
>
> In our experience the reactions encountered during gender trainings can be measured on a common scale. The participants have ranged from those who are open to new ideas and not afraid of questioning and challenges, to those who remain explicit in their opposition.
>
> The reactions of the latter can be summarised as:
>
> > "Women in India have the status of a goddess. They are not subordinate or secondary."
> >
> > "Women are women's worst enemies, they in fact oppress other women [mother-in-law, sister-in-law etc.]."
> >
> > "It is women who socialise children [as it is their prime responsibility to look after them] and it is they who inculcate gender differences."
> >
> > "Even when women are given opportunities, they do not avail them because they do not want to change their attitudes and behaviour."

"Men and women have different roles to perform in a society and there is no conflict in the given pattern that exists."

"Feminism and talking of equal rights for women is a western concept. If it is popularised in India, it will lead to broken families."

"Women perform household tasks because they love their children and husband. It should not be seen as a 'burden'."

These and many such reactions are common in most trainings. Responding to them has necessitated going beyond these statements into how they have been constructed over a period of time. They also reflect a fear that any acknowledgement of power relations within the family would put the whole institution in danger.

Understanding people's entrenched fears about taking on gender issues and the implications this may have for the very fundamental ways in which they view the world is an essential starting-point for gender trainers. We choose ultimately not to view disagreements as 'resistance' in the training environment, but as conflicts arising from the ways in which different people comprehend the world they live in, and organise that comprehension into simplistic categories. Through gender training we choose to reflect that world back to them through different lenses, with the ultimate hope that plurality of experience is respected and enriches development work to ensure that higher-level goals of well-being and justice are the active pursuit of those working in development.

Notes

[1]"Mainstreaming Gender Training for Civil Servants in India: A Systematic Approach", paper presented at the Gender Training Assessment Meeting, 7–9 July 1996 (APDC Kuala Lumpur).

[2]"Gender Trainings: Potential and Limitations", mimeo. 1996, Jaipur: Institute of Development Studies.

[3]"Promoting Gender-Sensitive Change within Bureaucracy: Role of Training", *Madhyam* 1995.

Notes on Contributors

NAILA KABEER is Fellow at the Institute of Development Studies, University of Sussex, where she has specialised in research, teaching and training in the field of gender. She has worked extensively on issues related to gender and development in Bangladesh, India and Vietnam. She is the author of *Reversed Realities: Gender Hierarchies in Development Thought*.

RAJNI PALRIWAL is Reader at the Department of Sociology, Delhi School of Economics. Her research interests include agrarian relations, women's work, kinship and gender relations and the women's movement and politics. She has contributed to books and journals, and is the author of *Changing Kinship, Family and Gender Relations in S.Asia: Processes, Trends and Issues.*

KARIN KAPADIA is South Asia Gender Adviser at the World Bank, Washington. She has taught at the University of Sussex, the School of Oriental and African Studies, London, and the London School of Economics. She has been published in many national and international journals and is author of *Siva and her Sisters: Gender, Caste and Class in Rural South India.*

SAROJINI GANJU THAKUR is a civil servant belonging to the Himachal Pradesh Cadre of the Indian Administrative Service. She is currently posted as Joint Secretary in the Department of Women and Child Development, Government of India, and is responsible for planning, monitoring, implementing and evaluating women's programmes at the national level.

MAITRAYEE MUKHOPADHYAY is Senior Gender Adviser at the Royal Tropical Institute in Amsterdam where she runs international courses on gender and development, provides technical advice to development agencies and undertakes research. She has worked on rural and urban development projects in India. Her most recent work, *Legally Dispossessed,* traces the relationship between Indian women and the state.

RANJANI K. MURTHY is an independent trainer and researcher based in Chennai working on the issues of gender, social relations and poverty. Her training-related work has been predominantly directed at NGO staff. She has co-authored *Addressing Poverty: Indian NGOs and Their Capacity Enhancement in the 1990s.*

RAMYA SUBRAHMANIAN has conducted trainings and worked on commissioned studies and consultancies on gender and development. She is presently a doctoral student at the Open University, UK, working on education administration.

MADHU SARIN is author of *Urban Planning in the Third World: The Chandigarh Experience* and *Joint Forest Management: The Haryana Experience*. She has published in both national and international journals and has been on several government committees and task forces. Her work on both urban and rural development issues has combined grassroots experience with policy analysis and advocacy to promote gender sensitive, equitable and decentralised natural resource planning and management.

SHOBHITA RAJGOPAL is Associate Fellow at the Institute of Development Studies, Jaipur. She has been researching issues related to women's development, women's empowerment and mainstreaming gender concerns in policy planning and implementation.

KANCHAN MATHUR is national level resource person on gender issues and has been involved in conducting trainings for development planners and practitioners, NGOs and public sector undertakings. She has written extensively for national and international journals on gender and development issues and has designed interventions for women's development, child labour and gender concerns in development policy and planning.

POORNIMA CHIKARMANE is Assistant Director of the Department of Adult and Continuing Education and Extension Work at the Pune Campus of the SNDT Women's University. She has worked on issues of women and children in the urban informal sector and has been involved in the training of police personnel, administrators and programme implementers, both in the government and NGO sectors.

This publication is an outcome of the research done by the Institute of Development Studies at the University of Sussex, and exerpiences of the participants of the Gender Planning Training Project (GPTP). GPTP was a joint collaboration of the Training Division, Department of Personnel & Training, Government of India, and the Department for International Development, UK, managed by the British Council. During 1993-1996 officials of several central and state government departments as well as trainers from the following institutions and NGOs participated in the project:

- Lal Bahadur Shastri National Academy of Administration, Mussoorie
- HCM Rajasthan Institute of Public Administration, Jaipur (and Udaipur campus)
- Administrative Training Institute, Mysore
- Madhya Pradesh Academy of Administration, Bhopal
- Uttar Pradesh Academy of Administration, Nainital
- Yeshwantrao Chavan Academy of Development Administration, Pune
- SVP National Police Academy, Hyderabad
- National Institute of Rural Development, Hyderabad
- Tata Institute of Social Sciences, Mumbai
- SNDT Women's University, Pune and Mumbai
- Mother Teresa Women's University, Kodai Kanal
- Avinashilingam Institute for Home Science & Higher Education, Coimbatore
- State Resources Centre, Jamia Milia Islamia, Delhi
- State Resource Centre, Indore
- National Council for Educational Research & Training, Delhi
- Maharashtra State Council of Education Research & Training, Pune
- Indira Gandhi National Forest Academy, Dehradun
- Dr BS Ambedkar National Institute of Social Science, Mhow
- SG Institute for Training of Youth in Leadership & Rural Development, Panchmari
- Institute of Development Studies, Jaipur
- Seva Mandir, Udaipur
- Sakti, Bangalore
- Uttarakhand Seva Nidhi, Almora
- Central Himalayan Rural Action Group, Nainital
- MP Bharat Gyan Vigyan Samiti, Bhopal